ESSAYS IN
SOCIOLOGICAL THEORY
Revised Edition

TALCOTT PARSONS

Essays in

Sociological Theory

REVISED EDITION

THE FREE PRESS, NEW YORK
COLLIER - MACMILLAN LIMITED, LONDON

Collier-Macmillan Canada, Ltd., Toronto, Ontario

FIRST FREE PRESS PAPERBACK EDITION 1964

Third Printing March 1966

Contents

Contents

ESSAYS IN
SOCIOLOGICAL THEORY
Revised Edition

Introduction

THE FIRST EDITION of this volume of Essays appeared in 1949. In the Introduction written at that time it seemed appropriate to say that it brought together work done by the author *since* the publication of his book, *The Structure of Social Action* in 1937. In preparing a new edition, the Free Press and the author thought in terms of work which lies *between* the aforementioned book and three new publications in the field of general theory which document a new phase in the development of the author's theoretical thinking. These are the monograph, *Values, Motives and Systems of Action,* written in collaboration with Edward A. Shils and published in the volume *Toward a General Theory of Action* (Harvard University Press, 1951) of which the two of us were co-editors; *The Social System* (Free Press, 1951); and the collection entitled *Working Papers in the Theory of Action* (Free Press, 1953), written in collaboration with Robert F. Bales and Edward A. Shils.

When the Free Press was considering the present new edition of the *Essays,* some of the papers printed in the *Working Papers* were either written or in process. The question arose as to whether any of these should be included in a new edition of the *Essays,* but at the time it seemed advisable to reserve all theoretical work done since the completion of *The Social System* for the separate publication of *Working Papers* and thus to confine the new edition of these *Essays* to work done before the new theoretical phase was under way. The present edition therefore was planned to end with the essay on "The Prospects of Sociological Theory," the author's presidential address before the American Sociological Society at its 1949 meeting, which was written in the midst of the work leading to *Toward A General Theory of Action* and points up the transition between these phases of intellectual development.

Since the *Working Papers* went to press, however, two other papers have been written which it has seemed advisable to include in the present collection. Both are to be published elsewhere but would through these channels have come to the attention of only rather restricted groups. Since they belong in the broad field of "application" of sociological theory and stand in the line of scientific development documented by these essays, they seemed to belong in the collection.

Within this general policy, several new items have thus been included in this new edition which were not part of the original one, and in order not to allow the volume to grow too large, three items in the earlier edition have been omitted.

The new additions fall into three classes. First, there are three papers which had been written before the publication of the first edition of these essays, but for reasons partly of space, and partly of balance, were not included in the volume at that time. These all fall in the "applied" category of essays in theory, dealing with large problems of the analysis and interpretation of institutional structures of the modern world, and dynamic processes of social change in it. The dominant focus of all three is on the political situation, a focus which is at least partly attributable to the urgencies of the time.

These three papers are, in order of their writing and placing in the new volume: (1) Chapter VI, "Democracy and Social Structure in Pre-Nazi Germany." This was written for and published in the first issue of the then new *Journal of Legal and Political Sociology* in 1942. It reflected the author's long-standing interest in problems of German society and forms a companion piece to the later paper on "Controlled Institutional Change." (2) Chapter VII, "Some Sociological Aspects of the Fascist Movements." This was written as the presidential address to the Eastern Sociological Society at its 1942 meeting, and was published in *Social Forces*, December, 1942. It attempts to generalize some of the insights developed in relation to Germany about the social background of the fascist movement, and to state them in terms of their relations to certain general features of modern Western society. (3) Chapter XIII, "The Population and Social Structure of Japan." This was published in the collaborative volume *Japan's Prospect* (D. G. Haring, Ed., Harvard University Press, 1946) by members of the faculty of the Harvard School for Overseas Administration. It is an attempt to extend to an Oriental society the same order of structural and dynamic analysis which had previously been developed in connection with Western countries.

The next three additions are papers written since the appearance of the first edition of these essays but prior to the general theoretical work cited above. These are (1) Chapter XV, "Social Classes and Class Conflict in the Light of Recent Sociological Theory." This was read at a meeting of the American Economic Association in December, 1948, which was concerned with assessment of the scientific influence of Marx in economics and sociology on the occasion of the hundredth anniversary of the *Communist Manifesto*. It was published in *Papers and Proceedings* of the *American Economic Review*, May, 1949. It is an attempt to bring to bear the main lines of modern sociological analysis on the problems of class conflict as stated in Marxist theory. (2) Chapter XVI, "Psychoanalysis and the Social Structure." This paper was read at a meeting of the American Psychoanalytic Association in May, 1948, and published in the *Psychoanalytic Quarterly*, July 1950. It is included because it states in rather general terms the author's approach to the relations between psychoanalysis and sociology. This theme has become a most important one in subsequent work. (3) The last addition in this group is the one already mentioned, Chapter XVII, "The Prospects of Sociological Theory," which points the way to the phase of theoretical work which was just beginning at the time it was written.

Finally, come the last two papers mentioned above which were written after those appearing in the *Working Papers*. The first of these, Chapter XVIII, is "A Sociologist Looks at the Legal Profession." This paper was read at the 50th Anniversary Symposium of the University of Chicago Law School in December, 1952. It is concerned with the similarities and differences between the place and functions of the legal profession in modern society and the medical profession which had been the object of considerable earlier study. It has proved possible in this paper to draw a closer analogy between the two professions than had at first seemed possible. The final paper added is "A Revised Analytical Approach to the Theory of Social Stratification." This paper was written for the *Reader in Social Stratification* edited by Bendix and Lipset. It attempts to bring the analysis of Chapter IV (written in 1940) up to date as a spelling out of general sociological theory in an important field of its application.

To make room for these additions, three chapters of the first edition of these essays have been omitted from the new one. The first of these is Chapter V, there entitled simply "Max Weber." This was by far the longest chapter in the book, and is omitted largely because it is readily available elsewhere in book form, not only in the first edition of these essays, but in its original place of publication as the Introduction to the translation of Weber's *Theory of*

Social and Economic Organization (Oxford University Press, 1947).
The second omission is Chapter I of the first edition, "The Position
of Sociological Theory." A good deal of its content is repeated
elsewhere, and it was felt that it was better to emphasize empirical
applications of theory in the new edition. Finally, Chapter III, "A
Selection from "Toward A Common Language for the Area of Social
Science " has also been omitted. This is largely because the classification set forth there is now completely obsolete, in the light of
the much more elaborate attempt at classification of institutional
patterns developed in Chapters III and IV of *The Social System*.
The main interest of the early version is as a first stage of the scheme
which has been much more fully developed in this later publication.

Besides the above changes in content, the new edition of these
Essays also differs in arrangement from the old. The balance between "pure" and "applied" theory has been altered in favor of the
latter sufficiently to make a separate section of papers with the
former emphasis less appropriate than before. Hence it has been
decided to reprint the papers in the order of their original publication without regard to subject-matter. This results in a few cases
in separating papers which belong closely together, as for example
that on Age and Sex and that on the American kinship system. But
perhaps this disadvantage is compensated for by giving the reader
a better opportunity to follow consecutively the process of development of theoretical thinking.

Karl Mannheim once stated that one of the principal differences
between European and American sociology lay in the concern of
the Europeans, especially on the Continent, with the diagnosis of
the larger social-political problems of their time, a trait of sociology
which connected it with the philosophy of history, while American
sociology had been much more concerned with specific and limited
empirical studies of phases of our own contemporary society. In
this respect the empirical preoccupations of most of these essays
clearly bear the imprint of the author's European training. But in
this empirical respect, as well as in respect to type of theory as
such, it seems legitimate to think of a process of convergence rather
than simply of two separate traditions of thought, and above all I
should like to argue that this interest in the larger social-political
problems does not mean the assimilation of sociology to the philosophy of history, as Alfred Weber above all has advocated and
carried it out. The interest in these broader problems in no way

involves the minimization or abandonment of the interest in acquiring for sociology the status of an empirical science with rigorous operational procedures and standards of validation.

In the recent theoretical work referred to above, my colleagues and I have strongly emphasized the fact that the theory of action, including its sociological branch, is applicable over a microscopic-macroscopic range. Sociologically speaking this reaches all the way from the analysis of the processes of interaction in temporary small groups to the processes in the most complex societies considered as total social systems. In this methodological situation, the study of the large-scale society, and the broad institutional structure of societies, of which Max Weber was the great master, has an exceedingly important place in the development of the relations between theory and empirical work.

If we are correct in our views about the range of applicability, there is no intrinsic reason why one rather than another "level" of the use of a conceptual scheme has any priority. It is a question of interest and of conceptions of the most strategic way to proceed in the furthering of sociological knowledge. In the light of this fact I should like to argue that broad comparative treatment of total social systems and of large-scale societies has had, in the light of the general state of sociological science in the last two generations, an important special place.

This is essentially because of the nature of the problems we sociologists have faced in making our conceptual schemes operationally testable according to the canons of the best scientific methods. The crux of the problem has been how to establish a fit between categories of data and the central concepts of *generalized* theoretical analysis. Broadly speaking we are only now *beginning* to get the kind of relation which combines empirical precision and high theoretical generality of implication in the *same* statements of fact. For the most part we have had to rest content with empirical statements which, as in the case for example of the net reproduction rate or the correlation between religious affiliation and voting behavior, might be extremely precise, but in theoretical terms must be interpreted to state *complex resultants* of the operation of a considerable and generally unknown number of variables of general significance to our science. But in physical science such concepts as temperature, velocity, momentum are both precisely determinable and are either the values of fundamental variables as such are very simple resultants. The great problem of the sciences of action in working toward empirical precision has been to break through this impasse of the lack of fit, and to do so in a situation where the fundamental variables it was desired to measure, were *unknown*. Common sense in this situation is likely to be as deceptive in our field as it is in physics. For example to common sense, density is "obviously" a fundamental property of physical objects; what *could* be more fundamental than the difference between a lead shot and a feather? But nevertheless density is, in the fundamental theory of mechanics, not treated as a fundamental variable, but as a resultant. There is no question but that many of the variables now thought to be most fundamental in the social sciences will turn out to be in the same category as density, not as mass or velocity. They are, that is to say, empirically crucial for many problems, but theoretically derivative, or (secondary).

In the light of very recent experience it seems that the very detailed and meticulous observation of interaction processes in small groups offered an opportunity to make the kinds of theoretical discriminations of empirically observable variables of which we are speaking, but in spite of the fact that such writers as Mead and Cooley have given us much insight about the problems of intimate interaction, until the present generation no one has had the imagination to develop a solid program of *detailed research* in this field. At the same time most of the data available on "intermediate" levels, especially before the development, which is itself recent, of sampling techniques, have been of the character of complex resultants illustrated by the net reproduction rate. In such a situation, increase in operational precision, *by itself* would not advance us toward our goal of "marrying" theory and operational procedures in the fruitful manner of the physical sciences.

It is in this connection that the macroscopic study of the large-scale society has acquired a certain special importance. The essential point is that the degree of precision which is theoretically significant is *relative*, relative that is to the theoretical discriminations which it is important to make.

Looking back, it can be seen that Toennies' famous discrimination of *Gemeinschaft* and *Gesellschaft* hit upon a quite fundamental line of distinction, which was not, to be sure, a distinction between two major variables in the usual sense, but which, if further analyzed, could lead to the definition of such variables as it has in fact, along with other sources, done. Toennies' empirical work was, however, highly impressionistic and not accompanied with at all precise conceptual analysis, to say nothing of research technique.

A much higher level, which represents the best of what is meant here by broad comparative study is found in two justly famous programs of research of the last generation, that of Max Weber in the comparative sociology of religion, and of Durkheim, in the field of rates of suicide. Weber essentially established certain broad differentiations of patterns of value-orientation, as we would now term them. He showed how these were related to the existential belief systems of the religious traditions in which they developed, and that these orientation patterns "corresponded" to the broad lines of differentiation of the social structures of the societies in which they had become institutionalized. This was the first major development in modern sociology in the systematic discrimination of major types of value system in terms directly articulated with the comparative analysis of social structures, which went well beyond the impressionistic level of a Toennies.

Weber was well trained in the techniques of historical research of his day, and was meticulously careful in his statements of fact. But he covered a range which would, and did, horrify the type of historian who believes that *only* establishment of detailed fact has scientific value. Moreover he necessarily ventured into a number of fields, such as Sinology and Indology, where in the nature of the case he could not himself be a competent expert in the detailed sense. But in exchange for this, using what was, from the point of view of the tradition of meticulous empirical scholarship a dubious procedure, he succeeded, as no one had done before him, in establishing broad lines of empirical differentiation which could be directly interpreted in terms of the theoretical scheme with which he had been working. He indeed used theoretical categories of the order of density, as for example "traditionalism," and much in his theoretical scheme has proved to need revision in the light of later developments. But by the use of the comparative method on the broadest scale, Weber, was carrying on *empirical* research which came closer to logic of the crucial experiment, than was the case for the work of almost any of the "empirical" sociologists whose coverage of the supposedly important facts of an empirical field was often much more "adequate" than his. The essential point is that the very breadth of the range Weber covered gave him, since he had a fruitful conceptual scheme, the opportunity to *select out* what for him were the *theoretically crucial* considerations of fact. Many details might remain unclear, but on the level of the research techniques he used, the *broad contrasts,* e.g. as between Chinese traditionalistic particularism and Western universalistic "rationalism," were unmistakable; and these contrasts have proved to be theoretically crucial.

Durkheim's work on suicide was in a sense intermediate between the broad comparative method and what might be called the "meticulous" ideal of operational procedure. He had statistical data of a sort and though his methods were, from the point of view of modern statistics, exceedingly crude, he showed considerable ingenuity in working out the most significant combinations of the data. But still the focus was the comparative method, the distinctions of rates of suicide by religious groups which he showed held up internationally; the differences between rates in armed forces and in the civil populations of the same countries, the variations of rates as a function of the business cycle. But Durkheim, as one of the great theorists of the history of sociology, was able to use these broad comparative differences to sharpen and refine his theoretical scheme. It was, crude as it was, empirical validation of highly generalized theory, and marked from that point of view a most important step in the development of the science.

This is the methodological context in which the empirical essays in this volume can claim to be contributions to empirical sociology and to the development of theory at the same time. In not a single case are they products of what, by current standards, would be called refined research technique; in this sense they can hardly claim to be "operational." They are, however, called essays in the "application" of theory in that in every case they represent attempts to bring to bear theoretical considerations in interpreting the various broad phenomena with which they are concerned. It matters profoundly to theory whether the theoretically expected relationships *in fact hold up* empirically. With respect to such matters as the distinctive character of the American middle-class urban kinship system, as contrasted for instance with that of classical China or of Japan, or to the major institutional pattern of medical practice in Western society as contrasted with that normal in "business" it can be claimed that they do stand up. Then however impressionistically these differences have been established, theory enables us to draw conclusions from them. We conclude for example that there is a relation between the specific structure of the American kinship system and the phenomena of our "youth culture," which have so often been attributed to the biological maturation process, but which are conspicuously absent in classical China. Or, the differences between the institutional pattern of medical practice and that of business can be shown to have a fundamental bearing on the psychotherapeutic component of the functions of medical practice.

The essential point of this discussion is that the gap between the empirical needs of the type of theory with which the author has been concerned, in the period represented by most of these essays, and the possibilities of most of the refined empirical operational techniques practiced in the same period has been such, that it is at least questionable whether confining attention to empirical problems to which the latter were best adapted would have served the empirical interests of theoretical development as well as the type of operationally crude empirical generalization represented in this volume has done. The gain in reliability and precision which such techniques could yield might well have been balanced by an exorbitant cost in the loss of freedom to investigate the empirical problems which seemed most crucial to the validation of the *strategic* theoretical ideas. In that case the distinctive contribution flowing from *some* kind of empirical testing of the kind of theoretical ideas in question might have been greatly diminished in favor of much better empirical work which was either in general less significant to theory, or at any rate was significant to a different order of theory.

I have wished to present this argument to the reader of these essays because the scientific functions of this order of crude empirical observation and generalization often tend to be overlooked when compared to the much greater sophistication and in one sense power of "real research." But in no sense do I wish to argue that this is an ideal or permanent state. Though it may very well prove to have a permanent place in our repertoire of procedures, it has its functions *above all* in the stage in which theory is beginning to "try its wings," when *some kind* of empirical guide-posts are absolutely essential. But when theory has developed far enough, its marriage with the sophisticated level of research technique can and must take place. We are, in my opinion, just beginning to enter the threshold of that era, with an increasing number of attempts to utilize more general theory in direct technical research, and conversely, to utilize technical research results for *technical* theoretical purposes.*

It is a commonplace that it is not possible to do certain kinds of things in the field of empirical validation and generalization without the development of the techniques to do them. But in some quarters there seems still to be a prevalent idea that theory, if it is in any sense good, cannot help making the connection if the techniques are available. Nothing could be further from the truth. Speaking from a good deal of experience in connection with the attempt to act as a "go-between" in arranging this marriage of theory and research technique, I can say that the amount of specifically *theoretical* work which is necessary is prodigious. The theoretical problems must be stated in a form which meets the operational requirements of the available techniques and at the same time permits high generality of reasoning about the implications of findings. For two parties to enter into a successful marriage *both* must have reached a certain level of maturity. The marriage, which we can expect soon to begin to produce offspring far surpassing the qualities of their parents, is only now becoming possible and only because the development of both partners has gone through a long series of preceding stages. This "father" of the new generation, if the role-designation for the theoretical partner may be permitted, had to go through his stages of playing cops and robbers and indians, before he was ready to do a man's job.

---

*The paper of Merton and Kit "Contributions to the Theory of Reference Group Behavior" is one of the best examples. Cf. *Continuities in Social Research*, Merton and Lazarsfeld, eds., The Free Press; 1950.

The Role of Ideas
in Social Action

THE SUBJECT of this paper has given rise to much controversy which has, on the whole, turned out to be strikingly inconclusive. It may be suggested that, in part at least, this is a result of two features of the discussion. On the one hand, sides have tended to be taken on the problem in too general terms. Ideas *in general* have been held either to have or not to have an important role in the determination of action. As opposed to this tendency, I shall attempt here to break the problem down into different parts, each of which fits differently into the analytical theory of action.

On the other hand, the discussion has, for the taste of the present writer, been altogether too closely linked to philosophical problems and has seldom been brought fairly into the forum of factual observation and theoretical analysis on the empirical level. This paper is to be regarded as a theoretical introduction to attempts of the latter sort.

I am far from believing that social or any other science can live in a kind of philosophical vacuum, completely ignoring all philosophical problems, but even though, as I have stated elsewhere,[1] scientific and philosophical problems are closely interdependent, they are nevertheless at the same time independent and can be treated in relative abstraction from each other. Above all, from the fact that this paper will maintain that ideas do play an important part in the determination of action, it is not to be inferred that its author is committed to some kind of idealistic metaphysics of the sort from which it has so often been inferred that ideas must arise through some process of "immaculate conception" unsullied by social and economic forces or that they influence action by some automatic and mysterious process of self-realization or "emanation" without relation to the other elements of the social system.

---

[1] *The Structure of Social Action,* 20 ff, New York, 1937.

The paper, then, will be devoted to the statement of a theoretical framework for the analysis of the role of ideas on an empirical, scientific basis. Without apologies, I shall start with an explicit definition of my subject matter. Ideas, for the purposes of this discussion, are "concepts and propositions, capable of intelligible interpretation in relation to human interests, values and experience." So far as, *qua* ideas, they constitute systems, the relations between these concepts and propositions are capable of being tested in terms of a certain type of norm, that of logic.

The definition just given is so stated that it can serve as the definition of a variable in a system of interdependent variables. That is, it is a combination of logical universals to which many different particulars, the values of the variable, may be fitted. Since the present concern is wholly scientific, the sole important questions to be asked are three: 1. Do differences which are accurately ascertainable obtain between the specific content of the ideas held by different individuals or groups in social systems at different times? 2. Is it possible to establish important relations between these differences and other observable aspects of, or events within, the same social systems? 3. Are these relations such that the ideas cannot be treated as a dependent variable, that is, their specific content deduced from knowledge of the values of one or more other observable variables in the same system? If all three of these questions can be answered in the affirmative, it may be claimed that ideas play an important role in the determination of social action in the only sense in which such a claim has meaning in science. Ideas would be an essential variable in a system of theory which can be demonstrated to "work," to make intelligible a complex body of phenomena. Whether in an ultimate, ontological sense these ideas are real, or only manifestations of some deeper metaphysical reality is a question outside the scope of this paper.

Ideas obviously could not be treated as a variable in systems of social action unless their specific content varied from case to case. But besides the variations of specific content from case to case, it may be possible, as has been suggested, to divide them into certain broad classes which differ appreciably from one another in their relations to action. How these classes shall be defined, and how many there are, are pragmatic questions in the scientific sense; the justification of making a distinction between any two classes is that their members behave differently in their relations to action. Whether this is the case or not is a question of fact. I shall outline such a classification and then present an analysis of the role of each so as to demonstrate the importance of making the distinctions.

The first class may be termed existential ideas. The concepts which comprise such ideas are the framework for describing or analyzing entities, or aspects or properties of them, which pertain to the external world of the person who entertains the ideas, the actor. These entities either are or are thought to be existent at the time, to have existed, or to be likely to exist. The reference is to an external "reality" in some sense. The ideas involve existential propositions relative to some phase or phases of this reality, real or alleged. The most general type of norm governing existential ideas is that of "truth."

Of existential, as of other ideas, it is convenient to distinguish two subclasses, the distinction between which is of cardinal importance. The one are empirical ideas, the concepts and propositions of which are, or are held to be, capable of verification by the methods of empirical science. All other existential ideas, on the other hand, I shall class together as nonempirical, regardless of the reasons why they are not scientifically verifiable.[2]

The second main class are what may be called normative ideas. These refer to states of affairs which may or may not actually exist, but in either case the reference is not in the indicative but in the imperative mood. If the state of affairs exists, insofar as the idea is normative the actor assumes an obligation to attempt to keep it in existence; if not, he assumes an obligation to attempt its realization at some future time. An idea is normative insofar as the maintenance or attainment of the state of affairs it describes may be regarded as an end of the actor. The states of affairs referred to may also be classified as empirical and nonempirical according to the above criteria.[3]

---

[2] This residual category is formulated for the immediate purposes in hand and its use is not to be held to imply that no distinctions between subclasses of nonempirical ideas are important for any other purposes.

[3] There is a third class of ideas which may be called "imaginative." The content of these refers to entities which are neither thought to be existent nor does the actor feel any obligation to realize them. Examples would be a utopia which is not meant as defining a program of action, or the creation of an entirely fictitious series of situations in a novel. At least the most obvious significance of such ideas in relation to action is as indices of the sentiments and attitudes of the actors rather than as themselves playing a positive role. To inquire whether indirectly they do play a role would raise questions beyond the scope of this paper and they will be ignored in the subsequent discussion. They are mentioned here only to complete the classification.

The first set of problems to be discussed concerns the role of empirical existential ideas. I think it fair to say that no branch of social science has been subjected to more thorough and rigorous analysis than this, so it forms an excellent starting point.[4] The context in which this analysis has taken place is the range of problems surrounding the concept of the rationality of action in the ordinary sense of the maximization of "efficiency" or "utility" by the adaptation of means to ends. It is the sense of rationality which underlies most current analysis of technological processes in science, industry, medicine, military strategy and many other fields, which lies at the basis of economic theory, and much analysis of political processes regarded as processes of maintaining, exercising, and achieving power.

The common feature of all these modes of analysis of action is its conception as a process of attaining specific and definite ends by the selection of the "most efficient" means available in the situation of the actor. This, in turn, implies a standard according to which the selection among the many possible alternative means is made. There is almost universal agreement that the relevant basis of selection in this kind of case involves the actor's knowledge of his situation, which includes knowledge of the probable effects of various possible alternative ways of altering it which are open to him. One of the necessary conditions of rationality of his action is that the knowledge should be scientifically valid.[5]

Valid empirical knowledge in this sense is certainly a system of ideas. It consists of concepts and propositions and their logical interrelations. Moreover, in all the above analyses of action, this knowledge is treated as a variable in the system of action; according to variations in its specific content, the action will be different. In explaining, above all, failure for the actual course of action to conform with a rational norm describing the "best" course, we continually refer to features of the store of knowledge of the actor. We say "He did not know . . . " with the implication that if he had, he would have acted differently, and "He supposed erroneously

---

[4] Much of this analysis is discussed in *The Structure of Social Action*. See esp. chap. 4, 161 ff.; chap. 5, 180 ff.; chap. 9, 344 ff.

[5] "Efficiency" involves choice among two or more alternative ways of attaining an end. The validity of knowledge alone is not a sufficient criterion to determine the relative efficiency of the different alternatives. Statement of the other necessary criteria would involve difficult questions far beyond the scope of this paper.

that . . . ," with the corresponding implication that if he had not been in error on the level of knowledge, he would also have acted differently. Thus, two of the coordinates of variation of knowledge which are relevant to its role in action are that in the direction of ignorance and of error. There is, for the attainment of any given end in any given situation, a certain minimum of valid knowledge which is adequate. If the knowledge actually falls short of this, if the actor is ignorant of any important features of the situation, or if his ideas are invalid, are in error, this is an adequate explanation of the failure of his action to be rational.

The analytical scheme in which the role of valid empirical knowledge in this sense has been most highly elaborated and conceptually refined is economic theory. Knowledge is a basically important variable in the system of economic theory, and he who would radically deny a role in action to ideas must find a satisfactory alternative explanation of all the uniformities of human action which have been established by two centuries of economic analysis, or demonstrate that the supposed uniformities do not exist.

But exactly the same thing is true of what we ordinarily call technology. The very processes of technological change to which many of our "materialists" assign so fundamental a role are in part a function of knowledge, i.e., of ideas, in exactly the same sense in which economic processes are. And there, far more than in the narrowly economic realm, knowledge has become a variable which we think of as to a high degree autonomous. For it takes, to a large extent, the form of theoretically systematized scientific knowledge rather than common sense. Surely the development of modern aniline dyes, the radio, or alloy steels, cannot be understood without reference to the essentially autonomous developments of science on which they depend.

Marxian theory has, however, classed technology among the "material" factors in social change, while "ideas" form part of the superstructure. Whence does this peculiar procedure derive? Two important sources of it may be noted. In the first place, Marxian theory has neither a rigorous concept of ideas, nor a classification of different kinds of ideas. Hence, when those ideas which Marxians habitually term "ideologies" behave differently from the scientific basis of technology, they tend to ignore the fact that the latter is also made up of ideas, and generalize the behavior of the former into that of ideas in general. Secondly, Marxian theory rests on an analytical basis essentially different from that which is the starting point of the present discussion. For it, the total concrete structure of the industrial enterprise is a "factor," technology, social organization and all. The present attempt is to break down entities like this into simpler elements, the classification of which cuts across the Marxian dichotomy of "ideal" and "material" factors. There is no inherent reason why the Marxian choice of variables should be ultimate. The only scientific test as between it and another, such as that under discussion here, is the pragmatic one: which is the more illuminating in the understanding of certain empirical problems.

Every human society possesses a considerable stock of empirically valid knowledge, both of the nonhuman environment in which its members act, and of themselves, and of each other. That this knowledge is empirical and not theoretically systematized in the sense of modern science does not alter the fact. Moreover, a very large part of the action of the members of all societies is to be understood in terms of this knowledge. Lévy-Bruhl's theory that primitive men do not think logically has, so far as it bears upon this point, been definitely discredited.[6]

But in addition to ideas which will stand the test of scientific validity, there are current in every society many ideas which in one respect or another diverge from this standard. So far as their reference is existential rather than normative or imaginative, the question arises as to what is the basis of this divergence. In answer to this question, a certain positivistic bias is very widely prevalent, and must be guarded against. It is the view, implicit or explicit, that divergence from the standard of empirical verifiability is always and necessarily a matter of empirical shortcomings in the sense that the ideas in question are not only, negatively, not verifiable, but that they can be shown to be *positively* wrong, that is, that the basis of their unverifiability is ignorance or error, or both. This judgment clearly implies that there is available an adequate positive scientific standard by which to judge them.

At least in the field of empirically known systems of existential ideas, it can be stated with confidence that this class, which may be called un-scientific ideas, does not exhaust the departures from empirical verifiability, but that, in addition, there is a class of con-

---

[6] See especially B. Malinowski, *"Magic, Science and Religion,"* ed. by Robert Redfield (Free Press, Glencoe, Ill., 1948).

cepts and propositions which are unverifiable, not because they are erroneous, but because, as Pareto put it, they "surpass experience." Such ideas as that the universe is divided between a good and an evil principle, that souls go through an unending series of reincarnations, that the only escape from sin is by divine grace, are in this category. They are *non*scientific rather than unscientific.[7]

What, then, can be said about the role of such nonscientific ideas? So far as they are existential rather than normative or imaginative in character, there are certain formal similarities with empirical, scientifically valid ideas. The latter may, in one aspect, be considered as mechanisms of orientation of the actor to his situation. Insofar as man is treated as a purposive being, attempting rationally to attain ends, he cannot be considered as fully oriented to his situation until, among other things, he has adequate knowledge of the situation in the respects which are relevant to the attainment of the ends in question, or other functionally equivalent mechanisms.

But the role of existential ideas has so far been considered only in one context, that of the basis of choice of means to given ends. There is in addition the necessity of cognitive orientation of another sort, an answer to the problem of justification of the ends which are in fact pursued.[8] If the justifications men give of why they should pursue their ultimate ends are systematically and inductively studied, one fact about them stands out. One very prominent component of all known comprehensive social systems of such justifications must be classed as nonempirical. The more the

---

[7] I do not wish to maintain that this distinction possesses ontological significance. To do so would be to alter the plane of the discussion of this paper, which has set out to adhere to the scientific level. Inevitably, the basis of the distinction must be found in current standards of scientific methodology. From this point of view, a nonempirical proposition is one, not only which cannot, because of practical difficulties, be verified with present techniques, but which involves, in the strict operational sense, "meaningless" questions, questions which cannot, in the present state of our scientific and methodological knowledge, be answered by a conceivable operation or combination of them. Whether, at some future time, a completely positivistic philosophy will be capable of demonstration is another question. But I should like to point out that objection to this distinction usually involves the positivistic philosophical position; it is arbitrarily laid down that all departures from the standard of empirical verifiability *must* be in terms of ignorance and error. The position taken here is such that the burden of proof is on him who would object to the distinction. It is his task to show empirically that what have here been called unscientific and nonscientific ideas in fact do not stand in different relations to action. This shifts the argument from the methodological to the factual plane.

[8] On this problem, see *The Structure of Social Action,* chap. 5, 205ff.

attempt is made to state the explicit or implicit major premises of such arguments clearly and sharply, the more evident it becomes that they are metaphysical rather than scientific propositions. This, I maintain, is true of all *known* social systems; whether it is ultimately possible to eliminate these nonempirical elements is not a relevant question in the present context.

But the mere demonstration that a certain class of phenomena exists does not prove that their description involves, for the purposes in hand, important variables. The question is not whether nonempirical existential ideas are always to be found in social systems, but whether important features of these social systems can be shown to be functions of variations in the content of these ideas. How is this problem to be attacked?

Most attempts in this field have been couched in terms of the historical or genetic method alone. Of course the only possible causal factors[9] in the genesis of any particular state of affairs are components of particular antecedent states of affairs in the same sequence. But even then causal relationship can be demonstrated only by the use of general concepts and generalized knowledge of uniformities. The question here at issue does not touch the explanation of particular facts, but the establishment of uniformities. The only possible procedure by which this can be done in our field is comparative method which permits the isolation of variables. It is the strict logical counterpart of experiment. One important reason for the unsatisfactory character of the discussion of these problems revolving about Marxism is the fact that it has been almost uniformly couched in genetic, historical terms, as the Marxian theory itself is, and analytical generalizations as to the role of ideas cannot in principle be either proved or disproved by such a method. Hence the indeterminate issue of the controversy.

By far the most significant empirical studies available in this particular field are those of Max Weber in the sociology of religion.[10] Weber was interested in a particular problem of historical imputation, that of the relative role of "material" factors and of

---

[9] "Factors" in the sense of concrete events or states of affairs, or parts or aspects of them, not of *generalized*, analytical elements like "mass" or "ideas." The two are often confused. See *The Structure of Social Action*, chap. 16, 610ff.

[10] *Gesammelte Aufsätze zur Religionssoziologie.* 3 vols. The most comprehensive secondary accounts in English are in L. L. Bennion, *Max Weber's Methodology*, and *The Structure of Social Action*, chaps. 14 and 15.

the religious ideas of certain branches of Protestantism in the genesis of what he called rational bourgeois capitalism. But Weber's methodological insight showed him that, in the absence of well-established general informities touching the role of ideas, it was hopeless to attack the problem by more and more elaborate genetic studies of the immediate historical background of modern capitalism. So he turned to the comparative method, the study of the influence of *variations* in the content of religious ideas.

A variable cannot, of course, be isolated unless other possibly important variables can, within a relevant range of variation, either be held constant or their independence demonstrated. Weber attempted to deal with this problem by showing that, in the different societies he treated, *before* the development of religious ideas in which he is interested, the state of the material factors and their prospective autonomous trends of development was, in the relevant respects, essentially similar. That is, for instance, in his three best worked out cases, those of China, India, and Western Europe, he attempted to estimate the relative favorableness or unfavorableness of the economic situations, the "conditions of production," to a capitalistic development. The outcome of his studies in this respect was the judgment that there is a high degree of similarity in all three societies in this respect, with, if anything, a balance of favorableness in favor of India and China.[11]

But the fact remains that only in Europe did the development of capitalism actually take place. What accounts for the radically different outcomes in the three civilizations? It is a fact that the development of religious ideas in the three cases took quite different courses. In relation to this variable, an adequate range of variation to account for the differentiation is demonstrable, whereas in the case of the material factors it is not. This places the burden of proof on him who would advance a materialistic explanation. He must show that differentiating elements on this level were present of which Weber did not take account.

However, Weber did not leave his account of the role of religious ideas at this point. In terms of a more generalized conceptual scheme, the "theory of action," or his *verstehende Soziologie*," he analyzed certain mechanisms by which ideas can and do exert an influence on action. On the basis of this analysis, he worked out

---

11 This part of Weber's work was not methodologically completely rigorous, but allowance for this does not affect his general conclusions.

what is the probable effect on certain aspects of secular social life of adherence to each of the dominant systems of religious ideas, Confucianism, Hinduism and Protestantism, and found these deductions verified in that the actual facts corresponded, as seen in comparative perspective, with expectations in terms of reasoning from this hypothesis.

He further strengthened his case by working out, in an elaborate analysis of evidence from various sources in terms of his conceptual scheme, an understanding of many of the specific mechanisms of the process by which this influence has probably been exerted and verified this analysis in considerable detail.

The result of this very comprehensive comparative study in all these phases was not only to build up a strong case for his original historical thesis, that the ideas of ascetic Protestantism actually did play an important causal role in the genesis of modern capitalism. It also resulted in the formulation of a generalized theory of the role of nonempirical existential ideas in relation to action. It is this which is of primary interest here.

It was not Weber's view that religious ideas constitute the principal driving force in the determination of the relevant kinds of action. This role is rather played by what he called religious interests. A typical example is the interest in salvation, an interest which has in turn a complex derivation from, among other things, certain stresses and strains to which individuals are sometimes subjected in social situations where frustration of the worldly ends seems inevitable and founded in the nature of things. But the mere interest in salvation alone is not enough. The question arises as to what kinds of specific action it will motivate. This, Weber's comparative analysis shows, will be very different according to the structure of the existential religious ideas according to which the individual achieves cognitive orientation to the principal nonempirical problems he faces in his situation.

For example, on the basis of the generally imminent, pantheistic conception of divinity of Indian philosophy, and more specifically of the doctrines of Karma and Transmigration, to seek salvation in a radical sense through concrete achievement in worldly spheres would be meaningless. If such action contravened the traditional order, it would be reprehensible for that reason and set the actor back on his quest for salvation; if not, it could only generate more Karma and lead to endless rebirths. The only meaning of salvation is escape from the "wheel of Karma" in completely otherworldly mystical and ascetic exercises. For the Calvinist, on the other hand, mystical union with the divine is entirely excluded by the absolute transcendentality of God. He has been placed in this world to do God's will in the building of the Kingdom. His eternal fate is settled by Predestination, but he can become certain of salvation through proving his faith by active labor in the vineyard, by doing God's will.

The function of religious ideas is, in relation to the interest in salvation, to "define the situation," to use W. I. Thomas' term. Only by reference to these ideas is it possible to understand, concretely, what specific forms of action are relevant to attainment of salvation, or certainty of it. Weber succeeded in showing that rational, systematic, workmanlike labor in a worldly calling has had this significance to ardent believers in Calvinism and related religious movements, whereas it would be totally meaningless to a believer in Karma and Transmigration on a pantheistic background no matter how strong his interest in salvation. In this sense, the content of the religious ideas is a significant variable in the determination of the concrete course of action.

So far discussion has been confined to the role of existential ideas. These have been dealt with in two quite different contexts. Empirical ideas have been analyzed in their relation to the problem of selection of means according to the norm of rationality. Non-empirical ideas, on the other hand, have been treated in relation to the teleological problem of orientation of the actor, the justification of selection of ends to pursue. There is a gap between these two treatments which must now be filled. Selection of means has no significance except in relation to ends, while what has been called teleological orientation is equally meaningless unless there is, facing actors, a problem of choice between alternative ends.

Indeed the whole analytical procedure which has here been followed implies that a fundamental role in action is played by normative elements.[12] In the first place, analysis of the underlying assumptions involved in treatment of empirical knowledge as an independent variable in the choice of means has shown that both a positive role of ends, and the existence of determinate relations of ends in a more or less well-integrated system are essential to the attribution of causal importance to knowledge. Rational action,

---

[12] The problem of the significance of normative elements in action is extensively treated throughout *The Structure of Social Action*.

in the sense of action guided by valid knowledge, is at the same time action which is normatively oriented. Similarly, the definition of the situation with reference to religious interests could have no meaning apart from the contention that it made a difference to the course of action what ends, among the various alternatives, were chosen.

Not only is action normatively oriented in the sense of pursuing ends, it is also subject to certain normative conditions, to rules which guide it. For instance, in pursuing the end of closing a profitable deal, a businessman may consider himself subject to the condition that it shall be done "honestly." From some points of view, such rules may be considered themselves as ends, but they are not the immediate ends of the course of action under analysis. They appear rather as considerations limiting the acceptable range of alternative means, choice among which is to be guided by considerations of rational efficiency.

Now both ends and guiding norms involve a cognitive element, an element of ideas, however little the normative pattern may be exhausted in these terms. That such an element is involved may be brought out by considering the implications of the questions which are inevitably asked when we try to understand action in terms of such normative elements. "What is the end . . . " of a given course of action;—for instance, what is meant by making a profitable deal; or "what do you mean . . . " by the norm to which a course of action is subject,—for instance, by honesty in making a deal? It is obvious that the answers to all questions must be in the form of propositions, that is, of ideas. But in this case, ideas are in some sense imputed, not only to the sociological observer of action, but to the actor himself. It is a question not of what honesty means to the observer, but to the actor. It means, for instance, among other things, that he should not attempt to get the other party's consent to the deal by making statements about his product as true which he knows to be false.

The essential point for present purposes is that, in so far as analysis of action in terms of orientation to ends and norms is scientifically useful at all, it implies two things: 1. That it is possible to impute to the actor with adequate precision for the purposes in hand, not only a "will" to attain certain ends or conform with certain norms, but a content of those ends and norms which is capable of formulation as a set of ideas. 2. That variations in this content stand in functional relations to the facts of the system of action other than the system of ideas of the actor.

Whether normative ideas constitute a variable independent of others in the system of action, is to be tested by essentially the same kind of procedure which was outlined in the case of Weber's treatment of religious ideas. Weber himself showed that it is a variable in part dependent on nonempirical ideas. This would make it, insofar, relatively independent of "material" factors. But at the same time, there is no essential reason why an important range of variability independent in turn of metaphysical and religious ideas does not exist.

The foregoing analysis of the role of ideas in action has been presented in general terms, with appeal to generally known facts, and to two bodies of technically specific evidence, that employed in economic and technological analyses of rational action, and in Max Weber's studies of the role of religious ideas. It is impossible within the limits of such a paper to detail any significant sample of the enormous mass of empirical evidence, from these and other sources, which supports the main lines of the analysis. I should not, however, like to close without mentioning one other set of considerations which seem to be greatly to strengthen the case for my thesis.

It has already been remarked that demonstration of causal relationship in any particular historical sequence cannot be derived from observation of the facts of that particular sequence alone; it is necessary to be able to apply to these facts generalized theoretical knowledge derived from comparative analysis of a series of different particular situations. Only by this procedure can variables be isolated and the functional relationships of their values be worked out and verified.

Hence the problem of the role of ideas cannot be treated adequately in terms of ad hoc *recitation of the facts of certain examples. It involves systematic theoretical analysis of action, of the relation of the same variables to many different concrete situations.* In both the two cases which have been most fully analyzed above, the theorems relative to the role of ideas are not isolated, but are an integral part of more comprehensive bodies of theory. Thus the analysis of the role of empirical ideas in rational action may be regarded as an application to this particular problem of one of the most highly developed bodies of generalized theoretical knowledge in the social field, economic theory. This has the effect of greatly strengthening the evidence for the particular theorem, for it is verified not only directly with reference to the kind of facts here discussed, but indirectly in that it is logically interdependent with all the other theorems of economic science. So far as they are mutually interdependent, the facts which support any one serve also to verify the others.

In the case of religious ideas, there is no such generally recognized and used body of theory into which the results of Weber's empirical studies can be fitted. But it has already been remarked that Weber himself did in fact develop a body of such theory to a high degree of systematization in the course of his studies. The theoretical structure he developed is, in his own work, applicable to, and verified in terms of, many other problems than that of the role of ideas. But more than this. My own recently published analysis of certain phases of the development of social theory in the last generation[13] has shown that in these theoretical results Weber converged with remarkable exactitude and detail on a structure in all essentials like that developed by other theorists with quite different starting points and empirical interests. In particular Durkheim, whose interest was not specifically in the problem of the role of ideas at all, but in the basis of social solidarity, arrived at a set of categories in the field of religion which corresponds point for point with that of Weber. Weber's theoretical analysis of the role of nonempirical ideas is in fact part of a much broader system of analytical social theory, the emergence of which can be traced in a number of sources quite independent of Weber.

Moreover not only did Weber, Durkheim, and others converge on this particular part of a theoretical system, dealing mainly with religion, but as, among other things, very important parts of the work of both men show, this common scheme of the sociology of religion is in turn part of a still broader theoretical system which *includes* the economic and technological analysis of the role of empirical knowledge in relation to rationality of action. Both sets of problems belong together, and are part of the same more generalized analysis of human action.[14]

---

[13] *The Structure of Social Action.* See esp. chaps. 17 and 18:

[14] The case of Pareto is particularly interesting in this respect. Pareto has been very widely heralded as one of the major prophets of anti-intellectualism, as one of the principal social theorists who radically denied an important role to ideas. Did he not lay particular emphasis on "nonlogical action"? To those who have followed the above argument closely, two facts should

To conclude. The actual controversy over the role of ideas has been much more a battle of the implications of rival philosophical and other extrascientific points of view than it has been the result of careful, empirical analysis of the facts. I suggest that leaving these philosophical considerations aside and embarking on such careful study will very probably result in much reduction of the difference of opinion. The thesis put forward in this paper seems to me not only to fit very important bodies of well established and carefully analyzed facts. It also fits in with a body of generalized theoretical knowledge of human social action, which has already accumulated a heavy weight of scientific authority behind it in a large number of different factual fields. This seems to me to justify taking the positive role of ideas as a working hypothesis for further empirical research. The result of such research will, as always, be to modify the formulations of the problem, and of theorems which appear to be verified, from forms which seemed acceptable when the research process began. But such modification is not "refutation" of a theory; it is the normal course of scientific progress to which the superseded theory itself makes an essential contribution.

---

make one suspicious of this interpretation. First, Pareto was well trained in economic theory, and insofar as he attributes importance to the elements it analyzes, to the "interests," he must, *ipso facto* attribute importance to ideas. But not only this; he makes the conception of rationality in precisely the technological-economic sense the starting point of his own broader analysis of action. Nonlogical action is precisely action insofar as it cannot be understood in terms of this standard of rationality.

It turns out on analysis that his main theoretical scheme as such involves no theorem at all as to the role of ideas, except empirical existential ideas. His actual thesis is, not that other ideas have no role, but that beyond the range of applicability of this kind of conception of rationality or logical action, the ideas which do have a role cannot claim empirical scientific validity. But in his actual treatment there is much evidence that he attributes a very important role to nonempirical existential and normative ideas. This conclusion is strongly confirmed by the circumstances that Pareto's general conceptual scheme converges in all essential respects with the broader more general theoretical structure of which I have spoken, which may also be found in the works of Max Weber and Durkheim. It would indeed be strange, in the light of this fact, if there were a radical disagreement between them on so basic a theorem as that of the role of ideas.

The interpretation of Pareto as a radical anti-intellectualist appears to arise mainly from two sources. On the one hand, there is, in the formulation of his approach to the analysis of action a source of anti-intellectualistic bias (*The Structure of Social Action*, 272, Note 1), which does not however play any substantive part in the main theoretical structure. This is indicative of the fact that his own theory was imperfectly integrated; and there are, underlying this, currents of thought which tend in this direction. But more important than this basis in Pareto's own work is the fact that the general majority of Pareto's interpreters have approached his work with an interpretive bias which enormously exaggerates the importance of these tendencies. The source of this bias is the fact that interpretation has been predominantly in terms of a positivistic system of general social theory. See *The Structure of Social Action*, chaps. 5-7.

II

The Professions
and Social Structure

COMPARATIVE STUDY of the social structures of the most important civilizations shows that the professions occupy a position of importance in our society which is, in any comparable degree of development, unique in history. Perhaps the closest parallel is the society of the Roman Empire where, notably, the Law was very highly developed indeed as a profession. But even there the professions covered a far narrower scope than in the modern Western world. There is probably in Rome no case of a particular profession more highly developed than in our own society, and there was scarcely a close analogy to modern engineering, medicine or education in quantitative importance, though all of them were developed to a considerable degree.

It seems evident that many of the most important features of our society are to a considerable extent dependent on the smooth functioning of the professions. Both the pursuit and the application of science and liberal learning are predominantly carried out in a professional context. Their results have become so closely interwoven in the fabric of modern society that it is difficult to imagine how it could get along without basic structural changes if they were seriously impaired.

There is a tendency to think of the development and application of science and learning as a socially unproblematical process. A vague sort of "curiosity" and beyond that mere possession of the requisite knowledge are held to be enough. This is evidenced by the air of indignant wonder with which technologically minded people sometimes cite the fact that actual technical performance is well below the theoretical potentialities of 100 percent efficiency. Only by extensive comparative study does it become evident that for even a moderate degree either of the development or the application of science there is requisite a complex set of social conditions which the "technologically minded" seldom think of, but incline to take for granted as in the nature of things. Study of the institutional framework within which professional activities are carried on should help considerably to understand the nature and functions of some of these social "constants."

The professions do not, however, stand alone as typical or distinctive features of modern Western civilization. Indeed, if asked what were the most distinctive features, relatively few social scientists or historians would mention the professions at all. Probably the majority would unhesitatingly refer to the modern economic order, to "capitalism," "free enterprise," the "business economy," or however else it is denominated, as far more significant. Probably the only major exception to this would be the relatively prominent attention given to science and technology, but even these would not be thought of mainly in relation to the professional framework, but rather as handmaidens of economic interests.

Not only is there a tendency to empirical concentration on the business world in characterizing this society, but this is done in terms which tend to minimize the significance of the professions. For the dominant keynote of the modern economic system is almost universally held to be the high degree of free play it gives to the pursuit of self-interest. It is the "acquisitive society," or the "profit system" as two of the most common formulas run. But by contrast with business in this interpretation the professions are marked by "disinterestedness." The professional man is not thought of as engaged in the pursuit of his personal profit, but in performing services to his patients or clients, or to impersonal values like the advancement of science. Hence the professions in this context appear to be atypical, to some even a mere survival of the mediaeval guilds. Some think that these spheres are becoming progressively commercialized, so that as distinctive structures they will probably disappear.

There are various reasons for believing that this way of looking at the "essence" of modern society is a source of serious bias in the sociological interpretation of the situation. The fact that the professions have reached a uniquely high level of development in *the same society* which is also characterized by a business economy suggests that the contrast between business and the professions which has been mainly started in terms of the problem of self-interest, is not the whole story. Possibly there are elements common to both areas, indeed to our whole occupational system, which are at least as important to their functioning as is self-interest to business, disinterestedness to the professions. The concrete inter-penetration of the two, as exemplified in the role of engineers and lawyers in the conduct of business enterprises would suggest that. The study of the professions, by eliminating the element of self-interest in the ordinary sense, would seem to offer a favorable approach to the analysis of some of these common elements. This paper will deal with three of them which seem to be of particular importance to the modern occupational structure as a whole, in-cluding business, the professions, and government.

But before entering on their discussion a further point may be noted. In much of traditional thought about human action the most basic of all differences in types of human motivation has been held to be that between "egoistic" and "altruistic" motives. Correlative with this there has been the tendency to identify this classification with the concrete motives of different spheres of activity: the business man has been thought of as egoistically pursuing his own self-interest regardless of the interests of others, while the profes-sional man was altruistically serving the interests of others regard-less of his own. Seen in this context the professions appear not only as empirically somewhat different from business, but the two fields would seem to exemplify the most radical cleavage conceiv-able in the field of human behavior.

If it can be shown that the difference with respect to self-interest does not preclude very important institutional similarities in other respects, a further possibility suggests itself. Perhaps even in this respect the difference is not so great as our predominantly economic and utilitarian orientation of thought would lead us to believe. Perhaps even it is not mainly a difference of typical motive at all, but one of the different situations in which much the same com-monly human motives operate. Perhaps the acquisitiveness of modern business is institutional rather than motivational.

Let us, however, turn first to the elements of the common insti-tutional pattern of the occupational sphere generally, ignoring for the moment the problem of self-interest. The empirical promi-nence of industrial technology calls attention immediately to one of them. Industrial technology in the modern world has become to a large extent "applied science." One of the dominant character-istics of science is its "rationality" in the sense which is opposed to "traditionalism." Scientific investigation, like any other human activity when viewed in terms of the frame of reference of action, is oriented to certain normative standards. One of the principal of these in the case of science is that of "objective truth." Whatever else may be said of this methodologically difficult conception, it is quite clear that the mere fact that a proposition has been held to be true in the past is not an argument either for or against it before a scientific forum. The norms of scientific investigation, the standards by which it is judged whether work is of high scientific quality, are essentially independent of traditional judgments.

What is true of science as such is in turn true of its practical applications. Insofar as a judgment of what is the "best" thing to do rests on scientific considerations, whether it be in technology or in medicine, the merely traditional way of doing it as "the fathers" have done it, fails to carry normative authority. The relevant questions are, rather, objective,—what are the facts of the situation and what will be the consequences of various alternative procedures? Furthermore rationality in this sense extends far beyond the boundaries of either pure or applied science in a technical sense. The business man, the foreman of labor, and not least the non-scientific professional man such as the lawyer, is enjoined to seek the "best," the most "efficient" way of carrying on his function, not to accept the time-honored mode. Even though the range of such rational considerations be limited by ends which are institutionally kept outside discussion, as the financial well-being of the enterprise or, as in the law, certain accepted principles of the Common Law, still, within the limits, traditionalism is not authoritative.

It should be noted that rationality in this sense is institutional, a part of a normative pattern: it is not a mode of orientation which is simply "natural" to men. On the contrary comparative study indicates that the present degree of valuation of rationality as opposed to traditionalism is rather "unnatural" in the sense that it is a highly exceptional state. The fact is that we are under continual and subtle social pressures to be rationally critical, particularly of ways and means. The crushing force to us of such epithets as "stupid" and "gullible" is almost sufficient indication of this. The importance of rationality in the modern professions generally, but particularly in those important ones concerned with the development and application of science serves to emphasize its role in the society at large. But this is even more impressively the case since here it is divorced from the institutionalized expectation of self-interest typical of the contractual pattern of business conduct.

In quite a different way the role of the professions serves to bring out a second widely pervasive aspect of our general occupational pattern. There is a very important sense in which the professional practitioner in our society exercises authority. We speak of the doctor as issuing "orders" even though we know that the only "penalty" for not obeying them is possible injury to the patient's own health. A lawyer generally gives "advice" but if the client knew just as well what to do it would be unnecessary for him to consult a lawyer. This professional authority has a peculiar sociological structure. It is not as such based on a generally superior status, as is the authority a Southern white man tends to assume over any Negro, nor is it a manifestation of superior "wisdom" in general or of higher moral character. It is rather based on the superior "technical competence" of the professional man. He often exercises his authority over people who are, or are reputed to be, his superiors in social status, in intellectual attainments or in moral character. This is possible because the area of professional authority is limited to a particular technically defined sphere. It is only in matters touching health that the doctor is by definition more competent than his lay patient, only in matters touching his academic specialty that the professor is superior, by virtue of his status, to his student. Professional authority, like other elements of the professional pattern, is characterized by "specificity of function." The technical competence which is one of the principal defining characteristics of the professional status and role is always limited to a particular "field" of knowledge and skill. This specificity is essential to the professional pattern no matter how difficult it may be, in a given case, to draw the exact boundaries of such a field. As in all similar cases of continuous variation, it is legitimate to compare widely separated points. In such terms it is obvious that one does not call on the services of an engineer to deal with persistent epigastric pain, nor on a professor of Semitic languages to clarify a question about the kinship system of a tribe of Australian natives. A professional man is held to be "an authority" only in his own field.

Functionally specific technical competence is only one type of case in which functional specificity is an essential element of modern institutional patterns. Two others of great importance may be mentioned to give a better idea of the scope of this institutional element. In the first place, in the classic type of "contractual relationship," rights and obligations are specifically limited to what are implicitly or explicitly the "terms of the contract." The burden of proof that it is really owed, is on him who would exact an obligation, while in many other types of relationship the opposite is true, the burden of proof that it is *not* due is on the one who would evade an obligation. Thus in an ordinary case of commercial indebtedness, a request for money on the part of one party will be met by the question, do I owe it? Whether the requester "needs" the money is irrelevant, as is whether the other can well afford to pay it. If, on the other hand, the two are brothers, any contractual agreements are at least of secondary importance; the important questions are, on the one hand, whether and how urgently the one needs the money, on the other whether the second can "afford" it. In the latter connection it comes down to a question of the possible conflict of this with what are recognized as higher obligations. In the commercial case it is not necessary even to cite what other possible uses for the money may be involved, the question is only *why* it should be paid. In the kinship case the question is immediately why the request should *not* be met, and the only satisfactory answer is the citing of higher obligations with which it conflicts. Commercial relations in our society are predominantly functionally specific, kinship relations, functionally diffuse.

Similarly if a doctor asks a patient a question the relevant reaction is to ask why he should answer it, and the legitimizing reply is that the answer is necessary for the specific function the doctor has been called upon to perform, diagnosing an illness for instance. Questions which cannot be legitimized in this way would normally be resented by the patient as "prying" into his private affairs. The patient's wife, on the other hand, would, according to our predominant sentiments, be entitled to an explanation as to why a question should *not* be answered. The area of the marriage relationship is not functionally specific, but diffuse.

Functional specificity is also essential to another crucial pattern of our society, that of administrative "office." In an administrative or bureaucratic hierarchy, authority is distributed and institutionalized in terms of office. By virtue of his office a man can do things, particularly in the sense of giving orders to others, which in his "private capacity" he would not be allowed to do at all. Thus the

treasurer of a company, in the name of the company, can sometimes sign checks for very large amounts which far exceed his
private resources. But the authority of office in this sense is strictly
limited to the powers of the particular office, as defined in the
structure of the hierarchy in question. Authority in this sense is not
enjoyed by virtue of a technical competence. The treasurer does
not necessarily have a skill in signing checks which is superior to
that of many of his subordinates. But this kind of authority shares
with that based on technical competence the fact that it is functionally specific. The officer of a concern is condemned or penalized
for exceeding his authority in a way similar to that in which a
doctor would be for trying to get his patient to do things not
justified as means of maintaining or improving his health. As in
the case of rationality, the concentration of much of our social
theory on the problem of self-interest has served to obscure the
importance of functional specificity, an institutional feature common to the professional and the commercial spheres. Again, as in
the case of rationality, this cannot be taken for granted as
"natural" to human action generally. The degree of differentiation
of these specific spheres of authority and obligation from the more
diffuse types of social relation—like those of kinship and generalized loyalty to "leaders"—which we enjoy, is most unusual in
human societies, and calls for highly specific explanation. It is one
of the most prominent features of the "division of labor."

It is not uncommon in sociological discussions today to distinguish between "segmental" and "total" bases in the relationships
of persons. What has above been spoken of as functional specificity
naturally applies only to segmental relationships. But relations
may be segmented without being functionally specific, in that the
separation of contents of the different relations in which a given
person stands need not be carried out primarily on a functional
basis. Friendships are usually segmental in this sense, one does
not share all his life and interests with any one friend. But aside
from structurally fortuitous variations due to the fact that there
may be different areas of common interest, friendships are more
apt to be differentiated on the bases of degrees of "intimacy" than
on that of the specific functional content. Hence the distinction
cuts across the one we have been discussing. But it serves to direct
attention to the third pattern element not taken account of in the
discussions of self-interest. The more two people's total personal-

ities are involved in the basis of their social relationship, the less it is possible for either of them to abstract from the particular person of the other in defining its content. It becomes a matter of what A means to B as a particular person. To a considerable extent in all three of the types of functionally specific pattern discussed above it is possible to abstract; to the professional man the other party is a "case" or a "client," to the business man a "customer," to the administrative officer a "subordinate." Cases, customers, and subordinates are classified by criteria which do not distinguish persons or the particular relations of persons as such. Cases are "medical" or "surgical," customers are "large" and "small," or good and poor credit risks, subordinates are efficient or inefficient, quick or slow, obedient or insubordinate. On the other hand in kinship relations such "objective" and universal bases of classification cannot be used. A's father is distinguished from all other males of an older generation, not by his physiological or pathological characteristics, not by his financial status, nor by his administrative qualities, but by virtue of the particular relation in which he stands to A.

The matter may be approached from a slightly different point of view. A heart specialist, for instance, may have to decide whether a given person who comes to his office is eligible for a relatively permanent relation to him as his patient. So far as the decision is taken on technical professional grounds the relevant questions do not relate to *who* the patient is but to *what* is the matter with him. The basis of the decision will be "universalistic," the consideration of whether he has symptoms which indicate a pathological condition of the heart. Whose son, husband, friend he is, is in this context irrelevant. Of course, if a doctor is too busy to take on all the new patients who apply, particularistic considerations may play a part in the selection, he may give special attention to the friend of a relative. But this is not the organizing principle of the doctor-patient relationship. Similarly within a relationship once established it is possible to make the same distinction with respect to the basis on which rights are claimed or obligations accepted. A patient's claim on his doctor's time is primarily a matter of the objective features of the "case" regardless of *who* the patient is, while a wife's claim on her husband's time is a matter of the fact that she is his wife, regardless, within limits, of what the occasion is. The standards and criteria which are independent of the particular social relationship to a particular person may be called universalistic, those which apply by virtue of such a relationship on the other hand are particularistic. Like all such analytical distinctions it does not preclude that both elements may be involved in the same concrete situation. But nevertheless their relative predominance is a matter of the greatest importance.

The fact that the central focus of the professional role lies in a technical competence gives a very great importance to universalism in the institutional pattern governing it. Science is essentially universalistic,—*who* states a proposition is as such irrelevant to the question of its scientific value. The same is true of all applied science. But the role of universalism is by no means confined to the professions. It is equally important to the patterns governing contractual relationships, for instance in the standards of common honesty, and to administrative office.

It is one of the most striking features of our occupational system that status in it is to a high degree independent of status in kinship groups, the neighborhood and the like, in short from what are sometimes called primary group relationships. It may be suggested that one of the main reasons for this lies in the dominant importance of universalistic criteria in the judgment of achievement in the occupational field. Where technical competence, the technical impartiality of administration of an office and the like are of primary functional importance, it is essential that particularistic considerations should not enter into the bases of judgment too much. The institutional insulation from social structures where particularism is dominant is one way in which this can be accomplished.

While there is a variety of reasons why disinterestedness is of great functional significance to the modern professions, there is equally impressive evidence for the role of rationality, functional specificity and universalism, as well as, perhaps, other elements which have not been taken up here. In both respects the importance of the professions as a peculiar social structure within the wider society calls attention to the importance of elements other than the enlightened self-interest of economic and utilitarian theory. On the one hand, it does so in that the institutional pattern governing professional activity does not, in the same sense, sanction the pursuit of self-interest as the corresponding one does in the case of business. On the other hand, the very fact that in spite of this difference the professions have all three of these other elements in common with the business pattern, and with other parts of our occupational structure, such as government and other administration, calls attention to the possibility that the dominant importance of the problem of self-interest itself has been exaggerated. This impression is greatly strengthened by the results of extensive comparative study of the relations of our own institutional structure to that of widely different societies which, unfortunately, it is impossible to report on in this paper.

Returning to the professions, however, study of the relation of social structure to individual action in this field can, as it was suggested earlier, by comparison throw light on certain other theoretically crucial aspects of the problem of the role of self-interest itself. In the economic and related utilitarian traditions of thought the difference between business and the professions in this respect has strongly tended to be interpreted as mainly a difference in the typical motives of persons acting in the respective occupations. The dominance of a business economy has seemed to justify the view that ours was an "acquisitive society" in which every one was an "economic man" who cared little for the interests of others. Professional men, on the other hand, have been thought of as standing above these sordid considerations, devoting their lives to "service" of their fellow men.

There is no doubt that there are important concrete differences. Business men are, for instance, expected to push their financial interests by such aggressive measures as advertising. They are not expected to sell to customers regardless of the probability of their being paid, as doctors are expected to treat patients. In each immediate instance in one sense the doctor could, if he did these things according to the business pattern, gain financial advantages which conformity with his own professional pattern denies him. Is it not then obvious that he is "sacrificing" his self-interest for the benefit of others?

The situation does not appear to be so simple. It is seldom, even in business, that the immediate financial advantage to be derived from a particular transaction is decisive in motivation. Orientation is rather to a total comprehensive situation extending over a considerable period of time. Seen in these terms the difference may lie rather in the "definitions of the situation" than in the typical motives of actors as such.

Perhaps the best single approach to the distinction of these two elements is in the question, in what do the goals of ambition consist? There is a sense in which, in both cases, the dominant goal may be said to be the same, "success." To this there would appear to be two main aspects. One is a satisfactory modicum of attainment of the technical goals of the respective activities, such as increasing the size and improving the portion of the business firm for which the individual is in whole or in part responsible, or attaining a good proportion of cures or substantial improvement in the condition of patients. The other aspect is the attainment of high standing in one's occupational group, "recognition" in Thomas' term. In business this will involve official position in the firm, income, and that rather intangible but none the less important thing, "reputation," as well as perhaps particular "honors" such as election to clubs and the like. In medicine it will similarly involve size and character of practice, income, hospital and possibly medical school appointments, honors, and again reputation. The essential goals in the two cases would appear to be substantially the same, objective achievement and recognition: the difference lies in the different paths to the similar goals, which are in turn determined by the differences in the respective occupational situations.

There are two particularly important empirical qualifications to what has been said. In the first place certain things are important not only as symbols of recognition, but in other contexts as well. This is notably true of money. Money is significant for what it can buy, as well as in the role of a direct symbol of recognition. Hence in so far as ways of earning money present themselves in the situation which are not strictly in the line of institutionally approved achievement, there may be strong pressure to resort to them so long as the risk of loss of occupational status is not too great.

This leads to the second consideration. The above sketch applies literally only to a well-integrated situation. In so far as the actual state of affairs deviates from this type the two main elements of success, objective achievement which is institutionally valued, and acquisition of the various recognition-symbols, may not be well articulated. Actual achievement may fail to bring recognition in due proportion, and vice versa achievements either of low quality or in unapproved lines may bring disproportionate recognition. Such lack of integration inevitably places great strains on the individual placed in such a situation and behavior deviant from the institutional pattern results on a large scale. It would seem that, seen in this perspective, so-called "commercialism" in medicine and "dishonest" and "shady" practices in business have much in common as reactions to these strains.

Even in these cases, however, it is dubious whether such practices result primarily from egoistic motivation in the simple sense of utilitarian theory. The following seems a more adequate account of the matter: "normally," i.e. in an integrated situation, the "interests" in self-fulfillment and realization of goals, are integrated and fused with the normative patterns current in the society, inculcated by current attitudes of approval and disapproval and their various manifestations. The normal individual feels satisfaction in effectively carrying out approved patterns and shame and disappointment in failure. For instance courage in facing physical danger is often far from "useful" to the individual in any ordinary egoistic sense. But most normal boys and men feel intense satisfaction in performing courageous acts, and equally intense shame if they have been afraid. Correlatively they are approved and applauded for courageous behavior and severely criticized for cowardice. The smooth functioning of the mechanisms of such behavior which integrates individual satisfactions and social expectations is dependent upon the close correspondence of objective achievement and the bases and symbols of recognition. Where this correspondence is seriously disturbed the individual is placed in a conflict situation and is hence insecure. If he sticks to the approved objective achievements his desires for recognition are frustrated; if on the other hand he sacrifices this to acquisition of the recognition symbols he has guilt-feelings and risks disapproval in some important quarters. Commercialism and dishonesty are to a large extent the reactions of normal people to this kind of conflict situation. The conflict is not generally a simple one between the actor's self-interest and his altruistic regard for others or for ideals, but between different components of the normally unified goal of "success" each of which contains both interested and disinterested motivation elements.

If this general analysis of the relation of motivation to institutional patterns is correct two important correlative conclusions follow. On the one hand the typical motivation of professional men is not in the usual sense "altruistic," nor is that of business men typically "egoistic." Indeed there is little basis for maintaining that there is any important broad difference of typical motivation in the two cases, or at least any of sufficient importance to account for the broad differences of socially expected behavior. On the other hand there is a clear-cut and definite difference on the institutional level. The institutional patterns governing the two fields of action are radically different in this respect. Not only are they different; it can be shown conclusively that this difference has very important functional bases. But it is a difference in definition of the situation. Doctors are not altruists, and the famous "acquisitiveness" of a business economy is not the product of "enlightened self-interest." The opinion may be hazarded that one of the principal reasons why economic thought has failed to see this fundamentally important fact is that it has confined its empirical attention to the action of the market place and has neglected to study its relations to other types of action. Only by such comparative study, the sociological equivalent of experimentation, is the isolation of variables possible.

These are a few of the ways in which a study of the professions can, indirectly and directly, throw light on some of the essential features of the occupational structure of modern society. In conclusion two further related lines of analysis may be suggested, though there is no space to follow them out. Naturally the occupational structure of any social system does not stand alone, but is involved in complex interrelationships, structural and functional, with other parts of the same social system. Above all most or at least many of these other structures involve quite different structural patterns from those dominant in the occupational sphere. In the case of the modern liberal state and the universalistic Christian churches there is a relatively high degree of structural congruence with the occupational system; hence the elements of conflict are more those of scope and concrete content of interests than of structural disharmony as such. But certain other parts of the system have structurally quite different institutional patterns. Among these notably are family and kinship, friendship, class loyalties and identifications so far as they are bound up with birth and the diffuse "community" of common styles of life, and loyalty to particular leaders and organizations as such, independently of what they "stand for." In all these cases though in different ways and degrees, particularism tends to replace universalism, and functional diffuseness, specificity. To a lesser degree they have tendencies to traditionalism. Absolute insulation of these other structures from that of the occupational sphere is impossible since the same concrete individuals participate in both classes. But much depends on the degree of relative insulation which it is possible to attain. In particular the kind of deviation from the norms of institutional integration in the occupational sphere which was discussed above creates a situation in which a breakdown of the institutional pattern itself in favor of one structurally similar to these other types can readily take place.

This danger is generally accentuated by the fact that the maintenance of the dominant pattern in the occupational sphere is subject to many severe strains. The reference is not to the problem of "enforcement" as such. There is much deviant behavior in violation of normative patterns which does not significantly involve the emergence of alternative normative patterns. The problem of keeping down the murder rate does not involve in any serious way a conflict of values in which one group stands out for the right to murder. But in certain situations such conflicts of values and resultant loyalties become of great importance. One prominent example may be cited.

Our administrative hierarchies, for instance, in a business corporation or a government agency, involve an institutional pattern which is predominantly universalistic and functionally specific. Authority is distributed and legitimized only within the limited sphere of the "office" and the claim to it is regulated by universalistic standards. But such a pattern is never fully descriptive of the concrete structure. The various offices are occupied by concrete individuals with concrete personalities who have particular concrete social relations to other individuals. The institutionally enjoined rigid distinction between the sphere, powers and obligation of office and those which are "personal" to the particular individuals is difficult to maintain. In fact in every concrete structure of this sort there is to a greater or less degree a system of "cliques." That is, certain groups are more closely solidary than the strict institutional definition of their statuses calls for and correspondingly, as between such groups there is a degree of antagonism which is not institutionally sanctioned. The existence of such clique structures places the individual in a conflict situation. He is for instance pulled between the "impartial," "objective" loyalty to his superior as the incumbent of an office, and the loyalty to a person whom he likes, who has treated him well, etc. Since in the society generally the patterns of personal loyalty and friendship are prominent and deeply ingrained, it is easy for these considerations gradually to come to predominate over the main pattern. Obligation to the duties of office, including submission to authority, is replaced by loyalty to an individual, that is, a particularistic is substituted for a universalistic basis. Similarly a superior in the clique structure may feel entitled to ask "favors" of his subordinates which go well beyond the strictly defined boundaries of their official duties, hence tending to break down the specificity of function. The processes involved are highly complex, but it is by no means impossible that they should be cumulative in one direction and lead to a serious impairment of the older occupational pattern. Indeed the evidence generally points to the conclusion that the main occupational pattern is upheld as well as it is by a rather precarious balance of social forces, and that any at all considerable change in this balance may have far-reaching consequences.

The importance of the professions to social structure may be summed up as follows: The professional type is the institutional frame work in which many of our most important social functions are carried on, notably the pursuit of science and liberal learning and its practical application in medicine, technology, law and teaching. This depends on an institutional structure the maintenance of which is not an automatic consequence of belief in the importance of the functions as such, but involves a complex balance of diverse social forces. Certain features of this pattern are peculiar to professional activities, but others, and not the least important ones, are shared by this field with the other most important branches of our occupational structure, notably business and bureaucratic administration. Certain features of our received traditions of thought, notably concentration of attention on the problem of self-interest with its related false dichotomy of concrete egoistic and altruistic motives, has served seriously to obscure the importance of these other elements, notably rationality, specificity of function and universalism. Comparison of the professional and business structure in their relations to the problem of individual motivation is furthermore a very promising avenue of approach to certain more general problems of the relations of individual motivation to institutional structures with particular reference to the problem of egoism and altruism. Finally, the often rather unstable relation of the institutional structures of the occupational sphere, including the professions, to other structurally different patterns, can throw much light on important strains and instabilities of the social system, and through them on certain of its possibilities of dynamic change.

III

The Motivation
of Economic Activities

SPECIALIZATION IS, without doubt, one of the most important factors in the development of modern science, since beyond a certain level of technicality it is possible, even with intensive application, to master only a limited sector of the total of human knowledge. But some modes of specialization are, at the same time, under certain circumstances, an impediment to the adequate treatment of some ranges of problems.

The principal reason for this limitation of the fruitfulness of at least some kinds of specialization lies in the fact that the specialized sciences involve a kind of abstraction. They constitute systematically organized bodies of knowledge, and their organization revolves about relatively definite and therefore limited conceptual schemes. They do not treat the concrete phenomena they study "in general" but only so far as they are directly relevant to the conceptual scheme which has become established in the science. In relation to certain limited ranges of problems and phenomena this is often adequate. But it is seldom, after such a conceptual scheme has become well worked out, that its abstractness does not sooner or later become a crucial source of difficulty in relation to some empirical problems. This is apt to be especially true on the peripheries of what has been the central field of interest of the science, in fields to which some of the broader implications of its conceptual scheme and its broader generalizations are applied, or in which the logically necessary premises of certain of these generalizations must be sought.

This has been notably the case with economics, precisely because, of all the sciences dealing with human behavior in society, it was the earliest to develop a well-integrated conceptual scheme and even today has brought this aspect of its science to a higher level of formal perfection than has any other social discipline. More than a century ago, however, economists began to be interested in the broader implications of their system and of the facts it had succeeded in systematizing. Perhaps more than in any other direction these "speculations" have concentrated on the range of problems which have been involved in the idea af "laissez-faire," of the functioning of a total economic system of "free-enterprise" untrammelled by controls imposed from without and without important relations to elements of human action which played no explicit part in the conceptual armory of economic theory.

Once the attention of the economist has extended to problems as broad as this, the problem of the motivation of economic activities, whether explicitly recognized or not, has inevitably become involved by implication. The equilibrating process of a free economy was a matter of responsiveness to certain types of changes in the situation of action, to the prices, the supplies, and the conditions of demand for goods. The key individual in the system, the business man, was placed in a position where money calculations of profit and loss necessarily played a dominant part in the processes of adjustment, when they were analyzed from the point of view of why the individual acted as he did. In a certain empirical sense it has seemed a wholly justifiable procedure to assume that he acted to maximize his "self-interest," interpreted as the financial returns of the enterprise, or more broadly, he could be trusted to prefer a higher financial return to a lower, a smaller financial loss to a greater.

From these apparently obvious facts it was easy to generalize that what kept the system going was the "rational pursuit of self-interest" on the part of all the individuals concerned, and to suppose that this formula constituted a sufficient key to a generalized theory of the motivation of human behavior, at least in the economic and occupational spheres. It is important to note that this formula and the various interpretations that were put upon it was not the result of intensive technical economic observation and analysis in the sense in which the theory of value and of distribution have been, but of finding a plausible formula for filling a logical gap in the closure of a system. This gap had to be filled if a certain order of broad generalization were to be upheld. Such current doctrines, outside the strictly economic sphere, as psychological hedonism, seemed to support this formula and to increase confidence in the universal applicability of the economic conceptual scheme.

In the meantime a good deal of work has been going on in other fields of the study of human behavior which has for the most part been rather rigidly insulated from the work of economists, but which bears on the problem of motivation, in ways which are applicable, among others, to the economic sphere. This has been true of social anthropology, and of parts of sociology and of psychology. Though there have been some notable examples of individual writers who, like Pareto, Durkheim, and Max Weber, have brought out various aspects of the interrelations of these fields with the problems of economics directly,[1] on the whole they seem to have remained insulated, so that it can scarcely be said that a well-rounded analysis of the problem, which takes account of the knowledge available on both sides, is, even in outline, well established as the common property of the social sciences. An attempt to present the outline of such an analysis is the principal object of the present paper.

On the economic side the impression has been widespread that a predominantly "self-interested" or "egotistic" theory of the motivation of economic activities was a logical necessity of economic theory. It can be said with confidence that careful analysis of the methodological status of economic theory as an analytical scheme demonstrates conclusively that this is not the case. There are, to be sure, certain necessary assumptions on this level. They are, I think, two. On the one hand, economic analysis is empirically significant only in so far as there is scope for a certain kind of "rationality" of action, for the weighing of advantages and disadvantages, of "utility" and "cost," with a view to maximizing the difference between them. In so far, for instance, as behavior is purely instinctive or traditional it is not susceptible of such analysis. On the other hand, its significance rests on there being an appreciable scope for the treatment of things and other people, that is of resources, in a "utilitarian" spirit, that is, within limits, as morally and emotionally neutral means to the ends of economic activity rather than only as ends in themselves. In both respects there is probably considerable variation between individuals and between societies.

---

[1] See the author's *The Structure of Social Action* (New York, 1937) for an analysis of this aspect of the work of these men.

But this does not necessarily have anything to do with "egoism" in the usual sense. It has already been pointed out that the immediate goal of economic action in a market economy is the maximization of net money advantages or more generally of the difference between utility and cost. Choices, so far as they are, in the immediate sense, "economically motivated" are, in the first instance, oriented to this immediate goal. It certainly is not legitimate to assume that this immediate goal is a simple and direct expression of the ultimate motivational forces of human behavior. On the contrary, to a large extent its pursuit is probably compatible with a considerable range of variation in more ultimate motivations. Indeed, it will be the principal thesis of the subsequent analysis that "economic motivation" is not a category of motivation on the deeper level at all, but is rather a point at which many different motives may be brought to bear on a certain type of situation. Its remarkable constancy and generality is not a result of a corresponding uniformity in "human nature" such as egoism or hedonism, but of certain features of the structure of social systems of action which, however, are not entirely constant but subject to institutional variation.

The theoretical analysis of economics is abstract, probably in several different senses. This is crucial to the argument because it is precisely within the area of its "constant" data or assumptions that the problems of the present discussion arise. To describe the kind of abstractness which is relevant here, perhaps the best starting point is a formula which has been much discussed in economics, but which can be given a much more specific meaning in modern sociological terms than it has generally had in economic discussions. It is that economic activity takes place within the "institutional" framework of a society; economic behavior is concretely a phase of institutional behavior.

Institutions, or institutional patterns, in the terms which will be employed here, are a principal aspect of what is, in a generalized sense, the social structure. They are *normative* patterns which define what are felt to be, in the given society, proper, legitimate, or expected modes of action or of social relationship. Among the various types of normative patterns which govern action there are two primary criteria which distinguish those of institutional significance. In the first place, they are patterns which are supported by common moral sentiments; conformity with them is not only a matter of expediency, but of moral duty. In the second place, they are not "utopian" patterns which, however highly desirable they may be regarded, are not lived up to except by a few, or by others in exceptional circumstances. Thus the extreme altruism of the Sermon of the Mount or extreme heroism are very widely approved but the ordinary individual is not *expected* to live up to them. When, on the other hand, a pattern is institutionalized, conformity with it is part of the legitimate expectations of the society, and of the individual himself. The typical reaction to infraction of an institutional rule is moral indignation of the sort which involves a feeling of being "let down." A person in a fiduciary position who embezzles funds, or a soldier who deserts is not doing what others feel they have a *right* to expect them to do.

Institutional patterns in this sense are part of the social structure in that, so far as the patterns are effectively institutionalized, action in social relationships is not random, but is guided and canalized by the requirements of the institutional patterns. So far as they are mandatory they in a sense directly "determine" action, otherwise they set limits beyond which variation is not permissible and sets up corrective forces.

Seen from this point of view, institutional structure is a mode of the "integration" of the actions of the component individuals. There are, it may be suggested, three principal ways in which it is functionally necessary that such a social system should be integrated if it is to remain stable and avoid internal conflicts which would be fatal to it. In the first place, the different possible modes of action and of relationship become differentiated. Some are socially acceptable and approved, others reprehensible and disapproved or even directly prohibited. But in any case this system of differentiated actions and relationships needs to be organized. Stability is possible only if within limits people do the right thing at the right time and place. It is furthermore exceedingly important that others should know what to expect of a given individual. Thus in all societies we find institutional definitions of *roles,* of the things given people are expected to do in different contexts and relationships. Each individual usually has a number of different roles, but the combinations of different roles vary with different "social types" of individuals.

Secondly, it is inherent in the nature of society that some individuals should be in a position to exercise influence over others.

Again it is necessary that there should be a differentiation between those modes of influence which are held permissible or desirable, and those which should be discouraged or even forbidden. Where the lines will be drawn will differ with the social roles of the persons concerned. The compulsion exercised by police officers will not be permitted to private individuals, for instance. Certain modes of influencing others, often regardless of the willingness of the others to be influenced, are often necessary to the performance of certain roles. Where such modes of influence are institutionally legitimized they may be called "authority." On the other hand, it is often socially necessary or desirable that some or all individuals should be protected from modes of influence which others would otherwise be in a position to exert. Such institutionalized protection against undesirable or unwanted influence may be called "rights." An institutionalized structure of authority and rights is a feature of every integrated social system.[2]

Finally, action generally is teleologically oriented to the attainment of goals and to conformity with norms. It is inherent in its structure that acts, qualities, achievements, etc., should be valued. It makes a difference on a scale of evaluation what a person is and what he does. This necessity of evaluation implies in turn the necessity of ranking, in the first place, qualities and achievements which are directly comparable; thus, if physical strength is valued, persons will in so far be ranked in order of their physical strength. Secondarily, this means that persons, as such, will be evaluated, and that where a plurality of persons are involved, they will, however roughly, be ranked. It is of crucial importance that the standards of ranking and their modes of application should, in the same social system, be relatively well integrated. This third aspect of institutional structure, then, is *stratification*. Every social system will have an institutionalized scale of stratification by which the different individuals in the system are ranked.

This institutional structure is found in social relationships generally and is as important in the sphere of economic activities as in any other. Every function at all well established in the economic division of labor comes to involve institutionally defined roles such as those of "banker," "business executive," "craftsman," "farmer," or what not. In connection with such a role there is a pattern of institutionally defined expectations, both positive and negative. Certain

2 Whether they are legally enforceable is secondary for present purposes.

of these economic roles involve institutional authority such as that of an employer in the role of supervisor over his workers. Again, in various respects, persons in economic roles are subject to the authority of others, notably of public officials in matters of taxation, labor legislation, and many other fields. They are institutionally expected to obey and usually recognize this authority. Persons in economic roles, further, enjoy certain institutionally protected rights, notably those we sum up as the institution of property, and in turn are institutionally expected to respect certain rights of others, to refrain, for instance, from coercing others or perpetrating fraud upon them. Finally, each of them has a place in the system of stratification of the community. By virtue of his occupation and his status in it, of his income, of his "reputation," and various other things, he is ranked high or low as the case may be.

So far an institutional structure has been described as an "objective" entity which as such would seem to have little to do with motivation. The terms in which it has been described, however, clearly imply a very close relation. Such a structure is, indeed, essentially a relatively stable mode of the organization of human activities, and of the motivational forces underlying them. Any considerable alteration in the latter or in their mutual relations would greatly alter it.

When we turn to the subjective side it turns out that one principal set of elements consists in a system of moral sentiments. Institutional patterns depend, for their maintenance in force, on the support of the moral sentiments of the majority of the members of the society. These sentiments are above all manifested in the reaction of spontaneous moral indignation when another seriously violates an institutional pattern. It may indeed be suggested that punishment and sanctions are to a considerable extent important as expressions of these sentiments, and as symbolizing their significance. The corresponding reaction to violation on the actor's own part is a feeling of guilt or shame which, it is important to note, may often be largely repressed. On the positive side the corresponding phenomenon is the sense of obligation. The well-integrated personality feels an obligation to live up to expectations in his variously defined roles, to be a "good boy" to be a "good student," an "efficient worker," and so on. He similarly has and feels obligations to respect legitimate authority in others, and to exercise it properly in his own case. He is obligated to respect the rights of others, and on occasion it may be a positive obligation from moral motives to insist on respect for his own rights. Finally, he is obligated to recognize the status of others with respect to stratification, especially, but by no means wholly, of those superior to himself. The element of obligation in this sense is properly treated as "disinterested." It is a matter of "identification" with a generalized pattern, conformity with which is "right." Within comparatively wide limits his personal interests in the matter in other respects are irrelevant.

The prevailing evidence is that the deeper moral sentiments are inculcated in early childhood and are deeply built into the structure of personality itself. They are, in the deeper senses, beyond the range of conscious decision and control, except perhaps, in certain critical situations, and even when consciously repudiated, still continue to exert their influence through repressed guilt feelings and the like. In situations of strain these may well come to be in radical opposition to the self-interested impulses of the actor; he is the victim of difficult conflicts and problems of conscience. But there is evidence of a strong tendency, the more that people are integrated with an institutional system, for these moral sentiments to be closely integrated with the self-interested elements, to which we must now turn.

If the above analysis is correct, the fact that concretely economic activities take place in a framework of institutional patterns would imply that, typically, such disinterested elements of motivation play a role in the determination of their course. This is not in the least incompatible with the strict requirements of economic theory for that requires only that, as between certain alternatives, choice will be made in such a way as to maximize net money advantages to the actor, or to the social unit on behalf of which he acts. Both in the ultimate goals to which the proceeds will be applied, and in the choice of means there is no reason why disinterested moral sentiments should not be involved. But there is equally no reason why, on a comparable level, elements of self-interest should not be involved also. Indeed, the distinction is not one of classes of concrete motives, but of types of element in concrete motives. In the usual case these elements are intimately intertwined.

There is, furthermore, no general reason to assume that "self-interest" is a simple and obvious thing. On the contrary, it appears to be a distinctly complex phenomenon, and probably the analytical distinctions to be made respecting it are relative to the level of analysis undertaken, hence to the problems in hand. Only such distinctions will here be made as seem essential to the main outline of a theory of motivation of economic activity.

The most general term which can be applied to this phase of motivation is, perhaps, "satisfaction." There is an interest in things and modes of behavior which yields satisfactions. One of the important components of this is undoubtedly "self-respect." So far, that is, as moral norms are genuinely built into the structure of personality the individual's own state of satisfaction is dependent on the extent to which he lives up to them. This is above all true with respect to the standards of his various roles, particularly, in our context, the occupational role, and to the place he feels he "deserves" in the scale of stratification.

Closely related to self-respect, indeed in a sense its complement, is what may, following W. I. Thomas, be called "recognition." To have recognition in this sense is to be the object of moral respect on the part of others whose opinion is valued. To be approved of, admired, or even envied, are flattering and satisfying to any ego. As the works of Mead and others have shown, the relations of self-respect and recognition are extremely intimate and reciprocally related. The loss of respect on the part of those from whom it is expected is one of the severest possible blows to the state of satisfaction of the individual.

Third, there is the element which lies closest to the pattern of economic analysis, the fact that we have an interest in a given complex of activities or relationships for "what we can get out of them." That is, they are, to a certain extent, treated as a means to something altogether outside themselves. This is the classic pattern for the interpretation of the significance of money returns. The pattern involves the assumption that there are certain "wants" which exist altogether independently of the activities by which the means to satisfy them are acquired. Though unjustified as a general interpretation of economic motivation, such a dissociation does, on a relative level, exist and is of considerable importance. In this, as in many other respects, the prevailing economic scheme is not simply wrong, but has not been properly related to other elements.

Fourth, there is another element which has played a prominent part in the history of economic thought—"pleasure." This may be conceived as a relatively specific feeling-tone which is subject to interpretation as a manifestation primarily of particular organic states. Of course pleasure may be one of the "ulterior" ends to which economic activities are means—it is certainly not, as the hedonists would have it, the sole one. It may also be present, and often is, in the actual activities performed in the pursuance of economically significant roles; most of us actually enjoy a good deal of our work. One fact, however, is of crucial significance. Pleasure, or its sources, is not, as the classical hedonists assumed, a biologically given constant, but is a function of the *total* personal equilibrium of the individual. It does seem to have a particularly close connection with organic states, but undoubtedly these in turn are greatly influenced by the emotional states of the individual, and through these, by the total complex of his social relationships and situation. Hence pleasure, as an element of motivation, can only in a highly relative sense be treated as an independent focus of the orientation of action.

Finally, there is still a fifth element in "satisfactions" which, though perhaps less directly associated with the economic field than with others, should be mentioned. Men have attitudes of "affection" toward other human beings, and somewhat similar attitudes toward certain kinds of inanimate objects. The "aesthetic emotion" very likely contains in this sense a component which is distinguishable from pleasure, by which one, for instance, can say "I am exceedingly fond of that picture." In the case of other human beings, however, this affectional attitude is often reciprocal and we may speak of a genuine egotistic interest in the affectional "response" of another, again to use Thomas's term. It is true that the institutional patterns governing economic relationships are, in our society, largely "impersonal" in a sense which excludes response from direct institutional sanction. It does, however, come in in at least two important ways. On the one hand, it is very prominent in the uses to which the proceeds of economic activity are put, constituting for one thing a prominent element of family relationships. On the other hand, on a non-institutional level, response relationships are often of great importance, concretely in the occupational situation and motivation of individuals. Thus a very important motive in doing "good work" may be its bearing on friendship with certain occupational associates.

In all these respects there is a further fundamental aspect of the motivational significance of a great many things which the traditional economic analysis does not take into account. Many of the most important relations of things to action lie in the fact that they are associated with one or more of these elements as symbols. An excellent example is that of money income. From the point of view of valuation it is probably fair to say that the most fundamental basis of ranking and status in the economic world is occupational achievement and the underlying ability. But for a variety of reasons it is difficult to judge people directly in these terms alone. Above all, in view of the technical heterogeneity of achievements it is difficult to compare achievements in different fields. But in a business economy it is almost inevitable that to a large extent money earnings should come to be accepted as a measure of such achievements and hence money income is, to a large extent, effectually accepted as a symbol of occupational status. It is hence of great importance in the context of recognition.

Once the institutional pattern in question comes to be thoroughly established, though it continues to be in part dependent on the moral sentiments underlying it, its maintenance by no means depends exclusively on these. There is, rather, a process of complex interaction on two levels at once, on the one hand between the disinterested and self-interested elements in the motivation of any given individual, on the other between the different individuals. The first aspect of interaction has already been outlined in discussing the content of the concept "self-interest." The general tendency of the second process, so far as the institutional system is integrated, is to reinforce conformity with the main institutional patterns through mechanisms which work out in such a way that, in his relations with others, the self-interest of any one individual is promoted by adhering to the institutional patterns.

It has already been pointed out that the normal reaction of a well-integrated individual to an infraction of an institutional rule is one of moral indignation. The effect of this is to change an otherwise or potentially favorable attitude toward the individual in question to an unfavorable one. There are, of course, many different variations of degree between the various possible effects of this. It may be a matter simply of lessened willingness to "cooperate" in the achievement of the first person's ends in ways in which the second is useful or necessary as a means. In the more extreme instances it may involve positive obstruction of his activities. It will certainly mean a lessening of the respect which is involved in recognition; again in the more extreme cases it may mean positive action to belittle and run down the offender's reputation and standing, dismissal from positions, withdrawal of honors, and the like.

It would be unusual, except in very extreme cases for direct pleasures to be involved, certainly in a physical sense. But in various subtle ways the disapproval of others, especially when it is intense enough to be translated into direct action, affects the sources of pleasure to which an individual has become accustomed. Finally, so far as people on whom he counts for response share the moral sentiments he has offended, this response, notably in "friendship," is likely to be lessened. In the extreme case again a friendly attitude may be transformed into a directly unfriendly one, indeed on occasion into bitter hatred.

Thus, even without taking account of the possible internal conflicts which violation of his own moral sentiments brings about, it can be seen that a very substantial component of the individual's own self-interest is directly dependent on his enjoying the favorable attitudes of others with whom he comes into contact in his situation. Even if he continues to "make money" as before, his loss from the point of view particularly of recognition and respect may be of crucial importance, and in the long run probably his income is (the better integrated the situation the more so) bound up with his maintenance of good relations with others in this sense.

It is now possible to bring out what is, in many respects, the most crucial point of the whole analysis. It is true that it has been argued that it is impossible to treat the self-interested elements of human motivation as alone decisive in influencing behavior, in the economic sphere or any other. But it is not this thesis which constitutes the most radical departure from a kind of common-sense view which is widely accepted among economists, as among other normal human beings. It is rather that the *content* of self-interested motivation itself, the specific objects of human "interests," cannot, for the purposes of any broad level of generalization in social science, be treated as a constant. That is, not only must the fact that people have interests be taken into account in explaining their behavior, but the fact that there are variations in their specific content as well. And these variations cannot, as economic theory has tended to do, be treated at random relative to the *social* structure, including in a very important sense that of the economic sphere of society itself. For it is precisely around social institutions that, to a very large extent, the content of self-interest is organized. Indeed, this organization of what are the otherwise, within broad limits, almost random potentialities of the self-interested tendencies of human action into a coherent system, may be said, in broad terms, to be one of the most important functions of institutions. Without it, society could scarcely be an order, in the sense in which we know it, at all. It thus depends on the standards according to which recognition is accorded, on the specific lines of action to which pleasure has become attached, on what have come to be generally accepted symbols of prestige and status, what, in concrete terms, will be the *direction* taken by self-interested activity and hence what its social consequences will be. Again this applies to what are ordinarily thought of as "economic" interests just as it does to any others.

The most convincing evidence in support of this thesis is to be derived from a broad comparative study of different institutional structures. Such a comparative study can go far to explain why, for instance, such a large proportion of Indian Brahmans have been interested in certain kinds of mystical and ascetic religious behavior, why so many of the upper classes in China have devoted themselves to education in the Confucian classics looking toward an official career as a Mandarin, or why the members of European aristocracies have looked down upon "trade" and been concerned, if they have followed an occupational career at all, so much with the armed forces of the state, which have counted specifically as "gentlemen's" occupations. There is, unfortunately, no space to go into this evidence.

It may be useful, however, to cite one conspicuous example from our own society, that of the difference between business and the learned professions. There are important differences between the institutional patterns governing these two sectors of the higher part of our occupational sphere, and perhaps the most conspicuous of these touches precisely the question of self-interest. The commonest formula in terms of which the difference is popularly expressed is the distinction between "professionalism" and "commercialism." Now in the immediately obvious sense the essence of professionalism consists in a series of limitations on the aggressive pursuit of self-interest. Thus medical men are forbidden, in the codes of medical ethics, to advertise their services. They are expected, in any individual case, to treat a patient regardless of the probability that he will pay, that he is a good "credit risk." They are forbidden to enter into direct and explicit price competition with other physicians, to urge patients to come to them on the ground that they will provide the same service at a cheaper rate. It is true that, in all this, infraction of the professional code would, in general, permit the physician to reap an immediate financial advantage which adherence to the code deprives him of. But it does not follow that, in adhering to the code as well as they do, medical men are actually acting contrary to their self-interest in a sense in which business men habitually do not.

On the contrary, the evidence which has been accumulated in the course of a study of medical practice[3] points to a quite different conclusion, which is that a principal component of the difference is a difference on the level of the institutional pattern, rather than, as is usually thought, a difference of typical motivation.[4] In both cases the self-interest of the typical individual is on the whole harnessed to keeping the institutional code which is dominant in his own occupational sphere. It is true that by advertising, by refusing to treat indigent patients, or in certain circumstances by cutting prices, the individual physician could reap an immediate financial advantage. But it is doubtful whether, where the institutional structure is working at all well, it is from a broader point of view to his self-interest to do so. For this would provoke a reaction, in the first instance among his professional colleagues, secondarily among the public, which would be injurious to his professional standing. If he persisted in such practices his professional status would suffer, and in all probability various more tangible advantages, such as habitual recommendations of patients by other physicians, would disappear or be greatly lessened. It is not suggested that the average physician thinks of it in these terms; for the most part it probably never occurs to him that he

---

[3] As yet unpublished.

[4] This is by no means meant to imply that there are no differences of typical motivation. Such differences could be accounted for either on the ground that the two occupational groups operated selectively on personality types within the population, or that they influenced the motivation of people in them. The essential point is that the treatment of the concrete differences of behavior as direct manifestations of differences of ultimate motivation alone is clearly illegitimate in that it fails to take account of the institutional factor. It is quite possible that the institutionalization of financial self-interest does, however, tend to cultivate a kind of egoism and aggressiveness in the typical business man which is less likely to be created in a professional environment.

might consider deviating from the code. But the underlying control mechanisms are present none the less.

In business the "definition of the situation" is quite different. Advertising, credit rating, and price competition are, for the most part, institutionally accepted and approved practices. It is not only not considered reprehensible to engage in them, but it is part of the institutional definition of the role of the "good" business man to do so.

It is true that in the professions money income is one of the important symbols of high professional standing. The more successful physicians both charge higher fees and receive larger total incomes. But there is still an important difference. There are in the first place important exceptions to the regularity of this relationship. There is probably nothing in the business world to correspond to the very high professional prestige of the "full-time" staff of the most eminent medical schools, even though their average income is markedly lower than that of the comparably distinguished men in private practice. There are probably very few resident physicians or surgeons in the teaching hospitals associated with such institutions as the Harvard Medical School who would refuse an opportunity to go on the full-time staff in order to enter private practice, even though the latter promised much larger financial returns.

But, beyond this, in business money returns are not only a symbol of status, they are to a considerable extent a direct measure of the success of business activities, indeed, in view of the extreme heterogeneity of the technical content of these, the only common measure. This situation is, however, being rapidly modified by the large-scale corporate organization of the business world. There "profit" applies only to the firm as a whole, for the individual it is primarily his office and his salary which count. This development is greatly narrowing the gap, in these respects, between business and the professions.[5]

It is thus suggested that the much talked of "acquisitiveness" of a capitalistic economic system is not primarily, or even to any very large extent a matter of the peculiar incidence of self-interested elements in the motivation of the typical individual, but of a

---

[5] This development involves a major change in the institutional setting of the problem of self-interest. Even though, as will be noted presently, in individual market competition, profit is an institutionally defined goal rather than a motive, it makes a considerable difference whether, as the older economists as-

peculiar institutional structure which has grown up in the Western world. There is reason to believe that the situation with respect to motivation is a great deal more similar in this area to that in other parts of our occupational structure which are not marked by this kind of acquisitiveness than is generally supposed.

Our occupational structure is above all one in which status is accorded, to a high degree, on the basis of achievement, and of the abilities which promise achievement, in a specialized function or group of functions. One may, then, perhaps say that the whole occupational sphere is dominated by a single fundamental goal, that of "success." The content of this common goal will, of course, vary with the specific character of the functional role. But whatever this may be, it will involve both interested and disinterested elements. On the disinterested side will be above all two components, a disinterested devotion to "good work" which must be defined according to the relevant technical criteria, and a disinterested acceptance of the moral patterns which govern this activity with respect to such matters as respecting the rights of others. On the side of self-interest in most cases the dominant interest is probably that in recognition, in high standing in the individual's occupational group. This will be sought both directly and through various more or less indirect symbols of status, among which money income occupies a prominent place. Part of the prominence of its place is undoubtedly a result of the fact that a business economy has become institutionalized in our society.[6]

---

sumed, the consequences of a business decision will react directly on the personal pocketbook of the person making the decision, or only on that of the organization on behalf of which he decides. The position of the business executive thus becomes to a very large extent a fiduciary position. There is little difference between the considerations which will influence the manager of an investment trust, especially of a conservative type, and the treasurer of a university or a hospital, even though one is engaged in profit-making business, the other is a trustee of an "altruistic" foundation. In both cases the individual concerned has certain obligations and responsibilities, and unless the situation is badly integrated institutionally, it will on the whole, though perhaps in somewhat different ways, be to his self-interest to live up to them relatively well.

[6] To avoid all possible misunderstanding it may be noted again that no claim is made that there are no important differences of motivation, above all that the business situation may not cultivate certain types of "mercenary" orientation. The sole important purpose of the present argument is to show that the older type of discussion which jumped directly from economic analysis to ultimate motivation is no longer tenable. The institutional patterns *always* constitute one crucial element of the problem, and the more ultimate problems of motivation can only be approached through an analysis of their role, not by ignoring it.

The traditional doctrine of economics that action in a business economy was primarily motivated by the "rational pursuit of self-interest" has been shown, in part to be wrong, in part to cover up a complexity of elements and their relationships of which the people who have used this formulation have for the most part been unaware. It may be hoped that the above exposition has, schematic as it has been, laid the foundations, in broad outline, of an account of the matter which will both do better justice to some of the empirical problems which confront the economist and will enable him to co-operate more fruitfully with the neighboring sciences of human behavior instead of, as has been too much the tendency in the past, insulating himself from them in a kind of hermetically sealed, closed system of his own.

It would, however, be unfortunate to give the impression that this account is by any means a complete one, suitable for all purposes, In closing, a further aspect of the problem which is of great empirical importance, but could not receive full discussion in the space available, may be briefly mentioned. The above analysis is couched in terms of the conception of an institutionally integrated social system. It is only in such a case that the essential identity of the direction in which the disinterested and the self-interested elements of motivation impel human action, of which so much has been made in this discussion, holds. Actual social systems are, in this sense, integrated to widely varying degrees; in some cases the integrated type is a fair approximation to reality, in others it is very wide of the mark. But even in developing a theory which is more adequate to the latter type of situation the integrated type is a most important analytical starting point.

There is a very wide range of possible circumstances which may lead individuals, in pursuing their self-interest, to deviate from institutionally approved patterns to a greater or less degree. Sometimes in the course of his life-history a far from perfect integration of personality is achieved, and the individual has tendencies of self-interest which conflict with his institutional status and role. Sometimes the social structure itself is poorly integrated so that essentially incompatible things are expected of the same individual. One of the commonest types of this structural malintegration is the case where the symbols of recognition become detached from the institutionally approved achievements, where people receive recognition without the requisite achievements and conversely, those with the achievements to their credit fail of the appropriate recognition. The result of all these various failures of integration is to place the individual in a conflict situation. He is, on the one hand, in conflict with himself. He feels urged to pursue his self-interest in ways which are incompatible with the standards of behavior in which he himself was brought up and which have been too deeply inculcated for him ever to throw off completely. On the other hand, objectively he is placed in a dilemma. For instance, he may live up to standards he values and face the loss of recognition and its symbols. Or he may seek external "success" but only by violating his own standards and those of the people he most respects. Usually both internal and external conflicts are involved, and there is no really happy solution.

The usual psychological reaction to such conflict situations is a state of psychological "insecurity." Such a state of insecurity in turn is well known to produce a variety of different more or less "neurotic" reactions by which the individual seeks to solve his conflicts and re-establish his security. One of the commonest of these is an increased aggressiveness in the pursuit of personal ambitions and self-interest generally.

It has been maintained that the institutionalization of self-interest accounts for one very important element of what is usually called the "acquisitiveness" of a capitalistic society. But it is far from accounting for all of it. Ours is a society which in a number of respects is far from being perfectly integrated. A very large proportion of the population is in this sense insecure to an important degree. It is hence suggested that another component of this acquisitiveness, especially of the kind which is most offensive to our moral sentiments, is essentially an expression of this widespread insecurity. Elton Mayo[7] coined an appropriate phrase for this aspect of the situation when he inverted Tawney's famous title and spoke of the "Acquisitiveness of a Sick Society." But it should be noted that this is an element which, along with the institutionalization of self-interest, is not adequately taken account of by the formula of the "rational pursuit of self-interest."

Many other points could doubtless be raised to show the incompleteness of the above outline of this problem. There is no doubt that in a great many respects its formulation will have to be altered

[7] In his *Human Problems of an Industrial Civilization* (New York, 1933). This type of element is probably prominently involved in the widespread complaints about the prevalence of "commercialism" in medicine.

as well as refined as our knowledge of the phenomena accumulates, as is the fate of all scientific conceptual schemes. In addition to whatever merit it may possess as a solution of this particular range of empirical problems, it is important for another reason. So far as it is substantiated it will help to demonstrate that many problems can be more fruitfully attacked by collaboration between the various social disciplines on a theoretical level than they can by any one of them working alone, no matter how well established its theoretical scheme may be for a certain range of problems.

An Analytical Approach to the
Theory of Social Stratification

SOCIAL STRATIFICATION IS regarded here as the differential ranking of the human individuals who compose a given social system and their treatment as superior and inferior relative to one another in certain socially important respects. Our first task is to discuss why such differential ranking is considered a really fundamental phenomenon of social systems and what are the respects in which such ranking is important. Ranking is one of many possible bases on which individuals may be differentiated.[1] It is only in so far as differences are treated as involving or related to particular kinds of social superiority and inferiority that they are relevant to the theory of stratification.

---

[1] Some writers (cf. P. A. Sorokin, *Social Mobility* [New York, 1927]) have distinguished what is here referred to as stratification as the "vertical" axis of differentiation of individuals from the "horizontal" axis. Correspondingly, when individuals change their status in the differentiated system, reference is made to vertical and horizontal mobility. This usage is dangerous. It states the analytical problem in terms of a two-dimensional spatial analogy. On the one hand, because stratification constitutes one important range of differentiation, it does not follow that all others can be satisfactorily treated as a single residual category. Thus sex differentiation, occupational differences apart from their relation to stratification, and differences of religious affiliation should not on a priori grounds be treated as if they all involved only values of a single variable with a common unit of variation, "horizontal distance." On the other hand, it is equally dangerous to assume a priori that stratification itself can be adequately described as variation on a single quantitative continuum, as the analogy of a dimension of rectilinear space suggests. There is a quantitative element involved in stratification as in most other social phenomena. This is inherent in its conception as a matter of ranking. But to assume that this exhausted the matter would be to assume that only the numbers and intervals were significant, which is by no means the case. As will appear below, there are also variations in the content of the criteria by which ranks are assigned which cannot, in the present state of knowledge, be reduced to points on a single quantitative continuum.

While of particular concern at present in relation to stratification, it may be pointed out that these considerations apply at the same time to any uncritical use of such concepts as "social space" and "social distance." The burden of proof in cases of their use should always be placed on their relevance to social facts and analytical schemes verified in the social field, not on the logic of deductions from analogies to physical space and distance.

Central for the purposes of this discussion is the differential evaluation in the moral sense of individuals as units. Moral superiority is the object of a certain empirically specific attitude quality of "respect," while its antithesis is the object of a peculiar attitude of "disapproval" or even, in the more extreme cases, of "indignation."[2]

In one sense, perhaps, the selection of moral evaluation as the central criterion of the ranking involved in stratification might be considered arbitrary. It is, however, no more and no less arbitrary than, for instance, the selection of distance as a basic category for describing the relations of bodies in a mechanical system. Its selection is determined by the place which moral evaluation holds in a generalized conceptual scheme, the "theory of action." The only necessary justification of such a selection at the outset is to show that the categories are applicable. In our ordinary treatment of social rank, moral evaluations are in fact prominently involved. The normal reaction to a conspicuous error in ranking is at least in part one of moral indignation,—either a person thinks he is "unjustly" disparaged by being put on a level with those who are really his inferiors, or his real superiors feel "insulted" by having him, in the relevant respects, treated as their equal.[3]

Consideration of certain aspects of social systems described in terms of the theory of action shows readily why stratification is a fundamental phenomenon. In the first place, moral evaluation is a crucial aspect of action in social systems. It is a main aspect of the broader phenomenon of "normative orientation," since not all normative patterns which are relevant to action are the object of moral sentiments. The second crucial fact is the importance of the human individual as a unit of concrete social systems. If both human individuals as units and moral evaluation are essential to social systems, it follows that these individuals will be evaluated as units and not merely with respect to their particular qualities,

---

[2] Perhaps Durkheim has done more than any other social theorist to make this phenomenon clear and to analyze its implications (see especially *L'Education morale* [Paris: F. Alcan, 1925], I, and *Les Formes elementaires de la vie religieuse* [Paris: F. Alcan, 1912; 2d ed., 1925], chap. iii): It is also involved in Max Weber's concept of legitimacy (*Wirtschaft und Gesellschaft* [Tübingen: Verlag von J. C. B. Mohr, 1925], chap. i, secs. 5, 6, 7). It is discussed and analyzed in Talcott Parsons, *The Structure of Social Action* (New York: McGraw-Hill Book Co., 1937), esp. Chaps. x, xi, and xvii.

[3] An excellent recent example of this is found in the results reported by F. J. Roethlisberger and W. A. Dickson, *Management and the Worker* (Cambridge, Mass., 1939), Part III, chap. xv.

acts, etc. Furthermore, this cannot merely be a matter of any given individual A's having moral attitudes toward any other given individual B, but it implies ranking. Unless there is to be a functionally impossible state of lack of integration of the social system, the evaluations by A and B of their associate C must come somewhere near agreeing; and their relative ranking of C and D must broadly agree where the necessity for comparison arises.[4] The theoretical possibility exists that not only any two individuals but all those in the system should be ranked as exact equals. This possibility, however, has never been very closely approached in any known large-scale social system. And, even if it were, that would not disprove the fundamental character of stratification, since it would not be a case of "lack" of stratification but of a particular limiting type. Stratification, as here treated, is an aspect of the concept of the structure of a generalized social system.[5]

There is, in any given social system, an actual system of ranking in terms of moral evaluation But this implies in some sense an integrated set of standards according to which the evaluations are, or are supposed to be, made. Since a set of standards constitutes a normative pattern, the actual system will not correspond exactly to the pattern. The actual system of effective superiority and inferiority relationships, as far as moral sanction is claimed for it, will hence be called the system of social stratification. The normative pattern, on the other hand, will be called the scale of stratification.

Since the scale of stratification is a pattern characterized by moral authority which is integrated in terms of common moral sentiments, it is normally part of the institutional pattern of the social system. Its general status and analysis falls into the theory of social institutions, and it is in these terms that it will be analyzed here.[6]

---

[4] The concept "integration" is a fundamental one in the theory of action. It is a mode of relation of the units of a system by virtue of which, on the one hand, they act so as collectively to avoid disrupting the system and making it impossible to maintain its stability, and, on the other hand, to "co-operate" to promote its functioning as a unity (cf. Parsons, *op. cit.*)

[5] A generalized social system is a conceptual scheme, not an empirical phenomenon. It is a logically integrated system of generalized concepts of empirical reference in terms of which an indefinite number of concretely differing empirical systems can be described and analyzed (see L. J. Henderson, *Pareto's General Sociology* [Cambridge: Harvard University Press, 1935], chap. iv and n. 3).

[6] The concept of institutions, like that of stratification, is central to the theory of action but cannot be analyzed here (cf. Parsons, *op. cit.*, chaps. x and xvii).

Before following out the problem of the structural differentiation of systems and scales of stratification, and some of the bases and functional consequences of such variations, it is well to discuss certain aspects of the relation of the individual actor to the scale of stratification. The main factual references will be to the type of system of stratification where, as in our own, there is a rather wide scope for, in Linton's term, the "achievement" of status.

From the point of view of the theory of action the actor is in part a "goal-directed" entity. One important aspect of this orientation is to be found in his sentiments as to the moral desirability of these goals, though they may, of course, at the same time have other sorts of significance. Not only are goals as such the objects of moral sentiments but this status is also occupied by persons and their attitudes to the actor, by things and their relations to the actor, and by social relationships. Many of the most important goals cluster about these things.

Second, any or all of these may have other types of significance to the actor than the moral. They may be sources of hedonic satisfaction or objects of affectional attitudes. The normal actor is, to a significant degree, an "integrated" personality. In general, the things he values morally are also the things he "desires" as sources of hedonic satisfaction or objects of his affection. To be sure, there are, concretely, often serious conflicts in this respect, but they must be regarded mainly as instances of "deviation" from the integrated type.

Finally, the importance of moral sentiments in action, together with the fact that action is directed toward goals, generally implies that the normal actor has moral sentiments toward himself and his acts. He either has a rather high degree of "self-respect" or in some sense or other feels "guilt" or "shame."

But this actor does not stand alone. He is, to a greater or less degree, integrated with other actors in a social system. This means, on the one hand, that there is a tendency for the basic moral sentiments to be shared by the different actors in a system in the sense that they approve the same basic normative patterns of conduct, while on the other, the other individuals become important to anyone; what they do, say, or even subjectively think and feel cannot be merely indifferent to him.

Through the differentiation of roles there is a differentiation in the specific goals which are morally approved for different individuals. But, so far as the society is morally and hence institutionally integrated, they are all governed by the same more generalized pattern. This common pattern is applied on the judgments of higher and lower as applied to individuals which thus form a convenient point of reference for systematizing the normative pattern itself. Self-respect, which, it may be said, is in the first instance a matter of living up to the moral norms the individual himself approves, becomes secondarily a matter of attaining or maintaining a position in terms of the scale of stratification.

This connection is reinforced by the interplay, in an institutionally integrated situation, between moral patterns and the self-interested elements of motivation. The actor has interests in the attainment of diverse goals, in hedonic satisfactions, in affectional response, and also in the recognition or respect of others. It is a simple corollary of the integration of moral sentiments that recognition, or moral respect on the part of others, is dependent on the actor on the whole living up to the moral expectations of these others. There is, furthermore, an important tendency for recognition and affectional response to go together. Loss of moral respect for a person makes it at least difficult to maintain a high level of affection for him. Loss of either or both tends also to entail withdrawal of sources of hedonic satisfaction as far as these are dependent on the actions of others. Failure to conform with institutionalized norms thus injures the individual's self-interest by leading to withdrawal of help and satisfactions; it can easily lead further into the "negative" reactions. Instead of merely refusing to be helpful, others may positively obstruct the attainment of one's goals. They may actively run down the individual's reputation, positively hate him, and seek to hurt him. All this is further accentuated by the fact that there is a need to "manifest sentiments by external acts,"[7] to pass over from hostile sentiments to overt action which is detrimental to the interests of the actors. Such overt action is all the more likely where the norms in question are solidly institutionalized. For, then, other actors have built up definite "expectations" of behavior on which they count; and, when these expectations are frustrated, they not merely "disapprove" but are directly "injured" and "let down."

Finally, there is much evidence that the more important moral patterns are not simply something which we rationally "accept."

---

[7] The title of Class III of Pareto's "residues."

They have been inculcated from early childhood and are deeply "introjected" to form part of the basic structure of the personality itself. Violation of them brings with it the risk not only of external sanctions but of internal conflict which is often of a really disabling magnitude.

It is thus not a question of whether institutional behavior is or is not self-interested. Indeed, if any given individual can be said to seek his own "self-interest" in this sense, it follows that he can do so only by conforming in some degree to the institutionalized definition of the situation. But this in turn means that he must to a large degree be oriented to the scale of stratification. Thus his motivation almost certainly becomes focused to a considerable extent on the attainment of "distinction" or recognition by comparison with his fellows. This becomes a most important symbol, both to himself and to others, of the success or lack of success of his efforts in living up to his own and others' expectations in his attempts to conform with value patterns. With particular reference to self-interest, distinction itself in this sense may and often does become an important direct goal of action. Thus stratification is one central focus of the structuralization of action in social systems.[8]

That action in a social system should, to a large extent, be oriented to a scale of stratification is inherent in the structure of social systems of action. But, though this fact is constant, the content of the scale, the specific standards and criteria by which individuals are ranked, is not uniform for all social systems but varies within a wide range. It follows from the definition of a scale of stratification adopted here that this variation will be a function of the more general variations of value orientation which can be shown empirically to exist as between widely differing social systems.[9] That there are wide variations in values is an established fact. In certain particular cases and respects it has also been established in what these variations consist. It can, however, scarcely be said that knowledge in this field is sufficiently far advanced for us to have available a generalized classification of possible value orientations which can simply be taken over and

---

[8] In the degree of its generality, "success" or "distinction" is a goal which is comparable with that of wealth or of power.

[9] For an empirical demonstration of this range of variation of fundamental value orientations see especially Max Weber's comparative studies in the sociology of religion (*Gesammelte Aufsatze zur Religionssoziologie* [3 vols.]; Tübingen: J. C. B. Mohr, 1934). A brief summary of certain aspects of these studies is given in Parsons, *op. cit.*, chaps. xiv and xv.

applied to the special features of the field of stratification. Starting with the implications of the fact of differential ranking of individuals in value terms, it is, however, possible to build up a classification of certain of the socially significant respects in which they are differentially valued. This classification in turn can be related to the classification of value systems in that the latter will supply the justifications of why discrimination in each of the respects treated here (or lack of it) is considered legitimate. The following is a classification of bases of differential valuation, which though by no means final and exhaustive, has been found to be relatively concrete and useful.

1. *Membership in a kinship unit.*—There is an aspect of differential status which is shared with other members of whatever in the society in question is an effective kinship unit. Membership in the unit may be held by virtue of birth, but it may also be by other criteria, as in the case of marriage by personal choice in our own society.

2. *Personal qualities.*—Personal qualities are any of those features of an individual which differentiate him from another individual, and which may be referred to as a reason for "rating" him higher than the other: sex, age, personal beauty, intelligence, strength, etc. In so far as personal effort may have an influence on these qualities, as in the case of "attractiveness" of women, it tends to overlap the next category, "achievements." From the present point of view, a quality is what for the purposes in hand is best treated as an aspect of what a person "is," not a result of what he "does." Concrete qualities range all the way from certain basic things altogether beyond personal control, such as the facts of sex and age, to those which are mainly achievements.

3. *Achievements.*—Achievements are the valued results of the actions of individuals. They may or may not be embodied in material objects. It is that which can be ascribed to an individual's action or agency in a morally responsible sense. Just as at one point achievements shade over into personal qualities, so at another they shade into the fourth category.

4. *Possessions.*—Possessions are things, not necessarily material objects, "belonging" to an individual which are distinguished by the criterion of transferability. Qualities and achievements as such are not necessarily transferable, though sometimes, and to a certain extent, they may be. Of course, concrete possessions may be the

results of one's own or another's achievements, and control over the qualities of persons may be a possession.

5. *Authority.*—Authority is an institutionally recognized right to influence the actions of others, regardless of their immediate personal attitudes to the direction of influence. It is exercised by the incumbent of an office or other socially defined status such as that of parent, doctor, prophet. The kind and degree of authority exercised is clearly one of the most important bases of the differential valuation of individuals.

6. *Power.*—It is useful to consider a sixth residual category of "power." For this purpose a person possesses power only in so far as his ability to influence others and his ability to achieve or to secure possessions are not institutionally sanctioned. Persons who have power in this sense, however, often do in practice secure a certain kind of direct recognition. Furthermore, power may be, and generally is, used to acquire legitimized status and symbols of recognition.

The status of any given individual in the system of stratification in a society may be regarded as a resultant of the common valuations underlying the attribution of status to him in each of these six respects.[10] A classification of types of scales, or rather several of them, can then be derived by a consideration of the variation in the emphasis placed on each of these categories by a given value system, and also of variations in the particular content of each category. Attention here will be confined to a very few cases which have been of great historical importance.

One of the most general distinctions which can be easily applied to stratification in terms of this scheme is that employed by Linton between "achieved" and "ascribed" status.[11] The relation of this very important dichotomy to this scheme is not simple. In general the criteria of ascribed status must be birth or biologically hereditary qualities like sex and age. But, in the socially defined role which accompanies such a status, there may be very important elements of expected achievement and resulting possessions. Other possessions, of course, may be associated with an ascribed status through

---

[10] It is clearly recognized that this proposition constitutes a statement of the problem, not a solution of it.

[11] R. Linton, *The Study of Man* (New York, 1936), chap. vii. "Status" is a term referring to any institutionally defined position of an individual in the social structure. Position in a scale of stratification is only one aspect of status. There is a certain loose tendency to make them coterminous.

the inheritance of property and the perquisites of office if the latter is filled by ascription rather than by achievement. The same is true of authority which may, at times, be directly inherited or may be attached to an office.

There is, however, another general relation between the six elements of stratificatory status which partly overlaps with the distinction of ascribed and achieved status but partly cuts across it. That is, in every known society membership in a solidary kinship unit is one fundamental element of the place of an individual in a system of stratification. There are, however, great variations in the way in which this takes place in the relation of kinship to the other elements. The basic elements of all kinship structure are birth and sexual union.[12] An individual becomes a member of a kinship group either by birth in one or by entering into a socially legitimized sexual union, a marriage.

The kinship groups centered about birth and sexual union are always to a certain extent "solidary" not only in the sense of mutual aid and support but also in the sense that they form units in the system of stratification of the society; their members are in certain respects treated as "equals" regardless of the fact that by definition they must differ in sex and age, and very generally do in other qualities, and in achievements, authority, and possessions. Even though for these latter reasons they are differently valued to a high degree, there is still an element of status which they share equally and in respect of which the only differentiation tolerated is that involved in the socially approved differences of the sex and age status. But as actually used, the term "social class" certainly covers a great deal of the ground involved in this basic phenomenon—the treatment of kinship groups as solidary units in the system of stratification. It is, therefore, proposed to define a social class here as consisting of the group of persons who are members of effective kinship units which, as units, are approximately equally valued. According to this definition, the class structure of social systems may differ both in the composition or structure of the effective kinship unit or units which are units of class structure and in the criteria by which such units are differentiated from one another. The class status of an individual is that rank in the system of stratification which can be ascribed to

---

[12] See Kingsley Davis and W. L. Warner, "Structural Analysis of Kinship," *American Anthropologist*, Vol. XXXIX, No. 2.

him by virtue of those of his kinship ties which bind him to a unit in the class structure. Kinship affiliation is thus always a basic aspect of the class status of an individual. It does not follow that his class status has always been determined by his kinship ties. Nor does it follow that the system of ranking of kinship units can be explained as derived from factors peculiarly associated with kinship.

There is a type of class structure in which class of birth is a sufficient criterion of an individual's rank in the scale of stratification throughout his life. Because of the close approach to its full realization in India, it is convenient to refer to this type as "caste." It is the case where the only relevant criterion of class status is birth and where the structure is one of hierarchically arranged hereditary groups, and no acquisition of authority, no qualities, achievements, or possessions can change an individual's rank. All hierarchical status is ascribed. From this type there is a gradual transition to an opposite pole—that in which birth is completely irrelevant to class status, the level being determined by some combination of the other elements.[13]

It is perhaps permissible to refer to this antithetical type as that of "equality of opportunity." But it should be noted how very formal this conception is. It says nothing whatever about either the combination of the other five elements of hierarchical status involved or the concrete content of any one. Groups of equals must, under a caste system, in the nature of the case be rigidly endogamous, for husband and wife are necessarily of the same class status. But in a system not resembling the caste type, husband and wife need not be rigidly equal by birth, although they become so by marriage, and a married couple and their children, even though equals at birth, may change their class status during their lifetimes. Generally speaking, of course, the more effectively solidary the extended kinship groups, especially as between the generations, the more closely the total class system will approach the caste pole.

This approach to the analysis of social class may help to throw light on some aspects of the class structure of contemporary American society. Broadly speaking there are two fundamental elements in the dominant American scale of stratification. We determine status very largely on the basis of achievement within an occupa-

---

[13] This is the limiting type where "class" disappears.

tional system which is in turn organized primarily in terms of universalistic criteria of performance and status within functionally specialized fields.[14] This dominant pattern of the occupational sphere requires at least a relatively high degree of "equality of opportunity" which in turn means that status cannot be determined primarily by birth or membership in kinship units.

But this occupational system with its crucial significance in the system of stratification coexists in our society with a strong institutional emphasis on the ties of kinship. The values associated with the family, notably the marriage bond and the parent-child relationship, are among the most strongly emphasized in our society.

Absolute equality of opportunity is, as Plato clearly saw, incompatible with any positive solidarity of the family. But such a relative equality of opportunity as we have is compatible not with all kinds of kinship systems but with certain kinds. There is much evidence that our kinship structure has developed in such a direction as to leave wide scope for the mobility which our occupational system requires while protecting the solidarity of the primary kinship unit.

The conjugal family with dependent children, which is the dominant unit in our society, is, of all types of kinship unit, the one which is probably the least exposed to strain and possible breaking-up by the dispersion of its members both geographically and with respect to stratification in the modern type of occupational hierarchy. Dependent children are not involved in competition for status in the occupational system, and hence their achievements or lack of them are not likely to be of primary importance to the status of the family group as a whole. This reduces the problem to that of possible competitive comparison of the two parents. If both were equally in competition for occupational status, there might indeed be a very serious strain on the solidarity of the family unit, for there is no general reason why they would be likely to come out very nearly equally, while, in their capacity of husband and wife, it is very important that they should be treated as equals.

One mechanism which can serve to prevent the kind of "invidious comparison" between husband and wife which might be disruptive of family solidarity is a clear separation of the sex roles such as to insure that they do not come into competition with each

---

[14] For an explanation of these terms in their application to the modern occupational system see Talcott Parsons, "The Professions and Social Structure," *Social Forces*, XVII (May, 1939), 457-67, included in the present volume.

other. On the whole, this separation exists in our society, and perhaps the above considerations provide part of the explanation of why the feminist movement has had such difficulty in breaking it down.

The separation of the sex roles in our society is such as, for the most part, to remove women from the kind of occupational status which is important for the determination of the status of a family. Where married women are employed outside the home, it is, for the great majority, in occupations which are not in direct competition for status with those of men of their own class.

Women's interests, and the standards of judgment applied to them, run, in our society, far more in the direction of personal adornment and the related qualities of personal charm than is the case with men. Men's dress is practically a uniform, admitting of very slight play for differentiating taste, in marked contrast with that of women. This serves to concentrate the judgment and valuation of men on their occupational achievements, while the valuation of women is diverted into realms outside the occupationally relevant sphere. This difference appears particularly conspicuous in the urban middle classes where competition for class status is most severe. It is suggested that this phenomenon is functionally related to maintaining family solidarity in our class structure.

The probability of this hypothesis is increased by two sets of contrasting facts. On the one hand, in such a society as that of eighteenth-century France, where the tone was set by a hereditary aristocracy, both sexes were greatly concerned with personal adornment and charm. This may in part be due to the fact that, since status was mainly hereditary, neither was in severe competition for status in such fields as the modern occupations. On the other hand, in many rural and peasant societies neither sex seems to be oriented in this direction. This suggests that, in our urban society with its competitive atmosphere, the qualities and achievements of the feminine role have come to be significant as symbols of the status of the family, as parts of its "standard of living" which reflect credit on it. The man's role, on the other hand, is primarily to determine the status of his family by "finding his level" in the occupational sphere.[15]

---

[15] Thorstein Veblen in *The Theory of the Leisure Class* (New York: Macmillan Co., 1899) called attention to some of the relevant features of the role of women but did not relate it in this way to the functional equilibrium of the social structure. Moreover, what Veblen means by "conspicuous consumption" is only one aspect of the feminine role and one which is associated more with certain elements of malintegration than with the basic structure itself.

From the fact that kinship affiliation is the primary criterion of the class status of an individual it does not, however, follow that the class structure of a society is to be biologically explained. Rather, all the factors involved in social phenomena generally are *prima facie* important in the determination of concrete kinship structures. The same is true of class. In a caste system no individual can change his status of birth, but it does not follow that elements other than birth are not important in the maintenance of a concrete caste system, that any great change in any one or more would not result in a change of the system. When there is a more or less open class system, on the other hand, it is to some combination of these other elements that one must look for the factors which lead to change of the class status of kinship groups.

There is a very complex system of mutual symbolic references by virtue of which primary criteria of status are reinforced by secondary criteria and symbols in various ways.[16] For the primary criteria one must look to the general common value system of the society and its history. The secondary criteria or symbols are often much more adventitious, the result of associations formed in particular historical circumstances which have come to be traditionally upheld. The primary criteria are those things which in relation to the dominant value system are "status-determining" attributes of the individual and which are valued for their own sake. The secondary criteria are those things which are regarded as normal accompaniments of the primary criteria or as normal effects of them.

Birth, of course, plays a prominent role among the primary criteria of class status in any system approaching the caste type. But birth is probably never alone adequate to define the social role, and hence the expected qualities, possessions, achievements, or authority of the occupant of a given hereditary status. There is, rather, a complex combination of these things ascribed to the occupant of such a status. An excellent example is the senatorial aristocracy of Republican Rome. Though not formally so, in effect this was a hereditary group, only members of the senatorial families being eligible for the kind of career which led to the higher magistracies

---

[16] The present distinction between primary and secondary criteria is a rough one. For many purposes it may well be necessary to refine the classification further. Besides their significance as criteria, many of the same elements may also have significance as causal factors in the distribution of individuals among statuses and in shifts in the system of stratification. It is impossible, within the limits of this paper, to enter into these complex problems.

and finally membership in the Senate. "New men," though not completely unknown, were very rare. But the young Roman of this class had to live up to a very rigorously defined pattern. He went through a career including military service and the holding of office. To be a good soldier, to run for office, to have the Roman aristocratic virtues, was compulsory for such a young man. Wealth was partly hereditary, partly an acquisition of office-holding. Far from being in a position simply to rest on the laurels of his birth the Roman aristocrat was subjected to a very severe discipline and was expected to live up to a high level of achievement. That none of the generals who led the earlier Roman conquests, first of Italy, then of Carthage, and in part of Greece and the East, was a professional soldier in our sense but an aristocratic amateur who was a soldier as part of his ascribed role as an aristocrat attests to the great power of such ascribed patterns. In certain respects the extraordinary discipline to which the Spartiates were subjected is an even more striking example. The essence of the matter is that a combination of elements other than birth becomes part of the ascribed pattern to which the incumbent of the status is socially expected to "live up."

Though birth is certainly in these circumstances a primary criterion of status, the basic "virtues" emphasized by the ascribed pattern are equally primary, and, once an individual is eligible by virtue of birth, these are the main points at which social pressure to maintain the pattern is applied. Wealth, however, is seldom a primary criterion. It may, however, play an important secondary role in that a certain "style of living" comes to be expected of the members of an aristocracy. A minimum of wealth is a necessary means of keeping this up, while unusual wealth may be a source of extra prestige, by enabling its holder to excel in many symbolically important respects. Sometimes an economic system may change so as seriously to endanger the position of such an aristocracy, by enabling persons not qualified by birth to take on many of the symbols of aristocratic status and at the same time making it impossible for members of the aristocracy to maintain them. The steady process by which Spartiate families dropped out because of inability to make their contributions to the mess is an excellent example.

Where status is mainly achieved, the situation is quite different. Birth cannot be a primary criterion but only a practical advantage in securing a differential access to opportunities, though in this respect it is of fundamental significance in our society and one of the main mechanisms by which a relative stability of the system of stratification is maintained.

But in our own society, apart from hereditary groups at the top in certain sections of the country, the main criteria of class status are to be found in the occupational achievements of men, the normal case being the married man with immature children. Authority is significant partly as a necessary means of carrying on occupational functions, but in turn the authority exercised is one of the main criteria of the prestige of an occupational status. Authority, especially that of office,[17] is again important as a reward of past achievements, the general structure of the pattern being a progressive rise to greater achievements and greater rewards concomitantly. Being permitted to perform the "higher" functions and being given the authority to do so constitute recognition of past achievements and of the ability necessary for further ones. Thus authority and office become secondary, symbolic criteria of status, because of their traditional association with achievement. But, once they have gained this significance as criteria, the incumbent of an office can enjoy its prestige independently of whether he actually has the requisite achievements to his credit or not.

The case of wealth as a criterion of status in our society is somewhat more complex. In spite of much opinion to the contrary, it is not a primary criterion, seen in terms of the common value system. Like office, its primary significance is as a symbol of achievement. But it owes its special prominence in that respect to certain peculiar features of our social system. That is, with a basic ethic which emphasizes individual achievement as the primary criterion of stratification, we have developed an economic system which to a hitherto unprecedented degree rests on a "business" or "capitalistic" basis. Our society is very highly specialized occupationally. The measures of achievement are technical and specific for each particular field. Hence it is difficult to compare relative achievements in different fields with one another. To be sure, there is a very rough general scale of prestige occupations which is at least relatively independent of income. Skilled labor ranks higher than unskilled labor; functions with an important intellectual com-

---

[17] Not only political office but, even more, offices held in business corporations and other "private" associations.

ponent which require "higher education" rank high. In particular, authority over others, in proportion to its extent, ranks high.

But in a business economy the immediate end of business policy must, in the nature of the case, be to improve the financial status of the enterprise. Regardless of the technical content of its operations, the earnings of a business have become the principal criterion of its success. It is not surprising that the same has, to a relatively high degree, come to be true of individuals in business. Hence, within the broad framework of the direct differential valuation of occupations and achievements as managerial, professional, skilled, unskilled, etc., there is an income hierarchy which, on the whole, corresponds to that of direct valuation.[18] This income hierarchy forms a most convenient point of reference for the determination of the status of an individual or of a family. Furthermore, within any particular closely knit group, it is fairly adequate as a criterion, since the more highly valued jobs are also the best paid. But in such a complex system as our own its adequacy is much more dubious. In particular, it is complicated by the inheritance of property, by the availability of means of making money which are of doubtful legitimacy in terms of the value system, and by the many relatively adventitious opportunities for money-making opened up by the rapid changes and fluctuations of a business system in a society which is to a high degree emancipated from the rigidities of traditionalism. Hence the same thing happens as with the case of authority. Wealth, which owes its place as a criterion of status mainly to its being an effect of business achievement, gains a certain independence so that the possessor of wealth comes to claim a status and to have it recognized, regardless of whether or not he has the corresponding approved achievements to his credit. In our society this is further complicated by the fact that there is a tradition of respect for inherited wealth which has never quite been extinguished, and where the status is ascribed and the wealth naturally never regarded as an effect of its possessors' achievements.

There is a further respect in which wealth has a peculiar significance in an "individualistic" society. Where status is ascribed, there is usually a fairly well-defined standard to which people are expected to live up. For the group in question there is something

---

[18] How this correspondence comes about is an interesting sociological problem. The one thing which can be said here with certainty is that an ordinary economic explanation, though true within certain limits, is quite inadequate to the general problem. The explanation is to a large extent institutional.

like a "ceiling" of adequate achievement, even though there are naturally different degrees of attainment. With respect to achieved status, on the other hand, the situation is different. Achievement is in a different sense competitive. There is a more or less indefinite scale of degrees of excellence in any one line. Even though for a professional group, like the medical, there is a fairly well-defined minimum of competence, from this minimum upward there is a gradual transition through a widely dispersed pyramid to the "top" of the profession. The fact that money is an infinitely divisible, quantitative medium of measurement makes it a peculiarly convenient criterion to designate the various steps in such a gradual pyramidal structure, particularly where other common measures such as direct technical criteria or hierarchy of office in directly comparable organizations are not readily available. It is, in fact, quite common to speak of "$5,000 men" or "$25,000 men," although it is realized that this is not alone an adequate measure of their status.

As in the case of ascribed status the role of money as a criterion of status is here strongly reinforced by the fact that its expenditure is largely for other symbols of status in turn. Though the "standard of living" of any group must cover their intrinsically significant needs, such as food, shelter, and the like, there can be no doubt that an exceedingly large component of standards of living everywhere is to be found in the symbolic significance of many of its items in relation to status. Indeed it may be said that there are two types of situations in which this is likely to be more important than otherwise—the case of an aristocracy the members of which maintain a conspicuously different style of life from that of the rest of the population and the case of a group who are involved in a highly competitive struggle for achieved status, where the status of a large proportion of them at any given time is either newly acquired or relatively insecure or both. Perhaps at no time in history have such a large proportion of a great population been "on the make" as in the United States of the early twentieth century.

One further important point is that the various items of a standard of living which are symbolic of status necessarily play their primary role in relation to class status, not to the other aspects of the status of the members of a family. This follows from the fact that income is allocated on a basis of the family as a unit. A very interesting point of view from which to conduct budget studies would be to determine the various different things which were thought necessary for each member of a family in order to maintain or to improve the class status of the family as a whole.

The difficulty of finding common measures of status when the primary criterion is occupational achievement has already been mentioned. To a certain extent we do, of course, have such common measures, above all the relatively vague scales of direct valuations and of income. But to a considerable extent this situation is met by a certain vagueness in the actual scale of stratification, so that it is only in a relatively rough and broad sense, not a precise and definite one, that a given individual or family is placed relative to others. There is a relatively broad range of the standard of living where anyone with a certain minimum of income can participate without having the question of his relative status raised. This is, for instance, true of many of the facilities open to the "public." In hotels, restaurants, theaters, etc., a certain minimum of dress and manners is required beyond the mere fact of being able to pay the direct charges. But this minimum is, for a certain class of facilities, possessed by people belonging to a rather wide range of class status. This is really an instance of a broader class of phenomena, those involved in the fact that very many social contacts in our society are "partial" or "segmental" and cover only an area of interests and values which can, to a relative degree, be isolated from class status. Another instance is the relative lack of integration as between different structures within the broader society, each of which involves a pretty definite stratification within itself, such as occupational groups of persons in regular daily contact, and "communities" of people whose mutual relations are very precisely defined.

This indefiniteness, among other things, makes possible two very important things for the functioning of an individualistic social system. In the first place, when the relatively adventitious circumstances of the economic and social situation lead to discrepancies between income and occupational status as otherwise judged, within certain limits too great a strain is not placed on the system. For example, it would be generally agreed that the difference between the top range of incomes earned, on the one hand, in business and the law, on the other, in university teaching and the ministry does not accurately measure the relative prestige of their incumbents. A world-famous scientist who is a university professor on a ten-thousand-dollar salary is not only at the top of his own profession but may be the full equal in status of a corporation lawyer whose income is ten times his own. But so long as the scientist is able to maintain a "respectable" standard of living, entertain his friends well, dress his family adequately, and educate his children well, the fact that he cannot afford the luxuries of a hundred-thousand-dollar income is a matter of relative indifference. He simply does not compete on the plane of "conspicuous consumption" which is open to the lawyer but closed to him.[19]

There is also another respect in which this vagueness is functionally important in our system. If the institutional pattern which bases class status on the occupational achievements of a man is not to be severely discredited, there must be considerable room for class mobility. But this means that there will inevitably be a process of "dispersion" of the members of the same kinship groups in the class structure. In particular, there will be dispersion as between parents and children and as between siblings. A son, for instance, may rise well above his father's status, or two brothers may fare very unequally. To be sure, this is partly taken care of by the weakening of at least parts of the kinship structure itself, in that the primary unit of kinship has become the immediate family of parents and immature children. The ties of independent children to their parents and of independent siblings to one another are greatly weakened. Above all, these are not any longer normally the day-to-day "community" ties which are inevitable as between those who share the life of a common household. But, of course, this does not mean that such ties have become of negligible importance. It is difficult to see how such powerful sentiments as those developed between parents and children during the dependent period could be simply dropped at maturity without serious effects.

The fact is that they are not. The vagueness of our class structure provides a kind of cushioning mechanism. For the fact that mature children ordinarily live in independent households is associated with the further fact that they are usually, to a large extent, members of independent "communities." Their mutual

---

[19] This is not to say that the discrepancy does not give rise to some strains which, however, are more likely to be felt by the scientist's wife and/or children than himself.

relations become highly segmental. When one visits the other, he is, from the point of view of the latter's community relationships, an "outsider," a stranger. So long as the discrepancy is not too great, it is then unnecessary for there to be any very exact determination of relatives class status, as there would have to be if both were permanent members of the same set of immediate community relationships, of the same "particular nexus." There will naturally be gossip which compares the relative status of the two, but this does not assume the same importance in the two cases. For instance, if two brothers are on the faculty of the same university, the question of their relative status is very acute. But if one is a physician in Boston and the other is in business in Chicago, such questions hardly arise at all unless the discrepancy of their relative "success" is very marked. One may say, then, that the vagueness of our class structure over relatively wide areas serves to protect the important residue of the more extended kinship relations from disruption in a society where class mobility is of fundamental functional importance. It would be expected that, wherever, in any particular situation, technical criteria of achievement were of particular importance in an occupational hierarchy, this vagueness of class status would tend to be especially marked, with even cases of what, from another point of view, would appear to be strange inhibitions on intimacy of social contact.

V

Age and Sex in the Social Structure of the United States

IN OUR SOCIETY age grading does not to any great extent, except for the educational system, involve formal age categorization, but is interwoven with other structural elements. In relation to these, however, it constitutes an important connecting link and organizing point of reference in many respects. The most important of these for present purposes are kinship structure, formal education, occupation and community participation. In most cases the age lines are not rigidly specific, but approximate; this does not, however, necessarily lessen their structural significance.[1]

In all societies the initial status of every normal individual is that of child in a given kinship unit. In our society, however, this universal starting point is used in distinctive ways. Although in early childhood the sexes are not usually sharply differentiated, in many kinship systems a relatively sharp segregation of children begins very early. Our own society is conspicuous for the extent to which children of both sexes are in many fundamental respects treated alike. This is particularly true of both privileges and responsibilities. The primary distinctions within the group of dependent siblings are those of age. Birth order as such is notably neglected as a basis of discrimination; a child of eight and a child of five have essentially the privileges and responsibilities appropriate to their respective age levels without regard to what older, intermediate, or younger siblings there may be. The preferential

---

[1] The problem of organization of this material for systematic presentation is, in view of this fact, particularly difficult. It would be possible to discuss the subject in terms of the above four principal structures with which age and sex are most closely interwoven, but there are serious disadvantages involved in this procedure. Age and sex categories constitute one of the main links of structural continuity in terms of which structures which are differentiated in other respects are articulated with each other; and in isolating the treatment of these categories there is danger that this extremely important aspect of the problem will be lost sight of. The least objectionable method, at least within the limits of space of such a paper, seems to be to follow the sequence of the life cycle.

treatment of an older child is not to any significant extent differentiated if and because he happens to be the first born.

There are, of course, important sex differences in dress and in approved play interest and the like, but if anything, it may be surmised that in the urban upper middle classes these are tending to diminish. Thus, for instance, play overalls are essentially similar for both sexes. What is perhaps the most important sex discrimination is more than anything else a reflection of the differentiation of adult sex roles. It seems to be a definite fact that girls are more apt to be relatively docile, to conform in general according to adult expectations, to be "good," whereas boys are more apt to be recalcitrant to discipline and defiant of adult authority and expectations. There is really no feminine equivalent of the expression "bad boy." It may be suggested that this is at least partially explained by the fact that it is possible from an early age to initiate girls directly into many important aspects of the adult feminine role. Their mothers are continually about the house and the meaning of many of the things they are doing is relatively tangible and easily understandable to a child. It is also possible for the daughter to participate actively and usefully in many of these activities. Especially in the urban middle classes, however, the father does not work in the home and his son is not able to observe his work or to participate in it from an early age. Furthermore many of the masculine functions are of a relatively abstract and intangible character, such that their meaning must remain almost wholly inaccessible to a child. This leaves the boy without a tangible meaningful model to emulate and without the possibility of a gradual initiation into the activities of the adult male role. An important verification of this analysis could be provided through the study in our own society of the rural situation. It is my impression that farm boys tend to be "good" in a sense in which that is not typical of their urban brothers.

The equality of privileges and responsibilities, graded only by age but not by birth order, is extended to a certain degree throughout the whole range of the life cycle. In full adult status, however, it is seriously modified by the asymmetrical relation of the sexes to the occupational structure. One of the most conspicuous expressions and symbols of the underlying equality, however, is the lack of sex differentiation in the process of formal education, so far, at least, as it is not explicitly vocational. Up through college, differentiation seems to be primarily a matter on the one hand of individual ability, on the other hand of class status, and only to a secondary degree of sex differentiation. One can certainly speak of a strongly established pattern that all children of the family have a "right" to a good education, rights which are graduated according to the class status of the family but also to individual ability. It is only in post-graduate professional education, with its direct connection with future occupational careers, that sex discrimination becomes conspicuous. It is particularly important that this equality of treatment exists in the sphere of liberal education since throughout the social structure of our society there is a strong tendency to segregate the occupational sphere from one in which certain more generally human patterns and values are dominant, particularly in informal social life and the realm of what will here be called community participation.

Although this pattern of equality of treatment is present in certain fundamental respects at all age levels, at the transition from childhood to adolescence new features appear which disturb the symmetry of sex roles, while still a second set of factors appears with marriage and the acquisition of full adult status and responsibilities.

An indication of the change is the practice of chaperonage, through which girls are given a kind of protection and supervision by adults to which boys of the same age group are not subjected. Boys, that is, are chaperoned only in their relations with girls of their own class. This modification of equality of treatment has been extended to the control of the private lives of women students in boarding schools and colleges. Of undoubted significance is the fact that it has been rapidly declining not only in actual effectiveness but as an ideal pattern. Its prominence in our recent past, however, is an important manifestation of the importance of sex role differentiation. Important light might be thrown upon its functions by systematic comparison with the related phenomena in Latin countries where this type of asymmetry has been far more accentuated than in this country in the more modern period.

It is at the point of emergence into adolescence that there first begins to develop a set of patterns and behavior phenomena which involve a highly complex combination of age grading and sex role elements. These may be referred to together as the phenomena of the "youth culture." Certain of its elements are present in pre-adolescence and others in the adult culture. But the peculiar combination in connection with this partciular age level is unique and highly distinctive for American society.

Perhaps the best single point of reference for characterizing the youth culture lies in its contrast with the dominant pattern of the adult male role. By contrast with the emphasis on responsibility in this role, the orientation of the youth culture is more or less specifically irresponsible. One of its dominant features themes is "having a good time" in relation to which there is a particularly strong emphasis on social activities in company with the opposite sex. A second predominant characteristic on the male side lies in the prominence of athletics, which is an avenue of achievement and competition which stands in sharp contrast to the primary standards of adult achievement in professional and executive capacities. Negatively, there is a strong tendency to repudiate interest in adult things and to feel at least a certain recalcitrance to the pressure of adult expectations and discipline. In addition to, but including, athletic prowess the typical pattern of the male youth culture seems to lay emphasis on the value of certain qualities of attractiveness, especially in relation to the opposite sex. It is very definitely a rounded humanistic pattern rather than one of competence in the performance of specified functions. Such stereotypes as the "swell guy" are significant of this. On the feminine side there is correspondingly a strong tendency to accentuate sexual attractiveness in terms of various versions of what may be called the "glamor girl" pattern.[2] Although these patterns defining roles tend to polarize sexually—for instance, as between star athlete and socially popular girl—yet on a certain level they are complementary, both emphasizing certain features of a total personality in terms of the direct expression of certain values rather than of instrumental significance.

---

[2] Perhaps the most dramatic manifestation of this tendency lies in the prominence of the patterns of "dating," for instance among college women. As shown by an unpublished participant-observer study made at one of the Eastern women's colleges, perhaps the most important single basis of informal prestige rating among the residents of a dormitory lies in their relative dating success—though this is by no means the only basis. One of the most striking features of the pattern is the high publicity given to the "achievements" of the individual in a sphere where traditionally in the culture a rather high level of privacy is sanctioned — it is interesting that once an engagement has occurred a far greater amount of privacy is granted. The standards of rating cannot be said to be well integrated, though there is an underlying consistency in that being in demand by what the group regards as desirable men is perhaps the main standard.

It is true that the "dating" complex need not be exclusively bound up with the "glamor girl" stereotype of ideal feminine personality — the "good companion" type may also have a place. Precisely, however, where the competitive aspect of dating is most prominent the glamor pattern seems heavily to predominate, as does, on the masculine side, a somewhat comparable glamorous type. On each side at the same time there is room for considerable differences as to just where the emphasis is placed — for example as between "voluptuous" sexuality and more decorous "charm."

One further feature of this situation is the extent to which it is crystallized about the system of formal education.[3] One might say that the principal centers of prestige dissemination are the colleges, but that many of the most distinctive phenomena are to be found in high schools throughout the country. It is of course of great importance that liberal education is not primarily a matter of vocational training in the United States. The individual status on the curricular side of formal education is, however, in fundamental ways linked up with adult expectations, and doing "good work" is one of the most important sources of parental approval. Because of secondary institutionalization this approval is extended into various spheres distinctive of the youth culture. But it is notable that the youth culture has a strong tendency to develop in directions which are either on the borderline of parental approval or beyond the pale, in such matters as sex behavior, drinking and various forms of frivolous and irresponsible behavior. The fact that adults have attitudes toward these things which are often deeply ambivalent and that on such occasions as college reunions they may outdo the younger generation, in drinking, for instance, is of great significance, but probably structurally secondary to the youth-versus-adult differential aspect. Thus the youth culture is not only, as is true of the curricular aspect of formal education, a matter of age status as such but also shows strong signs of being a product of tensions in the relationship of younger people and adults.

From the point of view of age grading, perhaps the most notable fact about this situation is the existence of definite pattern distinctions from the periods coming both before and after. At the line between childhood and adolescence "growing up" consists precisely in ability to participate in youth culture patterns, which are not, for either sex, the same as the adult patterns practiced by the parental generation. In both sexes the transition to full adulthood means loss of a certain "glamorous" element. From being the athletic hero or the lion of college dances, the young man becomes a prosaic business executive or lawyer. The more successful adults participate in an important order of prestige symbols but these are of a very dif-

---

[3] A central aspect of this focus of crystallization lies in the element of tension, sometimes of direct conflict, between the youth culture patterns of college and school life, and the "serious" interests in and obligations toward curricular work. It is of course the latter which defines some at least of the most important foci of adult expectations of doing "good" work and justifying the privileges granted. It is not possible here to attempt to analyze the interesting ambivalent attitudes of youth toward curricular work and achievement.

ferent order from those of the youth culture. The contrast in the case of the feminine role is perhaps equally sharp, with at least a strong tendency to take on a "domestic" pattern with marriage and the arrival of young children.

The symmetry in this respect must, however, not be exaggerated. It is of fundamental significance to the sex role structure of the adult age levels that the normal man has a "job," which is fundamental to his social status in general. It is perhaps not too much to say that only in very exceptional cases can an adult man be genuinely self-respecting and enjoy a respected status in the eyes of others if he does not "earn a living" in an approved occupational role. Not only is this a matter of his own economic support but, generally speaking, his occupational status is the primary source of the income and class status of his wife and children.

In the case of the feminine role the situation is radically different. The majority of married women, of course, are not employed, but even of those that are a very large proportion do not have jobs which are in basic competition for status with those of their husbands.[4] The majority of "career" women whose occupational status is comparable with that of men in their own class, at least in the upper middle and upper classes, are unmarried, and in the small proportion of cases where they are married the result is a profound alteration in family structure.

This pattern, which is central to the urban middle classes, should not be misunderstood. In rural society, for instance, the operation of the farm and the attendant status in the community may be said to be a matter of the joint status of both parties to a marriage. Whereas a farm is operated by a family, an urban job is held by an individual and does not involve other members of the family in a comparable sense. One convenient expression of the difference lies in the question of what would happen in case of death. In the case of a farm it would at least be not at all unusual for the widow to

---

[4] The above statement, even more than most in the present paper, needs to be qualified in relation to the problem of class. It is above all to the upper middle class that it applies. Here probably the great majority of "working wives" are engaged in some form of secretarial work which would, on an independent basis, generally be classed as a lower middle class occupation. The situation at lower levels of the class structure is quite different since the prestige of the jobs of husband and wife is then much more likely to be nearly equivalent. It is quite possible that this fact is closely related to the relative instability of marriage which Davis and Gardner (*Deep South*) find, at least for the community they studied, to be typical of lower class groups. The relation is one which deserves careful study.

continue operating the farm with the help of a son or even of hired men. In the urban situation the widow would cease to have any connection with the organization which had employed her husband and he would be replaced by another man without reference to family affiliations.

In this urban situation the primary status-carrying role is in a sense that of housewife. The woman's fundamental status is that of her husband's wife, the mother of his children, and traditionally the person responsible for a complex of activities in connection with the management of the household, care of children, etc.

For the structuring of sex roles in the adult phase the most fundamental considerations seem to be those involved in the inter-relations of the occupational system and the conjugal family. In a certain sense the most fundamental basis of the family's status is the occupational status of the husband and father. As has been pointed out, this is a status occupied by an individual by virtue of his individual qualities and achievements. But both directly and indirectly, more than any other single factor, it determines the status of the family in the social structure, directly because of the symbolic significance of the office or occupation as a symbol of prestige, indirectly because as the principal source of family income it determines the standard of living of the family. From one point of view the emergence of occupational status into this primary position can be regarded as the principal source of strain in the sex role structure of our society since it deprives the wife of her role as a partner in a common enterprise. The common enterprise is reduced to the life of the family itself and to the informal social activities in which husband and wife participate together. This leaves the wife a set of utilitarian functions in the management of the household which may be considered a kind of "pseudo-" occupation. Since the present interest is primarily in the middle classes, the relatively unstable character of the role of housewife as the principal content of the feminine role is strongly illustrated by the tendency to employ domestic servants wherever financially possible. It is true that there is an American tendency to accept tasks of drudgery with relative willingness, but it is notable that in middle class families there tends to be a dissociation of the essential personality from the performance of these tasks. Thus, advertising continually appeals to such desires as to have hands which one could never tell had washed dishes or scrubbed floors.[5] Organization about the function of housewife, however, with the addition of strong affectional devotion to husband and children, is the primary focus of one of the principal patterns governing the adult feminine role—what may be called the "domestic" pattern. It is, however, a conspicuous fact that strict adherence to this pattern has become progressively less common and has a strong tendency to a residual status—that is, to be followed most closely by those who are unsuccessful in competition for prestige in other directions.

It is, of course, possible for the adult woman to follow the masculine pattern and seek a career in fields of occupational achievement in direct competition with men of her own class. It is, however, notable that in spite of the very great progress of the emancipation of women from the traditional domestic pattern only a very small fraction have gone very far in this direction. It is also clear that its generalization would only be possible with profound alterations in the structure of the family.

Hence it seems that concomitant with the alteration in the basic masculine role in the direction of occupation there have appeared two important tendencies in the feminine role which are alternative to that of simple domesticity on the one hand, and to a full-fledged career on the other. In the older situation there tended to be a very rigid distinction between respectable married women and those who were "no better than they should be." The rigidity of this line has progressively broken down through the infiltration into the respectable sphere of elements of what may be called again the glamor pattern, with the emphasis on a specifically feminine form of attractiveness which on occasion involves directly sexual patterns of appeal. One important expression of this trend lies in the fact that many of the symbols of feminine attractiveness have been taken over directly from the practices of social types previously beyond the pale of respectable society. This would seem to be substantially true of the practice of women smoking and of at least the modern version of the use of cosmetics. The same would seem to be true of many of the modern versions of women's dress. "Eman-

---

[5] This type of advertising appeal undoubtedly contains an element of "snob appeal" in the sense of an invitation to the individual by her appearance and ways to identify herself with a higher social class than that of her actual status. But it is almost certainly not wholly explained by this element. A glamorously feminine appearance which is specifically dissociated from physical work is undoubtedly a genuine part of an authentic personality ideal of the middle class, and not only evidence of a desire to belong to the upper class.

cipation" in this connection means primarily emancipation from traditional and conventional restrictions on the free expression of sexual attraction and impulses, but in a direction which tends to segregate the elements of sexual interest and attraction from the total personality and in so doing tends to emphasize the segregation of sex roles. It is particularly notable that there has been no corresponding tendency to emphasize masculine attraction in terms of dress and other such aids. One might perhaps say that in a situation which strongly inhibits competition between the sexes on the same plane the feminine glamor pattern has appeared as an offset to masculine occupational status and to its attendant symbols of prestige. It is perhaps significant that there is a common stereotype of the association of physically beautiful, expensively and elaborately dressed women with physically unattractive but rich and powerful men.

The other principal direction of emancipation from domesticity seems to lie in emphasis on what has been called the common humanistic element. This takes a wide variety of forms. One of them lies in a relatively mature appreciation and systematic cultivation of cultural interests and educated tastes, extending all the way from the intellectual sphere to matters of art, music and house furnishings. A second consists in cultivation of serious interests and humanitarian obligations in community welfare situations and the like. It is understandable that many of these orientations are most conspicuous in fields where through some kind of tradition there is an element of particular suitability for feminine participation. Thus, a woman who takes obligations to social welfare particularly seriously will find opportunities in various forms of activity which traditionally tie up with women's relation to children, to sickness and so on. But this may be regarded as secondary to the underlying orientation which would seek an outlet in work useful to the community following the most favorable opportunities which happen to be available.

This pattern, which with reference to the character of relationship to men may be called that of the "good companion," is distinguished from the others in that it lays far less stress on the exploitation of sex role as such and more on that which is essentially common to both sexes. There are reasons, however, why cultural interests, interest in social welfare and community activities are particularly prominent in the activities of women in our urban communities. On the one side the masculine occupational role tends to absorb a very large proportion of the man's time and energy and to leave him relatively little for other interests. Furthermore, unless his position is such as to make him particularly prominent his primary orientation is to those elements of the social structure which divide the community into occupational groups rather than those which unite it in common interests and activities. The utilitarian aspect of the role of housewife, on the other hand, has declined in importance to the point where it scarcely approaches a full-time occupation for a vigorous person. Hence the resort to other interests to fill up the gap. In addition, women, being more closely tied to the local residential community, are more apt to be involved in matters of common concern to the members of that community. This peculiar role of women becomes particularly conspicuous in middle age. The younger married woman is apt to be relatively highly absorbed in the care of young children. With their growing up, however, her absorption in the household is greatly lessened, often just at the time when the husband is approaching the apex of his career and is most heavily involved in its obligations. Since to a high degree this humanistic aspect of the feminine role is only partially institutionalized it is not surprising that its patterns often bear the marks of strain and insecurity, as perhaps has been classically depicted by Helen Hokinson's cartoons of women's clubs.

The adult roles of both sexes involve important elements of strain which are both in certain dynamic relationships, especially to the youth culture. In the case of the feminine role, marriage is the single event toward which a selective process, in which personal qualities and effort can play a decisive part, has pointed. That determines a woman's fundamental status, and after that her role patterning is not so much status determining as a matter of living up to expectations and finding satisfying interests and activities. In a society where such strong emphasis is placed upon individual achievement it is not surprising that there should be a certain romantic nostalgia for the time when the fundamental choices were still open. This element of strain is added to by the lack of clear-cut definition of the adult feminine role. Once the possibility of a career has been eliminated there still tends to be a rather unstable oscillation between emphasis in the direction of domesticity or glamor or good companionship. According to situational pressures and individual character the tendency will be to emphasize one or another of these more strongly. But it is a situation likely to produce a rather high level of insecurity. In this state the pattern of domesticity must be ranked lowest in terms of prestige but also, because of the strong emphasis in community sentiment on the virtues of fidelity and devotion to husband and children, it offers perhaps the highest level of a certain kind of security. It is no wonder that such an important symbol as Whistler's mother concentrates primarily on this pattern.

The glamor pattern has certain obvious attractions since to the woman who is excluded from the struggle for power and prestige in the occupational sphere it is the most direct path to a sense of superiority and importance. It has, however, two obvious limitations. In the first place, many of its manifestations encounter the resistance of patterns of moral conduct and engender conflicts not only with community opinion but also with the individual's own moral standards. In the second place, it is a pattern the highest manifestations of which are inevitably associated with a rather early age level—in fact, overwhelmingly with the courtship period. Hence, if strongly entered upon serious strains result from the problem of adaptation to increasing age.

The one pattern which would seem to offer the greatest possibilities for able, intelligent, and emotionally mature women is the third— the good companion pattern. This, however, suffers from a lack of fully institutionalized status and from the multiplicity of choices of channels of expression. It is only those with the strongest initiative and intelligence who achieve fully satisfactory adaptations in this direction. It is quite clear that in the adult feminine role there is quite sufficient strain and insecurity so that widespread manifestations are to be expected in the form of neurotic behavior.

The masculine role at the same time is itself by no means devoid of corresponding elements of strain. It carries with it to be sure the primary prestige of achievement, responsibility and authority. By comparison with the role of the youth culture, however, there are at least two important types of limitations. In the first place, the modern occupational system has led to increasing specialization of the role. The job absorbs an extraordinarily large proportion of the individual's energy and emotional interests in a role the content of which is often relatively narrow. This in particular restricts the area within which he can share common interests and experiences with others not in the same occupational specialty. It is perhaps of considerable significance that so many of the highest prestige statuses of our society are of this specialized character. There is in the definition of roles little to bind the individual to others in his community on a comparable status level. By contrast with this situation, it is notable that in the youth culture common human elements are far more strongly emphasized. Leadership and eminence are more in the role of total individuals and less of competent specialists. This perhaps has something to do with the significant tendency in our society for all age levels to idealize youth and for the older age groups to attempt to imitate the patterns of youth behavior.

It is perhaps as one phase of this situation that the relation of the adult man to persons of the opposite sex should be treated. The effect of the specialization of occupational role is to narrow the range in which the sharing of common human interests can play a large part. In relation to his wife the tendency of this narrowness would seem to be to encourage on her part either the domestic or the glamorous role, or community participation somewhat unrelated to the marriage relationship. This relationship between sex roles presumably introduces a certain amount of strain into the marriage relationship itself since this is of such overwhelming importance to the family and hence to a woman's status and yet so relatively difficult to maintain on a level of human companionship. Outside the marriage relationship, however, there seems to be a notable inhibition against easy social intercourse, particularly in mixed company.[6] The man's close personal intimacy with other women is checked by the danger of the situation being defined as one of rivalry with the wife, and easy friendship without sexual-emotional involvement seems to be inhibited by the specialization of interests in the occupational sphere. It is notable that brilliance of conversation of the "salon" type seems to be associated with aristocratic society and is not prominent in ours.

Along with all this goes a certain tendency for middle-aged men, as symbolized by the "bald-headed row," to be interested in the physical aspects of sex—that is, in women precisely as dissociated from those personal considerations which are important to relation-

---

[6] In the informal social life of academic circles with which the writer is familiar there seems to be a strong tendency in mixed gatherings — as after dinner — for the sexes to segregate. In such groups the men are apt to talk either shop subjects or politics whereas the women are apt to talk about domestic affairs, schools, their children, etc., or personalities. It is perhaps on personalities that mixed conversation is apt to flow most freely.

ships of companionship or friendship, to say nothing of marriage. In so far as it does not take this physical form, however, there seems to be a strong tendency for middle-aged men to idealize youth patterns—that is, to think of the ideal inter-sex friendship as that of their pre-marital period.[7]

In so far as the idealization of the youth culture by adults is an expression of elements of strain and insecurity in the adult roles it would be expected that the patterns thus idealized would contain an element of romantic unrealism. The patterns of youthful behavior thus idealized are not those of actual youth so much as those which older people wish their own youth might have been. This romantic element seems to coalesce with a similar element derived from certain strains in the situation of young people themselves.

The period of youth in our society is one of considerable strain and insecurity. Above all, it means turning one's back on the security both of status and of emotional attachment which is engaged in the family of orientation. It is structurally essential to transfer one's primary emotional attachment to a marriage partner who is entirely unrelated to the previous family situation. In a system of free marriage choice this applies to women as well as men. For the man there is in addition the necessity to face the hazards of occupational competition in the determination of a career. There is reason to believe that the youth culture has important positive functions in easing the transition from the security of childhood in the family of orientation to that of full adult in marriage and occupational status. But precisely because the transition is a period of strain it is to be expected that it involves elements of unrealistic romanticism. Thus significant features of youth patterns in our society would seem to derive from the coincidence of the emotional needs of adolescents with those derived from the strains of the situation of adults.

A tendency to the romantic idealization of youth patterns seems in different ways to be characteristic of modern Western society as a whole.[8] It is not possible in the present context to enter into any extended comparative analysis, but it may be illuminating to call attention to a striking difference between the patterns associated with this phenomenon in Germany and in the United States. The German "youth movement," starting before the first World War,

---

[7] This, to be sure, often contains an element of romanticization. It is more nearly what he wishes these relations had been than what they actually were.

[8] *Cf.* E. Y. Hartshorne, "German Youth and the Nazi Dream of Victory," *America in a World at War, Pamphlet,* No. 12, New York, 1941.

has occasioned a great deal of comment and has in various respects been treated as the most notable instance of the revolt of youth. It is generally believed that the youth movement has an important relation to the background of National Socialism, and this fact as much as any suggests the important difference. While in Germany as everywhere there has been a generalized revolt against convention and restrictions on individual freedom as embodied in the traditional adult culture, in Germany particular emphasis has appeared on the community of male youth. "Comradeship" in a sense which strongly suggests that of soldiers in the field has from the beginning been strongly emphasized as the ideal social relationship. By contrast with this, in the American youth culture and its adult romanticization a much stronger emphasis has been placed on the cross-sex relationship. It would seem that this fact, with the structural factors which underlie it, have much to do with the failure of the youth culture to develop any considerable political significance in this country. Its predominant pattern has been that of the idealization of the isolated couple in romantic love. There have, to be sure, been certain tendencies among radical youth to a political orientation but in this case there has been a notable absence of emphasis on the solidarity of the members of one sex. The tendency has been rather to ignore the relevance of sex difference in the interest of common ideals.

The importance of youth patterns in contemporary American culture throws into particularly strong relief the status in our social structure of the most advanced age groups. By comparison with other societies the United States assumes an extreme position in the isolation of old age from participation in the most important social structures and interests. Structurally speaking, there seem to be two primary bases of this situation. In the first place, the most important single distinctive feature of our family structure is the isolation of the individual conjugal family. It is impossible to say that with us it is "natural" for any other group than husband and wife and their dependent children to maintain a common household. Hence, when the children of a couple have become independent through marriage and occupational status the parental couple is left without attachment to any continuous kinship group. It is, of course, common for other relatives to share a household with the conjugal family but this scarcely ever occurs without some important elements of strain. For independence is certainly the preferred pattern for an elderly couple, particularly from the point of view of the children.

The second basis of the situation lies in the occupational structure. In such fields as farming and maintenance of small independent enterprises there is frequently no such thing as abrupt "retirement," rather a gradual relinquishment of the main responsibilities and functions with advancing age. So far, however, as an individual's occupational status centers in a specific "job," he either holds the job or does not, and the tendency is to maintain the full level of functions up to a given point and then abruptly to retire. In view of the very great significance of occupational status and its psychological correlates, retirement leaves the older man in a peculiarly functionless situation, cut off from participation in the most important interests and activities of the society. There is a further important aspect of this situation. Not only status in the community but actual place of residence is to a very high degree a function of the specific job held. Retirement not only cuts the ties to the job itself but also greatly loosens those to the community of residence. Perhaps in no other society is there observable a phenomenon corresponding to the accumulation of retired elderly people in such areas as Florida and Southern California in the winter. It may be surmised that this structural isolation from kinship, occupational, and community ties is the fundamental basis of the recent political agitation for help to the old. It is suggested that it is far less the financial hardship[9] of the position of elderly people than their social isolation which makes old age a "problem." As in other connections we are very prone to rationalize generalized insecurity in financial and economic terms. The problem is obviously of particularly great significance in view of the changing age distribution of the population with the prospect of a far greater proportion in the older age groups than in previous generations. It may also be suggested that, through well-known psychosomatic mechanisms, the increased incidence of the disabilities of older people, such as heart disease, cancer, etc., may be at least in part attributed to this structural situation.

---

[9] That the financial difficulties of older people in a very large proportion of cases are real is not to be doubted. This, however, is at least to a very large extent a consequence rather than a determinant of the structural situation. Except where it is fully taken care of by pension schemes, the income of older people is apt to be seriously reduced, but, even more important, the younger conjugal family does not feel an obligation to contribute to the support of aged parents. Where as a matter of course both generations shared a common household, this problem did not exist.

VI

Democracy and Social Structure in Pre-Nazi Germany

FROM A SOCIOLOGICAL point of view, the "democratic," or better "liberal-democratic" type of society which has reached its highest degree of large-scale realization in such countries as England and the United States, has developed from a complex combination of structural elements. Some of these elements have been common to the Western world as a whole, while others have played a part particularly in these two countries. By contrast Germany presents a rather bewildering array both of similarities and of differences. This comparison will provide the main starting point of the present analysis of German social structure.[1]

On a common sense level, perhaps Germany's most conspicuous similarity especially with the United States, lies in the high development of industrialism, under the aegis of "big business." In particular this involves in the economy a high development of large scale organization, with a large, propertyless industrial class, a high concentration of executive authority and control of industrial property, and an important element of highly trained technical personnel, especially in engineering, but also in relation to legal and administrative functions. Certainly in no other country except the United States has the economy been so highly "bureaucratized" as in Germany.

In Germany, as in other industrial countries, this structure of modern industrial enterprise has been imbedded in a complex of other institutional features which in many ways are very similar. It has had a highly developed money economy. Only a relatively small fraction of the population has even approached self-suffi-

---

[1] In broad historical perspective, of course, France has a strong claim to be considered at least as important to "democracy" as the modern Anglo-Saxon countries. There are, however, notable differences the discussion of which would introduce too many complications to be dealt with in the limited space available. On another level, many of the smaller European countries and the British Dominions must be neglected for the same reason.

ciency. The great majority, on the contrary, have been mainly dependent on money income from salaries, wages or the profits of enterprise or disposal of services. To a high degree occupational status has been institutionally segregated from other not strictly functional bases of total status, though in this important respect there has certainly been a notable difference of degree especially from the United States. We have had no landed nobility, hardly an important class closely approaching the European peasantry, and a considerably smaller class of independent artisans and shop-keepers, whose status has in certain respects been similar to that of peasants.

Pre-Nazi Germany was also notable for the high development of the one-price system with its consequent restriction of the bargaining process to the larger-scale, hence often relatively highly organized, market situations. Indeed, by means of the development of cartels and collective bargaining through trade unions, Germany went further, at an earlier time, than any other country in the regulation of the exchange process. All this was backed by a firm and, on the whole, technically and impartially administered legal system in the fields of contract, monetary transactions and the like.

The similarity, in spite of certain differences, between Roman and Common Law, extends to the basic structure of the institution of property, especially by contrast with the feudal background of European society. There was full institutional segregation between ownership and either political authority or social status in other respects, combined with full alienability and centralization of all property rights in a single ownership—a condition which is an essential prerequisite of "capitalism" as well as of certain elements of personal freedom and of the mobility of resources, both human and non-human, which underlie the "liberal" type of industrial economy.

These similarities in the structure of the economy and of its more immediate institutional penumbra go so far that many writers, especially those inclined to Marxism, have strongly tended to treat the social structures of Germany and the United States as for most practical purposes identical. For them the appearance and political success of the Nazi movement in Germany would then indicate only relatively superficial differences perhaps of external conditions, or of the constitution in the formal, legal sense. It will, by contrast with that view, be the thesis of the present analysis that a divergence of political orientation so fundamental as that at present developing between the fascist and the liberal-democratic societies must go back to deeper structural sources than this view would indicate. On subtler institutional levels, important differences can be discerned even in the economy, but they can be more clearly brought out by noting their association with elements which contrast more obviously with our own.

It has thus long been clear to competent scholars that the German state differed markedly from its British or American counterparts. This difference may in the main be characterized in terms of its interdependent "feudal," militaristic, bureaucratic, and authoritarian features. The predominant impress of these elements came from Prussia, but the position of Prussia was sufficiently central strongly to color the whole of Germany.

Prussia, like England, has had a well-established "ruling class" even though the two have developed radically different patterns of life. In Prussia it has been a landed nobility with families settled on ancestral estates. Their status has involved complete local dominance over a subordinated rural population, with control of local government, with the lower classes kept in a state of economic dependency, and the enjoyment of a position of high social prestige enforced by rigid conventions. In the state itself, however, the primary mode of participation of this class has not been in the civil administration but in the armed forces. Members of the Prussian *Junker* families have, over a considerable period, set the "tone" of the officers' corps even though a majority of its members in recent times have not come from these families. The status of officer was that of maximum social prestige although not of impressive wealth or political influence in ordinary times— indeed there was a strong tradition of neutrality in ordinary political affairs.

Thus by virtue of its connection with the *Junker* nobility the German, especially the Prussian, officers' corps did not constitute an ordinary "professional" military force in the sense in which that is true of our regular army. This situation was further bolstered by two other circumstances. In the first place, the armed forces under the old German constitution were not under the control of the civil administration but were responsible directly to the Kaiser. This fact was not merely of constitutional significance but was indicative of the solidarity of social status between nobility and royalty, the two elements of the traditional "ruling class." The reciprocal solidarity is strongly indicated by the tendency of European royalty to emphasize their status as military commanders, for instance by making most public appearances in uniform even in peace time. Secondly, the officers' corps, in continuity with the whole Junker class, carried on a highly distinctive "style of life" which was in sharp contrast with everything "bourgeois," involving a strong contempt of industry and trade, of the bourgeois virtues, even of liberal and humane culture. Perhaps the most conspicuous symbol of this difference is the part played by the duel and its attendant code of honor. The most important criterion of eligibility to belong as a social equal was *Satisfaktionsfaehigkeit*, acceptability as an adversary in an "affair of honor." To be an officer one had also to be a "gentleman" in a technical sense which hardly included many elements of the population which we would consider high up in the middle class.

It has been remarked that toward the time of the first World War considerable bourgeois elements had penetrated into the officers' corps. They were, however, in Germany, predominantly what was called the "feudalized" bourgeoisie. That is, though sons of civil servants, professional men, even on occasion bankers or industrialists, they tended to take on the style of life of the *Junker* group rather than vice versa, and to be acceptable in proportion as they did so. One conspicuous phenomenon in this category was the place of the duelling "corps" in the universities.

Thus the "feudal-militaristic" elements have played a prominent role in the structure of the German state. Though not in any simple sense involved in "politics," they have been integral to the structure especially through their close connection with the monarchy and their position at the top of the scale of social prestige. The deposition of the monarchy and great reduction of the peace-time army after 1918 went far to remove this element from its central position on the formal level, but the process was not sufficiently thorough to break up its social identity nor to destroy its traditional prestige, especially in view of its close integration with other "conservative" elements in the social structure.

Along with the position of the *Junker* military element, the German state has been famous for the high development of its civilian administrative bureaucracy. As in the case of the *Junkers* the main outlines of this structural element ante-date, and are independent of, the development of industrialism in Germany. The bureaucracy does not, however, have the same continuity with "feudal" traditions, but developed as an aspect of the growth of centralized territorial monarchies in post-mediaeval times. It has been closely integrated with the adoption of Roman law and its teaching in the universities so that the bulk of administrative civil servants have had a university legal training. The judiciary has also, although a special branch, still been much more closely involved with this tradition than in the Anglo-Saxon countries. Indeed in Germany the legal profession as a whole has been far less independent of the state.

This famous German civil service has constituted a highly professionalized group, with a very high degree of formalization of status and of the operation of the organization. Specificity of status and powers in terms of formal legal definition have been carried very far. Impartiality and scrupulous precision in application of the law in meticulous detail has been the keynote. Again not only has impartial application of the law been called for, but there has been a strong tradition of aloofness from politics, of duty to carry out the legislation and decrees of the supreme authority without question.

Generally speaking the civil service has constituted for Prussia in particular the highest prestige element in the bourgeoisie. At court and in other "social" respects they have not been the equals of the nobility, but their sons could often become officers and even intermarriages with the nobility were not uncommon. A very strong sense of social superiority to most other bourgeois elements, particularly of a "capitalistic" tenor, except for the old "patricians" of the Hanseatic and other free cities, and latterly the most prominent business magnates, was conspicuous. University professors and the highest reaches of the independent liberal professions, as medicine and law, would be the closest below them in social prestige.

Unlike the *Junker* military element, the higher civil service was not, in the Weimar Republic, displaced from formal participation in the operation of Government. If anything their power was probably on the whole increased because short of really radical revolution their knowledge and competence in administrative affairs was indispensable for keeping the essential governmental services in operation in a time of crisis.

These two elements which were most closely involved in power and responsibility in the structure of the old German state were for the most part integrated together by the ideology which is perhaps best called "Prussian conservatism." It might be characterized as a combination of a patriarchal type of authoritarianism with a highly developed formal legalism. Government has constituted an *Obrigkeit*. Its role was by no means defined as "absolutism" in the sense of an unlimited right of those in authority to promote their own self-interest or indulge their personal whims. On the contrary, the pattern of "duty" as classically formulated by Kant was one of its keynotes. But this devotion to duty was combined with a strong sense of prerogative and authority which would not brook the "democratic" type of control by persons without authority, or any presumption, of elements not authorized by their formal status to interfere in the functions of duly constituted authority. Legitimacy and order were very strongly emphasized. At the same time it was a system of authority under law, and one principal keynote of the pattern of duty was scrupulous adherence to the law. The obverse of what seems to many Anglo-Saxons the petty proliferation of minor regulations, the ubiquitous notice that such and such is *Verboten*, was the meticulous incorruptibility of the administration.

Perhaps the master complex of ideological symbols of this system lay in Lutheranism. The ultimate legitimation of authority was the divine ordination of government and princes. Organizationally the Lutheran church and clergy were more closely bound up with the regime than perhaps any other major branch of Christianity in modern times—not only was it in Prussia the established church, but the pastor was directly a civil servant and the principal supervisor of the system of public education. But more on the ideological level, the realm of idealism and genuine wish-fulfillment is for the Lutheran exclusively subjective and spiritual. This world is dominated by sin, mitigated only by the restraining influence of ordained authority. Society is not and can never be a Kingdom of God on Earth, but is fundamentally a vale of tears. In its application to the role of authority, this pattern favors a certain realism, for instance with respect to the advisability of adequate military protection of one's territory but its benevolent patriarchalism readily slips over into a kind of harsh authoritarianism and even into a cynical pursuit of power in defiance of the welfare of the masses of people. Government is to it a grim business, of which war is a very typical and essential part.

It should not, of course, be forgotten that parliamentary government had developed in Imperial Germany to a considerable degree. But it is the above two elements in the state which were distinctive of Germany by contrast with the Western democracies, and which very greatly limited the decisiveness of the influence of the parliamentary element. This situation would seem to have a good deal to do with the tendency of German parliamentarianism, certainly more conspicuously than in either England or the United States, to become structured as a system of representation of rather specific interest groups such as agrarian interests, big business, labor unions, the Catholic Church, a tendency which came to full flower under the Weimar Republic and had a good deal to do with its instability.

The fact that a modern industrial economy developed in Germany in a society already to a large extent structured about the Prussian state and in the context of the pervasive configurational patterns of Prussian conservatism, undoubtedly colored the total development in many different respects. In the first place, "economic individualism" was never so prominent as in the Anglo-Saxon countries. Greater government participation in the affairs of the economy was taken for granted or not resisted, whether it was a question of government ownership and operation of the railways, or the fact that it was Germany which first introduced a comprehensive system of social insurance. It is undoubtedly significant that the "classical economics" never took real root in the German universities; for since it was never only a technical discipline but was also an ideology, it expressed an ideal of independence of "business" from the state and other "social" interests which was on the whole uncongenial to German mentality.

The same circumstances, however, favored the rapid growth of large-scale organization in the German economy, and its relatively close assimilation to the pattern of government bureaucracy. Particularly conspicuous in this respect is what to Anglo-Saxons appears to be a peculiar tendency towards the formalization of status in Germany, both in the economy and in other aspects of the society. Perhaps the best indication of this is the ubiquity of the use of titles. We give titles to high government officials, and various other persons in positions of dignity such as physicians, ministers and priests, sometimes officials of large organizations. But at least three differences are conspicuous as compared with pre-Nazi Germany. First, the system of titles is far less extensive. One could almost say that the prominence of formal rank and titles which we feel to be appropriate to armed services applies in Germany to the whole occupational world, reaching down even to statuses on the skilled labor level such as *Eisenbahneamter,* etc. The number of people who are plain Herr Braun or Herr Schmidt is relatively small. Secondly, titles are continuously used, so that in addressing a letter, or even in personal address it is a definite discourtesy to omit the full title. Thus anyone with any kind of a doctor's degree is always addressed as *Herr Doktor*—or so referred to—while we reserve this usage almost entirely for physicians. We often refer to, and even address titled people without the title— it would in Germany be disrespectful to refer to the Chancellor as Herr . . ., whereas speaking of "Mr. Roosevelt" instead of President Roosevelt is certainly not disrespectful. In Germany it would have had to be Herr Reichskanzler Dr. Bruening, or at least *Reichskanzler* Bruening. Closely related is the German tendency to use an accumulation of titles. Thus where on a letter we would write Professor John Smith, there it would have to be Herr Professor Doktor Johann Schmidt. Our tendency to ignore titles on occasion is related to the usage with other symbols of formal status such as uniforms. In peace time a military officer generally appears in civilian clothes, even at work, unless he is on military post or, for a naval officer, on shipboard. Even when the nation was imminently threatened by war we had the spectacle of the Army's Chief of Staff on an eminently official occasion, testifying before a Senate Committee, in civilian clothes. That would be completely unthinkable in Germany. Even in war time the President, though he is commander-in-chief of the armed forces, *never* wears a uniform. Finally, German titles are far more highly differentiated, both with respect to rank and to field of competence, than are ours. We have the one honorific title of "honorable" for high governmental officials; in Germany there are many graduations. The honorific title of *Rat* is differentiated into an indefinite number of subclasses according to the particular occupation of the incumbent *Kommerzienrat, Justizrat, Sanitaestsrat, Rechnungsrat,* etc. Finally there is, in general, a far greater insistence on meticulous observance of correct titles.[2]

Except for the status of nobility—including the title "von"—the primary content of this formalized status system in Germany was occupational. But the tendency to emphasize titles and other aspects of formal status even on what we would treat as "informal" occasions seems to indicate a difference from the predominant American pattern. With us, occupational status is to a relatively high degree segregated from the individual's "private life," while in Germany this seems to be considerably less the case; his specific formal status as it were follows him everywhere he goes. In social life generally he is less significant as a person, as John Smith, than he is as the incumbent of a formal status, as an official, an officer, a physician, a professor, or a worker.

Another aspect of this formalism is worthy of note. To an American the continual German insistence on titles connotes not only emphasis on formal status rather than individuality, it connotes also "formality" in the sense which is antithetical to the informality of intimacy or of friendship. To an American it is surprising that German students may associate for months and never speak to each other at all, or when they do, address each other as *Herr* and *Fraeulein,* when their American counterparts would be addressing each other by their first names. Similarly with us, colleagues of about the same age, especially if relatively young, almost always address each other by their first names; they do so in Germany only if they have a specifically intimate friendship. These differences of usage may be said to symbolize that to American sentiments, at all close association in common activities should include an element of friendship—he is not only my fellow student or colleague, but also my friend—while in Germany occupational association and friendship are specifically segregated. It is most untactful to "presume" a level of intimacy to which one is not entitled.[3]

---

[2] To relate an amusing instance:— as an official exchange student at a German university, I was formally received by the Rector of the University. After the interview a German student friend said, "I hope you addressed him correctly as *Euer Magnifizenz.*" When the reply was, "No, I said *Herr Professor,*" my student friend was genuinely shocked. To an American, however, the idea of addressing a rather seedy-looking elderly professor as "Your Magnificence" seemed more than a little ridiculous.

[3] From a superficial point of view the above two points might seem to be contradictory. This, however, is not the case. The German pattern seems to extend assimilation of other elements of status to formal occupational status considerably farther than ours does, and hence greatly to narrow down the

The above considerations suggest that differences which are perhaps most conspicuous to the social scientist in terms of the broader status-groupings of the state and the economy can be followed into the realm of the more intimate personal relationships. It surely would be remarkable if the order of difference which has been discussed did not extend into the realm of family structure, of the definition of sex roles, and the patterning of the relations of the sexes, within marriage and outside it.

In the first place, there would clearly seem to be in Germany a pattern of masculine superiority and a tendency to assume authority and prerogatives on the part of husbands and fathers which is much less pronounced in the United States. From the American point of view, particularly of women, German men tend to be dominating and authoritarian, and, conversely, to expect submissiveness and dependency on the part of their wives. This is perhaps particularly true in the middle classes. The "typical" German woman, especially if married, is thought of as a *Hausfrau* —significantly a word taken over untranslated into English to denote a social type, while "housewife" suggests rather a census classification. The Hausfrau is, perhaps, the antithesis of the "emancipated" woman—emancipated in any one of several directions. To the former applies the old adage of the three K's *Kinder, Kirche, Kueche.* Her life is concentrated on the home, on husband and children, and she participates little in the outside world, in community affairs, or even in cultural life. She tends to lack both "sex appeal" and other elements of "attractiveness." From the American point of view she does not dress well but is more "dowdy" than is accountable for in terms of lack of financial resources.

sphere of private individuality relative to the American pattern. But then a point is reached where matters concern a restricted sphere which is highly "private"—one's relations to one's true "friends." When this point is reached the segregation is far sharper than in the American case. The American pattern, on the other hand, does not go so far in extending the pattern of formal status beyond the immediate occupational context. Indeed, it minimizes it even there by admitting elements of "informality" which are structurally related to the friendship pattern in a way which would seem improper and undignified to most Germans. But there is a gradual transition, not marked by symbols of rigid distinction, between casual acquaintance with an occupational colleague through various degrees of intimacy to the most intimate friendship, which may or may not be with occupational associates, but certainly are not structurally required to be. In a sense the German system is more favorable to strict universalistic impartiality and less open to nepotism and other clique-like disturbances, but at the same time probably involves other elements of instability.

The difference is, of course, relative. Solid, conservative domesticity is very much a live ideal in the United States, but relatively less prominent. In Germany there has been "high society" with a great deal of aristocratic emancipation from moralistic domesticity, but one can say confidently that it has never been capable of really competing with its French counterpart. In the upper middle classes there have, especially in recent times, been many highly educated and cultured women, many of them leaders in the *Frauenbewegung.* Finally, gainful employment of married women outside the home has been as conspicuous in Germany as in other industrial countries, and has greatly modified this pattern for the working classes. But the quantitative difference of emphasis remains: more German women are Hausfrauen than American, and even the American woman who has no career or job, has on the average a different style of life, is more concerned with her personal appearance, with men other than her husband, and with impersonal interests outside her home. Above all on the ideological level there is, perhaps outside Catholic circles, a considerably more favorable attitude toward the non-domestic virtues in women. There is less tendency to encourage submissiveness and psychological dependency, less resentment at women "intruding" in the world of masculine affairs. The principal exception is probably in the areas of greatest intellectual, cultural, and "bohemian" emancipation which have probably been more extreme in Europe generally, including Germany, than in the United States at least until quite recently.

Closely related to this difference in feminine roles is a far lower development in Germany of the "romantic love" pattern. The love relationships of youth have been as it were "sentimentalized" in Germany to a considerable extent, but with a different emphasis. The *Maedchen* is more simple, sweet, and submissive, and less glamorous than her American counterpart. It is less a relation of equality. She is more apt, in the middle classes, to marry an established, somewhat older man. Related to this is another usage of titles, the fact that the German married woman takes not only her husband's surname, as with us, but also his title. She is addressed as *Frau Doktor, Frau Justizrat,* or *Frau Professor.* Would it not be legitimate to infer that while with us the primary emphasis is put on marriage to a particular man as an individual, in Germany it is put rather on his formal status. The significant thing is not that she is the wife of John Smith, but of *a* professor. The impression further is that the marriage relationship typically involves more impersonal attitudes, less emphasis on being "in love," as well as greater inequality so that to a certain extent the wife is classed with her children by contrast with the authority of the husband.

Rather generally speaking, there seems to be in Germany a good deal sharper segregation of the roles of the sexes than in the United States. With this, however, goes as a significant counterpart a strong tendency to emphasize, indeed to romanticize, the relationship of men to one another. On one level *Bruederschaft,* with its ritual oath and its symbolic use of *Du* as the form of address, is much more sharply emphasized than any particular form of masculine friendship with us, and seems to be invested with a very intense emotional significance. On another, comradeship, of which the relation of soldiers in the field is perhaps the prototype, is particularly idealized. Thus the main emphasis in the German Youth Movement was a romantic idealization of solidary groups of young men—sometimes with at least an undercurrent of homosexuality. The closest counterpart in our society is the romantization of the cross-sex love relationship.

The reader may quite reasonably ask what is gained by dwelling at such length on all these features of pre-Nazi German social structure, all of which are very well known, and a good many of which seem to have little to do with the issue of Germany's relation to democracy. The justification lies in the fact that they need to be brought to mind because of their bearing on what is doubtless still to many a very puzzling problem. We have seen that in many fundamental respects the social structure of Germany has been very similar to that of other Western industrial societies. Until 1918, to be sure, it did not have a democratic constitution politically, but surely it has become a commonplace of social science that the mere formal provisions of the constitution are quite secondary to the deeper-lying social structure. In that respect perhaps the most important feature of the German state, its administrative bureaucracy, was very far from being in radical conflict with at least liberal if not democratic patterns. Indeed, by contrast particularly with the American spoils system of the same era it might be considered to be in closer line with our own idealistic values because of its scrupulous adherence to the impartial "rule of law." Moreover, the collectivistic, if somewhat paternalistic, social welfare tendencies of the German state could go far to mitigate the more extreme consequences of rampant individualistic capitalism as it was found particularly in the United States. Then the one important thing would seem to have been the removal from power of the "feudal" elements of the old regime, an end which for all practical purposes was achieved with the revolution of 1918. The question is, why did this solution fail to stick, why did not Germany continue in what many have thought to be the main line of the evolution of Western society, the progressive approach to the realization of "liberal-democratic" patterns and values?

There can be no doubt that various kinds of external factors such as the treatment of Germany by the Allies after the last war, economic difficulties both in international trade and finance and internally to Germany and the like, played an important part. Perhaps these factors were even decisive in the sense that a more favorable set of circumstances in these respects would have tipped the total balance of forces so as to permit the democratic trend of evolution to continue uninterrupted. No doubt also the development of the relations of capital and labor, in the sense in which that tension is structurally inherent in all capitalistic industrial economies, played an important part. The Weimar regime put the Trade Unions and the parties of the left in a position of greatly enhanced power; wages were continually pushed up; and undoubtedly many business people became frightened and were ready to accept almost anything which would protect them from the danger of expropriation. Their fear was greatly enhanced by the ideological appeal to the danger of Communism which has been to a considerable degree effective in all the capitalistic countries.

But German National Socialism is a grand scale movement of a very particular type. It is, to be sure, nationalistic in opposition to the national humiliation and alleged submission to the enemies of Germany for which it purports to hold the men of Versailles and Weimar responsible. It is also anti-Communistic in that it purports to lead a great crusade against Bolshevism and to purge Europe forever from this "disease." But it is more than either or both of these. It is a revolutionary movement which, both in ideology and in actual policy, has already done much to alter fundamentally the broader social structure not only of the Weimar Republic but of the Germany which preceded and underlay it. National Socialism arose in a situation which quite understandably could have produced a strong nationalistic and conservative reaction, a reaction toward social patterns which, though in conflict with the leftward elements of the "liberal-democratic" tradition of the Western world, need not have removed Germany from the general sphere of Western civilization. But Nazi Germany is even today not a strong, national community with conservative leanings, as distinguished from the leftward leanings of British Labor or of the American New Deal. It is a radically new type of society which, if not interfered with, promises to depart progressively more radically from the main line of Western social development since the Renaissance. It is in the sources of this element of revolutionary radicalism in the Nazi movement that the interest of the present analysis is focussed.

In our common-sense thinking about social matters we probably tend greatly to exaggerate the integration of social systems, to think of them as neatly "exemplifying" a pattern type. For purposes of sheer comparative structural study this need not lead to serious difficulty, but when dynamic problems of directions and processes of change are at issue, it is essential to give specific attention to the elements of malintegration, tension and strain in the social structure.

In the first place, all Western societies have been subjected in their recent history to the disorganizing effects of many kinds of rapid social change. It has been a period of rapid technological change, industrialization, urbanization, migration of population, occupational mobility, cultural, political and religious change. As a function of sheer rapidity of change which does not allow sufficient time to "settle down," the result is the widespread insecurity —in the psychological, not only the economic sense—of a large proportion of the population, with the well-known consequences of anxiety, a good deal of free-floating aggression, a tendency to unstable emotionalism and susceptibility to emotionalized propaganda appeals and mobilization of affect around various kinds of symbols. If anything, this factor has been more prominent in Germany than elsewhere in that the processes of industrialization and urbanization were particularly rapid there. In addition, the strain and social upset of the last war were probably more severe than in the case of any other belligerent except Russia. On top of that came the political difficulties after 1918 and the inflation, finally exceedingly severe economic depression in the early thirties. Such a situation predisposes to radical emotional dissociation from the principal institutional statuses and roles of the existing order, but does not of itself give any clue to the direction which the structuring of definitions will take.

A second element of the situation is also common to all Western countries, but also perhaps somewhat more intense in Germany than elsewhere. A major aspect of the dynamic process of development in Western society ever since the Middle Ages has been a particular form of what Max Weber called the "process of rationalization." One of its central foci has been the continual development of science and the technologies derived from it in industry, in medicine, and in other fields. Closely related has been the development of bureaucratic organization, of economic exchange, and of the orientation of economic activity to capitalistic monetary calculation. Various aspects of the cultural tradition have also been affected in the form of the secularization of religious values, emancipation from traditional patterns of morality, especially in Christian form, and the general tendency of rational criticism to undermine traditional and conservative systems of symbols.

This process, looked at from the point of view of its dynamic impact on the social system, rather than the absolute significance of rationalistic patterns, has an uneven incidence on different elements in the social structure. In the first place, it tends to divide elements of the population according to whether they tend toward what are, in rationalistic terms, the more "progressive" or "emancipated" values of patterns of conduct, or the more conservative "backward," or traditional patterns. This introduces a basis of fundamental structuring in the differentiation of attitudes. It is a basis which also tends to coincide with other bases of strain in the structuring of interests, especially in that "capitalism" tends to be predominantly a phenomenon of emancipation which grows up at the expense of the "good old ways" and sound established values.

But not only does the process of rationalization structure attitudes. It is precisely the further effects of the dynamic process of change which are most important in this connection. In part this process is a principal source of the disorganization and insecurity discussed above as involved in *anomie*. In so far, however, as such disorganization is not specifically structured in other ways, it and its behavioral manisfestations tend to become structured in terms of their relation to this process. Hence manisfestations of these polar attitude patterns tend to bear the marks of psychological insecurity, to be "overdetermined." This is true on both sides: on the emancipated side in the form of a tendency to a compulsive "debunking" and denial of any elements of legitimacy to all traditional patterns, on the traditional side of a "fundamentalist" obstruction to all progress, a traditionalist literalism with strongly emotional attitudes.[4]

Though general to the Western world this situation has probably been more extreme in Germany because, relative to Western Europe and the United States, it has been more "conservative." Hence the impact of science, industrialism and such phenomena has been more unsettling and has led to more drastic extremes of attitudes. One significant symptom of this fact is to be found in the conspicuously greater tendency of German social thought to repudiate the primary rationalistic and emancipated ideological structures which have dominated the intellectual traditions of France and England. There has been conspicuously less intellectual "liberalism" in Germany—the obverse of the predominant "conservative" tendencies being the extreme of rationalistic radicalism found in Marxism.

One conspicuous tendency in this connection is for "fundamentalist" sentiments to crystallize about phenomena symbolic of the extremer forms of emancipation in defining what was dangerous to society. The coincidence in Nazi ideology of the Jews, capitalism, bolshevism, anti-religious secularism, internationalism, moral laxity, and emancipation of women as a single class of things to be energetically combatted is strongly indicative of this structuring.

In combination with certain peculiarities of the German cultural tradition, this situation helps to account for the fact that the German labor movement was considerably more extreme in the radical rationalistic direction than its counterparts in the Anglo-Saxon countries. Long before the British movement it was committed to a political socialist program, and this came to be formulated in terms of the strict Marxist ideology which, above all,

---

[4] This is, in the sense of Bateson, a particularly good example of the process of "Schismogenesis." See Gregory Bateson, *Naven*.

required drastic repudiation of traditional religious values. This undoubtedly made it easier for the labor movement to be defined as "dangerously radical" to the rest of the population, even apart from the growth of the Communist element during the later Weimar years.

One of the most important reactions to elements of strain of the sort just discussed, and certain more specific ones which will be taken up presently, is the formation of patterns of wishes or idealized hopes which, in the majority of cases, the established institutional patterns and their attendant situations do not permit to be fully realized. They hence tend to be projected outside the immediate social situation into some form of "idealized" life or existence. Since they are the results of certain emotional tensions which develop only in so far as people are imperfectly integrated with an institutionalized situation, they tend to involve a conspicuous element of "irrealism." They are associated with a negative valuation of the existing situation and, instead of a "realistic" orientation to its alteration in the direction of greater conformity with an ideal, involve an element of "escape." This phenomenon may be called "romanticism"—its essence is the dissociation of the strongest emotional values from established life situations—in the past or the future or altogether outside ordinary social life.[5] A most important question about any social system is that of its general predisposition to romanticism, and of the specific ways in which this tendency is structured.

In the Anglo-Saxon world it is probably true that there is on the whole a smaller predisposition to romanticism than in Germany because patterns which, in important respects, go back to Puritanism, canalize the orientation of action more in the direction of taking active responsibility for translating ideal patterns into reality. Associated with this, however, is a marked tendency to a kind of "utopianism," an attraction for many sorts of unrealistic blueprints for the "ideal society" where there will be perpetual peace, an elimination of all inequalities, of all irrationality or superstition, etc. This is a kind of romanticism which helps explain the appeal of the rationalistic movements of the left in these countries. In addition to that, however, there are two very important patterns of "individualistic" romanticism, the romanticism of personal "success" and romantic love. A very prevalent theme of American

---

[5] Perhaps only when the content of the "dream pattern" is secular should the term "romanticism" be used. Certain elements of other—worldly religious ideals are, however, closely related in psychological significance.

fiction is the boy whose abilities were such that he was *bound* to succeed. Its prevalence suggests a very high level of emotional investment in occupational functions. It is a pattern which, by contrast with the German, is also associated with the relative lack of formalism in our occupational system. Occupational functions are treated—however unrealistically—more as a matter of ability and achievement, and less as a matter of status for its own sake. The prominence of the pattern of romantic love, again however unrealistic it is, seems to indicate a particularly strong emphasis on the fusion of the sex relationship with the strongest bonds of personal intimacy and loyalty. That this is made the dominant ideal precisely of marriage, again relatively disregarding status as such, is striking. Both these romantic tendencies of American society, it may be noted, are not closely related to any form of political radicalism but tend, except in so far as their lack of realism leads to disillusionment, to reinforce the dominant institutional structure—or at least not to undermine it in a politcial direction.

The element of formalism in the patterning of the basic institutional system of Germany, which was discussed at some length above, seems to indicate a stronger general tendency to romanticism than exists in the Anglo-Saxon countries, in that institutionalized status tends to absorb less of the individual's emotional attachment. It is as if it were said: status is *only* formal; after all the most important things lie elsewhere. This impression is confirmed by the fact that Germany, precisely in the time when she was not dominated by a radical political movement, was known as the land of poets, philosophers and dreamers, of religious mysticism, of music. It has also been a land of peculiarly strong reaction against "bourgeois" values, an attitude which socialists and radicals, bohemian artists and intellectuals, and the Youth Movement have all had in common. Surely in recent times precisely the world of formal status structure has been the core of these bourgeois values.[6]

---

[6] Though there is no space available here to develop the point, it may be noted that there is strong evidence of a close connection between this combination of formalism and a tendency to romanticism, and the heritage of Lutheran Protestantism, precisely as distinguished from Calvinistic. For the Lutheran the true spiritual values could not be embodied in secular life, but only in the individual's completely intimate and personal communion with God. Secular duties were divinely ordained and conscientiously to be performed, above all the duty of submission to authority, but secular achievement was in no sense the real business of life, even in the service of the most exalted ideals. The world was essentially evil and could not be made a "Kingdom of God on Earth."

At the same time there were important structural reasons why two of the most important manifestations of romanticism in the Anglo-Saxon world could not be so important in Germany. A dominance of the personal success ideal was in conflict with the formalism of the status structure, as well as with the dominant position in the prestige scale of hereditary status groups. A corresponding role of the romantic love pattern was in part blocked by the connection of marriage with the formal status system, in part by the related difference in the definition of sex roles which made it difficult for a man and woman to be treated as equals in respect to the most profound emotional commitments of life. The kind of attachment to a woman which we idealize in the romantic pattern would, to most Germans, seem possible only to a soft, effeminate type of man, certainly not to the heroic type.

By virtue of its industrialization and urbanization, however, and of the impact in other respects of the rationalization process, the actual social life of Germany had developed for much of its population to a point where the older conservative patterns, especially in defining the role of youth, of sex relationships, and of women, could not serve as an adequate basis of institutional integration. "Leftist" radicalism appealed to organized industrial labor and to some intellectuals, but it had too narrow a base in the social structure to be stable. Sheer "emancipation," as practiced in bohemian circles, was not adequate and was too unstable, apart from the fact that both these phenomena inflamed conservative sentiment. At the same time among the middle class youth, among large numbers of women, and elsewhere in the society there were acute strains which strongly predisposed to romantic forms of expression.

The other side of the picture lies in the fact that the German situation presented possibilities for a structuring of these elements in a radically different direction from that predominant in most democratic societies. The traditions of national glory were bound up with conservative tendencies which were generally speaking stronger in the German social structure than elsewhere. An aspect of this was the appeal of military values with a strong tradition behind them which could become romanticized in terms of a "heroic" ideal[7] of the fighting man who could be propagandistically

---

[7] Dr. E. Y. Hartshorne has particularly called my attention to the possibility that romantization among Nazi Youth of the heroic life—and of the *Fuehrer*—might have functions similar to those of the pattern of romantic love in the United States.

contrasted with the money-grabbing capitalist of the "plutocracies." The whole appeal of nationalism could be mobilized in the same direction and combined with the reaction against all forms of dangerous radicalism. The military ideal forms in the nature of the case a strong contrast to the bourgeois stuffiness and safety-mindedness against which young people tended to react. Finally from the point of view of German women, a heroic ideal could mobilize their romantic idealization of men in a pattern which adequately fitted the German segregation of the sex roles, as the man in the role to which, of all roles, women were by tradition least suited, that of fighter.

To recapitulate: The Revolution of 1918 had the immediate effect of "Democratizing" Germany, of removing the "feudal" element and apparently bringing Germany at last into line with the other "progressive" industrial nations of the Western world. Why this result proved to be so unstable, so abruptly to overturn in favor of the most radical anti-liberal and anti-democratic movement of modern history, is certainly one of the most critical questions of the interpretation of social events of our time. Certainly political pressures on defeated Germany, economic dislocation, and such factors as the class struggle must be conceded to be highly important. The above analysis has, however, attempted to indicate, if only in a highly schematic way, that an equally important part has probably been played by factors distinctive to the social structure of Germany, in dynamic interrelation with the general processes of social development in Western civilization. From this point of view at least one critically important aspect of the National Socialist movement lies in the fact that it constitutes a mobilization of the extremely deep-seated romantic tendencies of German society in the service of a violently aggressive political movement, incorporating a "fundamentalist" revolt against the whole tendency of rationalization in the Western world, and at the same time against its deepest institutionalized foundations. The existence of such romantic elements is inherent in the nature of modern society. That, however, their manifestations should become structured in such a pattern and placed in the service of such a movement is understandable only in terms of specific features of the social structure of Pre-Nazi Germany which differentiated it from that of other Western countries.

VII

Some Sociological Aspects of the Fascist Movements

THE OLDER TYPE, especially of European, social theory was, very largely, oriented to the understanding, in broad terms, of the social situation of the writer's own time. Whatever was sound in these older attempts, as of a Comte, a Spencer or a Marx, tended to be so intimately bound up with scientifically dubious elements of grandiose speculative construction and methodological assumption and dogma that the whole genus of analysis has tended to become discredited as a result of the general reaction against speculative theories.

In the course of such reactions it is not uncommon for the baby to be thrown out with the bath, for elements of sound insight and analysis to be lost sight of through their seemingly inseparable involvement with these other elements. Perhaps in the last few years more strongly than at any other time have there been signs that warrant the hope of an ability in the social sciences to apply generalized theoretical analysis to such problems in a thoroughly empirical, tentative spirit which will make possible a cumulative development of understanding, relatively unmarred by scientifically irrelevant or untenable elements. The very breadth of the problem of diagnosis of the state of a great civilization creates a strong demand for such a method.

Perhaps the most dramatic single development in the society of the Western world in its most recent phase has been the emergence of the great political movements usually referred to as "Fascist." In spite of their uneven incidence, with Germany and Italy by far the most prominent centers, and their varying character in different countries, there is sufficient similarity to justify the hypothesis that the broad phenomenon is deeply rooted in the structure of Western society as a whole and its internal strains and conflicts. However much my own approach may turn out to differ from the Marxian this much must certainly be granted the latter—that it does relate Fascism to fundamental and generalized aspects of Western society.

As a starting point for the present analysis perhaps the common formula of characterization as the "radicalism of the right" is as satisfactory as any. It has at least the virtue of calling attention to two important points. In the first place Fascism is not "old conservatism" of the sort especially familiar before 1914, although elements which were once conservative in that sense have often been drawn into the Fascist movements. Secondly, it is definitely of the "right" in that it is specifically oriented in opposition to the political movements of the "left," notably of course communism.

Perhaps the most important reason why we are justified in speaking of "radicalism" lies in the existence of a popular mass movement in which large masses of the "common people" have become imbued with a highly emotional, indeed often fanatical, zeal for a cause. These mass movements, which are in an important sense revolutionary movements, are above all what distinguishes Fascism from ordinary conservatism. They are movements which, though their primary orientation is political, have many features in common with great religious movements in history, a fact which may serve as a guide to the sociological analysis of their origins and character.

A second important feature is the role played by privileged elite groups, groups with a "vested interest" in their position. While from some points of view the combination of these two elements in the same movement is paradoxical, it will be argued here that it is of the very essence of the phenomenon and perhaps more than anything else throws light on the social forces at work.

It has come to be a well-known fact that movements of religious proselytism tend to develop in situations involving a certain type of social disorganization, primarily that early though only roughly characterized by Durkheim as "anomie." Anomie may perhaps most briefly be characterized as the state where large numbers of individuals are to a serious degree lacking in the kind of integration with stable institutional patterns which is essential to their own personal stability and to the smooth functioning of the social system. Of this there are in turn perhaps two principal aspects. In the first place there seems to be a deep-seated need for a relative stability of the expectations to which action is oriented. The aspect of this on which Durkheim lays primary stress is the sufficiently clear definition of the goals of action—there can, he says, be no sense of achievement in progress toward the realization of an infinite goal. But goals are, to a very large extent defined by institutionalized expectations. This Durkheim illustrated by the inability of indefinite increase of wealth, once cut loose from definite standards, to satisfy ambition.

Similar considerations apply to other aspects of conduct. Expectations cannot be stable if the standards with which conformity is demanded are left so vague as not to be a real guide, or if the individual is subjected, in the same situation, to two or more conflicting expectations each of which advances claims to legitimacy which cannot be ignored.

The second, it would seem somewhat more difficult and complex aspect, lies in the need for a sufficiently concrete and stable system of symbols around which the sentiments of the individual can crystallize. In many different aspects of life highly concrete associations are formed which perhaps in many cases have no great intrinsic importance in themselves, but in that they become stabilized and perpetuated through a living social tradition perform a highly important function in integrating social groups and in stabilizing the orientation of individuals within them.

The general character of the typical reaction of the individual to anomie is that usually referred to in psychological terms as a state of insecurity. The personality is not stably organized about a coherent system of values, goals, and expectations. Attitudes tend to vacillate between indecision which paralyzes action—and all manner of scruples and inhibitions—and on the other hand compulsively "overdetermined" reactions which endow particular goals and symbols with an excess of hatred, devotion or enthusiasm over what is appropriate to the given situation. Generalized insecurity is commonly associated with high levels of anxiety and aggression, both of which are to an important extent "free-floating" in that they are not merely aroused in appropriate form and intensity by fear or anger-provoking situations but may be displaced onto situations or symbols only remotely connected with their original sources.

The present formulation of the psychological correlates of anomie has consciously adhered to the level closest to the more general character of social situations—lack of definition of goals and standards, conflicting expectations, inadequately concrete and stable symbolization. I am well aware that many psychologists find the deepest sources of insecurity to lie in the relations of the individual to his parents and others in the family in early childhood. The two approaches are by no means necessarily in conflict. There is much evidence that insecurity developed in adults from the sources here indicated affects their relations to their children and in turn the character formation of the latter, so that a cumulative vicious circle may work itself out.

An increase in anomie may be a consequence of almost any change in the social situation which upsets previous established definitions of the situation, or routines of life, or symbolic associations. To be sure, the members of some societies have average character types which are better able to withstand and adapt to rapid changes than are others—but in any case there is a limit to the extent and rapidity of change which can take place without engendering anomie on a large scale. There is ample evidence that the period immediately preceding our own time was, throughout the Western world, one of such rapid and fundamental change as to make this inevitable.

It was, in the first place, the period of the Industrial Revolution which, though going much farther back in history, tended cumulatively to gain in force throughout the nineteenth century and well into the twentieth. Though in widely differing degrees, most Western countries changed from predominantly agricultural to industrial and commercial societies, a change impinging not only on occupation but on the life of very large numbers of the population in many different aspects, especially in the tremendous growth of cities and the continual introduction of new elements into the standard of living.

Secondly, and intimately connected with this, the society has been subjected to many other influences adversely affecting situational stability. Migration of population from the rural areas to the growing urban concentrations has been only one phase of a tremendous and complex migration process which has necessitated the complex process of adaptation to new social environments—sometimes, as in the great bulk of immigration into the United States, assimilation to a drastically different cultural tradition with exposure to conflicting expectations and discrimination on ethnic lines. A somewhat different source of strain lies in the instability of the new economy— the exposure to cyclical fluctuations with unemployment and rapid and drastic changes in the standard of living. Inflation and many of the social and economic effects of war fit into the same general pattern.

Though it is perhaps more significant as a consequence of than as a causal factor in anomie, the fact is relevant that not only in women's dress but in any number of other fields our society is to a very high degree subject to rapid and violent changes of fad and fashion. No sooner have we become attached to a pattern than its social prestige melts away leaving the necessity to form a new orientation. This is especially true in the recreational and other expressional fields, but applies also to political and cultural ideas, and to many fields of consumption patterns.

Finally, the cultural development of the period has been preeminently one to undermine simplicity and stability of orientation. It has been to an extraordinary extent a period of the "debunking" of traditional values and ideas, and one in which for previously stable cultural patterns in such fields as religion, ethics, and philosophy, no comparably stable substitutes have appeared—rather a conspicuously unstable factionalism and tendency to faddistic fluctuation. Part of the situation is an inevitable consequence of the enormous development of popular education, and of the development of mass means of communication so that cultural influences which in an earlier time reached only relatively small "sophisticated" minorities now impinge upon a very large proportion of the total population.

Returning for a moment to the psychological level of consideration, one of the most conspicuous features of the present situation lies in the extent to which patterns of orientation which the individual can be expected to take completely for granted have disappeared. The complexity of the influences which impinge upon him has increased enormously, in many or most situations the society does not provide him with only one socially sanctioned definition of the situation and approved pattern of behavior but with a considerable number of possible alternatives, the order of preference between which is by no means clear. The "burden of decision" is enormously great. In such a situation it is not surprising that large numbers of people should, to quote a recent unpublished study,[1] be attracted to movements which can offer them "membership in a group with a vigorous *esprit de corps* with submission to some strong authority and rigid system of belief, the individual thus find-

---

[1] Theodore W. Sprague, "Jehova's Witnesses: a Study in Group Integration." Dissertation, Harvard University, 1942.

ing a measure of escape from painful perplexities or from a situation of *anomie*."

Thus the large-scale incidence of anomie in Western society in recent times is hardly open to doubt. This fact alone, however, demonstrates only susceptibility to the appeal of movements of the general sociological type of fascism but it is far from being adequate to the explanation of the actual appearance of such movements or above all the specific patterns in terms of which they have become structured. It is this latter problem which must next be approached.

The state of anomie in Western society is not primarily a consequence of the impingement on it of structurally fortuitous disorganizing forces though these have certainly contributed. It has, rather, involved a very central dynamic process of its own about which a crucially important complex of factors of change may be grouped, what, following Max Weber, may be called the "process of rationalization." The main outline of its character and influence is too familiar to need to be discussed in detail—but it must be kept clearly in mind as a basis for the subsequent analysis.

Undoubtedly the most convenient single point of reference is to be found in the patterns of science. The development of science is of course inherently dynamic and has a certain immediate effect in progressively modifying traditional conceptions of the empirical world. It is, however, its application in technology which provides the most striking source of cumulative social change, profoundly affecting the concrete circumstances of men's lives in a multitude of ways. Again it is not only that the explicit formal content of occupational roles is affected—this is the center from which many complex ramifications of change radiate into the informal and symbolic areas of men's working lives, and into their private lives through changes in their patterns of consumption, recreation, etc. Whatever the positive value of the changes, they always involve an abandonment of traditional orientation patterns, circumstances and definitions of the situation which necessitates a process of readjustment.

Though by no means simply an aspect of science and its application in technology a second dynamic complex is intimately related to it. It may be characterized as the treatment of a wide range of action patterns and contexts of human relationship in terms of orientation to relatively specific and limited goals. Perhaps the classic center of the complex is the field of "contractual" relationships, and its formulation at the hands of such theorists as Spencer and Tönnies provides the classic sociological characterization. Contractualism overlaps widely with the use of money and the wide extension of market relationships. This involves the enormous extension of the mobility of elements essential to coordinated human action and the extension of the possibility of focussing elements from many sources on the realization of a single goal. Codification and systematization of personal rights and individual liberties is another essential aspect as is the clear development of the modern institution of ownership in the sphere of property. The question of where ownership is lodged is not the primary issue—but rather the concentration of the various rights which taken together we call ownership into a single bundle rather than their dispersion; and by the same token their segregation from the other elements of the status of their holder.

By no means the least important element of this complex is the patterning of functional roles primarily about their functional content itself with clear segregation from other elements of the total social status of the individual—in kinship, local ties, even to a considerable extent social class and ethnic adherence. Though prominent in the case of independent roles such as those of private professional practice this patterning of functional roles is most prominent in the field of large-scale organization, indeed without it the latter as we know it would scarcely be conceivable at all.

The interdependence between the complex of science and technology on the one hand, and that just discussed on the other is exceedingly close. Some schools of thought, as of Veblen and Ogburn, give the former unquestioned primacy. This is at least open to serious question since it is only in relatively highly developed stages of the patterning of functionally specialized roles that the most favorable situation for the functioning of scientific investigation and technological application is attained. Less directly the mobility of resources through property and market relations, and the institutions of personal freedom all greatly facilitate the influence of science on social life.

Finally, science itself is a central part of the cultural tradition of our society. As such it is perhaps the most conspicuous embodiment of the more general pattern which may be called that of "critical rationality," differing from others primarily in the place accorded to the canons of empirical observation and verification. This same spirit of critical rationality has to an increasing extent ramified into many or even most other areas of the cultural tradition.

Notably of course it has permeated philosophical thought and the religious traditions of the various branches of Christianity. In this direction two consequences above all have appeared—the questioning of the cognitive status of the "non-empirical" elements of philosophical and religious thought, and the tendency to eliminate patterns and entities of primarily symbolic significance. The use of the categories of "ignorance" and "superstition" as sufficient characterizations of all thought not in conformity with the particular rational or pseudo-rational standards of the moment is an indication of the basic attitude.

The present concern is not whether the patterns of rationality in these different areas are in some sense superior to those they have tended to supplant, but rather the relation of their relatively rapid process of development to the functioning of the social system. It should be clear that their development is in itself perhaps the most important single source of anomie. Its significance in this respect is by no means simple and cannot be adequately analyzed here. It is partly a matter of the sheer rapidity of the process, which does not provide an opportunity for stable reorientation. Another aspect is the unevenness and incompleteness of its incidence so that it engenders conflicts in the social pressures impinging on the same groups and as between different groups. There is also the question whether, to balance its underminding effect on traditional patterns and values, it succeeds in providing even for the groups most thoroughly permeated, functionally adequate substitutes.

But beyond the significance as a source of temporary or permanent anomie, the process of rationalization has a further significance of crucial interest here. It is to it that we must look for the primary explanation of the structuring of attitudes and social organization so far as it can be treated as a response to the generalized condition of anomie. This question will have to be discussed on two primary levels, first that of the cognitive definition of the situation, second that of the differential affective appeal of the competing definitions of the situation which have come to be available.

The process of rationalization would scarcely have been of profound social importance if it had not affected large numbers of people in the immediate circumstances of their daily lives. But as an essential part of the same general cultural movement there has developed a tradition of "social thought" which, in a sufficiently broad perspective, can be seen to be highly distinctive in spite of its internal complexity. It has provided, above all, two interrelated

things, a diagnosis of the status of the society—particularly in relation to the traditional patterns and structures with which the process of rationalization has stood in conflict, and a frame of reference
for determining the proper attitudes of "reasonable" men toward
the social problems of the day. Its functioning as the "ideology" of
social and political movements is a natural consequence. In a very
broad sense it is the ideological patterns of the movements of the
"left" which are in question.

Such a tradition of thought is inevitably compounded of various
different elements which today we find it convenient to distinguish. In the first place, there are certain elements of genuine scientific insight which by contrast with previous stages may be considered new. Undoubtedly the "utilitarian" pattern of analysis of
the division of labor and exchange and the corresponding analysis
of the functioning of a system of competitive market relationships
—in short the "classical economics"—is largely in this category. With
the shift on this level from "economic individualism" in the direction of socialism, especially Marxism, certain changes of emphasis
on different factors have occurred but a fundamental constancy of
cognitive pattern, the "utilitarian," has remainded.

From the perspective of a later vantage point we can now see
that in spite of the undoubtedly sound elements there have from a
scientific point of view been certain shortcomings in this scheme of
thought. Attention has been concentrated on one sector of the total
structure of a social system—that of contract, exchange, monetary
transactions—and others such as family life have been neglected.
But even within the area of focussed attention the "fallacy of misplaced concreteness" has, understandably enough, played a prominent role. The prominent patterns of thought have, that is, been
inadequately placed in perspective and integrated with other elements of a total social system.

The scientifically relevant element has, at the same time, been
closely related to certain patterns of value orientation—with both a
positive and a negative aspect. In one connection the new social
thought expressed a revolt against the old order and a rationalization or justification of the changes introduced by the process of
rationalization. Its primary targets of attack have been traditionally
established statuses of prestige, authority and privilege and the
traditionalized patterns themselves which have been integrated
with these. Positively, the rights of the individual both as against

other human agencies and as against tradition itself have provided the main focus. A fundamental trend toward egalitarianism has also been prominent. Broadly the pattern can be described as one of "emancipation" from the control of forces without rational sanction, from unjust authority, from monopoly and competitive privilege, from the "tyranny" of ignorance and superstition.

Finally, apart both from questions of science and of ethical value the tendency has, it has been noted, been to extend patterns of rationality into the metaphysical realm. Science has been taken as the prototype of all sound cognitive orientation and all elements of tradition not scientifically defensible have tended to be "debunked." Here of course traditional religion has been the primary object of attack.

In the earlier phases of its development this scheme of thought overwhelmingly embodied positive value attitudes. It defined the situation for the emergence and establishment of a new and magnificent social order, for freedom against tyranny, for enlightenment against ignorance and superstition, for equality and justice against privilege, for free enterprise against monopoly and the irrational restrictions of custom.

Gradually, however, with the growing ascendancy of the associated patterns, in certain directions certain elements of the scheme of thought have with altered emphasis and formulation come to be built into a pattern embodying quite different value attitudes. This has centered primarily on the developed system of emancipated and rationalized economic organization. The liberation of free enterprise from the tyranny of monopoly and custom has, it is said, led only to the system of capitalistic exploitation. The "profit motive" has become the object of deep reproach. Inequality, unemployment, and new forms of unjust privilege have been brought into the limelight. Political liberation from the tyrannical Bourbons has led only to a new enslavement under the "executive Committee of the Bourgeoisie."

This new negative orientation to certain primary aspects of the maturing modern social order has above all centered on the symbol of "capitalism," which in certain circles has come to be considered as all-embracing a key to the understanding of all human ills as Original Sin once was. But it is important to note that the main intellectual movements within which this has developed have retained, even in an extreme form, the rationalized patterns in other connections, particularly in attitudes toward ignorance and superstition— lurking behind which economic interests are often seen—and many other symbolic and unrationalized patterns of thought and social behavior. What in terms of the recent situation is "leftist" social thought is overwhelmingly "positivistic" as well as utilitarian.

With the wisdom of hindsight, it can now be clearly seen that this rationalistic scheme of thought has not been adequate to provide a stably institutionalized diagnosis of even a "modern" social system as a whole, nor has it been adequate to formulate all of the important values of our society, nor its cognitive orientation to the world. It has been guilty of the fallacy of misplaced concreteness in neglecting or underestimating the role of what Pareto has called the "non-logical" aspects of human behavior in society, of the sentiments and traditions of family and informal social relationships, of the refinements of social stratification, of the peculiarities of regional, ethnic or national culture—perhaps above all of religion. On this level it has indeed helped to provoke a most important "anti-intellectualist" reaction.

On another level it has "debunked" many of the older values of our cultural tradition, and above all the cognitive patterns of religion, to a point well beyond that to which common values and symbols in the society had moved. Even apart from questions of its metaphysical validity it cannot be said adequately to have expressed the common orientations of the members of the society.

But on top of these inherent strains a crucial role has been played by the emergence within the rationalized cultural tradition itself of a definition of the situation which has thoroughly "debunked" many of the institutionalized products of the process of rationalization itself. Surely the stage was set for a combination of this definition of the situation with a reassertion of all the patterns which the utilitarian scheme had omitted or slighted—an acceptance of its own indictment but a generalization of the diagnosis to make "capitalism" appear a logical outcome of the whole process of rationalization itself, not merely of its perversion, and the fact that in certain directions it had not been carried far enough. By the same token it is possible to treat both capitalism and its leftist antagonists, especially communism, not as genuine antagonists but as brothers under the skin, the common enemy. The Jew serves as a convenient symbolic link between them.

This reaction against the "ideology" of the rationalization of society is one principal aspect at least of the ideology of fascism.

It characteristically accepts in essentials the socialist indictment of the existing order described as capitalism, but extends it to include leftist radicalism and the whole penumbra of scientific and philosophical rationalism.[2]

The ideological definition of the situation in terms of which the orientation of a social movement becomes structured is of great importance but it never stands alone. It is necessarily in the closest interdependence with the psychological states and the social situations of the people to whom it appeals. We must now turn to the analysis of certain effects of the process of rationalization on this level.

The fundamental fact is that the incidence of the process within the social structure is highly uneven—different elements of a population become "rationalized" in different degrees, at different rates, and in different aspects of their personalities and orientations.

It may be said that both traditional and rationalized patterns are, to a high degree, genuinely institutionalized in our society. Indeed the distinction is itself largely relative and dynamic rather than absolute, and both are functionally essential to an even relatively stable society. Some elements of the population are relatively securely integrated but with varying emphasis in one direction or the other. Thus the best integrated professional groups would lean in the rational direction, certain rural elements in the traditional.

This difference of incidence has important consequences on both the structural and the psychological levels. Structurally it differentiates the social system broadly along a continuum of variation from the most highly traditionalized areas which have been least touched by the more recent phases of the process of rationalization to the most "emancipated" areas which tend at least partly to institutionalize the most "advanced" of the rationalized patterns or those which are otherwise most thoroughly emancipated from the traditional background.

For these and other reasons certain areas of the social structure have come to stand out conspicuously. In the first place is the area of "intellectualism" emancipated from the patterns and symbols of traditional thought, secondly of urbanism particularly on the metropolitan scale with its freedom from particularistic controls, its cosmopolitanism and general disrespect for traditional ties. Third is the

---

[2] I am aware of the importance of other aspects of the total fascist pattern such as its romanticism and a tendency to ethical nihilism, but cannot stop to analyze them here.

area of economic, technological, and administrative rationalization in the market system and large-scale organization, especially toward the top, with its responsiveness to *ad hoc* situations and its relation to conflicting codes. Fourth is the area of "cultural" emancipation in literature and the arts with its high susceptibility to unstable faddism, and its association with bohemianism. Finally there is the moral emancipation of "Society" with its partial permeation of the upper middle class, the adoption of manners and folkways not in keeping with various traditional canons of respectability, all the way from women smoking to polite adultery.

The uneven incidence of these various forms of emancipation results in an imperfect structural integration with latent or overt elements of conflict and antagonism. These conflicts in turn readily become associated with the tensions involved in other structural strains in the society. In particular may be mentioned here first, the difficult competitive position of the lower middle class, near enough to the realization of success goals to feel their attraction keenly but the great majority, by the sheer relation of their numbers to the relatively few prizes, doomed to frustration. Secondly, the particular strains in the situation of youth engendered by the necessity of emancipation from the family of orientation and exposure to the insecurities of competitive occupational adjustment at about the same stage of the life cycle, and third, the insecurity of the adult feminine role in our urban society.[3]

An element of at least latent antagonism between relatively emancipated and relatively traditionalized elements of the society would exist even if all its members were perfectly integrated with institutional patterns, if there were no anomie. But we have seen that anomie exists on a large scale. In relation to the above discussion, however, two principal foci, each with a tendency to a different structuring of attitudes need to be distinguished. On the one hand certain of the population elements involved in the spearheads of the processes of emancipation and rationalization are subject to a high incidence of it with its attendant insecurity. These elements tend to find the main points of reference of their orientations in the relatively well institutionalized rational and emancipated patterns

[3] A colleague (E. Y. Hartshorne in an unpublished paper) has noted that in Germany the most conspicuous support of the Nazis came from the lower middle class, from youth, and from women. On the two latter factors see the author's paper "Age and Sex in the Social Structure of the United States," (*American Sociological Review*, Vol. 7, October, 1942) reprinted in this volume.

—in science, liberalism, democracy, humanitarianism, individual freedom. But being insecure they tend to "overreact" and both positively and negatively to be susceptible to symbolizations and definitions of the situation which are more or less distorted caricatures of reality and which are overloaded with affect. Thus negatively the traditional order from which emancipation has been taking place is characterized overwhelmingly as embodying ignorance, superstition, narrow-mindedness, privilege, or in the later stages, acquisitive capitalistic exploitation. On the positive side there has been not only a marked abstractness but also some form of naive rationalistic utopianism. The pattern tends to bear conspicuous marks of the psychology of compulsion. It is held that if only certain symbolic sources of evil, superstition, or privilege or capitalism were removed "everything would be all right" automatically and for all time. Indeed there is every reason to believe that the psychology of this type of insecurity has had much to do with the cognitive biases and inadequacies of utilitarian thought as sketched above. It has contributed largely to the currency of a definition of the situation which contains conspicuous elements of utopianism and of distorted caricature.

The other type of reaction has been prominent in those areas of the society where traditional elements have formed the institutionalized points of reference for orientation. There the principal sources of anomie have often been derived from situational factors such as technological change, mobility and ethnic assimilation with relatively little direct relation to rationalized ideological patterns. There insecurity has tended to be structured in terms of a felt threat to the traditionalized values. The typical reaction has been of an over-determined "fundamentalist" type. Aggression has turned toward symbols of the rationalizing and emancipated areas which are felt to be "subversive" of the values. Naturally there has at the same time been an exaggerated assertion of and loyalty to those traditional values. The availability of ready-made caricatured definitions of the situation and extreme symbols has of course greatly facilitated this structuring. The use of such slogans as "capitalism," has made it possible to exaggerate the "rottenness" of the whole modern society so far as it has departed from the good old values.

In the complex process of interaction in Western society between imperfectly integrated institutional structures, ideological definitions of the situation, and the psychological reaction patterns typical of anomie, at a certain stage in the dynamic process of its development this new structured mass movement has come upon the scene and at certain points in the Western world has gained ascendancy. It is perhaps safe to conclude from the above analysis that its possibility is at least as deeply rooted in the social structure and dynamics of our society as was socialism at an earlier stage.

Before turning to another phase of the problem a word may be said about the role of nationalism in the present context. Though not, in terms of the "old regime," itself strictly a traditional value, the complex of sentiments focussing on national cultures has involved many of these traditionalistic elements—varying in specific content from one case to another. Ever since the French Revolution a functional relationship between the rise of nationalism and the process of rationalization has been evident—they have developed concurrently.

For a variety of reasons nationalistic sentiment has been perhaps the readiest channel for the fundamentalist reaction to flow into. The national state assumed great actual importance. The actual or potential enemy in the power system of states, differing in national tradition, has formed a convenient target for the projection of many aggressive affects, At the same time many of the emancipated areas of the social structure have been defined as "international" and could be regarded as subversive of national interest, honor, and solidarity. Finally, nationalism has been a kind of lowest common denominator of traditionalistic sentiments. Above all, the humblest insecure citizen, whatever his frustrations in other connections, could not be deprived of his sense of "belonging" to the great national community.

Undoubtedly one of the most important reasons for the different degrees of success of the fascist movement in different countries has lain in the differing degrees in which national traditions and with them pride and honor, have been integrated with the symbols of the rationalized patterns of Western culture. In the United States, on the one hand, the great national tradition stems from the Enlightenment of the eighteenth century — liberty, democracy, the rights of the individual are our great slogans. A radically fundamentalist revolt would have to overcome the enormous power of these symbols. In Germany on the other hand the political symbols of a liberal democratic regime could be treated as having been ruthlessly imposed on a defeated and humiliated Germany by the

alien enemy. National sentiments instead of being closely integrated with the existing regime could readily be mobilized against it.

The second important element of the fascist movements, that of
"vested interests" can be much more briefly treated. It is one of the
most fundamental theorems of the theory of institutions that in proportion to the institutionalization of any pattern a self-interest in
conformity with it develops. Self-interest and moral sentiments are
not necessarily antithetical, but may, and often do, motivate conduct in the same direction. Though this is true generally, it has a
particularly important application to statuses involving prestige and
authority in the social system. There, on top of the broader meaning of an interest in conformity, there is an interest in defending
higher status and its perquisites against challenge from less privileged elements. For this reason the reaction of privileged elements
to insecurity is almost inevitably structured in the direction of an
attitude of defense of their privileges against challenge. For the
same reason any movement which undermines the legitimacy of
an established order tends to become particularly structured about
an overt or implied challenge to the legitimacy of privileged statuses within it.

Western society has in all its recent history been relatively highly
stratified, involving institutionalized positions of power, privilege,
and prestige for certain elements. In the nature of the case the sentiments and symbols associated with these prestige elements have
been integrated with those institutionalized in the society as a
whole. In so far, then, as the process of rationalization and other
disorganizing forces have undermined the security of traditional
patterns the status and the bases of the legitimacy of privileged elements have inevitably been involved. But in addition to this they
have been affected by threats to the legitimacy and security of their
own position in the social structure. This situation tends to be particularly acute since the process of more general change is regularly
accompanied by a process of the "circulation of the elite."

It is in the nature of a highly differentiated social structure that
such privileged elements should be in a position to exercise influence on the power relations of the society through channels other
than those open to the masses, through political intrigue, financial
influence, and so on. Hence, with the progressive increase in the
acuteness of a generalized state of anomie it is to be expected that
such elements, which have been privileged in relation to a tradi-

ditional social order should, within the limits provided by the particular situation, develop forms of activity, sometimes approaching conspiratorial patterns, which in these terms may be regarded as a defense of their vested interests. Exactly what groups are involved in this phenomenon is a matter of the particular structural situation in the society in question.

The general phenomenon would seem to be clear enough. It is also not difficult to understand the tendency for elite elements whose main patterns go far back into the older traditional society to become susceptible to the fascist type of appeal—such as the landed nobility and higher clergy in Spain, or the Junker class in Germany. But there is a further complication which requires some comment.

The process of institutional change in the recent history of our society has brought to the fore elite elements whose position has been institutionalized primarily about the newer rationalized patterns. The most important are the business and professional elites. The latter are, except where radical fascist movements have immediately threatened to gain the ascendancy, perhaps the securest elite elements in the modern West.

The position of the business elite has, however, been much more complex. It gained for a time a position of great ascendancy, but for various reasons this rested on insecure foundations. With the "leftward" turn in the movement of ideology its position came under strong attack as the key element of capitalism. With its position thus threatened by the leftward sweep of the process of rationalization the legitimacy, the moral validity of its position was under attack, and its actual vested interests became less and less secure. From this point of view Fascism has constituted in one respect a continuation, even an intensification of the same threat. The threat has been made concrete by the rise to power of a new political elite with the means in hand to implement their threat.

At the same time fascism has seemed to stand, in the logic of the sentiments, for "sound" traditional values and to constitute a bulwark against subversive radicalism. Very concretely it has been instrumental in breaking the power of organized labor. At the same time on the level of power politics there has been a distinct area of potential mutual usefulness as between a political movement of the fascist type and entrenched business interests. This has been especially true because of the fascist tendency immediately to mobilize the economy in preparation for war.

The relation between fascism and vested interests in general may thus be regarded as a constant. In the case of the older traditional interests it is relatively unequivocal, but in that of business it is highly ambivalent. Especially where, as in Germany, business interests have not been closely integrated with strong liberal institutions the relationship has tended to be very close. But even there the movement can by no means be considered a simple expression of these vested interests and there are elements in the Nazi movement which may, in a certain state of the internal balance of power, turn out to be highly subversive of business.

In such brief space it has been possible to analyze only a few aspects of the very complex sociological problem presented by the fascist movement—the analysis is in no sense complete. But perhaps it will serve in a humble way to illustrate a direction in which it seems possible to utilize the conceptual tools of sociology in orienting ourselves, at least intellectually, to some of the larger aspects of the tragic social world we live in. To consider the possibility of going farther, of predicting the probable social consequences, of possible outcomes of the war and considering what we can do about fascism in other than a strictly military sense would raise such complex issues even on the scientific level, that it is better not even to attempt to touch upon them here.

VIII

Propaganda and Social Control

PROPAGANDA IS ONE kind of attempt to influence attitudes, and hence directly or indirectly the actions of people, by linguistic stimuli, by the written or spoken word. It is specifically contrasted with rational "enlightenment," with the imparting of information from which a person is left to "draw his own conclusions," and is thus a mode of influence mainly through "non-rational" mechanisms of behavior. Hence the apparent justification of treating it as a psychological problem, since psychology is the science of the mechanisms of behavior. But the same mechanisms operate in very different situations, cultures and social structures and in people with very different character or personality structures. While most psychologists would readily admit the existence of such variations they would tend to treat them as matters of common sense. To the sociologist, however, explicit analysis of these states of the social system provides precisely the problems he is interested in investigating. Why, for instance, have Germany and Japan become militantly aggressive powers while the United States has not? This is surely not in any ordinary sense a problem of psychology.

Even in a single person the "social" component of his situation and personality cannot be ignored, although for some purposes it need not be treated as a set of variables. But most propaganda is oriented to the influencing not of single persons, but of large numbers in such a way that its effectiveness will lead to an appreciable alteration of the "state of the social system" of which they are a part. On this level the structure of that social system is decidedly in the category of variables, and since there is every reason to believe that analysis of the dynamics of social systems is beyond the resources of psychology alone, scientific help from other quarters becomes indispensable.

The first problem then, is that of outlining the principal elements of a social system, other than the psychological mechanisms of its component persons, so as to provide a systematic setting for studying the operation of these mechanisms and their concrete conse-quences, especially on a mass level. The essential components from this point of view may be said to be three, the institutional struc-ture, the concrete situation of action, and the cultural tradition.

Institutions in the present sense are patterns governing behavior and social relationships which have become interwoven with a system of common moral sentiments which in turn define what one has a "right to expect" of a person in a certain position. The sim-plest way of treating the institutional significance of these senti-ments and expectations is to conceive them as applying to the definition of the statuses and roles of persons, that is, the "positions" in the social system, relative to other persons, to which they are treated as legitimately entitled, and the legitimate expectations of performance—including abstention—on the part of the persons occupying the given status. The institutional structure of a social system then, is the totality of morally sanctioned statuses and roles which regulate the relations of persons to one another through "locating" them in the structure and defining legitimate expectations of their attitude and behavior.

Every social system is a *functioning entity*. That is, it is a system of interdependent structures and processes such that it tends to maintain a relative stability and distinctiveness of pattern and be-havior as an entity by contrast with its—social or other—environ-ment, and with it a relative independence from environmental forces. It "responds," to be sure, to the environmental stimuli, but is not completely assimilated to its environment, maintaining rather an element of distinctiveness in the face of variations in environ-mental conditions. To this extent it is analogous to an organism.

Since institutional patterns form the focal structural element of social systems,[1] it is of fundamental importance that in any given case the basic institutional patterns constitute a relatively integrated system and not a mere agglomeration of distinct elements or "traits." The structural interrelations of the different parts of an institutional system are closely interdependent with the "functional needs" of the social system as a whole which include, of course, the biological and psychological needs of its component persons, but also those structures and mechanisms necessary for the aggre-

---

[1] This proposition of course cannot be justified in the scope of a brief article. For an extended treatment of the problem see Parsons, Talcott, *The Structure of Social Action;* New York, McGraw-Hill, 1937 (xii and 817 pp) — especially Chapters X and XV.

gate to function as a unit in terms of its own distinctive patterns and situations. Institutions are not independent entities—from a certain point of view they are rather relatively stable crystalizations of uniformities in the processes of action and interaction of human personalities. But in the present state of social science, knowledge of the institutional structure of a social system is as essential to the understanding of its functioning as is knowledge of anatomy essential to understanding the physiological functioning of an organism. In neither case can the structure be derived, and especially its variations from system to system, from dynamic analytical considerations alone. At best there is only fragmentary insight on this level.

Implicitly or explicitly then, sociological analysis must operate with a generalized system of institutional structure such that it supplies generalized categories adequate to the *complete*[2] description of a functioning institutional system. Although there is much difficulty in detail, it may be said that this possibility exists in current sociology, and it is most important to make systematic and explicit use of it. One of the commonest sources of fallacious conclusions lies in the tendency to treat certain aspects of a social structure without taking account of their interdependence. Whether or not this abstraction is legitimate depends of course on the particular case, but often, while plausible, it is not.

Just as it is dangerous to ignore the interdependence of institutional patterns with each other, so is it also dangerous to ignore their interdependence with the other elements of the social system, with the situation of action and the cultural tradition. From the point of view of any given person the institutionalized patterns of his own society constitute one of the most fundamental aspects of the concrete situation in which he acts. In his role of son, husband, father, doctor, citizen or church member, institutional patterns define the goals he is expected to pursue, the means among which he may choose, and the sentiments and attitudes he should manifest. Conversely they also go far to define the behavior and attitudes he can expect from others with whom he stands in social relationships, whether they are previously known to him as persons or not. From the point of view of the social system, the institutional patterns are, in one principal respect, agencies of the "control" of the behavior of its members, in that they keep it in line with the established structure and functional requirements of the social system.

---

[2] Not in detail, but in terms of functionally essential aspects.

Although institutional patterns thus involve very important elements of orientation to the situations which people face, they are by no means exhaustive. With respect to the action of persons they fail to include certain factors. In the first place there is generally, although in widely varying degree, a range of toleration within which action, within an institutionalized status and role, can vary without being treated as "deviant," within which the specific details are contingent on particular personalities and circumstances. Secondly, the existence of deviant behavior itself is a fact of paramount importance which is part of the situation others must face, although appropriate reactions to it, as will be seen, may be institutionalized to a greater or lesser extent. In relation to the non-human situation there is likewise a range of detailed variation, and of elements of change and uncertainty. Hence it is not possible to understand the concrete behavior of persons in a social system without reference to the concrete situations faced by its members. It should also be obvious that, since institutional patterns and situations are *inter*-dependent, situational pressure may constitute one important factor in the modification of institutions.

Finally, it should be noted that institutionalization of patterns is a matter of degree and that hence there may be an indistinct borderline where orientation to particular situations is only partially determined by institutional norms even within the realm where this is intrinsically possible.

As distinct from its normative aspects, in relation to the situation of action, the principal function of institutional patterns may, following W. I. Thomas, be said to be to "define the situation." The significance of a situation is never simply given in its intrinsic "nature"; rather a selection is made of those aspects which are functionally related to the particular orientations, values, interests, and sentiments of the person. A tract of land, for example, represents an aspect of the physical environment which would be quite differently "defined" by a geologist surveying the topography of the region, by a farmer whose produce is grown upon it, and by a military officer interested in making the area secure against enemy attack, and these differing definitions would lead to correspondingly different actions on the part of each. Insofar as one plays an institutionalized role in interaction with other institutionalized roles, the alternatives for action are presented to him in terms of an institutional definition of the situation.

There is, however, no rigid line between what is given in the situation and what is imputed to it by the person, although if his definition of the situation is sufficiently seriously "unrealistic," it will entail pragmatic consequences. There is, however, a continuum between empirically correct, although selective, definitions, through various kinds and degrees of "distortions" to completely erroneous definitions. In the field of social relationships a still further factor of flexibility comes in because here action is itself a function of institutionalized definitions of social situations, so that the definitions are, within considerable limits, not anchored in empirical realities which are independent of the social system itself. Hence, there is an important area of "socially[3] arbitrary" variation in the definition of situations. It is probably true that elements of unrealistic distortion of non-social empirical reality can become relatively stably institutionalized. Although imposing a functional handicap on the social system, this may well be counterbalanced by other aspects of their functional significance.[4] But if this is true where there are external empirical checks, it is doubly so within the sphere of social arbitrariness. What is, in terms of a previous set of institutional patterns, a seriously distorted definition of the situation may well become very thoroughly institutionalized through an important change in the social system.

The function of institutional patterns in defining the situation of action provides a convenient link between them and the cultural tradition, as well as between them and the situation itself. The cultural tradition is an exceedingly heterogeneous category including science, common-sense knowledge, religious and philosophical ideas, value patterns, art and other expressional forms which have an important degree of general acceptance and continuity in a social system, even though the acceptance is uneven, and the continuity involves continual change, so long as it is not mere random variation. What they have in common is their "ideal" existence, the fact that they are "eternal" objects, as such neither physi-

---

[3] Although not in the same sense or degree *individually arbitrary*.

[4] For example, there is reason to believe that the attitudes toward health and disease officially held by the Christian Science church are not merely "one view" but in the light of medical science contains important elements of positive error and distortion of established truth. But it does not follow from this, if true, that Christian Scientists as a group are in the same proportion an "unhealthy" or disturbing element in the social system. Orientation to health and disease is only one of many factors which would have to be taken into account in arriving at a judgment on such a question. And certainly their position is quite firmly institutionalized within their own group.

cal nor social, which stand in relation to systems of human action. The functional relation of the different elements of a cultural tradition to social action is exceedingly varied, but there is always some degree of integration both as between themselves and with the other elements of action.

Since institutional patterns consist of norms defining what action and attitudes are legitimately expected of people, they are, in one aspect, actually part of the cultural tradition. In the aspect of institutionalized patterns they have, to quote Durkheim, a "constraining" or controlling influence on action, while in the role of part of the cultural tradition they are involved in the different standards by which its elements are evaluated and subject to selective pressures, in terms of cognitive validity, moral judgment and conformity with human interests and sentiments. It is primarily through their involvement in the cultural tradition that institutional patterns are interwoven with the primary orientation systems of the members of a society, with their empirical and non-empirical "beliefs," their moral values and the specific structuring of their goals and wishes.

The primary focus of institutions is the definition of expectations with respect to action in concrete human social relationships. Only a small part, however, of the total cultural tradition bears directly on this field. Other elements are primarily significant in orientation to the empirical situation, or to the problems of meaning in relation to basic frustrations and uncertainties. Still others are primarily significant in symbolic and other expressional roles. Even these elements, are, however, subject to a kind of "secondary" institutionalization in that conformity with certain beliefs, or acceptance and admiration of certain expressional forms, comes to be obligatory and a test of full participation in certain social statuses. Hence, no part of the cultural tradition is completely indifferent to the balance of interdependent forces in a social system.

A particularly crucial role is, however, played by those elements which are most closely involved in the definition of the situation of action. Of these, in turn, three important classes may be analytically distinguished, even though they merge into each other. First are the primary institutionalized patterns and values which, in the nature of the case, are close to typical action and social relationship situations, but often are not explicitly formulated at all, while in any case questions of "interpretation" and application to particular concrete situations are left open in an important degree. Second is the system of beliefs and orientations which give these primary institutionalized values their "meaning," which, on appropriate levels, help to make holders of them psychologically secure. Finally, third, is the set of explicit diagnoses of particular situations and justification of actual or projected courses of action in them, especially in those of critical significance to the social system as a whole, such as revolutions, wars and great religious movements. It should be abundantly clear that with respect to all of these there is, in any complex and dynamically changing social system, room for a large variety of factors of uncertainty and flexibility in many different directions.

Clarity and definiteness as well as integration of the different elements on both cultural and action levels, are, for a variety of reasons, of very great functional importance for the stability of social systems. They are, for equally important reasons, exceedingly difficult to obtain. Rigid enforcement of "official" definitions always sets up serious strains because of the difficulty of adapting to changes both in situations and in the cultural tradition, many of the elements of which are inherently dynamic, and almost always involves serious strains in the social structure itself.

Every social system, functionally regarded, faces a control problem on the level of overt behavior. Even a moderate level of the integration of the complex elements of a system of social action is no more to be taken for granted as in the "nature" of the human material which makes it up than is the analogous integration of one of the higher organisms in the physio-chemical nature of the proteins, carbohydrates, and other chemical substances which make up the body. In both cases highly specific mechanisms are functionally essential to the maintenance of the equilibrium of the system. The direct obverse of the functional necessity of integration is the existence of many important tendencies and seeds of deviant behavior.[5]

---

[5] It is impossible to take space here to go into the analysis of these seeds. One of them undoubtedly lies in the inevitable lack of full congruence between the distribution of hereditary constitutional tendencies in a population and the functional requirements to the institutionalized system of statuses and roles—*any* population and *any* institutionalized system. Compare Davis, Kingsley, "The Child and the Social Structure." *J. Educational Sociol.* (1940) 14:217-229: Another lies in the fact that any institutional structure at certain points imposes strains on a person which are too severe to be adequately counteracted by the existing control mechanisms, but lead to deviant behavior by some persons. Still another lies in the fact that socialization at one stage of the life cycle probably sometimes positively unfits the person for the roles he must assume in a later stage. There are doubtless various others.

From what is now very well known of the types of systems most closely analogous to the social, the physiological system of the organism and the psychological system of the personality, it would be surprising indeed if a highly important functional role were not played by control mechanisms, and if these were perfectly obvious to the "naked eye" of common sense.

It seems to be inherent in the structure of human action that there are, fundamentally, two kinds of channels through which "pressure" to control behavior may be exerted—whether "deliberately" by any controlling agency or unconsciously is indifferent for present purposes. On the one hand, the appeal may be to what psychoanalysts call the "reality principle," and the mechanism will then operate through the actual or potential alteration of the situation in which people act. It will consist either in revealing previously unknown aspects of the situation, or in actually or potentially altering it to the actor's advantage or disadvantage through the imposition of positive or negative "sanctions." This mode of control is of course effective only to the extent that action is actually motivated in reality terms, is integrated, that is, in particular ways. On the other hand, appeal may be made to the "state of mind" or the "sentiments" of the actor relatively independently of potential alterations in the situation in which he acts. This in turn may take the form of an attempt, whether or not it is clear to the person what is being done, to change his "attitudes" or to influence his definition of the situation.[6] It is in this latter category that propaganda falls, as one important mechanism for controlling action—not of course necessarily in the interest of checking deviant tendencies, quite possibly of promoting them—through appeal to the "subjective" non-situational aspects of action.

Further progress in the analysis of the actual and potential roles of propaganda would, in view of the preceding considerations, seem to be involved with analysis of the functional mechanisms which, apart from any deliberate process of propagandizing, operate in

---

[6] For reasons which cannot be gone into here it may be assumed that definitions of the situation which are markedly deviant from either empirical reality or institutionalized patterns or both cannot be "gotten across" through mechanisms of cognitive "persuasion" alone, but must link up somewhere with sentiments through non-rational mechanisms.

Underlying this whole problem is the very fundmanetal one of the modes and mechanisms of the "introjection" of institutional patterns, both norms and definitions of the situation, and their relation to the problems of integration both of personality and of social systems.

any relatively smoothly functioning social system to control deviant tendencies, through acting upon the sentiments of actors. Before explicitly taking up the potential role of propaganda it will prove illuminating to discuss certain critical points in the social system at which it seems possible to impute rather specific controlling functions to aspects of the institutionalized patterns.

Attention may first be called to the fact that control functions may reasonably be attributed to the most ordinary patterns of interaction between persons. Two primary facts seem to underlie this, that there is an essential factor of "resistance" to the fulfillment of normative expectations and obligations, so that stimulus from the actual or anticipated reactions of others has an important functional significance and, secondly, that the incidence of "neurotic" mechanisms and reaction patterns is universal although varying enormously in degree. In the first context tendencies to "laxity," to letting down standards, are checked by the fact that the actor is involved in social relationships in such a way that, usually both through situational and subjective channels, the tendency is at an early stage subject to check. For each person this situation is above all brought about through the complex of introjected moral sentiments which are interwoven with what is usually called his "self-respect." There are usually also important concrete connections with affectional ties and with other elements of sentiment and interest. This complex of mechanisms may in broad terms be said to operate successfully short of two main types of limits. On the one hand, one's deviant tendencies to laxity may become extreme enough and sufficiently interwoven with his character structure so that he ceases without unbearable conflict to "care" enough and is no longer adequately responsive to the explicit or implicit disapproval of others. On the other hand, there may be a more or less cumulative vicious circle so that the same tendencies are at work in a whole group of persons in such a way that the deviant tendencies of each reinforce those of the others, instead of performing the normal function of "bringing back into line."

There seems to be much evidence that all the principal psychological mechanisms which play the predominant role in "neurotic" character patterns constitute in an important sense exaggerations of "normal" reactions to situations of emotional strain. Neurotic "aggressiveness" in an exaggeration of normal anger at an interference with legitimate expectations, neurotic anxiety an exaggeration of fear in the face of real danger. What characterizes the neurotic pattern is, above all, an element of cognitive distortion in the definition of the situation and, emotionally, "over-reaction," an intensity of affect which is out of proportion to what would be appropriate to the real situation.[7] But elements of this distortion and exaggeration are the most commonplace phenomena in the behavior of all "normal" people under various kinds of stress. What seems to characterize the normal person as distinguished from the neurotic is the relative absence or far smaller degree of rigidity in the relation of his reaction pattern to the situation. He is relatively speaking responsive to the "reality" situation. Hence, on the cognitive level, his rationalizations do not tend to build up cumulatively into more and more logically elaborated and "watertight" systems which are increasingly impervious to facts or institutionalized patterns, but tend to be corrected by reference to them. Emotionally, in a similar way, the over-reaction tends to subside, to fall into line with what is treated as a normal reaction to the type of situation in question.

Now from the psychological point of view a vital criterion of normality is sensitiveness to the reality principle, or responsiveness to situational influences. But from the *sociological* point of view it is essential to keep in mind that *one* of the most fundamental aspects of reality of the situation consists in the actual and anticipated reactions of other persons. On occasion these other people doubtless do "diagnose" the neurotically deviant tendency of the actor and act deliberately to counteract it. But it is safe to say that far more frequently they quite automatically and without premeditation—in so far as they are not neurotic themselves—react in the *right* way in order to help bring the potential deviant back "into line." The exact psychological mechanisms by which this takes place cannot be elaborated here, and are in any refined sense beyond the competence of a sociologist. But the *fact* that such a process of reciprocal control reaction is continually going on in ordinary social relationships, especially the more intimate ones such as marriage, friendship and close occupational collaboration, undoubtedly has prime functional significance to the social system. It is one of the most important channels by which, as a dynamic process, the functional integration of the social system is maintained. Institutionally established behavior and reaction patterns undoubtedly

---

[7] In a very large proportion of cases these reactions result in significant part from the operation of the mechanisms of "projection" or "displacement" so that the affect is not really "appropriate" to the manifest object or situation.

have, among others, this latent function, that they provide the right stimuli to other persons to prevent them from embarking on too widely deviant trends of behavior.[8]

It is known, however, that the working of these mechanisms is, in any complex society, highly imperfect. A great deal of deviant behavior actually occurs—what then? There is evidence that every social system possesses more or less well-developed "secondary" defenses against deviance, with either or both of two immediate functions: either to bring a person back into line by processes inaccessible to ordinary social relationships, or where this fails to insulate him from reciprocal influence on others so that he becomes at least relatively harmless. It is in this light that a brief discussion of certain aspects of modern medical practice will be entered upon.

The ostensible character of medical practice, its manifest function, is as that of a machinery for harnessing deliberate rational action, through the knowledge and skill of highly trained experts, to the practical problem of cure, or sometimes prevention, of "disease" in the person, of restoring or maintaining his "health." The knowledge and skill of the modern physician have, moreover, consisted, at least until very recently, overwhelmingly in knowledge of "organic medicine," of aspects of the *biological* sciences and techniques based upon them. There can be no doubt of the real importance of these elements to the problem of health nor of the very striking achievements of modern medicine in such fields as the control of infectious diseases through application to them of the findings of bacteriology and immunology—and more recently certain forms of chemotherapy—and aseptic surgery, in considerable part also a result of bacteriological discoveries.

The only question is that of the exhaustiveness of the conception of medical practice as "applied biological science," whether it is adequate to the total concrete significance of the relation of a patient to a physician in its bearing on his health. There can be little doubt that there is a great deal more to it than that.

On one level, recognition that this is so has been clearly implied in a formula which has been widely current in the medical profes-

---

[8] Functional analysis of this situation is relatively easy where it concerns the maintenance of patterns essential to the functioning of the particular concrete reciprocal relationships — such as in a marriage, although even here there is much actual deviance. It becomes much more difficult when it concerns the maintenance of sentiments essential to a large-scale social system in situations outside the immediate experience of most of its individual members; for instance in a peaceable society, willingness—and actual emotional capacity—to risk life and limb in fighting for national interests.

sion at least ever since the rise to prominence of "scientific medicine"—the formula that in addition to the "science of medicine," which may be taken to include the practical application of exact biological and biochemical knowledge, there has always been, in a position of great importance, something called the "art of medicine." This might most specifically be described as all those "intangibles" in the function of the doctor which were most important to the "human" problems of practice,—regard for the personal problems and idiosyncrasies of the patient, the famous "bedside manner," and various things of that sort. The use of the term "art" has suggested that these functions are not subject to scientific "codification" and that they are most effectually carried out through the "personality" of the physician.

The first of these presumptions has, for at least a considerable part of the area, been questioned by one of the most conspicuous developments of medicine in the past generation, that of psychiatry and the psychological aspects of the problems of disease. It had, of course, long been known that there was such a thing as "mental disease" where the pathology was not so much organic as behavioral; that is, people did not think or act according to social expectations. But even here, with relatively little success except in a few cases such as syphilitic paresis and brain tumors, there has been a strong tendency to attempt to reduce mental diseases to manifestations of organic pathological states. But more recently much attention has been devoted to two other very large fields where what in some sense were considered "pathological" phenomena in a person have been treated as "psychogenic," the "psychoneuroses" and psychosomatic disorders. In the former group there existed for the most part—except in conversion hysteria—neither somatic symptoms nor evidence of somatic aetiological factors. In the latter in one group, the so-called "functional" disorders, the symptoms were somatic in the form of pain or disturbance of function, but no organic lesions to account for them could be found. In another group, however, it was found that very definite organic lesions could be made to respond to psychotherapeutic measures and aetiologically a crucial influence could be attributed to psychic factors. Thus the "psychic factor in disease"—an exceedingly wide variety of diseases —has come, in what are on the whole scientifically the most advanced medical circles, to play a central part in their whole orientation to the care of patients.

The fact that in all these respects both mental patients and those with functional or organic disabilities are, in a large range of cases, open to deliberate psychotherapeutic influence, not only opens up a very large field for the present practice but also for the future development of medicine. It also strongly suggests, and the suggestion is confirmed by much other evidence, that a very important part has been played in previous and also current medical practice by what may be called "unconscious" psychotherapy, that the way in which doctors have in fact handled patients has had an important effect on their states of health through their mental and emotional states as well as acting directly on the physiological systems of their bodies. Much of the art of medicine has consisted in this kind of unconscious psychotherapy. The same considerations also go far to explain the undoubted therapeutic success in considerable degree, of much, from the point of view of modern scientific medicine, "unsound" treatment of health problems, all the way from some of the current medical "cults" through Christian Science healing to primitive health magic.

The emergence of the importance of the psychic factor further throws into relief the fact, which has been more or less clear to many practitioners for a long time, that "health" is not simply a state of the biological organism, but is a matter of a person's total adjustment to his life situation. Not the least important among the aspects of this situation are his social relations, and at least one aspect of lack of adequate adjustment to others in the social system is its bearing on various forms of ill health.

This further suggests that the conscious or unconscious psychotherapeutic significance of the role of the physician is not confined to what, in the ordinary sense, the doctor "does" to or for his patient, but involves the specific structure of the kind of social relations in which the latter is placed when he turns to medical aid in his difficulties. In other words, even if what the doctor "does" is therapeutically useless or even in not too great a degree positively harmful, the net effect on the patient *may* be therapeutically beneficial. How can this be?

There are certain striking differences between the patterning of the role of the physician and that of most other roles with which the normal person is brought into ordinary interpersonal relations in life. The latter tend to be, like the "job" situation, either highly impersonal and very strictly functional, often involving an element of impersonal authority, or, if they are intimate they are, like the relations of kinship and friendship, highly particularistic and involved with a reciprocity of moral judgment and personal sentiment.

The doctor is analogous to the patient's most intimate kin and friends in that he is a person who can almost without limit be trusted, both in the sense that his disinterestedness is assured, and in the sense that, often beyond even the level of personal intimacies, he can be taken into confidence in matters touching the most private and intimate affairs and sentiments of the patient. To a considerable degree this "trustworthiness" rests on his reputation for technical competence, as a person who can be relied upon to "help" someone who is in need of help.

But at the same time there are very striking differences from the more intimate ordinary social relations. It is an essentially asymmetrical relationship in that the doctor does not admit his patient to intimacies with himself, does not "reveal" himself to the patient, physically or mentally. He is a person of a specific "dignity" who is "aloof" from the network of the personal relations of the patient, who does not participate in reciprocities with him.[9]

Although enjoying, indeed needing, this particular dignity, he specifically does not turn it into a certain kind of authoritarian role, above all he generally does not manifest moral judgments of his patient, but treats the case as a "problem" to be diagnosed and treated in a "scientific" spirit. The patient need not be afraid that he will be blamed or punished for his shortcomings; he will rather be understood and helped. Conversely, he will often fail to find approval or sympathy where in ordinary relations he would be entitled to expect them.

Although the physician does not in the ordinary sense assume an authoritarian role, these aspects of the pattern of medical practice do endow him with a very important kind of authority. He is in a position to exercise great influence even though his "orders" are not, in the usual sense, backed by coercive sanctions. He has great prestige resting on the reputation that members of his profession possess high levels both of technical competence and of moral integrity.

One of the focal patterns on which this professional prestige and its resulting authority rest is that of responsibility. As a technical

---

[9] Where he is also a personal friend there is generally a marked tendency to segregation of the two roles.

expert he must assume responsibility in relation to all laymen since they are not competent to have a reliable judgment of his diagnoses, decisions, or therapeutic procedures. But the technical aspect of his responsibility is heightened in significance by its relation to the moral aspect. For his very technical superiority to the layman, in combination with the seriousness of the interests which depend upon his action, means that he holds enormous potential power to exploit the patient.

A very notable fact about medical practice is the small extent to which enforcement of the responsible use of the prestige and power of the role is achieved by a system of formal controls and sanctions. Neither the law of the state nor the disciplinary machinery of medical societies plays a major role. Indeed what impresses the outside observer most forcibly is the ineffectiveness of these controls and the lack of reliance upon them. On this level the medical man enjoys an extraordinary range of freedom. But the potentialities of abuse are so great that the existence of a ramified system of informal control of the practitioner himself as well as the patient is strongly indicated.

Acceptance of authority without coercive sanctions is understandable only in terms of a fundamental trust in the person in the position of authority—what physicians call "confidence." This is true for any case of technical competence but is doubly important in the medical case because all schools of psychiatry seem to be agreed that it is essential to psychotherapy, in any form, conscious or unconscious. When one adds to this the very formidable element of uncertainty which renders the physician in a very large proportion of cases unable to guarantee success and in fact often exposes him to failure, the average effectiveness of his authority becomes very impressive indeed. It is highly improbable that the high degree of average confidence in physicians actually found in *our* society can be adequately explained either by realistic appreciation of the technical achievements of medicine or by the impression made by particular personalities as such. The institutionalization of the role is evidently of paramount importance.

Returning to the case of the relationship between the patient and doctor, in by far the most sophisticated form this factor of "confidence" has been analyzed and consciously made use of by psychoanalysts, especially in their treatment of the phenomena of transference." Apart from specific interpretations and other positive

therapeutic measures taken, a major factor in the therapeutic results of analytic treatment is held to lie in the fact that the analyst
is, so far as possible, a "neutral screen" on which the patient projects his affects and definitions of situations in human relations. The
very discrepancy between the attitudes the patient manifests
toward his analyst, and what the analyst actually is to him, is a
major factor in forcing the patient to analyze his own reactions and
investigate the deeper sources of his failure to adapt to reality more
generally. This "neutrality" of the analyst is aided by various devices such as keeping out of the patient's sight so that gesture and
facial expression cannot supply clues to react to, and confining the
relationship to stated appointments of stated length so that it is
subject to a minimum of manipulation in terms of the patient's immediate feelings and rationalizations.

Underlying all this is a most important consideration. In ordinary
social relations it can be said that there is a mutual obligation to
take the other party at his face value, to "take him seriously" as it
were. It is this very obligation, and its reciprocal expectations, which
creates a primary opening for the operation of the vicious circles
which may eventuate in neuroses, for by distorting the cognitive
definition of the situation by rationalization, by concealing—usually
unconsciously— actual motives and putting up an acceptable front,
one forces others into the fulfillment of the obligations of their
statuses and roles although one is not "really" in terms of actual
social values entitled to this fulfillment. The striking thing here
about the role of the physician is his ability to avoid being put in
this position. He does not "argue" with his patient about his rationalizations and his motives; to do so would grant a status of reciprocity which he cannot grant. But neither does he accept the
patient's rationalizations at their face value, and while he does not
"refute" them, it is quite clear to the patient from his behavior that
he does not accept them. This again forces the patient to further
analysis of his own motives.

It is clear that it is only in terms of a certain form of definition
of roles that such a situation becomes possible. The physician must
have some kind of authority which justifies to the patient his failure
to treat him as ordinary people would, and along with this he must
secure acceptance of his refusal to be drawn into the particular
nexus of the patient, to become an intimate friend, a parent, a
lover, or a personal enemy. On the patient's side the predominant

element seems to be the definition of his own role as a "patho-logical case," and hence as in need of help. In so far as he has "put himself in the hands" of a physician he implicitly accepts the latter's authority, based on his competence and integrity and, however much at times he may rebel, accepts the obligation to re-examine his own rationalizations and underlying motives again and again.

The therapeutic essence of the definition of role of the psychia-trist or psychoanalyst seems to be the ability to break through the vicious circle of rationalization and deviance of the neurotic mech-anisms. This in turn has two aspects. On the one hand it relieves the patient of certain pressures to which he is subject in ordinary life, notably perhaps the pressure of moral responsibility, but also more broadly of the normal consequences of expressing himself with complete freedom, either in the form of moral blame or pun-ishment or aggressive reactions, or of the acceptance of respon-sibility for maintaining and living up to the obligations of an institutionally defined relation in the case of positive relations. The price he pays for this extraordinary freedom, which need not be pleasurable, is the acceptance of a status of dependency, the admis-sion he is "sick" and in need of help. It is, of course, of fundamental social significance that it is essential to the pattern of medical prac-tice that this dependency should not be permanently maintained, but should be eliminated as rapidly as possible and the patient put "back on his own feet."

The other side of the picture is the steady discipline to which the patient is subjected in the course of his treatment. While the fact that he is required and allowed to express himself freely may pro-vide some immediate satisfactions, he is not really allowed to "get away" with their implications for the permanent patterning of his life and social relations, but is made, on progressively deeper levels, conscious of the fact that he cannot "get away" with them. The physician places him in a kind of "experimental situation" where this is demonstrated over and over again. In both respects the therapeutic effect would not be possible without the institutional patterning of the physician's role which has become established in the Western world. There is probably more than either historical connection or intrinsic relatedness to the technical tradition of medicine in the fact that psychoanalysis has insisted so strongly that the analyst assume formally the role of the physician.

What is true of psychoanalysis at one extreme is, with various modifications and many differences of degree, apparently true of medical practice as a whole, though of course in merely binding up a cut finger this aspect of the physician's role is for minor significance.

This situation in medical practice has two types of significance for the broader problems of this paper. In the first place it is a particularly striking case of the existence of relatively unconscious automatic control mechanisms in society which tend to counteract the vicious-circle mechanisms of at least one broad class of deviant tendencies on the behavioral level. Psychoanalysts have tended to become relatively self-conscious about the positive therapeutic significance of the patterning of the analyst's role, and to use this quite deliberately, though even they are probably far from having exhausted the subject. But even in much practice of psychiatry there is relatively little self-consciousness of this and even less in most of organic medicine. Indeed at one stage the very effectiveness of the control mechanisms seemed to be dependent on their latent functions remaining unrecognized, on both physician and patient thinking the former was concerned solely with acting on the physiological equilibrium of the patient's body, through biological techniques.

Secondly, for the treatment of patients, as the case of psychoanalysis most completely and dramatically shows, the institutionalized role of physician provides a particularly strategic vantage point from which to apply deliberate psychotherapeutic techniques. The question then arises whether for mass tendencies to deviance, rather than individual pathology, there is any analogous vantage point or set of them which can be used for deliberate propagandistic control. If there is it would seem likely that, like the role of physician, it—or they—would involve a considerable measure of latent, unconscious control function apart from deliberate control policies. It is, furthermore, reasonable to suppose that systematic recognition of the mechanisms by which unconscious control operates on the social level might contribute significantly to the formulation of propaganda policies.

It has become clear from the foregoing analysis that the institutional patterns of society perform important automatic control functions on at least two different levels, that of ordinary "personal" social relations and of the institutionalization of medical practice. In the latter case it should be kept clearly in mind that not only does the physician "control" his patient but, in order to be in a position to do so, he must himself be controlled, he must adhere sufficiently closely to an institutionalized definition of his role, and to a situation which is enforced overwhelmingly by automatic, informal mechanisms.

While the first type of control is broadly common to all social systems the second is, in an at all comparable level of development, peculiar to the modern Western world. In view of this fact it would be surprising if the fundamental structural and functional aspects of it should be confined to the one relatively narrow functional sphere of medical practice.

By contrast with the area of "personal" relations, that of medical practice is particularly characterized by three broad institutional features. It is "functionally specific" as opposed to "diffuse" in that it defines the role with reference to a specific content of function and segregates this "area," that of the professional relations, from any other of potential relation between the parties. A physician's peculiar "rights" in relation to his patient, as to confidential information and of access to the body, are defined and limited by the relevance to the performance of his professional role, dealing with matters of health. The same is true of authority, which does not involve a generalized superiority of status, but is limited to the health context. Finally the physician's obligations to his patient are equally defined and limited by this context. He is not, for instance, under obligation to help the patient financially except in so far as it concerns making adequate treatment of his health problems possible. This functional specificity is one of the principal conditions for "insulating" the physician from involvement in the patient's "particular nexus" or set of personal relations, which makes the previously mentioned "aloofness" possible.

Secondly, the professional pattern is "affectively neutral" as contrasted with a positively affective pattern. That is, in his professional capacity the physician is expected to avoid emotional involvements with his patient, either affection or hatred, moral approval or disapproval. He should be "objective" and "impersonal," treat the patient's condition as a problem, a "case." This again is essential to insulation from the patient's system of personal relations and plays an important role in making conscious and unconscious psychotherapy possible.

Finally the professional pattern is "universalistic" as opposed to "particularistic." The patient is again significant in a technical context rather as a "case" than as a "person." it is not the significance of that patient as a person, either in terms of personal relations or of institutionalized social status, not "who" he is, but "what is the matter" with him, which defines the relationship. All cases of typhoid, or schizophrenia should be treated alike, subject to technically founded variations, regardless of "who" they are. This universalism is an essential element of scientific objectivity and without it a high development of medicine as applied science would not be possible.

The combination of these broad features of institutional patterns is, as shown by comparative study of different societies, very unevenly distributed both historically and geographically. The extensity of the area of the social structure in which the combination is highly developed is, indeed, one of the most conspicuous features of modern Western society. It underlies traditions of civil rights before the law, of the freedom of the person, of contract and market relations, of large-scale organization in general and the structure of political and other authority as well as the development and application of science. Its functional significance is manifold and by no means confined to the type of control function which is relevant to this paper. It is, for instance, difficult to suppose that the institutional regulation of marked relations connected with the "one-price system" and the control of tendencies to force and fraud are very directly related to the "psychological" level which is most relevant to the propaganda problem in the sense in which the patterns governing medical practice are.

For certain rough purposes the pathological patterns in the person in relation to which psychotherapy has significance may be classified in terms of two elements, "rationalizations" and "attitudes." The first is the individual counterpart of definitions of the situation, or an important aspect of them, on the social level. The second formulates the "emotional" or "affective" element. From this distinction it is possible, in making the transition from the personal to the social level, to investigate what are rough functional equivalents in the social system of the control functions of the physician in his relation to the patient. Very great care must, however, be taken to avoid misleading analogies, and to base conclusions only on the actual nature of the respective systems.

There is probably no such thing as deviance without some important element of institutionalized definition of the situation. To be "sick" and thus an appropriate person to be the patient of a physician is to be placed in an institutionally defined role. Two important

things are, however, to be noticed about this. In the first place the
sick person by the very fact of being defined as such is in a certain
sense insulated from normal interaction with the rest of the social
system. His role is by definition an undesirable one to be escaped
from as rapidly as possible. Although he is generally not, like the
criminal, morally blamed for his condition, it is not a "legitimate"
one. Above all—in so far as he is defined as pathological he is deprived in the relevant respects of any claim to be a source of influence or a model to emulate. Hence, deviance which takes this
form is prevented from influencing the structure of the social system. In the second place, sick people do not compose a "group"
or a "movement" but only a statistical class. It is in the nature of
the role that its incumbents cannot become integrated into a structurally significant group.

It should, however, be quite clear that the same fundamental
psychological processes and reaction patterns are involved in types
of deviance from an established set of institutionalized roles and
definitions of the situation which lead to structural innovation, to
the acceptance of shifts in the established definitions of the situation
by large numbers of people which are definitely structured departures from the norm, and similarly to inappropriate attitudes. The
differences from the individual level here are two. Negatively there
is successful avoidance of being placed in a social category such as
the "pathological" which would deprive the innovation of a claim
to legitimacy. Positively, attitudes and definitions of the situation
become structured for large numbers in a sufficiently uniform way
so that, relative to the existing social structure, the adherents of
the new patterns form a definitely structured group. In addition to
these mass reaction phenomena come others for which there is no
counterpart on the individual level, namely leadership and social
organization of groups, which perform important functions in crys-
tallizing more or less diffuse deviant tendencies in specific directions.

The existence of these possibilities of deviant structuring on the
social level implies, to one familiar with the functional approach,
the corresponding existence in the social system of automatic control mechanisms which, however imperfectly they function, in
normal circumstances somehow serve to keep the amount of deviance down to a relatively low level, whereas the elements of strain
and disorganization present in all complex social systems would,
without them, lead to far more serious instability.

In the case of individual pathologies the subject matter of the rationalizations which are of greatest importance to the maintenance of symptoms tends to be focused primarily about the "personal" problems of the patient. Problems of the definition of the situation for the social system as a whole are relatively remote from the more immediate preoccupations of the person and from his most concrete emotionally significant experience. On this account they are probably on the whole less rigidly determined by emotional compulsions, but at the same time both because of the complexity of the issues and the relative remoteness are less subject to effective control in terms of the reality principle. The combination of these two factors[10] would indicate a relative fluidity in many aspects of the cultural tradition of a society which heightens the significance of the control problem. Moreover, in our own society, the prominence of the element of "rationality," of freedom from traditionalistic stereotyping, works in the same direction in that it deprives cultural tradition to a considerable extent of the influence of powerful stabilizing forces.

An approach to the problem of what sort of mechanisms operate to stabilize the cultural tradition may be made by recalling the fact that the medical profession itself owes a very important part of its institutionalized status and thus of its direct and indirect therapeutic effectiveness to its integration with one fundamentally important part of the cultural tradition, namely certain branches of science. The prominence of magical healing in place of even relatively primitive "medical science" in most societies, and the place in our own of the health "cults," of innumerable health superstitions, and of such phenomena as Christian Science, strongly suggests that "belief" in the efficacy and superiority of scientific medicine is by no means to be taken for granted. Informally the degree of stability is associated with the fact that medical science is a part of the whole tradition of scientific culture, and of the associated fields of rational-liberal learning which is characteristic of Western society as a whole, and which has tremendous social prestige, especially in that it has become so strongly integrated with the way of life of the principal prestige classes in society.

On the more formal side it is of very great importance that medical training is placed under the auspices of the universities. This

---

[10] That is provided there are not "watertight" technical criteria by which to keep "beliefs" in line. Relative weakness in this respect is characteristic of almost all cultural fields, even of science.

fact not only articulates the "applied" side of medical knowledge and skill formally with more or less "pure" scientific research in medical fields, the bulk of which is carried on in the laboratories of university medical schools and teaching hospitals affiliated with them. It also articulates the medical sciences with the other sciences which do not have primarily medical fields of application, and finally with other fields of learning, such as humanities, which are not ordinarily thought of as scientific. The universities, in short, are the primary formal carriers of the great Western rational-liberal cultural tradition. Direct affiliation of the medical profession with them—which is true of the other principal professions as well—integrates it directly with this cultural tradition. Medical practice is by no means a matter simply of intelligent men using their general intelligence to deal with a certain type of practical problems.

But perhaps even more important than this formal affiliation with universities is the informal integration, largely within the academic framework, with the general patterns governing the perpetuation, advancement, and transmission of science and liberal learning. Just as in the case of medicine, it is quite clear for this broader field that the integration of the broader cultural tradition is not brought about automatically by the intrinsic nature of the subject matter. There are many areas and elements of uncertainty in practically all fields. Even within the academically formal rubrics there is a very high degree of specialism which makes exact appraisal of achievement difficult, even if it is intrinsically possible, and finally in the university faculty as a whole there is a very great heterogeneity of fields. One of the conspicuous symptoms of the need for control in this area is the chronic tendency for academic disciplines in almost all fields to split up into "schools." Careful study of these shows that they bear in large measure and to a very important extent the marks of operating psychologically as rationalizations. Although generally by no means without important elements of technical justification, the doctrines of a given school always show elements of bias which can be related to complex affective backgrounds.

At the same time that this need for control is so conspicuous, it seems quite clear that it is not primarily accomplished by the informal control system any more than is true of the medical case. For instance the pattern of academic freedom gives the university professor a range of freedom in the conduct of his professional function which is hardly exceeded by any group whose work is carried out in the context of large organizations. This freedom undoubtedly has important functions in lending him dignity and encouraging a high sense of professional responsibility, but it is also directly incompatible with stringent control through the machinery of formal organization. Closely related to this is the institution of tenure. Once in the status of a permanent position, a university teacher can only be dismissed for "cause," which means gross malfeasance in office. In fact this sanction is very seldom invoked—perhaps one might say that there is as great a reluctance on the part of university administrations to resort to it as there is of medical societies to take formal disciplinary action against their members.

The importance of the institutional patterning of the academic role for the present paper lies in the fact that included in the subjects of professional competence of academic men are precisely those fields of the cultural tradition which, in Western society, have been most central to the definitions of the situation which have, on the one hand, been institutionalized in the social structure, and which are, on the other hand, the necessary starting points for any deviant definitions which could conceivably help to crystallize important processes of structural change. In this connection three groups of disciplines are of primary importance. Philosophy and theology have tended to be the places in which the more abstract and generalized formulations of basic orientations have taken place, including both intellectual ideas as to "man's place in the universe" and the fundamental ethical ideas. Secondly, law has the longest and most sophisticated tradition of thinking with respect to the embodiment of common values in practical social relations. Finally, much more recently than the others, the social sciences, with varying emphasis in different cases have been particularly important in the diagnosis of the situation of society, the meanings of various phases of its history and of tendencies to change.[11]

Of course definitions of the situation on all of these levels are by no means in any simple sense a creation of the academic disciplines. They are far more deeply rooted in the institutional structure itself and in the related popular ideas and sentiments. But it is precisely one of the most important facts about modern Western society that to a very great extent the primary institutionalized bearers of its main cultural traditions and leaders of its thought are highly

---

[11] Specific cases of the relevance of these disciplines to the problems of "ideology" will be taken up in the second paper.

professionalized groups without whose role the distinctive characteristics of cultural traditions would be very greatly altered. Hence, short of a very profound revolution, any important changes must articulate with them, especially with the universities, and conversely through both obvious and obscure channels they undoubtedly exert an enormous influence on the functioning of the social system in this context. Furthermore, this field provides a particularly striking illustration of the working of automatic control mechanisms which are built into the institutional structure.

The academic structure would at the present time seem to be significant overwhelmingly in relation to definitions of the situation rather than to the direct control of attitudes, though the segregation is never anywhere nearly absolute. Historically, however, two great professional groups, the clergy and the law, have conspicuously combined these two functions in a sense somewhat comparable to the medical case, although in relation to very different social functions. In the case of the clergy this was far more conspicuously true than it is now in the time when the clergy had a far stronger position of leadership in the community as a whole. But even now it is undoubtedly of considerable importance. It is notable that in the critical situation in Europe in recent years where the government structure has come under the control of revolutionary elements, the clergy have tended to become leading symbolic spokesmen of the historic values of the society, as in the case of both Protestant and Catholic clergy in Germany who have made by far the most effective protests against the Nazi regime, and just recently, in France, the clerical protests against the deportation of Jews.

A particularly interesting feature of the role of the clergy lies in its transitional character between the medical case and others the influence of which is significant primarily on the social level. In his role as a personal adviser and spiritual guide to the parishioner the clergyman has long been known to perform functions which have at least an element of unconscious psychotherapy—most conspicuously of course in the Catholic confessional. But unlike the medical man he does it in a way which attempts directly to influence his parishioner to conformity with a system of values and religious ideas which define the situation for an organized social group as a whole if not the whole society. The medical man is using both the cultural tradition and the institutional patterning of his own role

—more or less consciously—to influence the patient in a direction established as a goal by common values. The clergyman, on the other hand, is directly seeking to bring—or keep—his parishioner in conformity with a normative tradition, both to get him to accept the definition of the situation current in his denomination and to have the proper attitudes.

In this connection it is highly significant that ever since a decisive point in the early history of Catholic Christianity the status of the religious professional has been defined as an "office." The sacramental authority of the priest did not inhere in any personal quality of his own, such as saintliness, but was derived from ordination. It was an "impersonal" authority resting on integration with a universalistically defined tradition. Moreover, it applied only within the sphere of religious affairs and did not extend into secular spheres; it was, that is, functionally specific. Although the Reformation brought about important changes in the organization of religion, it did not disturb this fundamental pattern.

It can be seen that this pattern of office with its segregation of the sphere of religious authority from the "personal" character and affairs of the incumbent has important similarities with the role of the physician. It is a role of a specific dignity and prestige so structured as to insulate its performer from personal involvement with those with whom he has to deal. It lends him this dignity by virtue of the legitimation of a universalistic social tradition which, however different in content from medical science, is still in many respects similar as a source of impersonal authority.

In more detail it would be extremely illuminating, if space permitted, to analyze the similarities in the ways in which the medical, the academic, and the clerical roles exert a steady discipline on the people to whom they are subjected. The church service, it may be suggested, exerts an important influence in this way. By the doctrinal content of sermons and scriptural readings it serves to stabilize the definition of the situation, while at the same time through the collective ritual observance in hymn-singing, prayer, and in other ways, it has an important influence on attitudes.[12] The im-

---

[12] See Durkheim, Emile, *Elementary Forms of the Religious Life;* The Free Press, Glencoe, Ill., 1947 (xi and 456 pp.), for what is probably the classic analysis of the social functions of religious ritual. Durkheim, by his concentration on primitive society seems to have neglected the importance of the definition of the situation. The analogy to psychotherapy, and the psychological mechanisms involved in the "integrating" influence of ritual would repay far more careful study than they have received.

portance of the minister or priest as the focal center of this system of social interaction is clear.

Both the service itself, and more broadly, it seems certain, the particular mode of definition of the clerical role, have an important bearing on the integrating functions of religion in society. In particular its form in Western Christianity has immense importance for the influence of the Western type of cultural tradition.

For two reasons a few brief words may now be said about certain aspects of the institutionalization of government, with special reference to the problem of attitudes. On the one hand, it is the primary focus, in certain fundamental respects, of the integration of the national social system as a whole, and is hence of key importance to any consideration of the state of the system. On the other hand, for the same reasons it provides the most important single strategic vantage point for implementing any deliberate policy of control.

The functional problem is particularly clear in this case, especially to certain modern trends of thinking about politics. The position of government in the social structure is such that it more or less inevitably becomes the principal focus of whatever more general struggle for power is going on in the society, almost regardless of the particular content of the interest or "cause" which any group promotes. This is true of any complex society, but in addition our particular form of democratic government would seem to accentuate the situation in that it formally structuralizes the conflict of interests into a struggle of "partisan" groups for "power," that is, control of the machinery of government, and, short of that, "influence," the ability to get governmental agencies to serve the interests[13] of their particular groups. Thus the "administration" always consists of the spokesmen of some combination of interests, and various branches of government, especially Congress, are very much open to pressure. Finally, the intrinsic pressure of interest groups is accentuated by a further factor. All structures or personalities with an institutionalized prestige status are to a prominent

---

[13] The essentials of this phenomenon are independent of the quality of motivation of the members and leaders of the group in question. For instance large elements of the backing of the prohibition movement may well have been singularly free from "self-interest" in the usual sense, overwhelmingly concerned with an application of pure religious ethics. The Anti-Saloon League was not on that account any less a "pressure" group.

degree symbols on which affects are projected or displaced which are generated in connection with other aspects of a person's life.[14] This phenomenon is particularly important in a complex, rapidly changing society where there is a great deal of personal insecurity. Its immediate effect is to accentuate the divisive tendencies of the formal recognition of partisanship. Prominent political leaders are not only supported or opposed realistically according to the effectiveness with which they promote or obstruct the interests and causes with which the citizen is identified. They are also unrealistically inflated into heroes or bogeymen as the case may be, and hence ideologically the opposition between conflicting partisan groups and their leaders tends to be defined as far deeper than it really is.

In view of all this it may seem remarkable that this system of government can function at all. The answer must clearly be that there is another side to the picture, that there are patterns with positively integrating functions. Informally there is much in the "democratic tradition" which has this significance. There is the acceptance of the results of an election as expressing the popular will and hence as being binding on the nation as a whole. Conversely there are the formal constitutional and informal restraints which prevent those in power from using their power too much in a partisan interest, or from promoting that interest by illegitimate means, such as abridging the constitutional freedoms of opponents.

There are also, besides the constitution itself, structures and patterns which embody and symbolize integrating functions for the nation as a whole. The Federal judiciary, especially the Supreme Court, is to a considerable extent kept out of partisan politics. Furthermore, elective officers, such as the president, have a double character. On the one hand the incumbent is a party leader with a partisan mandate. But on the other hand his *office* is institutionally representative of the nation as a whole and its common traditions. In many ways this integral character is emphasized. To take one

---

[14] The phenomena of transference illustrate this phenomenon in classic form in relation to the physician. The same thing, is pre-eminently true of universities which are everywhere the object of deeply ambivalent attitudes which are conspicuously unrealistic on both sides—the prominence of "town and gown" feeling and the ease with which charges of "radicalism" can be brought against academic institutions are illustrations of the negative aspect. A corresponding political example of projection of negative affect was the "hate Roosevelt" pattern so prominent in the business classes a few years ago—surely not simply an objective appraisal of the New Deal.

example, when Mr. Roosevelt made a radio address he was not introduced as *Mr.* or even *President Roosevelt,* certainly not as the Leader of the Democratic Party, but "Ladies and Gentlemen, the President of the United States" is the accepted formula. Similarly even in cases of the most bitter partisan hostility to the particular incumbent, a certain respect for the dignity of the office is generally clearly discernible.[15] The same can be said of many lesser offices of the government. In connection with many of its administrative agencies the element of partisanship is much less conspicuous. Even though originally established by partisan administrations, they have for all practical purposes come to be accepted by the public as a whole.

Perhaps the most conspicuous phenomenon in this whole field, which relates it to the cases already discussed, is the tendency to the *segregation* of the two aspects of the government structure. If this did not exist there would be danger that the whole structure would be drawn into the partisan struggle and there would be no adequate structure of symbols on which to form sentiments of common loyalty and integration. It is closely parallel to the impersonal components of the role of the physician on which "confidence" in him is focused, and to the academic and clerical roles as "representative" of an objectively impersonal cultural tradition.

These examples are perhaps sufficient to establish in a general way that control mechanisms, the operation of which is not a matter of the deliberate "policy" of any group, or even of their manifest functions, pervade the whole structure, and play an essential role in the functioning of the social system. In particular, in conformity with the character of its institutions and peculiar cultural tradition, society has evolved a complex of mechanisms of a particular sort centering in roles of high prestige characterized by universalism, functional specificity and affective neutrality. Medical practice represents one particular type of a much larger class of roles which is specialized in the direction of exerting a particular kind of influ-

---

[15] For example, at the time of the Harvard Tercentenary celebration some Harvard alumni of the bitterly anti-Roosevelt school would even go so far as to say the whole thing would be spoiled if "that man" were permitted to be present. But one very quickly also had occasion to hear the reaction, "After all, he *is* President of the United States," and for any academic institution to have the President, regardless of "who" he might be, as an alumnus and a guest could scarcely be treated as anything but an honor. On the same occasion a similar but for many perhaps an even more acute conflict arose over the official role of Governor James M. Curley.

ence upon persons. The others in different ways suggest how analogous modes of influence on the social structure might be exerted by deliberately working "along with" existing control mechanisms as conscious psychotherapy takes advantage of the patterning of the physician's role.

What has previously been called "propaganda" is essentially a technique which is capable of use in the service of any goal. From the point of view of the present paper, that of relevance to the state of integration of a social system, three kinds of propaganda may be differentiated according to their orientation to different goals. One type is "revolutionary" in that it is oriented to the "conversion" of people to a pattern of values and definition of the situation which is specifically in conflict with fundamental aspects of the existing basic institutional structure and its attendant values and definitions. The "propaganda" of a strictly otherworldly religious movement which wishes to wean its adherents from all emotional attachment to "worldly" things, including performance of the obligations of their institutionalized social roles, is revolutionary in the present sense just as much as is that of a social or political movement whose goal is revolutionary change in the social structure.

A second fundamental type of propaganda is the "disruptive." Its goal is not winning people over to an alternative set of values and definitions of the situation, but undermining their attachment to the existing institutional system as such. There is of course a disruptive aspect in any system of revolutionary propaganda, but the relatively pure disruptive type was developed on a grand scale in Nazi propaganda toward the democracies. There was relatively little attempt to convert Americans to Nazi values. It was rather an attempt to weaken them by playing systematically and deliberately on the elements of tension, conflict and lack of clear and confident orientation in their society. It tried to foment conflict, to undermine confidence in authority and leadership, to play upon latent feelings of anxiety and guilt so as generally to paralyze capacity for decision and action. Indeed this has, to a very considerable extent, come to be regarded as the type case of propaganda in general.

But the same basic insights are applicable in a very different orientation of policy, that of "reinforcement," of strengthening attachment to the basic institutional patterns and cultural traditions of the society and deliberately and systematically counteracting the

very important existing deviant tendencies.[16] Few would question
that this is the direction that propaganda should take in relation to
the internal situation since, in this great crisis, it is fundamentally
preservation of continuity with the great traditions and institutional
patterns of Western society which is at stake.

Shaping the basic orientation of propaganda policy as one of
reinforcement means not only in the most general sense directing it
to support of the sentiments and definitions of the situation which
connect Americans with the continuity of their institutional and
cultural heritage. It must take account of certain particular features
of that heritage which are essential to its connection with the kind
of social control mechanisms which have previously been discussed.

The findings of sociology and anthropology with respect to the
importance of cultural relativity are such that any proposition with
respect to the more universal significance of the institutionalized
patterns of any particular social system should be put forward with
great caution. Yet it is highly probable that the findings of modern
psychology with respect to what constitutes psychological "maturity"
will not come to be completely relativized as applicable only to this
society. This is particularly true of what psychoanalysts have called
the "reality principle," a maximization of which is a principal criterion of strong "ego development," and what may be called
"affective reciprocity," the ability affectively to take account of the

---

[16] Perhaps two principal objections will be raised to a deliberate propaganda
policy of the "reinforcement" type directed toward the home front. One is that
such a policy would tend to freeze the *status quo* and perpetuate the evils of the
existing social order. One's attitude on this question will depend on the degree
of radicalism with which he interprets those evils. If it is sufficiently great, if
society is to him fundamentally corrupt, the only acceptable propaganda policy
will be a frankly revolutionary one. But general support of a reinforcement program does not commit one to freezing the *stats quo*. On the contrary, by contrast with the fascist alternative, all the main potentialities of reform in society,
of a more "democratic" way of life, are bound up with the maintenance of a basic
continuity with the fundamentals of Western institutional and cultural tradition.

The other objection is that propaganda, "fooling" and "working on" people
is incompatible with our basic values—the public must be taken fully into government's confidence and treated as responsible adults. This view is largely a
compound of utopianism and rationalistic bias. In a certain sense by the same
token medical practice should be abolished since it is incompatible with the
human dignity of a sick person to submit to being helped by someone more competent than himself—or the teaching function should be completely de-institu-
tionalized to permit students to "stand on their own feet." Realistically the
alternatives are not "paternalism" *versus* complete independence of all persons,
but a conscientious exercise of power in fiduciary terms in conformity with the
basic patterns of the society or abuse of power in some direction. Deliberate
"propaganda" is only an extension of the general use of the power of government.
It is not whether it should be used but *how* which is the problem for serious discussion. Unconscious propaganda influence on a considerable scale is in any
case inevitable.

feelings of others and not to define situations in a grossly "one-sided" manner. Certainly the high incidence of science and rational techniques in a society tend to indicate a peculiarly high development of the "reality principle" in one direction. Hence its predominance may be said to transcend the element common to all social structures, realistic adaptation to the existing institutionalized structure, whatever it may be. But the elements of universalism and functional specificity found in all of the cases previously analyzed are all cases of a specifically high degree of institutionalization of pattern elements which play a fundamental role in encouraging reactions of emotional maturity.

Whatever there may be of any more generalized significance in the institutionalization of these patterns, there can be no doubt that reinforcement of them is fundamental to the cultivation of maturity in our society—psychotherapy which consisted in "conversion" of the person to drastically otherworldly cults would, however much it solved his practical problems, be something drastically different from that of modern medicine. It is, conversely, clear that the psychology of most movements which tend to a drastic break with this same institutional heritage, especially perhaps those of the fascist type, is one which exploits precisely the opposite elements of character structure, those most closely bound up with "neurotic" types of reaction pattern, ideological distortion and affective over-reaction.

It is the principal thesis of this paper that the structure of Western society in its relation to the functions of social control provides an extraordinary opening for the deliberate propaganda of reinforcement as an agency of control. Just as deliberate psychotherapy in the medical relationship is in a sense simply an extension of functional elements inherent in the structure of the role of physician, so, on the social level, the propaganda of reinforcement would be simply an extension of many of the automatic but latent functions of existing institutional patterns.

Indeed, as a result of the above analysis it can safely be said that consideration of the role of the propaganda agency as analogous to that of the psychotherapist is more than a mere analogy. Social control in the sense of this discussion is after all in the last analysis a process of influencing, through psychological mechanisms, first the behavior, more deeply, through the process of socialization especially, the character structure of humans. In its non-deliberate functional significance the institution of medical practice is an integral part of a far more generalized institutional structure and system of social control. The fundamental orientations inherent in its patterning, especially the role of the reality principle and psychological maturity form an aspect, an "application" in one context, of configurational principles common to the institutional structure as a whole. With proper precautions for taking account of the difference of level, to treat propaganda policy as a kind of "social psychotherapy" is to act directly in accordance with the essential nature of this social system.

The first maxim is that, quite apart from what it deliberately does in dealing with particular tendencies to deviance which arise, the agency or agencies should assume a role as closely analogous to that of physician as is possible in the circumstances. Specifically it should so far as possible identify itself with those elements of the institutional patterning of government and other structures in the society which are symbolic of the integration of the society as a whole. In relation to government this means above all that it should avoid involvement in any of the internal struggles for power of partisan groups; both in its constitution and publicly conspicuous personnel it should be as close as possible to the ideal of an impartial judiciary.

It should also take advantage of other formally institutionalized elements in the society which fit into the same general type of pattern, perhaps especially the academic and the religious, although on account of the element of ambivalence in public attitudes to academic persons and institutions here great caution is called for— it would be unfortunate to allow a symbol like that of the early New Deal "brain trust" to become current.

Also more informally it is essential to establish a position of impersonal authority. This, in the medical case, involves primarily two elements, technical competence and moral integrity in relation to the fundamental goals of medical practice. Since there is as yet in society no professional group which has come to be defined to the public in general as possessing technical competence in "social psychiatry"—perhaps someday some of the social sciences will achieve this—the next best seems to be the deliberate cultivation of a reputation for scrupulously truthful reporting of information, the sources of which the public cannot have direct access to. Information is of great intrinsic importance in itself. But what is involved here is its indirect importance, as establishing the authority of the propaganda agency, and a disposition to turn to it for "help" in matters where a person is necessarily incompetent. Exercising judgment as to whether or not information needs to be withheld for military reasons is by no means incompatible with effective use of this possibility.

The analogy to the moral integrity of the physician is somewhat more complex. It is true the physician avoids expressing moral judgments of much of his patient's conduct and this is one primary source of his ability to "get at" his patient. But he does not assume a morally nihilistic attitude. Above all in relation to the definition of his own role certain moral fundamentals are taken for granted, especially his obligation to do his best for the patient and conversely the patient's obligation to give him full "cooperation," including complete truthfulness in relevant subjects. More broadly this pattern implicity assumes agreement on certain moral fundamentals of our institutionalized patterns, especially those involved in the acceptance of "mature adjustment" as a goal of therapy. Similarly a propaganda agency can quite self-consciously take for granted what are in the first instance moral fundamentals about its own role, its fiduciary position on behalf of the national welfare and its moral integrity in fulfilling its obligations. Implicitly this would carry with it acceptance of the fundamental orientation of national policy toward the war, above all, and acceptance of the principal fundamentals of the historic institutionalized values and cultural tradition.

It can probably be said with confidence that it is generally best not to "argue" these things explicitly, but rather to take them for granted. This is not, however, to evade the moral questions involved. Rather, when occasion arises, it is quite legitimate to react strongly in the assertion of the relevant values. Generally speaking a good physician does not permit a patient to "get away" with a challenge to his moral integrity. He has no hesitation in reacting strongly.

A few words may be said about the technique of handling particular problems once the requisite generalized role has been established. Above all such an agency would not be an organ of "instruction" of the public in the ordinary rationalistic sense. Its function especially would *not* be to "refute" undesirable opinions and definitions of the situation. Its main function would rather be to keep the central definitions of the situations and symbols continually, but not too obtrusively, before the public. Just how it should be worked out in detail is a very complicated and technical subject.

Whether and in what circumstances and ways it should emulate the deliberate psychotherapist by, at strategic moments, offering "interpretations" of "pathological" behavior, is a most interesting question, but surely not one to be settled without much analysis and experience.

Finally, it should be clear that one main index of whether or not such an agency were effectively performing its functions would be that it would become the object of "transferences," of the projection of affects which were not appropriate to what it had actually done, both positive and negative. This should provide positive opportunities for extending its usefulness.

The intention of this last discussion has not been to work out a blueprint of a propaganda agency, or to deliver or imply any judgment on the adequacy of existing agencies of our government.[17] It has been possible only to draw certain broad implications from the very general analysis of the problem which has occupied the main part of the paper. In relation to practical policy, the most it can do is to point a general direction.

As in all such cases, getting closer to detailed practical policy would involve further analysis of the particular problems that have to be faced. A psychiatrist does not deal with neuroses in general, but with a particular patient with particular problems. It is proposed in a subsequent article to analyze certain salient features of the contemporary American social system in so far as they bear upon the problem of possible deliberate control by propaganda methods. This will raise the questions of what are the principal deviant tendencies in this situation, how are they rooted in the conflicts, strains, and malfunctioning of the social system, and in what ways and how far are they accessible to control by this kind of technique.

---

[17] It should be clear that, consciously or unconsciously, a good many of these functions have in fact been to a considerable extent performed by government agencies, most conspicuously by the presidency. Surely one of the main bases for referring to Mr. Roosevelt as an exceptionally good "politician" has been his ability to assume this type of role. Above all he must be conscious of often having been the object of "negative transference" and it would seem, has on the whole acted in the proper way to deal with such phenomena. An analysis of his public reactions to the various waves of public opinion toward the war from the fall of France to Pearl Harbor would be extremely illuminating. One of the most interesting phases is that of the timing as well as the content of major speeches, which are, in a sense, analogous to the interpretations of a psychoanalyst. Perhaps one of the most important things for a very high executive to learn is not to speak publicly too much, too often, or at the wrong times.

IX

The Kinship System of the Contemporary United States

IT IS A REMARKABLE fact that, in spite of the important interrelations between sociology and social anthropology, no attempt to describe and analyze the kinship system of the United States in the structural terms current in the literature of anthropological field studies exists. This is probably mainly accounted for by two facts; on the sociological side, family studies have overwhelmingly been oriented to problems of individual adjustment rather than comparative structural perspective; while from the anthropological side, a barrier has grown out of the fact that a major structural aspect of a large-scale society cannot be observed in a single program of field research. To a considerable extent the material must come from the kind of common sense and general experience which have been widely held to be of dubious scientific standing.

There are two particularly cogent reasons why an attempt to fill this gap is highly desirable. In the first place, an understanding of the kinship system on precisely this structural level is of the greatest importance to the understanding of the American family, its place in the more general social structure, and the strains and psychological patterning to which it is subject.[1] Secondly, our kinship system is of a structural type which is of extraordinary interest

[1] Probably the most significant contribution to this field thus far has been made by Kingsley Davis in a series of articles starting with his "Structural Analysis of Kinship" (*America Anthropologist*, April, 1937), in collaboration with W. Lloyd Warner, and going on to "Jealousy and Sexual Property" (*Social Forces*, March, 1936), "The Sociology of Prostitution" (*American Sociological Review*, October, 1937), "The Child and the Social Structure" (*Journal of Educational Sociology*, December, 1940), "The Sociology of Parent-Youth Conflict" (*American Sociological Review*, August, 1940.)

I am greatly indebted to Dr. Davis's work, starting with the significance of his first article, for the systematic relating of the biological and the social levels of kinship structure. Much of the present analysis is implicit in his later articles, which have proved to be very suggestive in working out the somewhat more explicit formulations of the present study.

in relation to the broader problems of typology and systematic functional dynamics of kinship generally. As a type which, to the writer's knowledge, is not closely approached in any known non-literate society, its incorporation in the range dealt with by students of kinship should significantly enrich their comparative perspective.[2]

It can perhaps be regarded as established that, with proper precautions, analysis of kinship terminology can serve as a highly useful approach to the study of the functioning social structure. In the case of the English language two precautions in particular, over and above those commonly observed, need to be explicitly mentioned. Such analysis alone cannot serve to bring out what is distinctively American because the terminology has been essentially stable since before the settlement of America, and today there is no significant terminological difference between England and the United States. Moreover, the differences in this respect between English and the other modern European languages are minor. Hence all analysis of terminology can do is indicate a very broad type within which the more distinctively American system falls.

As shown in the accompanying diagram[3] the American family is perhaps best characterized as an "open, multilineal, conjugal system."

The conjugal family unit of parents and children is one of basic significance in any kinship system. What is distinctive about our system is the absence of any important terminologically recognized

---

[2] It is proposed in a later article to enter into certain of these comparative problems of kinship structure in an attempt to arrive at a higher level of dynamic generalization about kinship than has yet come to be current in the sociological or even the anthropological literature.

[3] The diagramming conventions adopted in this paper [see note in second paragraph, above] are somewhat different from those commonly used by anthropologists. They are imposed by the peculiar structural features of our system, especially—

a) Its "openness," i.e., absence of preferential mating. Hence the two spouses of any given conjugal family are not structurally related by family of orientation and it is not possible to portray "the" system in terms of a limited number of lines of descent. Each marriage links ego's kinship system to a complete system.

b) The consequent indefinite "dispersion" of the lines of descent.

The best that can be done in two dimensions is to take *ego* as a point of reference and show *his* significant kin. It is strictly impossible to diagram the system as a whole—that would require a space of n-dimensions. Similarly, "vertical" and "horizontal" or "lateral" "axes" have only a very limited meaning. "Lines of descent" and "generations" are significant. But there is a geometrically progressive increase in the number of lines of descent with each generation away from ego and the distinctions cannot be made in terms of a linear continuum. I am indebted to Miss Ai-li Sung of Radcliffe College for assistance in drafting the diagram.

Figure 1
The American Kinship System

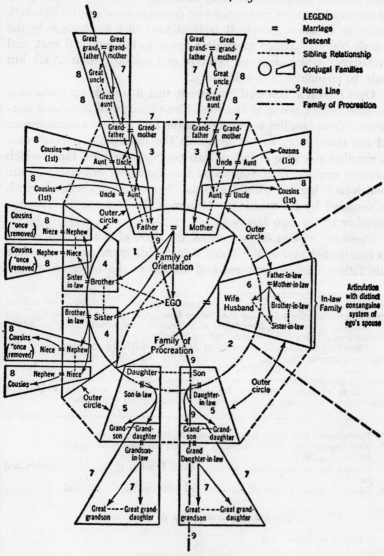

LEGEND

= Marriage

→ Descent

---→ Sibling Relationship

○ ◁ Conjugal Families

⁹ Name Line

—·—· Family of Procreation

Types of Families:

1. Ego's family of orientation (1 only)
2. Ego's family of procreation (1 only)
3. First-degree ascendant families (2)

(continued on foot of page 180)

units which cut across conjugal families, including some members and excluding others. The only instances of such units are *pairs* of conjugal families each with *one* common number. Terminologically, in common speech, it is significant that we have only the words "family," which generally[4] refers to the conjugal unit, and "relatives," which does not refer to *any* solidarity unit at all, but only to anyone who is a kinsman.

Ours then is a "conjugal"[5] system in that it is made up *exclusively* of interlocking conjugal families. The principle of structural relation of these families is founded on the fact that, as a consequence of the incest tabu, *ego* is always in the structurally normal[6] case a member not of one but of two conjugal families, those which Warner usefully distinguishes as the "family of orientation," into which he is born as a child, and the "family of procreation," which is founded by his marriage. Moreover, he is the *only*[7] common member of the two families.

From *ego's* point of view, then, the core, of the kinship system is constituted by families *1* and *2* in the diagram, in the one case his father, mother, brothers and sisters, in the other his spouse

---

[4] The most important exception is its usage in upper class circles to denote what Warner calls a "lineage," i.e., a group possessing continuity over several generations, usually following the "name line," e.g., the "Adams family." See W. L. Warner and Lunt, *Social Life of a Modern Community*. The significance of this exception will be commented upon below.

[5] See Ralph Linton, *The Study of Man*, Ch. VIII, for the very useful distinction between "conjugal" and "consanguine" kinship types.

[6] Excluding, af course, those who do not marry. But failure to marry has no positive structural consequences in relation to kinship—only negative.

[7] It is of course possible for two pairs—or even more—of siblings to intermarry. This case is, however, without structural significance.

---

4. First-degree collateral families (number indefinite, 2 types)
5. First-degree descendant families (number indefinite, 2 types)
6. In-law family (1 only)
7. Second-degree ascendant and descendant families (4 ascendant, descendant indefinite, 4 types)
8. Second-degree collateral families (all children ego's cousins)

Structural Groupings of Families:

I. 1 + 2 — Inner circle
II. 3, 4, 5 + 6 — Outer circle
III. 1, 2, 3, 5, 7 — Families in line of descent
IV. 4, 8 — Collateral families
V. 2, 6 — Articulation of consanguine systems

No difference according to sex of ego, except in the term for spouse and the fact that, if ego is female, name line does not extend below ego in line of descent.

(wife or husband according to *ego's* sex), sons and daughters. Monogamy is reflected in the fact that *parent* and *other parent's spouse* are terminologically identical, modified only by the prefix "step" to take account of second or later marriages, and in the fact that the terms "father" and "mother," "husband" and "wife" can each apply to only *one* person at a time. It is also notable that no distinction on the basis of birth order is made—all brothers are terminologically alike. But most notable of all is the fact that *none* of these seven kinship personalities is terminologically identified with *any* relative outside the particular conjugal family in which he is placed. A brother is specifically distinguished from any male cousin, the father from any uncle, the mother from any aunt, etc. These two conjugal families may conveniently be treated as constituting the 'inner circle" of the kinship structure. Relative priorities within them will be discussed below.

Now *each* member of *ego's* inner kinship circle is the connecting link with one other terminologically recognized conjugal family. Moreover he links the family of orientation or procreation, as the case may be, with *only* one farther conjugal family, and each individual with a separate one. The kinship personalities of this "outer circle" are not, however, always terminologically separate, a fact which will be shown to be of paramount importance.

The first pair of outer circle families, which may be called the "first ascendant," are the families of orientation of *ego's* parents. Besides the articulating personality, each consists of the four kinship personalities of grandfather, grandmother, uncle, and aunt. The most significant fact is the lack of terminological distinction between the paternal and the maternal families of orientation—grandparents, uncles and aunts are alike regardless of which "side" they are on. The only important exception to this lies, not in kinship terminology as such but in the patrilineal inheritance of the family name, giving rise to a unilateral "name line" (9). Since the same principle of lack of distinction by sex of intervening relative applies to still higher ascendant generations—the four great-and eight great-great-grandfathers—it is perhaps more accurate to speak of a "multilineal" than a "bilateral" system. Anyone of an indefinite number of lines of descent *may* be treated as significant. Above all, the extension from the principle of *bi*laterality, as applied to the first ascendant (and descendant) families, to that of *multi*lineality in succeeding generations is completely incompatible with any tendency to *bifurcate* the kin group on the basis of lines of descent.

The same fundamental principles govern the terminology of the first collateral families (4), the families of procreation of *ego's* siblings; and the first descendant families (5), the families of procreation of his children. It is noteworthy that siblings' spouses are terminologically assimilated to sibling status with the suffix "in-law"—generally not used in address or the more intimate occasions of reference—and that nephews and nieces are the same whether they are brothers' or sisters' children and regardless of the sex of *ego*. Similarly spouses of children are assimilated to the status of children by the same terminological device and sons' and daughters' children are all indiscriminately grandchildren. Finally, both siblings-in-law and children-in-law are terminologically segregated from *any* kinship status relative to *ego* except that in the particular conjugal family which is under consideration.

The last outer circle family, the "in-law" family (6), has a very particular significance. It is the only one of those to which *ego's* inner circle is linked to which he is not bound by descent and consanguinity but only by affinity, and this fact is a paramount importance, signalizing as it does the openness of our system. Preferential mating on a kinship basis, that is, is completely without structural significance, and every marriage in founding a new conjugal family brings together (in the type case) two completely unrelated kinship groups which are articulated on a kinship basis *only* in this one particular marriage. Seen from a somewhat more generalized point of view, if we take the total inner and outer circle group of *ego's* kin as a "system," it is articulated to another entirely distinct system of the same structure by *every* peripheral relative (i.e., who is not a connecting link between the inner and outer circles), except in the direct lines of descent. The consequence is a maximum of dispersion of the lines of descent and the prevention of the structuring of kinship groups on any other principle than the "onion" principle, which implies proportionately increasing "distantness" with each "circle" of linked conjugal families.[8]

Another way of throwing the significance of this basic open-multi-lineal structure into relief is to recall the fact that *ego's* family of orientation and his in-law family are, from the point of view of his

---

[8] In any finite population, lines of descent are bound to cross somewhere, and in our society the marriage of fairly close relatives is not infrequent. But there is no consistent pattern in this intermarriage, and it is hence without structural consequences.

Most of the essentials of an open conjugal system can be maintained, while a high level of generation continuity in at least one line is also main-

children, both first ascendant families whose members are equally grandparents, aunts and uncles.

In principle it is possible to distinguish, beyond the outer circle, further layers of the "onion" indefinitely. It is, however, significant that our kinship terminology ceases at this point to apply at all specific terms, fundamentally recognizing only two elements. First is the line of descent (8) designated by the ascendant and descendant family terms with the addition of the reduplicating prefix "great" —e.g., great-grandfather and great-grandson. Second is the indiscriminate category "cousins" into which all "collaterals" are thrown, with only the descriptive[9] devices of "first," "third," "once removed," etc., to distinguish them by.

How far can this distinctive terminology be said to "reflect" the actual institutional structure of kinship? In a broad way it certainly does. We clearly have none of the "extended" kin groupings so prevalent among non-literate peoples, such as patrilineal or matrilineal clans. We have no exogamy except that based on "degree" of relationship. We have no preferential mating—all these are a matter of the simplest common knowledge. But to get a clearer conception of the more specific structure it is essential to turn to a different order of evidence.

In the first place, the importance of the isolated conjugal family is brought out by the fact that it is the normal "household" unit. This means it is the unit of residence and the unit whose members as a matter of course pool a common basis of economic support, especially with us, money income. Moreover, in the typical case neither the household arrangements nor the source of income bear any specific relation to the family of orientation of either spouse, or, if there is any, it is about as likely to be to the one as to the other. But the typical conjugal family lives in a home segregated from those of both pairs of parents (if living) and is economically

---

tained, by a systematic discrimination between lines of descent—especially through primogeniture. The extent to which this has and has not occurred is the most important range of variation within the basic pattern and will have to be discussed in some detail below.

[9] It should perhaps be explicitly stated that though sometimes called a "descriptive" system by some of the older anthropologists, our terminology is by no means literally descriptive of exact biological relationships. Above all it fails to distinguish relatives whose relation to *ego* is traced through different lines of descent. But it also fails to distinguish by birth order, or to distinguish siblings' spouses from spouses' siblings—both are brothers- or sisters-in-law. Finally, as just noted, it stops making distinctions very soon, treating all collaterals as "cousins."

independent of both. In a very large proportion of cases the geographical separation is considerable. Furthermore, the primary basis of economic support and of many other elements of social status lies typically in the husband's occupational status, his "job," which he typically holds independently of any particularistic relation to kinsmen.

The isolation of the conjugal unit in this country is in strong contrast to much of the historic structure of European society where a much larger and more important element have inherited home, source of economic support, and specific occupational status (especially a farm or family enterprise) from their fathers. This of course has had to involve discrimination between siblings since the whole complex of property and status had to be inherited intact.[10]

Hence considerable significance attaches to our patterns of inheritance of property. Here the important thing is the absence of any specific favoring of any particular line of descent. Formally, subject to protection of the interests of widows, complete testamentary freedom exists. The American law of intestacy, however, in specific contrast to the older English Common Law tradition, gives all children, regardless of birth order or sex, equal shares. But even more important, the actual practice of wills overwhelmingly conforms to this pattern. Where deviations exist they are not bound up with the kinship structure as such but are determined by particular relationships or situations of need. There is also noticeable in our society a relative weakness of pressure to leave all or even most property to kin.[11]

It is probably safe to assume that an essentially open system, with a primary stress on the conjugal family and corresponding absence of groupings of collaterals cutting across conjugal families, has existed in Western society since the period when the kinship terminology of the European languages took shape. The above evidence, however, is sufficient to show that within this broad type the American system has, by contrast with its European forbears, developed far in the direction of a *symmetrically multilineal type*. This relative absence of any structural bias in favor of solidarity with the ascendant and descendant families in any one line of descent has

---

[10] Though perhaps the commonest pattern, primogeniture has by no means been universal. Cf. Arensberg and Kimball, *Family and Society in Ireland*, and G. C. Homans, *English Villagers of the 13th Century*.

[11] Indeed a wealthy man who completely neglected philanthropies in his will would be criticized.

enormously increased the structural isolation of the individual conjugal family. This isolation, the almost symmetrical "onion" structure, is the most distinctive feature of the American kinship system and underlies most of its peculiar functional and dynamic problems.

Before entering into a few of these, it should be made clear that the incidence of the fully developed type in the American social structure is uneven and important tendencies to deviation from it are found in certain structural areas. In the first place, in spite of the extent to which American agriculture has become "commercialized," the economic and social conditions of rural life place more of a premium on continuity of occupation and status from generation to generation than do urban conditions, and hence, especially perhaps among the more solidly established rural population, something approaching Le Play's *famille souche* is not unusual.

Secondly, there are important upper class elements in this country for which elite status is closely bound up with the status of ancestry, hence the continuity of kinship solidarity in a—mainly patrilineal— line of descent, in "lineages."[12] Therefore in these "family elite" elements the symmetry of the multilineal kinship structure is sharply skewed in the direction of a patrilineal system with a tendency to primogeniture—one in many respects resembling that historically prevalent among European aristocracies, though considerably looser. There is a tendency for this in turn to be bound up with family property, especially an ancestral home, and continuity of status in a particular local community.

Finally, third, there is evidence that in lower class situations, in different ways both rural and urban, there is another type of deviance from this main kinship pattern. This type is connected with a strong tendency to instability of marriage and a "mother-centered" type of family structure—found both in Negro and white population elements.[13] It would not disturb the multilineal symmetry of the

---

[12] Cf. Warner and Lunt, *op. cit.*, and A Davis and Gardner, *Deep South*:

[13] Cf. Davis and Gardner, *op. cit.*, Ch. VI, E. Franklin Frazier, *The Negro Family in the United States*, and Lynd, *Middletown in Transition*. Mrs. Florence Kluckhohn of Wellesley College has called my attention to a fourth deviant type which she calls the "suburban matriarchy." In certain suburban areas, especially with upper-middle class population, the husband and father is out of the home a very large proportion of the time. He tends to leave by far the greater part of responsibility for children to his wife and also either not to participate in the affairs of the local community at all or only at the instance of his wife. This would apply to informal social relationships where both entertaining and acceptances of invitations are primarily arranged by the wife or on her initiative.

system but would favor a very different type of conjugal family, even if it tended to be as nearly isolated as the main type from other kinship groups. This situation has not, however, been at all adequately studied from a functional point of view.

Thus what is here treated as the focal American type of kinship structure is most conspicuously developed in the urban middle class areas of the society. This fact is strong evidence of the interdependence of kinship structure with other structural aspects of the same society, some of which will be briefly discussed below.

In approaching the functional analysis of the central American kinship type, the focal point of departure must lie in the crucial fact that *ego* is a member not of one but of two conjugal families. This fact is of course of central significance in all kinship systems, but in our own it acquires a special importance because of the structural prominence of the conjugal family and its peculiar isolation. In most kinship systems many persons retain throughout the life cycle a fundamentally stable—though changing—status in one or more extended kinship units.[14] In our system this is not the case for anyone.

The most immediate consequences lie in the structural significance of the marriage relationship, especially in relation to the lines of descent and to the sibling tie. *Ego*, by marriage, that is, is by comparison with other kinship systems drastically segregated from his family of orientation, both from his parents—and their forbears —and from his siblings. His first kinship loyalty is unequivocally to his spouse and then to their children if and when any are born. Moreover, his family of procreation, by virtue of a common household, income, and community status, becomes a solidarity unit in the sense in which the segregation of the interests of individuals is relatively meaningless, whereas the segregation of these interests of *ego* from those of the family of orientation tends relatively to minimize solidarity with the latter.

The strong emphasis for *ego* as an adult on the marriage relationship at the expense of those to parents and siblings is directly correlative with the symmetrical multilineality of the system. From the point of view of the marriage pair, that is, neither family of orientation, particularly neither parental couple, has structurally sanctioned priority of status. It is thus in a sense a balance of

---

[14] This is conspicuously true, for example, in a unilateral clan system, of the members of the sex group on which the continuity of the clan rests. The situation of the other, the "out-marrying," sex, is, on the other hand, quite different.

power situation in which independence of the family of procreation is favored by the necessity of maintaining impartiality as between the two families of orientation.[15]

From this it seems legitimate to conclude that in a peculiar sense which is not equally applicable to other systems the marriage bond is, in our society, the main structural keystone of the kinship system. This results from the structural isolation of the conjugal family and the fact that the married couple are not supported by comparably strong kinship ties to other adults. Closely related to this situation is that of choice of marriage partner. It is not only an open system in that there is no preferential mating on a kinship basis, but since the new marriage is not typically "incorporated" into an already existing kinship unit, the primary structural reasons for an important influence on marriage choice being exerted by the kin of the prospective partners are missing or at least minimized.

It is true that something approaching a system of "arranged" marriages does persist in some situations, especially where couples brought up in the same local community marry and expect to settle down there—or where there are other particularistic elements present as in cases of "marrying the boss's daughter." Our open system, however, tends very strongly to a pattern of purely personal choice of marriage partner without important parental influence. With increasing social mobility, residential, occupational and other, it has clearly become the dominant pattern. Though not positively required by the kinship structure, freedom of choice is not impeded by it, and the structure is probably, in various ways, connected with the motivation of this freedom, an important aspect of the "romantic love" complex.

A closely related functional problem touches the character of the marriage relationship itself. Social systems in which a considerable number of individuals are in a complex and delicate state of mutual interdependence tend greatly to limit the scope of "personal" emotional feeling or, at least, its direct expression in action. Any considerable range of affective spontaneity would tend to impinge on

---

[15] See Simmel's well-known essay on the significance of number in social relationships. (*Soziologie*, Ch. II). This is an illuminating case of the triadic" group. It is not, however, institutionally that of *tertius gaudens* since that implies one "playing off the other two against each other," though informally it may sometimes approach that. Institutionally, however, what is most important is the requirement of impartiality between the two families of orientation. Essentially the same considerations apply as between an older couple and two or more of their married children's families of procreation—impartiality irrespective of sex or birth order is expected.

the statuses and interests of too many others, with disequilibrating consequences for the system as a whole. This need to limit affective spontaneity is fundamentally why arranged marriages tend to be found in kinship systems where the newly married couple is incorporated into a larger kin group, but it also strongly colors the character of the marriage relationship itself, tending to place the primary institutional sanctions upon matters of objective status and obligations to other kin, not on subjective sentiment.[16] Thus the structural isolation of the conjugal family tends to free the affective inclinations of the couple from a whole series of hampering restrictions.

These restrictive forces, which in other kinship systems inhibit affective expression, have, however, positive functional significance in maintaining the solidarity of the effective kinship unit. Very definite expectations in the definition of role, combined with a complex system of interrelated sanctions, both positive and negative, go far to guarantee stability and the maintenance of standards of performance. In the American kinship system this kind of institutionalized support of the role of marriage partner through its interlocking with other kinship roles is, if not entirely lacking, at least very much weaker. A functionally equivalent substitute in motivation to conformity with the expectations of the role is clearly needed. It may hence be suggested that the *institutional* sanction placed on the proper subjective sentiments of spouses, in short the expectation that they have an obligation to be "in love," has this significance. This in turn is related to personal choice of marriage partner, since affective devotion is, particularly in our culture, linked to a presumption of the absence of any element of coercion. This would seem to be a second important basis of the prominence of the "romantic complex."

Much evidence has accumulated to show that conformity with the expectations of socially structured roles is not to be taken as a matter of course, but that often there are typically structured sources of psychological strain which underlie socially structured mani-

---

[16] This tendency for multiple-membered social systems to repress spontaneous manifestations of sentiment should not be taken too absolutely. In such phenomena as cliques, there is room for the following of personal inclinations within the framework of institutionalized statuses. It is, however, probable that it is more restrictive in groups where, as in kinship, the institutionalized relationships are particularistic and functionally diffuse than in universalistic and functionally specific systems such as modern occupational organizations. In the latter case personal affective relationships can, within considerable limits, be institutionally ignored as belonging to the sphere of "private affairs."

festations of the kind which Kardiner has called "secondary institutions."[17]

Much psychological research has suggested the very great importance to the individual of his affective ties, established in early childhood, to other members of his family of orientation. When strong affective ties have been formed, it seems reasonable to believe that situational pressures which force their drastic modification will impose important strains upon the individual.

Since all known kinship systems impose an incest tabu, the transition from asexual intrafamilial relationships to the sexual relation of marriage—generally to a previously relatively unknown person —is general. But with us this transition is accompanied by a process of "emancipation" from the ties both to parents and to siblings, which is considerably more drastic than in most kinship systems, especially in that it applies to both sexes about equally, and includes emancipation from solidarity with *all* members of the family of orientation about equally, so that there is relatively little continuity with *any* kinship ties established by birth for anyone.

The effect of these factors is reinforced by two others. Since the effective kinship unit is normally the small conjugal family, the child's emotional attachments to kin are confined to relatively few persons instead of being distributed more widely. Especially important, perhaps, is the fact that no other adult woman has a role remotely similar to that of the mother. Hence the average intensity of affective involvement in family relations is likely to be high. Secondly, the child's relations outside the family are only to a small extent ascribed. Both in the play group and in the school he must to a large extent "find his own level" in competition with others. Hence the psychological significance of his security within the family is heightened.

We have then a situation where at the same time the inevitable importance of family ties is intensified and a necessity to become emancipated from them is imposed. This situation would seem to have a good deal to do with the fact that with us adolescence—and beyond—is, as has been frequently noted, a "difficult" period in the life cycle.[18] In particular, associated with this situation is the prominence in our society of what has been called a "youth culture," a distinctive pattern of values and attitudes of the age groups

---

[17] See Abraham Kardiner, *The Individual and His Society*.

[18] Cf. the various writings of Margaret Mead, especially her *Coming of Age in Samoa* and *Sex and Temperament*.

between childhood and the assumption of full adult responsibilities. This youth culture, with its irresponsibility, its pleasure-seeking, its "rating and dating," and its intensification of the romantic love pattern, is not a simple matter of "apprenticeship" in adult values and responsibilities. It bears many of the marks of reaction to emotional tension and insecurity, and in all probability has among its functions that of easing the difficult process of adjustment from childhood emotional dependency to full "maturity."[19] In it we find still a third element underlying the prominence of the romantic love complex in American society.

The emphasis which has here been placed on the multilineal symmetry of our kinship structure might be taken to imply that our society was characterized by a correspondingly striking assimilation of the roles of the sexes to each other. It is true that American society manifests a high level of the "emancipation" of women, which in important respects involves relative assimilation to masculine roles, in accessibility to occupational opportunity, in legal rights relative to property holding, and in various other respects. Undoubtedly the kinship system constitutes one of the important sets of factors underlying this emancipation since it does not, as do so many kinship systems, place a structural premium on the role of either sex in the maintenance of the continuity of kinship relations.

But the elements of sex-role assimilation in our society are conspicuously combined with elements of segregation which in many respects are even more striking than in other societies, as for instance in the matter of the much greater attention given by women to style and refinement of taste in dress and personal appearance. This and other aspects of segregation are connected with the structure of kinship, but not so much by itself as in its interrelations with the occupational system.

The members of the conjugal family in our urban society normally share a common basis of economic support in the form of money income, but this income is not derived from the co-operative efforts of the family as a unit—its principal source lies in the remuneration of occupational roles performed by individual members of the family. Status in an occupational role is generally, however, specifically segregated from kinship status—a person holds a "job" as an individual, not by virtue of his status in a family.

---

[19] Cf. N. J. Demerath, *Schizophrenia and the Sociology of Adolescence.* Dissertation, Harvard University, 1942, (unpub.)

Among the occupational statuses of members of a family, if there is more than one, much the most important is that of the husband and father, not only because it is usually the primary source of family income, but also because it is the most important single basis of the status of the family in the community at large. To be the main "breadwinner" of his family is a primary role of the normal adult man in our society. The corollary of this role is his far smaller participation than that of his wife in the internal affairs of the household. Consequently, "housekeeping" and the care of children is still the primary functional content of the adult feminine role in the "utilitarian" division of labor. Even if the married woman has a job, it is, at least in the middle classes, in the great majority of cases not one which in status or remuneration competes closely with those held by men of her own class. Hence there is a typically asymmetrical relation of the marriage pair to the occupational structure.

This asymmetrical relation apparently both has exceedingly important positive functional significance and is at the same time an important source of strain in relation to the patterning of sex roles.[20]

On the positive functional side, a high incidence of certain types of patterns is essential to our occupational system and to the institutional complex in such fields as property and exchange which more immediately surround this system. In relatively common-sense terms it requires scope for the valuation of personal achievement, for equality of opportunity, for mobility in response to technical requirements, for devotion to occupational goals and interests relatively unhampered by "personal" considerations. In more technical terms it requires a high incidence of technical competence, of rationality, of universalistic norms, and of functional specificity.[21] All these are drastically different from the patterns which are dominant in the area of kinship relations, where ascription of status by birth plays a prominent part, and where roles are defined primarily in particularistic and functionally diffuse terms.

It is quite clear that the type of occupational structure which is so essential to our society requires a far-reaching structural segregation of occupational roles from the kinship roles of the

[20] Cf. Talcott Parsons, "An Analytical Approach to the Theory of Social Stratification" (*American Journal of Sociology*, May, 1940); and "Age and Sex in the Social Structure of the United States" (*American Sociological Review*, October, 1942). Both reprinted in this volume.

[21] For the meaning of these technical terms, see Talcott Parsons, "The Professions and Social Structure" (*Social Forces*, May 1939), reprinted in this volume.

same individuals. They must, in the occupational system, be treated primarily as individuals. This is a situation drastically different from that found in practically all non-literate societies and in many that are literate.

At the same time, it cannot be doubted that a solidary kinship unit has functional significance of the highest order, especially in relation to the socialization of individuals and to the deeper aspects of their psychological security. What would appear to have happened is a process of mutual accommodation between these two fundamental aspects of our social structure. On the one hand our kinship system is of a structural type which, broadly speaking, interferes least with the functional needs of the occupational system, above all in that it exerts *relatively* little pressure for the ascription of an individual's social status—through class affiliation, property, and of course particular "jobs"—by virtue of his kinship status. The conjugal unit can be mobile in status independently of the other kinship ties of its members, that is, those of the spouses to the members of their families of orientation.

But at the same time this small conjugal unit can be a strongly solidary unit. This is facilitated by the prevalence of the pattern that normally only *one* of its members has an occupational role which is of determinate significance for the status of the family as a whole. Minor children, that is, as a rule do not "work," and when they do, it is already a major step in the process of emancipation from the family of orientation. The wife and mother is either exclusively a "housewife" or at most has a "job" rather than a "career."

There are perhaps two primary functional aspects of this situation. In the first place, by confining the number of status-giving occupational roles of the members of the effective conjugal unit to one, it eliminates any competition for status, especially as between husband and wife, which might be disruptive of the solidarity of marriage. So long as lines of achievement are segregated and not directly comparable, there is less opportunity for jealousy, a sense of inferiority, etc., to develop. Secondly, it aids in clarity of definition of the situation by making the status of the family in the community relatively definite and unequivocal. There is much evidence that this relative definiteness of status is an important factor in psychological security.[22]

---

[22] An example of disturbing indeterminacy of family status without occupational competition between husband and wife is the case where inherited wealth and family connections of a wife involve the couple in a standard of living and

The same structural arrangements which have this positive functional significance also give rise to important strains. What has been said above about the pressure for thoroughgoing emancipation from the family of orientation is a case in point. But in connection with the sex-role problem there is another important source of strain.

Historically, in Western culture, it may perhaps be fairly said that there has been a strong tendency to define the feminine role psychologically as one strongly marked by elements of dependency. One of the best symbols perhaps was the fact that until rather recently the married woman was not *sui juris,* could not hold property, make contracts, or sue in her own right. But in the modern American kinship system, to say nothing of other aspects of the culture and social structure, there are at least two pressures which tend to counteract this dependency and have undoubtedly played a part in the movement for feminine emancipation.

The first, already much discussed, is the multilineal symmetry of the kinship system which gives no basis of sex discrimination, and which in kinship terms favors equal rights and responsibilities for both parties to a marriage. The second is the character of the marriage relationship. Resting as it does primarily on affective attachment for the other person as a concrete human individual, a "personality," rather than on more objective considerations of status, it puts a premium on a certain kind of mutuality and equality. There is no clearly structured superordination-subordination pattern. Each is a fully responsible "partner" with a claim to a voice in decisions, to a certain human dignity, to be "taken seriously." Surely the pattern of romantic love which makes his relation to the "woman he loves" the most important single thing in a man's life, is incompatible with the view that she is an inferior creature, fit only for dependency on him.

In our society, however, occupational status has tremendous weight in the scale of prestige values. The fact that the normal married woman is debarred from testing or demonstrating her fundamental equality with her husband in competitive occupational achievement, creates a demand for a functional equivalent. At least in the middle classes, however, this cannot be found in the utilitarian functions of the role of housewife since these are treated as relatively menial functions. To be, for instance, an excellent

---

social relations to which the husband's occupational status and income would not give access. Such a situation is usually uncomfortable for the husband, but also very likely for the wife.

cook, does not give a hired maid a moral claim to a higher status than that of domestic servant.

This situation helps perhaps to account for a conspicuous tendency for the feminine role to emphasize broadly humanistic rather than technically specialized achievement values. One of the key patterns is that of "good taste," in personal appearance, house furnishings, cultural things like literature and music. To a large and perhaps increasing extent the more humanistic cultural traditions and amenities of life are carried on by women. Since these things are of high intrinsic importance in the scale of values of our culture, and since by virtue of the system of occupational specialization even many highly superior men are greatly handicapped in respect to them, there is some genuine redressing of the balance between the sexes.

There is also, however, a good deal of direct evidence of tension in the feminine role. In the "glamor girl" pattern, use of specifically feminine devices as an instrument of compulsive search for power and exclusive attention are conspicuous. Many women succumb to their dependency cravings through such channels as neurotic illness or compulsive domesticity and thereby abdicate both their responsibilities and their opportunities for genuine independence. Many of the attempts to excel in approved channels of achievement are marred by garishness of taste, by instability in response to fad and fashion, by a seriousness in community or club activities which is out of proportion to the intrinsic importance of the task. In all these and other fields there are conspicuous signs of insecurity and ambivalence. Hence it may be concluded that the feminine role is a conspicuous focus of the strains inherent in our social structure, and not the least of the sources of these strains is to be found in the functional difficulties in the integration of our kinship system with the rest of the social structure.[23]

Finally, a word may be said about one further problem of American society in which kinship plays a prominent part, the situation of the aged. In various ways our society is oriented to values particularly appropriate to the younger age groups so that there is a tendency for older people to be "left out of it." The abruptness of "retirement" from occupational roles also contributes. But a

---

[23] There is no intention to imply that the adult masculine role in American society is devoid of comparably severe strains. They are not, however, *prima facie* so intimately connected with the structure of kinship as are those of the feminine role.

primary present concern is one implication of the structural isolation of the conjugal family. The obverse of the emancipation, upon marriage and occupational independence, of children from their families of orientation is the depletion of that family until the older couple is finally left alone. This situation is in strong contrast to kinship systems in which membership in a kinship unit is continuous throughout the life cycle. There, very frequently, it is the oldest members who are treated with the most respect and have the greatest responsibility and authority. But with us there is no one left to respect them, for them to take responsibility for or have authority over.

For young people not to break away from their parental families at the proper time is a failure to live up to expectations, an unwarranted expression of dependency. But just as they have a duty to break away, they also have a right to independence. Hence for an older couple—or a widow or widower—to join the household of a married child is not, in the terms of the kinship structure, a "natural" arrangement. This is proved by the fact that it is seldom done at all except under pressure, either for economic support or to mitigate extreme loneliness and social isolation.[24] Even though in such situations it may be the best solution of a difficult problem it very frequently involves considerable strain, which is by no means confined to one side. The whole situation would be radically different in a different kind of kinship structure. It may be surmised that this situation, as well as "purely economic" questions, underlies much of the current agitation for old age pensions and the appeal of such apparently fantastic schemes as the Townsend Plan.

In this brief paper there can be no pretense of anything approaching an exhaustive functional analysis of the American kinship system or of its structural interdependence with other aspects of our social structure. A few problems of this order have been presented, beyond a direct descriptive analysis of the kinship structure as such, to illustrate the importance of a clear and thorough grasp of this structure in the understanding of many problems of the func-

---

[24] These pressures are, of course, likely to be by far most acute in the case of widows and widowers, especially the former. They are also considerably the more numerous, and often there is no other at all tolerable solution than to live in the family of a married child. Being joined and cared for by an unmarried child, especially a daughter, is another way out for the aged which often involves acute tragedies for the younger person.

tioning of American society, including its specific pathology. This, by and large, sociological students of the Amercian family have failed to provide or use systematically. It is as a contribution toward filling the gap in our working analytical equipment that the present paper has been conceived.

X

The Theoretical Development of the Sociology of Religion

A CHAPTER IN THE HISTORY OF MODERN SOCIAL SCIENCE

THE PRESENT PAPER will attempt to present in broad outline what seems to the writer one of the most significant chapters in the recent history of sociological theory, that dealing with the broader structure of the conceptual scheme for the analysis of religious phenomena as part of a social system. Its principal significance would seem to lie on two levels. In the first place, the development to be outlined represents a notable advance in the adequacy of our theoretical equipment to deal with a critically important range of scientific problems. Secondly, however, it is at the same time a particularly good illustration of the kind of process by which major theoretical developments in the field of social theory can be expected to take place.

Every important tradition of scientific thought involves a broad framework of theoretical propositions at any given stage of its development. Generally speaking, differences will be found only in the degree to which this framework is logically integrated and to which it is explicitly and self-consciously acknowledged and analyzed. About the middle of the last century or shortly thereafter, it is perhaps fair to say, generalized thinking about the significance of religion to human life tended to fall into one of two main categories. The first is the body of thought anchored in the doctrinal positions of one or another specific religious group, predominantly of course the various Christian denominations. For understandable reasons, the main tenor of such thought tended to be normative rather than empirical and analytical, to assure its own religious position and to expose the errors of opponents. It is difficult to see that in any direct sense important contributions to the sociology of religion as an empirical science could come from this source.[1] The other main category may be broadly referred to as that of positivistic thinking. The great stream of thought which culminated in the various branches of utilitarianism, had, of course, long been much concerned with some of the problems of religion. In its concern with contemporary society, however, the strong tendency had been to minimize the importance of religion, to treat it as a matter of "superstition" which had no place in the enlightened thinking of modern civilized man. The result of this tendency was, in the search for the important forces activating human behavior, to direct attention to other fields, such as the economic and the political. In certain phases the same tendency may be observed in the trend of positivistic thought toward emphasis on biology and psychology, which gathered force in the latter part of the nineteenth century and has continued well into our own.

Perhaps the first important change in this definition of problems, which was highly unfavorable to a serious scientific interest in the phenomena of religion, came with the application of the idea of evolution to human society. Once evidence from non-literate societies, not to speak of many others, was at all carefully studied, the observation was inescapable that the life of these so-called "primitive" men was to an enormous degree dominated by beliefs and practices which would ordinarily be classified according to the common-sense thinking of our time as magical and religious. Contemporary non-literate peoples, however, were in that generation predominantly interpreted as the living prototypes of our own prehistorical ancestors, and hence it was only natural that these striking phenomena should have been treated as "primitive" in a strictly evolutionary sense, as belonging to the early stages of the process of social development. This is the broad situation of the first really serious treatment of comparative religion in a sociological context, especially in the work of the founder of modern social-anthropology, Tylor,[2] and of Spencer,[3] perhaps the most penetrating theorist of this movement of thought. Though there was here a basis for serious scientific interest, the positivistic scheme of thought imposed severe limitations on the kind of significance

---

[1] It was far less unfavorable to historical contributions than to those affecting the analytical framework of the subject.

[2] *Primitive Culture.*

[3] Esp. *Principles of Sociology*, Vol. I.

which could be attributed to the observed phenomena. Within the positivistic schema, the most obvious directions of theoretical interpretation were two. On the one hand, religious phenomena could be treated as the manifestations of underlying biological or psychological factors beyond the reach of rational control, or interpretations in terms of subjective categories. Most generally this pattern led to some version of the instinct theory, which has suffered, however, some very serious scientific handicaps in that it has never proved possible to relate the detailed variations in the behavioral phenomena to any corresponding variations in the structure of instinctual drives. The whole scheme has on the level of social theory never successfully avoided the pitfalls of reasoning in a circle.

The other principal alternative was what may be called the "rationalistic" variation of positivism,[4] the tendency to treat the actor as if he were a rational, scientific investigator, acting "reasonably" in the light of the knowledge available to him. This was the path taken by Tylor and Spencer with the general thesis that primitive magical and religious ideas were ideas which in the situation of primitive men, considering the lack of accumulated knowledge and the limitations of the technique and opportunities of observation, it would reasonably be expected they would arrive at. With beliefs like that in a soul separable from the body, ritual practices in turn are held to be readily understandable. It is, however, a basic assumption of this pattern of thinking that the only critical standards to which religious ideas can be referred are those of empirical validity. It almost goes without saying that no enlightened modern could entertain such beliefs, that hence what we think of as distinctively religious and magical beliefs, and hence also the accompanying practices, will naturally disappear as an automatic consequence of the advance in scientific knowledge.

Inadequate as it is in the light of modern knowledge, this schema has proved to be the fruitful starting-point for the development of the field, for it makes possible the analysis of action in terms of the subjective point of view of the actor in his orientation to specific features of the situation in which he acts. Broadly speaking, to attempt to deal with the empirical inadequacies of this view by jumping directly, through the medium of anti-intellectualistic psy-

---

[4] See the author's *The Structure of Social Action*, Chaps. II and III.

chology, to the more fundamental forces activating human behavior, has not proved fruitful. The fruitful path has rather been the introduction of specific refinements and distinctions within the basic structural scheme with which "rationalistic positivism" started. The body of this paper will be concerned with a review of several of the most important of these steps in analytical refinement, showing how, taken together, they have led up to a far more comprehensive analytical scheme. This can perhaps most conveniently be done in terms of the contributions of four important theorists, Pareto, Malinowski, Durkheim, and Max Weber, none of whom had any important direct influence on any of the others.

It is of primary significance that Pareto's[5] analytical scheme for the treatment of a social system started precisely with this fundamental frame of reference. Like the earlier positivists, he took as his starting-point the cognitive patterns in terms which the actor is oriented to his situation of action. Again like them, he based his classification on the relation of these patterns to the standards of empirical scientific validity—in his terms, to "logico-experimental" standards. At this point, however, he broke decisively with the main positivistic tradition. He found it necessary, on grounds which in view of Pareto's general intellectual character most certainly were primarily empirical rather than philosophical, to distinguish two modes of deviance from conformity with logico-experimental standards. There were, on the one hand, the modes of deviance familiar to the older positivists, namely the failure to attain a logico-experimental solution of problems intrinsically capable of such solution. This may be attributable either to ignorance, the sheer absence of logically necessary knowledge of fact, or possibly of inference, or to error, to allegations of fact which observation can disprove or to logical fallacy in inference. In so far as cognitive patterns were deviant in this respect, Pareto summed them up as "pseudo-scientific" theories. Failure to conform with logico-experimental standards was not, however, confined to this mode of deviance, but included another, "the theories which surpass experience." These involved propositions, especially major premises, which are intrinsically incapable of being tested by scientific procedures. The attributes of God, for instance, are not entities cap-

---

[5] *The Mind and Society.* See also the author's *The Structure of Social Action,* Chap. V–VII; and "Pareto's Central Analytical Scheme,"*Journal of Social Philosophy,* I, 1935, 244-262.

able of empirical observation; hence propositions involving them can by logico-experimental methods neither be proved nor disproved. In this connection, Pareto's primary service lay in the clarity with which the distinction was worked out and applied, and his demonstration of the essentially prominent role in systems of human action of the latter class of cognitive elements. It is precisely in the field of religious ideas and of theological and metaphysical doctrines that its prominence has been greatest.

Pareto, however, did not stop here. From the very first, he treated the cognitive aspects of action in terms of their functional interdependence with the other elements of the social system, notably with what he called the "sentiments." He thereby broke through the "rationalistic bias" of earlier positivism and demonstrated by an immense weight of evidence that it was not possible to deal adequately with the significance of religious and magical ideas solely on the hypothesis that men entertaining them as beliefs drew the logical conclusions and acted accordingly. In this connection, Pareto's position has been widely interpreted as essentially a psychological one, as a reduction of non-logical ideas to the status of mere manifestations of instinct. Critical analysis of his work[6] shows, however, that this interpretation is not justified, but that he left the question of the more ultimate nature of non-cognitive factors open. It can be shown that the way in which he treated the sentiments is incompatible in certain critical respects with the hypothesis that they are biologically inherited instinctual drives alone. This would involve a determinacy irrespective of cultural variation, which he explicitly repudiated.

It is perhaps best to state that, as Pareto left the subject, there were factors particularly prominent in the field of religious behavior which involved the expression of sentiments or attitudes other than those important to action in a rationally utilitarian context. He did not, however, go far in analyzing the nature of these factors. It should, however, be clear that with the introduction, as a functionally necessary category, of the non-empirical effective elements which cannot be fitted into the pattern of rational techniques, Pareto brought about a fundamental break in the neatly closed system of positivistic interpretation of the phenomena of religion. He enormously broadened the analytical perspective

---

[6] Cf. *The Structure of Social Action,* 200 ff., 241 ff.

which needed to be taken into account before a new theoretical integration could be achieved.

The earlier positivistic theory started with the attempt to analyze the relation of the actor to particular types of situations common to all human social life, such as death and the experience of dreams. This starting-point was undoubtedly sound. The difficulty lay in interpreting such situations and the actor's relations to them too narrowly, essentially as a matter of the solution of empirical problems, of the actor's resorting to a "reasonable" course of action in the light of beliefs which he took for granted. Pareto provided much evidence that this exclusively cognitive approach was not adequate, but it remained for Malinowski[7] to return to detailed analysis of action in relation to particular situations in a broader perspective. Malinowski maintained continuity with the "classical" approach in that he took men's adaptation to practical situations by rational knowledge and technique as his initial point of reference. Instead of attempting to fit all the obvious facts positively into this framework, however, he showed a variety of reasons why in many circumstances rational knowledge and technique could not provide adequate mechanisms of adjustment to the total situation.

This approach threw into high relief a fundamental empirical observation, namely that instead of there being one single set of ideas and practices involved, for instance in gardening, canoe-building, or deep-sea fishing in the Trobriand Islands, there were in fact two distinct systems. On the one hand, the native was clearly possessed of an impressive amount of sound empirical knowledge of the proper uses of the soil and the processes of plant growth. He acted quite rationally in terms of his knowledge and above all was quite clear about the connection between intelligent and energetic work and a favorable outcome. There is no tendency to excuse failure on supernatural grounds when it could be clearly attributed to failure to attain adequate current standards of technical procedure. Side by side with this system of rational knowledge and technique, however, and specifically not confused with it, was a system of magical beliefs and practices. These beliefs concerned the possible intervention in the situation of forces and entities which are "supernatural" in the sense that they are

---

[7] See esp. *"Magic, Science, and Religion,"* by Bronislaw Malinowski, edited by Robert Redfield, the Free Press, Glencoe, Ill.

not from our point of view objects of empirical observation and experience, but rather what Pareto would call "imaginary" entities, and on the other hand, entities with a specifically sacred character. Correspondingly, the practices were not rational techniques but rituals involving specific orientation to this world of supernatural forces and entities. It is true that the Trobriander believes that a proper performance of magic is indispensable to a successful outcome of the enterprise; but it is one of Malinowski's most important insights that this attribution applies only to the range of uncertainty in the outcome of rational technique, to those factors in the situation which are beyond rational understanding and control on the part of the actor.

This approach to the analysis of primitive magic enabled Malinowski clearly to refute both the view of Lévy-Bruhl,[8] that primitive man confuses the realm of the supernatural and the sacred with the utilitarian and the rational, and also the view which had been classically put forward by Frazer[9] that magic was essentially primitive science, serving the same fundamental functions.

Malinowski, however, went beyond this in attempting to understand the functional necessity for such mechanisms as magic. In this connection, he laid stress on the importance of the emotional interests involved in the successful outcome of such enterprises. The combination of a strong emotional interest with important factors of uncertainty, which on the given technical level are inherent in the situation, produces a state of tension and exposes the actor to frustration. This, it should be noted, exists not only in cases where uncontrollable factors, such as bad weather or insect pests in gardening, result in "undeserved" failure, but also in cases where success is out of proportion to reasonable expectations of the results of intelligence and effort. Unless there were mechanisms which had the psychological function of mitigating the sense of frustration, the consequences would be unfavorable to maintaining a high level of confidence or effort, and it is in this connection that magic may be seen to perform important positive functions. It should be clear that this is a very different level of interpretation from that which attributes it only to the primitive level of knowledge. It would follow that wherever such uncertainty elements enter into the pursuit of emotionally important goals, if

---

[8] *Primitive Mentality.*

[9] *The Golden Bough.*

not magic, at least functionally equivalent phenomena could be expected to appear.[10]

In the case of magic, orientation to supernatural entities enters into action which is directed to the achievement of practical, empirical goals, such as a good crop or a large catch of fish. Malinowski, however, calls attention to the fact that there are situations which are analogous in other respects but in which no practical goal can be pursued. The type case of this is death. From the practical point of view, the Trobrianders, like anyone else, are surely aware that "nothing can be done about it." No ritual observances will bring the deceased back to life. But precisely for this reason, the problem of emotional adjustment is all the greater in importance. The significance both practically and emotionally of a human individual is of such a magnitude that his death involves a major process of readjustment for the survivors. Malinowski shows that the death of another involves exposure to sharply conflicting emotional reactions, some of which, if given free range, would lead to action and attitudes detrimental to the social group. There is great need for patterns of action which provide occasion for the regulated expression of strong emotions, and which in such a situation of emotional conflict reinforce those reactions which are most favorable to the continued solidarity and functioning of the social group. One may suggest that in no society is action on the occasion of death confined to the utilitarian aspects of the disposal of the corpse and other practical adjustments. There is always specifically ritual observance of some kind which, as Malinowski shows, cannot adequately be interpreted as merely acting out the bizarre ideas which primitive man in his ignorance develops about the nature of death.

Malinowski shows quite clearly that neither ritual practices, magical or religious, nor the beliefs about supernatural forces and entities integrated with them can be treated simply as a primitive and inadequate form of rational techniques or scientific knowledge; they are qualitatively distinct and have quite different functional

---

[10] For example, the field of health is, in spite of the achievements of modern medicine, even in our own society a classical example of this type of situation. Careful examination of our own treatment of health even through medical practice reveals that though magic in a strict sense is not prominent, there is an unstable succession of beliefs which overemphasize the therapeutic possibilities of certain diagnostic ideas and therapeutic practices. The effect is to create an optimistic bias in favor of successful treatment of disease which apparently has considerable functional significance.

significance in the system of action. Durkheim,[11] however, went farther than Malinowski in working out the specific character of this difference, as well as in bringing out certain further aspects of the functional problem. Whereas Malinowski tended to focus attention on functions in relation to action in a situation, Durkheim became particularly interested in the problem of the specific attitudes exhibited toward supernatural entities and ritual objects and actions. The results of this study he summed up in the fundamental distinction between the sacred and the profane. Directly contrasting the attitudes appropriate in a ritual context with those towards objects of utilitarian significance and their use in fields of rational technique, he found one fundamental feature of the sacred to be its radical dissociation from any utilitarian context. The sacred is to be treated with a certain specific attitude of respect, which Durkheim identified with the appropriate attitude toward moral obligations and authority. If the effect of the prominence which Durkheim gives to the conception of the sacred is strongly to reinforce the significance of Malinowski's observation that the two systems are not confused but are in fact treated as essentially separate, it also brings out even more sharply than did Malinowski the inadequacy of the older approach to this range of problems which treated them entirely as the outcome of intellectual processes in ways indistinguishable from the solution of empirical problems. Such treatment could not but obscure the fundamental distinction upon which Durkheim insisted.

The central significance of the sacred in religion, however, served to raise in a peculiarly acute form the question of the source of the attitude of respect. Spencer, for instance, had derived it from the belief that the souls of the dead reappear to the living, and from ideas about the probable dangers of association with them. Max Müller and the naturalist school, on the other hand, had attempted to derive all sacred things in the last analysis from personification of certain phenomena of nature which were respected and feared because of their intrinsically imposing or terrifying character. Durkheim opened up an entirely new line of thought by suggesting that it was hopeless to look for a solution of the problem on this level at all. There was in fact no common intrinsic quality of things treated as sacred which could account for the attitude of respect.

---

[11] *The Elementary Forms of the Religious Life.* See also *The Structure of Social Action,* Chapter XI.

In fact, almost everything from the sublime to the ridiculous has in some society been treated as sacred. Hence the source of sacredness is not intrinsic; the problem is of a different character. Sacred objects and entities are symbols. The problem then becomes one of identifying the referents of such symbols. It is that which is symbolized and not the intrinsic quality of the symbol which becomes crucial.

At this point Durkheim became aware of the fundamental significance of his previous insight that the attitude of respect for sacred things was essentially identical with the attitude of respect for moral authority. If sacred things are symbols, the essential quality of that which they symbolize is that it is an entity which would command moral respect. It was by this path that Durkheim arrived at the famous proposition that society is always the real object of religious veneration. In this form the proposition is certainly unacceptable, but there is no doubt of the fundamental importance of Durkheim's insight into the exceedingly close integration of the system of religious symbols of a society and the patterns sanctioned by the common moral sentiments of the members of the community. In his earlier work,[12] Durkheim had progressed far in understanding the functional significance of an integrated system of morally sanctioned norms. Against this background the integration he demonstrated suggested a most important aspect of the functional significance of religion. For the problem arises, if moral norms and the sentiments supporting them are of such primary importance, what are the mechanisms by which they are maintained other than external processes of enforcement? It was Durkheim's view that religious ritual was of primary significance as a mechanism for expressing and reinforcing the sentiments most essential to the institutional integration of the society. It can readily be seen that this is closely linked to Malinowski's view of the significance of funeral ceremonies as a mechanism for reasserting the solidarity of the group on the occasion of severe emotional strain. Thus Durkheim worked out certain aspects of the specific relations between religion and social structure more sharply than did Malinowski, and in addition put the problem in a different functional perspective in that he applied it to the society as a whole in abstraction from particular situations of tension and strain for the individual.

---

[12] Especially *De la division du travail* and *Le suicide*. See also *The Structure of Social Action*, Chap. VIII, X.

One of the most notable features of the development under consideration lay in the fact that the cognitive patterns associated with religion were no longer, as in the older positivism, treated as essentially given points of reference, but were rather brought into functional relationship with a variety of other elements of social system of action. Pareto in rather general terms showed their interdependence with the sentiments. Malinowski contributed the exceedingly important relation to particular types of human situation, such as those of uncertainty and death. He in no way contradicted the emphasis placed by Pareto on emotional factors or sentiments. These, however, acquire their significance for specifically structured patterns of action only through their relation to specific situations. Malinowski was well aware in turn of the relation of both these factors to the solidarity of the social group, but this aspect formed the center of Durkheim's analytical attention. Clearly, religious ideas could only be treated sociologically in terms of their interdependence with all four types of factors.

There were, however, still certain serious problems left unsolved. In particular, neither Malinowski nor Durkheim raised the problem of the relation of these factors to the variability of social structure from one society to another. Both were primarily concerned with analysis of the functioning of a given social system without either comparative or dynamic references. Furthermore, Durkheim's important insight into the role of symbolism in religious ideas might, without further analysis, suggest that the specific patterns, hence their variations, were of only secondary importance. Indeed, there is clearly discernible in Durkheim's thinking in this field a tendency to circular reasoning in that he tends to treat religious patterns as a symbolic manifestation of "society," but at the same time to define the most fundamental aspect of society as a set of patterns of moral and religious sentiment.

Max Weber approached the whole field in very different terms. In his study of the relation between Protestantism and capitalism,[13] his primary concern was with those features of the institutional system of modern Western society which were most distinctive in differentiating it from the other great civilizations. Having established what he felt to be an adequate relation of congruence between the cognitive patterns of Calvinism and some of the principal institutionalized attitudes towards secular roles of our own society,

---

[13] *The Protestant Ethic and the Spirit of Capitalism.*

he set about systematically to place this material in the broadest
possible comparative perspective through studying especially the
religion and social structure of China, India, and ancient Judea.[14]
As a generalized result of these studies, he found it was not possible to reduce the striking variations of pattern on the level of
religious ideas in these cases to any features of an independently
existent social structure or economic situation, though he continually insisted on the very great importance of situational factors in
a number of different connections.[15] These factors, however, served
only to pose the problems with which great movements of religious
thought have been concerned. But the distinctive cognitive patterns
were only understandable as a result of a cumulative tradition of
intellectual effort in grappling with the problems thus presented
and formulated.

For present purposes, even more important than Weber's views
about the independent causal significance of religious ideas is his
clarification of their functional relation to the system of action. Following up the same general line of analysis which provides one of
the major themes of Pareto's and Malinowski's work, Weber made
clear above all that there is a fundamental distinction between the
significance for human action of problems of empirical causation
and what, on the other hand, he called the "problem of meaning."
In such cases as premature death through accident, the problem of
how it happened in the sense of an adequate explanation of empirical causes can readily be solved to the satisfaction of most minds
and yet leave a sense not merely of emotional but of cognitive frustration with respect to the problem of *why* such things must happen. Correlative with the functional need for emotional adjustment
to such experiences as death is a cognitive need for understanding,
for trying to have it "make sense." Weber attempted to show that
problems of this nature, concerning the discrepancy between normal human interest and expectations in any situation or society
and what actually happens are inherent in the nature of human
existence. They always pose problems of the order which on the
most generalized line have come to be known as the problem of
evil, of the meaning of suffering, and the like. In terms of his com-

---

[14] *Gesammelte Aufsätze zur Religionssoziologie.* See also *The Structure of
Social Action,* Chaps. XIV, XV, and XVII.

[15] See especially his treatment of the role of the balance of social power in
the establishment of the ascendancy of the Brahmans in India, and of the international position of the people of Israel in the definition of religious problems for
the prophetic movement.

parative material, however, Weber shows there are different directions of definition of human situations in which rationally integrated solutions of these problems may be sought. It is differentiation with respect to the treatment of precisely such problems which constitute the primary modes of variation between the great systems of religious thought.

Such differences as, for instance, that between the Hindu philosophy of Karma and transmigration and the Christian doctrine of Grace with their philosophical backgrounds are not of merely speculative significance. Weber is able to show, in ways which correlate directly with the work of Malinowski and Durkheim, how intimately such differences in doctrine are bound up with practical attitudes towards the most various aspects of everyday life. For if we can speak of a need to understand ultimate frustrations in order for them to "make sense," it is equally urgent that the values and goals of everyday life should also "make sense." A tendency to integration of these two levels seems to be inherent in human action. Perhaps the most striking feature of Weber's analysis is the demonstration of the extent to which precisely the variations in socially sanctioned values and goals in secular life correspond to the variations in the dominant religious philosophy of the great civilizations.

It can be shown with little difficulty that those results of Weber's comparative and dynamic study integrate directly with the conceptual scheme developed as a result of the work of the other writers. Thus Weber's theory of the positive significance of religious ideas is in no way to be confused with the earlier naively rationalistic positivism. The influence of religious doctrine is not exerted through the actor's coming to a conviction and then acting upon it in a rational sense. It is rather, on the individual level, a matter of introducing a determinate structure at certain points in the system of action where, in relation to the situation men have to face, other elements, such as their emotional needs, do not suffice to determine specific orientations of behavior. In the theories of Malinowski and Durkheim, certain kinds of sentiments and emotional reactions were shown to be essential to a functioning social system. These cannot stand alone, however, but are necessarily integrated with cognitive patterns; for without them there could be no coordination of action in a coherently structured social system. This is because functional analysis of the structure of action shows that situations must be subjectively defined, and the goals and values to which action is oriented must be congruent with these definitions, must, that is, have "meaning."

It is of course never safe to say a scientific conceptual scheme has reached a definitive completion of its development. Continual change is in the nature of science. There are, however, relative degrees of conceptual integration, and it seems safe to say that the cumulative results of the work just reviewed constitute in broad outline a relatively well-integrated analytical scheme which covers most of the more important broader aspects of the role of religion in social systems. It is unlikely that in the near future this analytical scheme will give way to a radical structural change, though notable refinement and revision is to be expected. It is perhaps safe to say that it places the sociology of religion for the first time on a footing where it is possible to combine empirical study and theoretical analysis on a large scale on a level in conformity with the best current standards of social science and psychology.

When we look back, the schemes of Tylor and Spencer seem hopelessly naive and inadequate to the modern sociologist, anthropologist, or psychologist. It is, however, notable that the development sketched did not take place by repudiating their work and attempting to appeal directly to the facts without benefit of theory. The process was quite different. It consisted in raising problems which were inherent in the earlier scheme and modifying the scheme as a result of the empirical observation suggested by these problems. Thus Malinowski did not abandon all attempt to relate magic to rational technique. Not being satisfied with its identification with primitive science and technology, he looked for specific modes of difference from and relation to them, retaining the established interpretation of the nature and functions of rational technique as his initial point of reference. It is notable again that in this process the newer developments of psychological theory in relation to the role of emotional factors have played an essential part. The most fruitful results have not, however, resulted from substituting a psychological "theory of religion" for another type, but rather from incorporating the results of psychological investigation into a wider scheme.

In order for this development to take place it was essential that certain elements of philosophical dogmatism in the older positivism should be overcome. One reason for the limitations of Spencer's insight lay in the presumption that if a cognitive pattern was significant to human action, it must be assimilable to the pattern of science. Pareto, however, showed clearly that the "pseudoscientific" did not exhaust significant patterns which deviated from scientific standards. Malinowski went further in showing the functional relation of certain non-scientific ideas to elements of uncertainty and frustration which were inherent in the situation of action. Durkheim called attention to the importance of the relation of symbolism as distinguished from that of intrinsic causality in cognitive patterns. Finally, Weber integrated the various aspects of the role of non-empirical cognitive patterns in social action in terms of his theory of the significance of the problems of meaning and the corresponding cognitive structures, in a way which precluded, for analytical purposes, their being assimilated to the patterns of science.[16] All of these distinctions by virtue of which the cognitive patterns of religion are treated separately from those of science have positive significance for empirical understanding of religious phenomena. Like any such scientific categories, they are to the scientist sanctioned by the fact that they can be shown to work. Failure to make these distinctions does not in the present state of knowledge and in terms of the relevant frame of reference[17] help us to understand certain critically important facts of human life. What the philosophical significance of this situation may be is not as such the task of the social scientist to determine. Only one safe prediction on this level can be made. Any new philosophical synthesis will need positively to take account of these distinctions rather than to attempt to reinstate for the scientific level the older positivistic conception of the homogeneity of all human thought and its problems. If these distinctions are to be transcended it cannot well be in the form of "reducing" religious ideas to those of science —in the sense of Western intellectual history—or vice versa. The proved scientific utility of the distinctions is sufficient basis on which to eliminate this as a serious possibility.

---

[16] See the writer's paper, "The Role of Ideas in Social Action," *American Sociological Review*, III, 1938, for a general analytical discussion of the problem included in the present volume.

[17] Every treatment of questions of fact and every empirical investigation is "in terms of a conceptual scheme." Scientifically the sole sanction of such a conceptual scheme is its "utility," the degree to which it "works" in facilitating the attainment of the goals of scientific investigation. Hence the conceptual structure of any system of scientific theory is subject to the same kind of relativity with "arbitrariness." It is subject to the disciplining constraint both of verification in all questions of particular empirical fact, and of logical precision and consistency among the many different parts of a highly complex conceptual structure. The "theory of social action" is by now a theoretical structure so highly developed and with so many ramifications in both these respects that elements structurally essential to it cannot be lightly dismissed as expressing only "one point of view."

XI

The Present Position and Prospects of Systematic Theory in Sociology

THE GENERAL NATURE *and Functions of Systematic Theory*. It is scarcely too much to say that the most important single index of the state of maturity of a science is the state of its systematic theory. This includes the character of the generalized conceptual scheme in use in the field, the kinds and degrees of logical integration of the different elements which make it up, and the ways in which it is actually being used in empirical research. On this basis the thesis may be advanced that sociology is just in the process of emerging into the status of a mature science. Heretofore it has not enjoyed the kind of integration and directed activity which only the availability and common acceptance and employment of a well-articulated generalized theoretical system can give to a science. The main framework of such a system is, however, now available, though this fact is not as yet very generally appreciated and much in the way of development and refinement remains to be done on the purely theoretical level, as well as its systematic use and revision in actual research. It may therefore be held that we stand on the threshold of a definitely new era in sociology and the neighboring social science fields.

"Theory" is a term which covers a wide variety of different things which have in common only the element of generalized conceptualization. The theory of concern to the present paper in the first place constitutes a "system" and thereby differs from discrete "theories," that is, particular generalizations about particular phenomena or classes of them. A theoretical system in the present sense is a body of logically interdependent generalized concepts of empirical reference. Such a system tends, ideally, to become "logically closed," to reach such a state of logical integration that every logical implication of any combination of propositions in the system is explicitly stated in some other proposition in the same system.[1]

In a highly developed system of theory there may be a wide variety of different types of generalized concepts and functions which they may serve. A thorough discussion of the possibilities cannot be undertaken here, so attention will be confined to those most vital to the general status of the scientific field. The two most general functions of theory are the facilitation of description and analysis. The two are most intimately connected since it is only when the essential facts about a phenomenon have been described in a carefully systematic and orderly manner that accurate analysis becomes possible at all.

The basic category of all scientific description seems to be that of empirical system. The empirical references of statements of fact cannot be isolated from each other, but each describes one aspect or feature of an interconnected whole which, taken as a whole, has some measures of independent significance as an entity. Apart from theoretical conceptualization there would appear to be no method of selecting among the indefinite number of varying kinds of factual observation which can be made about a concrete phenomenon or field so that the various descriptive statements about it articulate into a coherent whole, which constitutes an "adequate," a "determinate" description. Adequacy in description is secured in so far as determinate and verifiable answers can be given to all the scientifically *important* questions involved. What questions are important is largely determined by the logical structure of the generalized conceptual scheme which, implicitly or explicitly, is employed.

Specific descriptive propositions often refer to particular aspects or properties of an empirically existent set of phenomena. Such propositions are, however, empirically meaningless unless the "what" which they qualify is clearly and determinately conceived and defined. This "what," the interconnected empirically existent phenomena which constitute the field of description and analysis for a scientific investigation, is what is meant by an empirical "system." It is that which can, for scientific purposes, be treated at the same time as a body of phenomena sufficiently extensive, complex and diversified so that the results of their study are significant and not merely truistic, and sufficiently limited and simplified so that the

[1] For a fuller development of this view of theory, see the author's *The Structure of Social Action*, (New York: McGraw-Hill Co., 1937), especially Chaps. I and XIX.

problems involved are manageable and the investigator does not get lost in the maze.

The functions of a generalized conceptual scheme on the descriptive level seem to be performed mainly in terms of two types of conceptual elements. The first consists in what is called the "frame of reference." This is the most general framework of categories in terms of which empirical scientific work "makes sense." Thus, in classical mechanics, three-dimensional rectilinear space, time, mass, location, motion are the essential elements of the frame of reference. Every descriptive statement, to be applicable to a mechanical system must be referable to one or more "particles" each with a given mass, capable of location in space, changing its location in time through motion, etc. Besides providing the specific categories in terms of which a system is described, the function of the frame of reference is above all to provide a test of the determinacy of the description of a system. It is a logical implication of the structure of the conceptual system that there is a limited number of essential categories, specific values for which must be obtained before the description can be determinate. Its use is the only way of locating the important gaps in available knowledge.

The second level is that of the structure of systems as such. Phenomena which are significantly interrelated, which constitute a system, are intrinsically interrelated on the structural level. This fact seems to be inherent in the most general frame of reference of empirical knowledge itself, which implies the fundamental significance of the concept of system as that is taken for granted here. Structure is the "static" aspect of the descriptive mode of treatment of a system. From the structural point of view a system is composed of "units," of sub-systems which potentially exist independently, and their structural interrelations. Thus a system in mechanics is "made up" of particles as its units. The structure of the system consists in the number of particles, their properties, such as mass, and their interrelations, such as relative locations, velocities and directions of motion.

The functions of the frame of reference and of structural categories in their descriptive use are to state the necessary facts, and the setting for solving problems of dynamic analysis, the ultimate goal of scientific investigation. Besides the immense possibilities of variation in the scope of analysis, there are two aspects of the goal itself; first the "causal explanation" of past specific phenomena or processes and the prediction of future events; second, the attainment of generalized analytical knowledge, of "laws" which can be applied to an indefinite number of specific cases with the use of the appropriate factual data. The attainment of the two goals, or aspects of the same goal, go hand in hand. On the one hand specific causal explanation is attainable only through the application of some generalized analytical knowledge; on the other, the extension of analytical generalization is only possible by generalization from empirical cases and verification in terms of them.

In both respects scientific advance consists especially in the gradual widening of the scope of dynamic analysis. Even the simplest rational practical activity would be impossible without the ability to establish a dynamic relation between a single, simple "necessary condition" and a consequent effect under the assumption that in a relevant degree "other things are equal." This, applied in a particular case, implies some degree of generalization that this *kind* of factor is a necessary condition of the kind of effect, thus, that "boiling" for a certain length of time—i.e., a generalized *type* of antecedent process—is necessary if potatoes are to be "cooked"—i.e., reach a certain kind of observable state. This *kind* of common-sense analysis merges gradually into science in proportion to the complexity of the system of dynamically interdependent variables which can be treated together, and to the breadth of applicability to particular situations of the analytical generalizations commanded.

Sometimes one aspect is predominant in the development of a body of scientific knowledge, sometimes the other. Where, however, breadth of applicability can be attained only through extreme simplicity in the relations of variables, only a secondary order of scientific significance can be attributed to the results. For where only very simple relationships, or only those of two or three variables, can be involved in a dynamic generalization it must inevitably remain undesirably abstract in the sense that in very few cases of concrete empirical systems, will these relationships and these variables be the only or the predominant ones involved in the solution of the pressing empirical problems. Hence, the ideal of scientific theory must be to extend the dynamic scope of analysis of complex systems as a whole as far as possible. It is the attainment of this ideal which presents the greatest theoretical difficulties to science.

Put a little differently, the essential feature of dynamic analysis in the fullest sense is the treatment of a body of *interdependent* phenomena simultaneously, in the mathematical sense. The simplest case is the analysis of the effect of variation in one antecedent factor, but this ignores the reciprocal effect of these changes on this factor. The ideal solution is the possession of a logically complete system of dynamic generalizations which can state all the elements of reciprocal interdependence between all the variables of the system. The ideal has, in the formal sense, been attained only in the systems of differential equations of analytical mechanics. All other sciences are limited to a more "primitive" level of systematic theoretical analysis.

For this level of dynamic analysis to be feasible, there seem to be two essential necessary conditions. On the one hand, the variables need to be of an empirical character such that the particulars within the generalized categories are in actuality the relevant statements of fact about a given state of the empirical system as indicated by the structure of problems of the science. On the other hand, the formal logical character of these concepts must be such as to be susceptible to special types of technical manipulation. The only kind of technical manipulation so far available which makes simultaneous dynamic analysis of interdependence of several variables in a complex system possible in a completely rigorous sense, is the mathematics of the differential calculus and some of its more refined derivatives.

To be susceptible of this type of analytical manipulation a variable must be of a very particular sort—it must vary only in numerically quantitative value on a continuum. This requirement greatly narrows the range of observational possibility. In many cases even where numerical continua can be observed they are not necessarily the variables of greatest empirical significance.

The most essential condition of successful dynamic analysis is continual and systematic reference of every problem to the state of the system as a whole. If it is not possible to provide for that by explicit inclusion of every relevant fact as the value of a variable which is included in the dynamic analysis at that point, there must be some method of simplification. Logically, this is possible only through the removal of some generalized categories from the role of variables and their treatment as constants. An analytical system of the type of mechanics does just this for certain elements *outside* the system which are conditional to it. But it is also logically feasible *within* the system. This is essentially what happens when structural categories are used in the treatment of dynamic problems.

Their function is to simplify the dynamic problems to the point where they are manageable without the possibility of refined mathematical analysis. At the same time the loss, which is very great, is partly compensated by relating all problems explicitly and systematically to the total system. For the structure of a system as described in the context of a generalized conceptual scheme is a genuinely technical analytical tool. It ensures that nothing of vital importance is inadvertently overlooked, and ties in loose ends, giving determinancy to problems and solutions. It minimizes the danger, so serious to common-sense thinking, of filling gaps by resort to uncriticized residual categories.

It should be noted that in mechanics the structure of the system does not enter in as a distinct theoretical element. For descriptive purposes, it is of course relevant for any state of the system. But on the dynamic plane it dissolves into process and interdependence. This calls attention to the important fact that structure and process are highly relative categories. Structure does not refer to any ontological stability in phenomena but only to a relative stability—to sufficiently stable uniformities in the results of underlying processes so that their constancy within certain limits is a workable pragmatic assumption.

Once resort is made to the structure of a system as a positive constituent of dynamic analysis there must be a way of linking these "static" structural categories and their relevant particular statements of fact to the dynamically variable elements in the system. This link is supplied by the all-important concept of *function*. Its crucial role is to provide criteria of the *importance* of dynamic factors and processes within the system. They are important in so far as they have functional significance to the system, and their specific importance is understood in terms of the analysis of specific functional relations between the parts of the system and between it and its environment.

The significance of the concept of function implies the conception of the empirical system as a "going concern." Its structure is that system of determinate patterns which empirical observation shows, within certain limits, "tend to be maintained" or on a somewhat more dynamic version "tend to develop" according to an empirically constant pattern (e. g. the pattern of growth of a young organism).

Functional significance in this context is inherently teleological.

A process or set of conditions either "contributes" to the maintenance (or development) of the system or it is "dysfunctional" in that it detracts from the integration, effectiveness, etc., of the system. It is thus the functional reference of all particular conditions and process *to the state of the total system as a going concern* which provides the logical equivalent of simultaneous equations in a fully developed system of analytical theory. This appears to be the only way in which dynamic *inter*dependence of variable factors in a system can be explicitly analyzed without the technical tools of mathematics and the operational and empirical prerequisites of their employment.

The logical type of generalized theoretical system under discussion may thus be called a "structural-functional system" as distinguished from an analytical system. It consists of the generalized categories necessary for an adequate description of states of an empirical system. On the one hand, it includes a system of structural categories which must be logically adequate to give a determinate description of an empirically possible, complete empirical system of the relevant class. One of the prime functions of *system* on this level is to ensure completeness, to make it methodically impossible to overlook anything important, and thus explicitly to describe *all* essential structural elements and relations of the system. For if this is not done implicitly, uncriticized allegations about the missing elements will always play a part in determining conclusions and interpretations.

On the other hand, such a system must also include a set of dynamic functional categories. These must articulate directly with the structural categories—they must describe processes by which these particular structures are maintained or upset, and the relations of the system to its environment are mediated. This aspect of the system must also be complete in the same sense.

On a relatively complete and explicit level this type of generalized system has been most fully developed in physiology[2] and more recently if less completely in psychology. The anatomical structure of the organism is an essential fixed point of reference for all physiological analyses of its functioning. Function in relation to the maintenance of this structure in a given environment is the source of criteria for the attribution of significance to processes such as

---

[2] For the place of structural-functional analysis in physiology, see especially W. B. Cannon, *The Wisdom of the Body*, (New York: W. W. Norton and Co., 1932).

respiration, nutrition, etc., and of their dynamic interdependence. In recent psychology, it is "character structure" or personality which plays the role analogous to that of anatomical structure in biology while "motives" in relation to situations are the dynamic elements.

II

Unsatisfactory Types of Theory in Recent Sociology. It is the primary thesis of this paper that the structural-functional type of system is the one which is most likely and suitable to play a dominant role in sociological theory. In varying degrees it has, though largely implicitly and in a fragmentary fashion, been in actual use in the field. But until quite recently the predominant trends of thought in this field have been such as to prevent its emergence into the central explicit position which would allow it to develop freely all its potentialities for fruitful integration of the science. On the one hand, there has been a school of empiricism which was blind to the functions of theory in science—often mistakenly thinking it was following the model of the physical sciences. On the other hand, what has gone by the name of "theory" has consisted mainly in conceptual structures on quite a different level from what is here meant by a generalized theoretical system.

One major strand of thought in the history of sociological theory has been that closely associated with, indeed merging into, the philosophy of history. The central interest here has been in the establishment of a highly generalized pattern in the processes of change of human societies as a whole, whether it be linear evolutionism, cyclical or dialectic process, etc. Perhaps the evolutionary anthropologists like Tylor and Morgan have been most prominent here. But it also, in certain respects, includes Marx and his followers, Veblen and many others.

The element of generality which justifies calling these writers particularly theorists lies in the comprehensiveness of the empirical generalizations they have formulated and attempted to establish. The theory of analytical mechanics, or of general physiology, on the other hand, does not *as such* contain any empirical generalizations at all. It is a set of *tools* by which, working on adequate data, both specific empirical solutions and empirical generalizations can be arrived at. To make empirical generalization the central focus of theory in a science is to put the cart before the horse. In proportion as a generalized theoretical system is really perfected, and, what necessarily goes with it, empirical research and knowledge of fact builds up, it becomes possible to attain more and more comprehensive empirical generalizations. Indeed it can be said that any system of sound empirical generalizations implies a generalized theoretical system.

But concentrating theoretical attention on this level of empirical generalization to the exclusion of the other is very risky. Such systems have had a notorious tendency to overreach the facts and their own analytical underpinning and by and large have not, in the meanings originally meant by their authors, stood the test of competent criticism. On this level no competent modern sociologist can be a Comtean, a Spencerian, or even a Marxian.

The prominence of this tendency has had two very serious unfavorable consequences. First it has, by focussing attention at the wrong place, impeded the progress of the subject. It has attempted to attain, at one stroke, a goal which can only be approached gradually by building the necessary factual foundations and analytical tools. It is not surprising that such ill-advised attempts should lead to difficulties. As these have become increasingly formidable and evident, the second consequence has appeared. Since "theory" has been so largely identified with such attempts at comprehensive empirical generalization, their failure has discredited not only themselves, which is only right and proper, but also everything else which has gone by the name of theory. This reaction has contributed greatly to a kind of "empiricism" which has blindly rejected the help of theoretical tools in general. While one tendency, it may be said, has sought to create a great building by a sheer act of will without going through the requisite of technical procedures, the other has tried to make a virtue of working with bare hands alone, rejecting all tools and mechanical equipment.

A second major strand of "theoretical" thinking in sociology has been that which has attempted to assess the importance of various "factors" in the determination of social phenomena. Usually it has taken the form of attempting to prove the exclusive or predominant importance of one such factor—geographic, biological, economic or what not.

This type of theorizing, though in a different way, also puts the cart before the horse. It also involves a kind of generalization which can only be soundly established as a *result* of the kind of investigation in which generalized theory, in the present sense, is an indispensable tool. If it is sound it, like the other, will *imply* a system of theory, and will depend upon it. But it is unlikely that such an un-criticized implicit system will be as adequate as one which has been carefully and explicitly worked out in direct relation to the facts.

Indeed a very large part of this "factor" theorizing has had the effect, if not the function, of evading the problem of a generalized theory of *social* systems. It has tended to do this in two ways. The major trend, particularly in Anglo-Saxon countries, has been to at-tribute the principal role to factors which are not specific to social systems, notably the environmental (e.g., geographical), and the biological and the economic.

In the first two of these cases the most important elements of theoretical generality have already been thoroughly worked out by investigations in other fields which have high prestige in the scientific world. Though on principle new discoveries in any field of application should lead to revision of the theoretical structure of a science, in fact, in the case of biology, for instance, there was little chance of human social tail being able to wag the dog of all known lower organic species. If, on the one hand, it was assumed that men, being organisms, were subject to biological laws, and, on the other, that the theory of natural selection was fully established as explaining the process of development of organic species in gen-eral, the predominant tendency would naturally be simply to seek in human social development examples of the working of the prin-ciples of natural selection without too much attention to the dis-tinctive features of human society in other respects. Thus both economic competition and international rivalries have been widely interpreted in these terms. This has led to widespread neglect of the fundamental canon of science, the need to study in the very first instance the facts of the *particular* phenomena.

This unfortunate effect has been reinforced by another circum-stance. Until recently it has been rare to find very much insight into the senses in which scientific theory on practically all levels is abstract. Thus natural selection has been interpreted as a general-ized description of *the* process by which change in organic species came about—not as the formulation of *certain elements* in the pro-cess which might have a more or less dominant role relative to others in different cases. The effect of this tendency to "empirical closure" of a system is to make its application to any given field, especially a new one, a rigidly simple question of whether it "applies" or not. Application is interpreted in "all or none" terms—it is either a case or not. If it is in any sense a case, then there is no incentive to look further and study the interdependence of the factors thus formulated with others which might be involved, since the latter are assumed not to exist or to be unimportant.[3]

A slightly different though closely analogous situation occurs when the factors singled out are of certain types predominantly observed in human social behavior, but are treated in such a way as to ignore major elements of the context in which they operate in social systems.

A leading example of this type is the kind of theory which lays primary emphasis on rational adaptation of means to given ends in technological or economic contexts. This tendency has been predominant in the whole "utilitarian" tradition of social thought since Locke and in a modified form is decisive for Marx and Veblen. As I have shown in other connections this mode of treatment of social action as a whole has implied a very specific form of generalized theoretical system which has very seriously broken down in the course of the last generation of theoretical work.[4] The key to this process of breakdown is the emergence into a position of central prominence of certain modes and factors in the integration of social systems which could not be taken account of in utilitarian terms.

The utilitarian type of factor analysis is analogous to the environmental and biological in that it singles out elements which also can be treated in complete abstraction from social systems as such. Actual rational behavior is not, of course, observed apart from social situations. But the implicit conceptual scheme is such that other elements, of a "social" rather than a biological or environmental character, enter only in the role of conditions of the situation in which people act. They become, that is, theoretically equivalent to the physical environment and are thus deprived of any distinctive theoretical role in the social system of action itself.

All of the above factor theories have impeded the development of a theory of social systems by imposing an implicit generalized conceptual scheme which denied the empirical relevance of a distinctively social system—as a generalized theoretical system or a class of empirical systems. There would be no objection to this if the

---

[3] The above is what Whitehead has called "the fallacy of misplaced concreteness."

[4] See Talcott Parsons, *The Structure of Social Action*, Chaps. III, XII.

resulting theoretical structures had proved to be adequate for the solution of the pressing ranges of empirical problems which have dominated social science. At point after point, however, this empirical inadequacy has come to be exposed and has necessitated theoretical reconstruction.[5] A common strategy has been the retreat from one lost factor theory to another—thus from a rational utilitarian type to a bio-psychological instinct theory or one of natural selection. None of these has, however, provided more than temporary relief from the relentless pressure of empirical criticism and developing empirical knowledge.

It is not surprising that in this atmosphere attempts should have been made to elevate the neglected distinctively "social" elements into a dominant factor in the same sense—to oppose a "sociologistic"[6] theory to an economic or biological one. The most notable example of this possibility is what is in part the actual significance, but still more the predominant interpretation, placed upon Durkheim's famous formula that "society is a reality *sui generis*" which "constrains" the thought, feelings and actions of individuals. If however this alternative is taken as simply another "factor" theory it involves the same theoretical and empirical difficulties which all other similar constructions do. It throws light on some empirical problems but only at the cost of increasing difficulties in other directions.[7]

Not the least deleterious effect of the "factor" type of theorizing, to which it is even more subject than the empirical generalization type, is the division of the field into warring "schools" of thought. On this basis every school has some solid empirical justification but equally each, as a result of the need for closure of the system, involves insuperable difficulties and conflicts with other interpretations of the same phenomena. Professional pride and vested interests get bound up with the defense or promotion of one theory against all others and the result is an impasse. In such a situation it is not surprising that theory as such should be discredited and many

---

[5] Two conspicuous fields are the breakdown of the theories of social evolution of the Spencerian type, and the growing dissatisfaction with an individualistic utilitarian interpretation of the modern industrial economy.

[6] A term used by P. A. Sorokin in *Contemporary Sociological Theories*, New York: Harper and Bros., 1928).

[7] It is the author's contention that progress toward the formulation of a genuine structural-functional system is a far more important aspect of Durkheim's work. See *The Structure of Social Action*, Chaps. VIII-XI and Section III below.

of the sanest, least obsessive minds become disillusioned with the
whole thing and become dogmatic empiricists, denying as a matter
of principle that theory can do anything for science. They feel it
is, rather, only a matter of speculative construction which leads
away from respect for facts, and that thus the progress of science
can consist *only* in the accumulation of discrete, unrelated, un-
guided discoveries of fact.

Such empiricists often invoke the supposed authority of the natural sciences. But the whole history of science shows that this is a
gross misinterpretation. Perhaps the most extraordinary view is the
relatively common contention that the glory of physics is mathematical method, while at the same time "theory" is an unnecessary
impediment. But methematics in physics *is* theory. The greatness
of Newton and Laplace, of Einstein and Heisenberg is as theorists
in the strictest sense. A science of physics without higher mathematics would be the real equivalent of the empiricists' ideal for
social science. This shows quite clearly that what we need is not
a science purified of theoretical infection—but one with the nearest
possible approach to an *equivalent* of the role of mathematical
analysis in physics. The trouble with sociology has not been that
it has had too much theory but that it has been plagued with the
wrong kinds and what it has had of the right has been insufficiently
developed and used to meet the need.

III

Approaches to a Generalized Social System. In various partial
aspects of the field of human social behavior highly developed
theoretical schemes of what are here considered the right kind
have existed. This is notably true of economic theory, especially
since the discovery of the principle of marginal utility, and of psychological theory, especially since Freud.

Economics has directly followed the methodological model of
analytical mechanics and has been able to do so because, uniquely
among social disciplines, it can deal primarily with numerically
quantitative continua as variables. It has proved possible in principle to describe the state of a price economy in terms of the values
of the variables of a system of simultaneous differential equations,
though it is not possible operationally to ascertain the exact values
of the variables nor would it be mathematically possible to solve
the equations because of their excessive complexity. Hence most
actual working economic analysis has had to fall back on more

"primitive" analytical methods, and use the system of differential equations only as a methodological model.

But even more serious than this limitation has been the difficulty of fitting economic theory into the broader context of the social system as a whole. This was not a serious problem to the classical economists since they implicitly assumed a "utilitarian" system which gave economic "factors" the dominant dynamic role.[8] The general direction of solution seems to be that technical economic analysis makes sense only in the context of an "institutional" structure of social relationship patterns which is not, as such, part of the system dynamically treated by economic theory, but must constitute a set of constant data for it. Exactly what this means when the institutional data are treated on structural-functional terms while the economic data are not, remains on the whole an unsolved problem.

It is significant that concern with economic theory as well as training in mathematics and physics constituted the background of by far the most important attempt so far made to build up a generalized analysis of social systems as a whole in a dynamic analytical system on the model of mechanics—that of Pareto.[9] Pareto's attempt undoubtedly put systematic theoretical thinking about social systems on a new level; it is unique in the literature for its comprehensiveness and the sophistication of its understanding of the physical science model. And yet it must be regarded as a relative failure.

Pareto started with the view that economic theory had become a genuine dynamic system, but it was, relative to concrete social problems (including those which are usually classed as "economic"), empirically inadequate because unduly abstract. Hence he sought to analyze the most important missing variables in a total social system in terms of their dynamic interdependence with those of economics. He took the "logical action," which is involved in the economic as well as certain other phases of the orientation of action, as a starting point and attempted to analyze the remaining residual category of nonlogical action inductively in order to reveal the principal variables.

The result is highly complex and not very satisfactory. He isolated three variables which are very heterogeneous relative to one

---

[8] See *The Structure of Social Action,* Chaps. III and IV.

[9] *Cf.* L. J. Henderson, *Pareto's General Sociology: A Physiologist's Interpretation,* (Cambridge: Harvard University Press, 1937) Parsons, *The Structure of Social Action,* Chaps. V-VII.

another. The most satisfactorily analyzed, the "derivations," proves
to be empirically the least significant. Even this, however, cannot
be reduced to variation on a continuum but its values must be
treated in terms of a four-fold qualitative classification. The same
is true of the most important, the "residues," except that here the
classification is far more complex and its basis of principle in the
structure of social systems of action far less clear. Indeed it gives
the impression of a great deal of arbitrariness. Finally, with the
fourth variable, social heterogeneity, Pareto shifts to an altogether
different level. The first three referred immediately to elements of
the motivation or orientation of the action of individuals. The
fourth refers to an aspect of the structure of a system of social relationships. Its appearance may be taken as an indication of the extreme difficulty of operating in this field without structural categories. Its relevance to Pareto's principal empirical generalizations
is very clear and it serves the function of giving empirical relevance
to his analytical scheme. But strictly speaking it has no place in the
latter as a variable but should, with the aid of the relevant data,
be derivable from the system of variables.

It was said above that Pareto's attempt was a *relative* failure.
He certainly succeeded in avoiding all the principal theoretical
difficulties discussed above. His system is an extraordinarily useful
instrument of criticism. It also, when skillfully used as by Pareto
himself, yields important though rather general empirical insights.
But it has signally failed to work as a direct source of detailed
analytical tools in detailed research. What is successfully established
is too vague and general. The gaps have to be filled by arbitrary *ad
hoc* constructions and classifications or by the introduction of structural categories which are merely tolerated, not systematically
developed.

The conclusion is that Pareto took what is, in the present state
of sociological knowledge, the less fruitful alternative. A structural-
functional system must sacrifice much of the dynamic flexibility
Pareto aimed at. But it can hope to counterbalance this by a great
gain in explicit systematic determinacy and precision in detailed
analytical use.

The other alternative, the structural-functional type, also has
important antecedents. The most important of these are the following four:

1. The developments of modern dynamic and clinical psychology
which conceive the human individual as a dynamic structural-func-

tional system. Psychoanalytic theory has been the most important single influence in this field but stands by no means alone. This psychological theory is highly important both as a methodological model for that of a social system and as itself providing some of the most essential components of it.

2. Modern social and cultural anthropology, especially that with something of a "functional" slant though by no means confined to those writers usually designated as belonging to the functional school. Probably Malinowski's is so far the most important single name. Perhaps the basic point is that the scale of non-literate societies has been small and there has been no established division into different specialisms in dealing with it. Hence the anthropologist, when dealing with a society, was more likely than other social scientists to see it as a single functioning system.

3. Durkheim and his followers. As has been noted above, Durkheim in many respects tended to set a "sociologistic" factor theory over against the individualistic factor theories current in his day. But along with this heading there is a more important strand in his thought which gained increasingly in strength in the course of his career. This was a genuinely structural-functional treatment of the social system—with a gradual clarification of the more important elements of it. This is above all evident from the way in which he treated empirical problems, in his analysis of the stability of a system of functionally differentiated roles in his *Division of Labor*, in his study, *Le Suicide*, and in his interpretation of religious ritual in *The Elementary Forms of the Religious Life*.

4. Max Weber. In part Weber can serve as a type case of the more generalized thinking of the historical disciplines in the institutional field. But also, in reaction against the individualistic factor theories of his time, he went much farther than any other writer toward the underpinning of empirical study of comparative institutions with a generalized theoretical scheme. Incomplete though this was, it converged with Durkheim's scheme and supplemented it in the directions where comparative structural perspective is most important.[10]

---

[10] In addition to the *The Structure of Social Action,* Chaps. XIV-XVII, see the author's introduction to Weber's *Theory of Social and Economic Organization* (translated from *Wirtschaft und Gesellschaft,* Part I).

IV

Outline of a Structural-Functional Theory of Social Systems.
Limitations of space forbid following out the substantive problems
in the development of the present state of the structural-functional
theory of social systems. It is, however, contended that, developing
with particular clarity though by no means exclusively in the above
four sources, we now have the main outline of an articulated system
of structural-functional theory available and in actual use. The final
section of this paper will be devoted to an exceedingly bare and
general sketch of this main outline. Of necessity most of the details
will have to be omitted. As in every developing theoretical structure, there are innumerable difficulties and unsolved problems
which also cannot be entered into.

The first essential of a generalized theoretical system is the "frame
of reference." For the social system in question it is quite clear that
it is that of "action" or perhaps better "actor-situation" in a sense
analogous to the organism-environment frame of reference of the
biological sciences.

The actor-situation frame of reference is shared with psychology,
but for a social system it takes on the added complication introduced by the treatment of a plurality of *inter* acting actors in situations which are in part discrete, in part shared in common.

The unit of all social systems is the human individual *as actor,*
as an entity which has the basic characteristics of striving toward
the attainment of "goals," of "reacting" emotionally or affectively
toward objects and events, and of, to a greater or less degree, cog-
nitively knowing or understanding his situation, his goals and himself. Action is, in this frame of reference, inherently structured on a
"normative," "teleological," or possibly better, a "voluntaristic" system of "coordinates" or axes. A goal is by definition a "desirable"
state of affairs, failure to attain it a "frustration." Affective reaction
includes components of pleasurable or painful significance to the
actor, and of approval or disapproval of the object or state which
occasions the reaction. Finally, cognitive orientation is subject to
standards of "correctness" and "adequacy" of knowledge and understanding.

This essential "normative orientation" of action directs attention
to the crucial role of the "patterns" which define the desirable
direction of action in the form of goals and standards of behavior.
This system of normative patterns seems to be best treated as *one*

very important element of the "culture" of the group, which also includes cognitive patterns of "ideas," symbols and other elements. From the present point of view, however, a social system is a system of action, i.e., of motivated human behavior, not a system of culture patterns. It articulates with culture patterns in one connection just as it does with physical and biological conditions in another. But a "system of culture" is a different order of abstraction from a "social system" though it is to a large degree an abstraction from the same concrete phenomena.[11]

In all this, the point of view of interpretation of action has a peculiar duality. One essential component is its "meaning" to the actor, whether on a consciously explicit level or not. The other is its relevance to an "objective" concatenation of objects and events as analyzed and interpreted by an observer.

In a sense this basic frame of reference consists in the outline of the structural categories of human personality in a psychological sense, in terms of the particular values of which each particular character structure or sequences of action must be described and analyzed. But the structure of social systems cannot be derived directly from the actor-situation frame of reference. It requires functional analysis of the complications introduced by the interaction of a plurality of actors.

Even in abstraction from social relationships, features of the situation of action and the biologically determined needs and capacities of an individual provide certain fixed points of determination in the system of action. The functional needs of social integration and the conditions necessary for the functioning of a plurality of actors as a "unit" system sufficiently well integrated to exist as such impose others.

But functional needs, whether their ultimate sources be biological, socio-cultural or individual are, so far as they are dynamically relevant to this conceptual scheme, satisfied through *processes of action*. The need to eat is biologically determined, but the human processes of food production and the variations in the social customs of food taste and consumption are no more biologically determined than any other social phenomena, such as, for instance

---

[11] For the distinction between action and culture, see *The Structure of Social Action*, Chap. XIX, pp. 762 ff. This view differs from that of culture and social system set forth in Kluckhohn and Kelly, "The Concept of Culture," in Ralph Linton, ed., *The Science of Man in the World Crisis*, Columbia University Press.

the production and enjoyment of symphonic music. Hence, the ultimate "source" of needs is not relevant except in so far as it affects the structure and orientation of social systems of action, especially by providing "foci" around which attitudes, symbols and action patterns cluster.

A structure is a set of relatively stable patterned relationships of units. Since the unit of social system is the actor, social structure is a patterned system of the social relationships of actors. It is a distinctive feature of the structure of systems of social action, however, that in most relationships the actor does not participate as a total entity,[12] but only by virtue of a given differentiated "sector" of his total action. Such a sector, which is the unit of a system of social relationships, has come predominantly to be called a "role."[13] Hence, the previous statement must be revised to say that social structure is a system of patterned relationships of actors in their capacity as playing roles relative to one another. Role is the concept which links the subsystem of the actor as a "psychological" behaving entity to the distinctively *social* structure.

Two primary questions arise in following on beyond this point. First, what is the nature of this link, what is social structure from the point of view of the actor playing his roles within it? Second, what is the nature of the "system" of the patterned relationships of social structure?

The clue to the first question is found in the normative-voluntaristic aspect of the structure of action. From the point of view of the social system, a role is an element of generalized patterning of the action of its component individuals. But this is not merely a matter of statistical "trend." It is a matter of goals and standards. From the point of view of the actor, his role is defined by the normative expectations of the members of the group as formulated in its social traditions. The existence of these expectations among his fellows constitutes an essential feature of the situation in which any given actor is placed. His conformity with them or lack of it brings consequences to him, the sanctions of approval and reward, or of condemnation and punishment. But more than this, they constitute part of his own personality. In the course of process of socialization he absorbs—to a greater or less degree—the standards and ideals of

---

[12] In the sense in which a given brick as a whole is or is not "part" of a given wall.

[13] This concept has been used above all by Ralph Linton in *The Study of Man*, (New York: D. Appleton-Century Co., 1936). See especially Chap. VIII.

his group so that they become effective motivating forces in his own conduct, independently of external sanctions.

From this point of view the essential aspect of social structure lies in a system of patterned expectations defining the *proper* behavior of persons playing certain roles, enforced both by the incumbents' own positive motives for conformity and by the sanctions of others. Such systems of patterned expectations, seen in the perspective of their place in a total social system and sufficiently thoroughly established in action to be taken for granted as legitimate, are conveniently called "institutions." The fundamental, structurally stable element of social systems then, which, according to the present argument, must play a crucial role in their theoretical analysis, is their structure of institutional patterns defining the roles of their constituent actors.

Seen from the functional point of view, institutionalized roles constitute the mechanism by which extremely varied potentialities of "human nature" become integrated in such a way as to dovetail into a single integrated system capable of meeting the situational exigencies with which the society and its members are faced. Relative to these potentialities they have two primary functions: first, the *selective* one of bringing out those possibilities of behavior which "fit" the needs and the tolerances of the particular patterned structure and by-passing or repressing the others; secondly, through interactive mechanisms the maximum of motivational backing for action in conformity with the expectations of roles must be secured. Above all, *both* the disinterested motives associated with "conscience" and "ideals" and the self-interested ones must be mobilized in the interest of the *same* directions of behavior.

The second main problem is that of the structure of institutions themselves as a system. They are resultants of and controlling factors in the action of human beings in society. Hence, as a system they must at the same time be related to the functional needs of their actors as individuals and of the social systems they compose. Thus, the basic structural principle, as in the case of anatomy, is that of functional differentiation. The functional reference, however, is in the social case more complex since *both* functional needs of the actor and those of the social system are intertwined.

Any scheme for analyzing such a functionally differentiated structure is necessarily complex and there is presumably no single "right" one. A basic three-fold scheme has, however, proved very useful and seems of highly generalized significance.[14] In the first place, there are "situational" institutions or patterns. These are cases of the organization of roles about aspects of the situation in which actors and social systems are placed. Leading examples are kinship roles, organized about the biological relatedness of individuals through descent, and in part at least, political institutions, organized about solidarity with respect to the use and sufferance of force within a territorial area.

The second class are "instrumental" institutions, patterned about the attainment of certain classes of goals as such. For example, a given technology like that of modern medicine is pursued within the framework of an institutionalized role, that of physician. Finally, third, there are "integrative" institutions, those primarily oriented to regulating the relations of individuals so as to avoid conflict or promote positive cooperation. Social stratification and authority are primary examples.

Since relative valuation of personal qualities and achievements is inevitable in a system, it is, thus essential that these valuations be integrated in an ordered system of ranking, the system of stratification of a society. Similarly the potentialities of deviant behavior and the need for detailed coordination of the action of many people are, in any at all complex society, such that spontaneous response to unorganized controls cannot be relied upon. Some persons and organized agencies must be in a position within limits to repress deviance or its consequences or to ensure effective cooperation. Again, it is essential to the integration of a society that such control over others be institutionally ordered and regulated and constitute a system of roles of legitimate authority. This is an important factor in the effectiveness of the control since it makes possible appeal to a sense of moral obligation, and makes it possible to regulate authority which, if misused, has serious, disruptive potentialities.

The importance of conceiving institutions as a functionally differentiated system lies in making it possible to place changes in any one part of it in the perspective of their interdependence in the system as a whole. In so far as the system is adequately formulated in generalized terms and is structurally complete, it ensures that explicit attention will be given to every major possibility of the repercussions of a change in different directions.

---

[14] See "Toward a Common Language for the Area of Social Science," Part II, mimeographed for use by students in Harvard College (reprinted in the original edition of this volume.)

Dynamic analysis is not, however, possible in terms of the systematic treatment of institutional structure alone. This involves the possibility of generalized treatment of the behavioral tendencies of the human actors, in the situations in which they are placed and subject to the expectations of their institutionalized roles. In the most general terms such generalization depends on a theory of the "motivation" of human behavior.

The ultimate foundations of such a theory must certainly be derived from the science of psychology. But both because the "idiosyncratic" element in the behavior and motivation of individuals is so great and because the levels of abstraction current in psychology have been what they have, it has not been possible, in general, to derive an adequate theory of the motivation of socially structured mass phenomena through the simple "application" of psychological generalizations. The relationship between the psychological level and behavior in social systems is complex, but light is thrown on it in terms of the psychological implications of the conception of role.

This is above all true in two directions. The early tendency of psychology was to consider "personality" as largely an expression of genetic constitution or of unique idiosyncrasy. Study of socialization in a comparative perspective is, however, demonstrating that there are important elements of uniformity in the "character structure" of those who have been socialized in the same cultural and institutional system, subject to variations according to different roles within the system.[15] Though the limits of applicability of this conception of a character structure appropriate to a given role structure are as yet by no means clear, its general theoretical significance is established. In so far as it applies, the pattern of motivation to be used in explaining behavior in an institutionalized role is not derived directly from the "propensities of human nature," in general. It is a matter of such components *organized* into a particular structure. Such a structured personality type will have its own appropriate patterns of motivation and tendencies of behavior.

The other principal direction of development is different. It concerns the area within which there is, in any given social system, a range of flexibility in behavior on a psychological level. Evidence, particularly from complex societies, points to the view that this range is relatively wide for large proportions of the population and

---

[15] See, for instance, Abram Kardiner, *The Individual and His Society*, (New York: Columbia University Press, 1939), and various recent writings of Margaret Mead.

that the distribution of character types more or less successfully fulfilling the requirements of a given role also covers a wide range.

The fundamental mechanism here is what may be called the "structural generalization of goals" and of other aspects of orientation. As W. I. Thomas puts it, one of the fundamental functions of institutions is to "define the situation"[16] for action. Once a situation is institutionally defined and the definition upheld by an adequately integrated system of sanctions, action in conformity with the relevant expectations tends, as pointed out, to mobilize a wide variety of motivational elements in its service. Thus, to take one of the most famous examples, the "profit motive," which has played such a prominent part in economic discussion, is not a category of psychology at all. The correct view is rather that a system of "free enterprise" in a money and market economy so defines the situation for the conducting or aspiring to the conduct of business enterprise, that they must seek profit as a condition of survival and as a measure of success of their activities. Hence, whatever interests the individual may have in achievement, self-respect, the admiration of others, etc., to say nothing of what money will buy, are channeled into profit-making activity.[17] In a differently defined situation, the same fundamental motives would lead to a totally different kind of activity.[18]

Thus, in analyzing the dynamic problems of a social system, it is not enough to apply "psychology" to the behavior of individuals in the relevant "objective" situations. It is necessary to qualify the interpretation of their "reactions" in terms of the evidence on at least two other problems—what can be known about a character structure "typical" of that particular social system and particular roles within it, and what will be the effect of the structurally generalized goals and orientations resulting from the "definitions of the situation" current in the society.

But with due regard of this type of qualification, it remains true that the basic dynamic categories of social systems are "psycho-

---

[16] See especially his *The Unadjusted Girl*, (Boston: Little, Brown, and Co., 1927), Introduction.

[17] See Talcott Parsons, "The Motivation of Economic Activity," *Canadian Journal of Economics and Political Science*, 6: 187-203, May, 1940. For a further analysis of the relation of role-structure to the dynamics of motivation see Talcott Parsons, "Propaganda and Social Control," *Psychiatry*, 5: 551-572, November, 1942. Both are reprinted in the present volume.

[18] See B. Malinowski, *Coral Gardens and their Magic*, (London: G. Allen and Unwin, 1935), vol. I, Chap. I, Sec. 9.

logical." The relation of psychology to the theory of social systems appears to be closely analogous to that of biochemistry to general physiology. Just as the organism is not a category of general chemistry, so social system is not one of psychology. But within the framework of the physiological conception of what a functioning organism is, the *processes* are chemical in nature. Similarly, the *process* of social behavior as of any other are psychological. But without the meaning given them by their institutional-structural context they lose their relevance to the understanding of social phenomena.

However sketchy and inadequate the above outline may be, it may be hoped that it does give an idea of the main character of the emerging structural-functional theory of social systems. It remains to raise the question of what aspect of that theory may be considered specifically sociological.

It is of course possible to consider sociological theory as concerned with the total theory of social systems in general. It seems, however, undesirable to do this since it would make of sociology such an extremely comprehensive discipline, including as it would have to, for instance, both the major part of psychology and all of economic theory. The most important alternative is to treat sociology as the science of institutions in the above sense or more specifically of institutional structure. This would, as here conceived, by no means limit it to purely static structural analysis but could retain a definite focus on problems of structure, including structural change. Dynamic, particularly psychological, problems would enter into sociology in terms of their specific relevance to this context.[19]

This view leaves room for a clear distinction from psychology as the general science of human personality structure and motivation. It is quite clear that many of the concrete problems of psychology in this sense are not sociological at all. For example, sociological considerations would be secondary and peripheral in the whole field of clinical psychology. The two sciences are, however, necessarily closely interdependent and data concerning the role structure of the social system are at least implicity involved in practically all

---

[19] This is in slightly modified form essentially the view put forth in *The Structure of Social Action*, Chap. XIX. Institutions are those elements of the structure of social systems which most distinctively embody the patterns of "common value integration" of a system of action.

concrete psychology problems. This, however, is not an unusual situation in the relationship of different sciences.

This view also makes it possible to distinguish sociology from economic theory. Economic theory is concerned with certain distinctive dynamic processes which go on within social systems. A situation where it is relevant in more than the broadest respects is confined to certain distinctive types of social systems, notably those where there is an important degree of primary orientation to considerations of optimum utilization of resources and of cost. Such a situation presupposes in the first place a distinctive institutional structure. In the second place, as a consequence of this, it presupposes the organization of motives about certain types of structurally generalized goals. But, given these conditions, the distinctive dynamic consequences of economically oriented action must be analyzed in terms of a specific technical conceptual scheme. As Pareto and many others have been well aware, this scheme is highly abstract and the larger aspects of the dynamics of total economic systems will inevitably involve interdependence with non-economic variables.

In some respects analogous to the distinctive features of a market or price economy is the emergence in complex social systems of certain prominent functionally differentiated structures. Perhaps the most important of these is that of government. It is always possible to make a study of such structures and the relevant social processes the subject of a relatively independent science. So far, however, in none of these cases has a distinctive analytical scheme appeared which would give that science a theoretical status analogous to that, for instance, of economics. Thus, it is highly questionable whether "political theory" in a scientific rather than an ethical and normative sense should be regarded as a fundamental element of the theory of social systems. It seems more logical to regard it as a field of application of the general theory of social institutions but one which is sufficiently differentiated to be treated as an independent discipline for many purposes. The same general considerations apply to other aspects of structural differentiation, such as, for example, that of religion.

Finally, there is a question as to whether anthropology should be considered in a theoretical sense an independent science. As the study of non-literate societies, it is of course a pragmatic field of specialization of considerable significance, in some ways analogous to the field of government. In so far, however, as its theoretical concern is with the study of social systems as such, there seems to be no reason to regard social anthropology as a distinctive theoretical discipline. In the relevant respects, it must be regarded as a branch of sociology, and in its other aspects, of economics, government and so on. There is, however, one problem, analysis of which might modify this view. To many of its proponents, the distinctive feature of anthropology is that it is the science of *culture,* not of social systems. It is implicit in the above analysis that culture, though empirically fundamental to social systems and in one sense a component of them, is not in the theoretical sense exclusively a social phenomenon. It has been pointed out above that the study of the structure of cultural patterns *as such* and of their structural interdependence is a legitimate abstraction from the concrete phenomena of human behavior and its material consequences, which is quite different from their study in the context of interdependence in a social system. It is perfectly clear that this study is not equivalent to the study of institutions as aspects of a social system. If the focus of theoretical interest of anthropology is to develop in this direction, two important consequences would seem to follow. First, it is quite clear that its traditional primary concern with non-literate peoples cannot be upheld. The culture of non-literate peoples is neither more nor less a subject for the differentiation of a science than is their institutional structure. Secondly, it is particularly important to clarify the generalized relationship between culture and social structure. A great deal of confusion appears to be prevalent on this point among both sociologists and cultural anthropologists.

XII

The Problem of Controlled Institutional Change

THE MEMBERS OF the Conference reached definite agreement on the important conclusion that the sources of German aggressive expansionism are not merely a matter of the particular recent situation in which the German nation has been placed, or of the character and policies of a particular régime which can be expected to vanish with the fall of the régime. Although drawn out and accentuated by these factors, the more important sources lie deeper and would not necessarily be seriously affected by chances at these levels.

The principal emphasis of the Conference was on the existence of a typical German character structure which predisposes people to define all human relations in terms of dominance, submission, and romantic revolt. It was, however, also agreed that such a typical character structure, although probably an independent factor[1] of great significance, is supported by, and closely interdependent with, an institutional structure of German society. The interdependence is such that on the one hand any permanent and far-reaching change in the orientation of the German people probably cannot rest on a change of character structure alone, but must also involve institutional change; otherwise, institutional conditions would continue to breed the same type of character structure in new generations. On the other hand, it may prove that a direct attack on character structure as such is less promising than one through other forces that operate on the institutional system and which, through changes in that, may serve to create conditions favorable to a change in character structure.

---

[1] Exactly how far it is an independent factor is exceedingly difficult to judge since only actual uniformities of behavior are available as direct evidence. Hence, for certain purposes character structure and institutional structure may be treated as different abstractions from the same facts. Even so far as they are actually independent permanent change of character structure is dependent upon institutional change.

Analytical Introduction
INSTITUTIONS IN THE SOCIAL SYSTEM

The institutional structure of a society must be regarded as a special aspect of the total social system. Especially for purposes of considering the possibilities of dynamic change in institutions it is essential to treat them systematically and explicitly in terms of their interdependence with the other principal elements of the system.

Institutions are those patterns which define the essentials of the legitimately expected behavior of persons insofar as they perform *structurally important roles* in the social system. There are, of course, many degrees of conformity or lack of it, but a pattern is "institutionalized" only insofar as at least a minimum degree of conformity is legitimately expected—thus its absence treated with sanctions at least of strong disapproval—*and* a sufficient degree of conformity on the part of a sufficient proportion of the relevant population exists so that this pattern defines the *dominant* structural outline of the relevant system of concrete social relationships. It is the *structurally* significant elements of the total concrete relationship pattern which are institutionally relevant. What these are cannot be decided in terms of the subjective sentiments of participant observers but only in the perspective of structural analysis of the social system.

Institutional patterns are the "backbone" of the social system. But they are by no means absolutely rigid entities and certainly have no mysteriously "substantial" nature. They are only relatively stable uniform resultants of the processes of behavior of the members of the society, and hence of the forces which determine that behavior. Their relative stability results from the particular structure of interdependence of those forces, and institutional structure is subject to change as a function of any one of many different kinds of change in the underlying system of forces. Their relatively stable role in social systems, however, indicates that institutionalized patterns do in fact mobilize a combination of forces in support of their maintenance which is of primary significance in the total equilibrium of a social system. Analysis of the nature and principal components of this combination is the first requisite of an approach to the problem of institutional change.

Furthermore, institutionalization is a *general* phenomenon of all extensive and permanent social systems. Hence, the broad outline of the problem concerns elements which are universal to all societies and does not depend upon specialized knowledge of the particular society in question. A general analysis of the problem can be presented first[2] and then applied to the particular facts and circumstances of the case.

The uniformities of human behavior must be analyzed in terms of the structure of motivational forces on the one hand, and of the situation in which they have to operate, on the other. In looking for the structure of forces underlying institutions, it is important to keep in mind that *both* elements of the determination of human behavior are involved in a peculiar kind of interdependence. For in social relationships it is the *expected* and actual behavior and manifestation of the sentiments of others which is the most important component of the situation in which any one person acts. Hence, to a very large extent, the structure of the situation is dependent on the stability of the motivational structure of the members of the society at large. So long as a stable structure is maintained this accounts for the interlocking of so many motivational elements in support of the same goals and standards. It above all accounts for the cardinal fact of institutional behavior, that in an integrated system "self-interested" elements of motivation and disinterested moral sentiments of duty tend to motivate the *same* concrete goals.

Such an interlocking is, however, never complete. There are important elements of the situation of action of different classes of persons which are not primarily dependent on the crystallized sentiments of others. Conversely, there are unstable elements in the motivation structure of persons. It is at these two points that the principal openings for institutional change are to be sought. It is a further implication of the general character of institutions that the consequences of changes at these points may be more important than would appear at first sight because any change at these points will *interact* with the other elements of the system and may well set up cumulative tendencies to change.

Before exploring these possibilities further, however, it is necessary to develop a somewhat clearer picture of the main elements of stability in an institutional system. It is these which have to be modified to achieve fundamental changes.

---

[2] This analysis is of course generalized from the study of many empirical cases—not simply deduced from general considerations.

Factors of Rigidity: *"Vested Interests"*

It is inherent in the nature of an institutional system that it should create, and is in part supported by, a complex system of vested interests. Even on occasion in conflict with very deep-rooted moral sentiments, people will often be powerfully motivated by considerations of interest. There is no question of the importance of interests but only of the perspective in which they are seen in the total social system and of the nature of the structure of motivational elements referred to as an interest.

Among "interests" in general those which may be called "vested" are distinguished by the fact that they are oriented to the maintenance of objects of interest which have already become established. This means that to a greater or less degree the status and situations and their perquisites to which such interests are attached already involve some element of legitimacy or claim to it. To attempt to deprive a person or a group of something in which they enjoy a vested interest thus involves not only imposing the frustrations attendant to the deprivation as such but also to a greater or less degree outrages the moral sentiments surrounding the claim of legitimacy. The resistance of the people or groups affected is thus strengthened by their sense of injustice. Furthermore, the same fact enables them to rally support for their claims from people who do not share the same interests. The obverse of this, finally, is the fact that among those who oppose a vested-interest group there is likely to be an element of sense of guilt arising from the fact that they share the same patterns of value. This introduces an element of ambivalence which in an important sense weakens the position of the attacker. If the guilt is repressed, however, it may make the actual attack more extreme than it would otherwise have been. But in such cases the attacker may be highly vulnerable to the proper kind of attempt to change his attitudes.

The structure of interests in a group is a function both of the structure of the realistic situations in which people act and of the "definitions" of those situations which are institutionalized in fhe society. It is this latter fundamental aspect which is most likely to be misunderstood in common sense thinking, since one is prone to assume that what people want to "get out of" a realistic situation, or avoid in it, is universal, a matter of "human nature." The actual tendency is to project one's own definitions of situations onto the action of other people and societies. An actor thinks of what he would want in such a situation.

The consequence of the role of institutionalized definitions of situations in the structuring of interests is at some points to introduce elements of rigidity, which would not otherwise exist, of flexibility at others. In the first case it delays or altogether blocks what might otherwise be felt to be a "natural" reaction to a change in the realistic situation.[3] It is, therefore, never safe to count on the effect of changing a situation on the structure of interests without specifically investigating the definitions of situations within the groups involved.

The effect of a change in the realistic situation while an institutionalized definition remains unchanged is to create a strain. The line of least resistance in reaction to this strain will usually be to attempt more aggressively than before to reassert the old definition of the situation and to shape the realistic situation in conformity with it. This total reaction involving above all the appropriate emotional components is what is generally meant by talking about the behavior of "the vested interests." For constructive change to take place it is therefore not only necessary to provide realistic opportunities which can be utilized to satisfy the interests of groups. It is also necessary to have some mechanism for coping with these other aspects of the problem. Two things are above all important. First, to provide new alternative definitions of the situation which give the new realistic opportunities positive meaning. It is particularly important that these should not be too far removed from the symbols and prestige standards previously current. Secondly, the emotionally aggressive defensiveness must be dealt with. This is to a large extent a reaction to a sense of insecurity, and requires some kind of measures of reassurance.

Of course, there are occasions where it is not possible to redefine the situation so that an interest group will fit into a new situation. Then its compulsory repression is the only way. But here, besides the question of adequate means of compulsion, a most important consideration is that of the moral position of the compelling agent. For the moral sentiments which legitimize an interest are shared by,

---

[3] A dramatic example is the "suicidal mania" of Japanese soldiers. To the Occidental a hopeless situation where no further contribution to the cause is possible is an occasion for honorable surrender. To most Japanese, apparently, surrender under any circumstances is an intolerable disgrace. This is a matter of differences in the *definition* of the situation, not of the *realistic* situations themselves.

and shade into, those of other groups. For the long run effect the moral isolation and insulation of a group which has to be frustrated is at least as important as the physical capacity to carry it through.

The converse of this difficulty lies in the fact that rational adaptation to realistic situations *is* a fundamental component of human social behavior. Hence, change of situation plus sheer cognitive enlightenment about its possibilities can often effect important changes. It must, however, to exploit this possibility, operate so as to avoid too serious conflict with the forces just discussed. Above all the change must be such as not to be interpreted—psychologically, not intellectually alone—as threatening security in those things in which members of the group have important emotional investment.

The phenomenon of vested interests thus proves to be a special case of the general integration of diverse motivational forces about an institutional structure. It is exceedingly difficult to say that the elements of self-interest are *the* decisive factors in most cases. It is the mutual reenforcement of the different elements which is the principal source of rigidity—interest taken alone is probably one of the factors most accessible to change.

A particularly important class of cases of this mutual reenforcement is that where group solidarities are involved. In a functionally differentiated society like that of the modern Occident, in perhaps a majority of groups solidarity is secondary to the functional significance of the roles of the members. But even here, sentiments of solidarity readily acquire a prominent place. Insofar as this happens the security of their members becomes associated with the status of the group as such, rather than fulfillment of the functional norms which ideally govern its role; and sanctions come to be applied to what is interpreted as loyalty to the group rather than functionally adequate achievement. Once such patterns of group solidarity are firmly established a serious obstacle to change is introduced. Appeals to a group in terms of functional values may be ineffective unless they can also carry the sentiments of group solidarity with them. Such sentiments are particularly difficult to deal with when the members of the group feel insecure,[4] because this creates a "defensive" attitude system.

---

[4] Guilt may be an important element in this insecurity. Where people are really uneasy about the moral justification of their position, they may defend it with all the emotional intensity of fanaticism. In this case the "ethics" of group loyalty is often used to rationalize away the deeper moral conflict.

The concept of "vested interest" thus serves as a key to the problem of rigidity in an institutional system because it is the most conspicuous pattern of behavior which appears in particular groups in resistance to change or threats of it. As such, however, it applies to particular groups. It is a mode of focusing all the principal components of motivation on such resistance. But any one group is structurally interdependent with others in the same social system. Moreover, the same persons play a variety of different roles as members of different groups.

It is a cardinal fact of social change that it impinges unevenly on the different parts of the society it affects. It alters the status and role of some groups but not directly of others. Or it may alter the situation or definition of it of the members of a group in *one* of their roles—for example, occupational; but not directly in another—for example, kinship. But it is in the nature of this structural interdependence of groups and roles in a social system that alteration in any one will set up waves of repercussion in many others. The different structural elements of a social system are "geared in" to one another. The factors of stability or rigidity just discussed are present in each one. Change at one point sets up a strain in neighboring parts of the system. One fundamental and immediate possibility of reaction to the strain is the vested-interest reaction—to activate an emotionally defensive resistance to the change. After the problem of overcoming this pattern of reaction at the points where the forces of change impinge most immediately on the system itself, the next problem is that of preventing the development of this barrier to its structurally necessary repercussions beyond these points.

This is a basically important consideration since if the defensive reaction becomes sufficiently firmly consolidated, one of two things must happen. Either the reaction will be so powerful as to eliminate the change and, if not restore the previous balance, lead to a quite different direction of change. Or, short of this, there will be a permanent state of malintegration and tension which will prevent stable institutionalization of the new patterns even within their primary area of application. Not only will there be elements of group conflict but, perhaps even more important, a large number of persons will be caught in a pattern of conflicting pressures and ambivalent attitudes as "marginal men." For the patterns dominant in one set of roles a person plays will conflict more or less seriously with those in others. The resulting situation of insecurity for many produces a high degree of instability of overt attitudes and behavior.

An example of fundamental significance in modern Western society is the tension between occupational and family roles. The occupational system has, through the inherently dynamic character of modern technology and of the development of large-scale organization, been a focus of continual change, profoundly altering the pattern of the occupational role. On the whole the forces for change operating *directly* on the family have not been so strong and have been of a different, largely an ideological, character. Hence, the defensive reaction pattern has been particularly strong in the family and in those agencies which, like the churches, have assumed the role of guardians of the integrity of its traditional patterns. As so often happens, only a very vague insight into the real sources of the changes has existed, so the hostility generated has largely been discharged upon scapegoats, prominent among which has been the "younger generation."

Two further features of the "psychological" structure of social systems are of very general significance for the present discussion. First, psychologists have strongly emphasized the importance of emotional attitudes toward those objects which impinge directly upon the everyday emotional life of a person, particularly those concrete persons with whom he is placed in immediate contacts: his own parents, siblings, spouse, or "boss." It is readily understandable that he should have strong and often complicated emotional feelings toward them. But it is also true that people have very strong feelings about objects, patterns, and symbols which are relatively remote from their personal experiences and interests. Indeed, for most of a population most of the time the majority of those objects which are essential to the structuring and behavior of large-scale social units are in this category. Thus, in time of peace a potential national enemy, the ideal of equality of opportunity or the flag can arouse very powerful reactions. Of course, reflection and analysis shows that even people's immediate interests are in fact dependent on these things and what they symbolize. But the intellectual complexity of the relation is too great for it to account adequately for the emotional reaction. This must depend on nonrational mechanisms to an even higher degree than reactions to immediate objects. The nature of these mechanisms is a problem of great importance.

It is clear that the connection may be relatively loose between these two basic levels and that attitudes toward the remoter objects may be subject to change by psychological techniques which would not operate successfully to change a man's attitude toward his mother or his "boss." It is essential to keep this in mind in discussing problems of ideology, political attitudes and the like.

The second important fact is that the conception of a completely integrated social system is a limiting case. Every at all complex society contains very important elements of internal conflict and tension. In some respects this is an impediment to change since patterns of defensive vested-interest behavior already exist in important cases as responses to conflict with other internal elements. But it also almost certainly means that there are "allies" within the social system itself which can be enlisted on the side of change in any given direction.

In particular, Germany is not, relatively to the rest of the Western world, a completely "sealed off" unique society. Many of its most important culture patterns and structural elements shade imperceptibly into those on the democratic side of the conflict. They are genuinely institutionalized in Germany or have been very incompletely eradicated under the Nazi régime. They constitute fundamentally important avenues of approach to change in the other, the conflicting elements.

This lack of full integration has a further consequence: it means that the underlying institutional foundations of national behavior are not as firm as they would be in a better integrated system. Indeed, one factor in the violence of these manifestations in the case of Germany lies in the conflict; part of the energy has the function of repressing the sentiments and patterns opposed to the recent course. The expectation may then be that not too radical an alteration in the *balance* of forces could have "disproportionately" great effects on immediate behavior. This is, indeed, what happened in the shift from Weimar to the Nazi régime. The Germany of Weimar was not spurious—a "deceitful mask" as many are now inclined to feel. That would be as serious an error as the previous one of supposing that it was the one "true Germany" once the "bad" monarchy had been eliminated.

But of course merely shifting the balance till the scale tips is not a radical cure—it would take too little to shift it back again. But it can be an early phase of a farther-reaching process—the obverse of what the Nazi régime has hoped it was accomplishing.

Channels of Influence

To recall a previous starting point: human behavior may be influenced either through the situations in which people must act, or through "subjective" elements—their sentiments, goals, attitudes, definitions of situations. This classification may serve for orinetation to the analysis of the elements of flexibility, hence possible openings for control, of a social system.

The first must be differentiated according to whether it is the situation external to the social system as a whole, which is independent of its internal institutional structure, or the immediate situations in which large classes of people act—of which institutional patterns themselves constitute a crucial element—which is to be deliberately controlled. In the latter case only certain elements of situations are subject to control as a *means* of bringing about institutional change; others must be a result of it.

A second essential discrimination is between using control of the situation to suppress a structural element or manifestation, and using it to alter it by making available new channels of expression for the same basic sentiments and goals—so that the sense of continuity need not be lost.

Turning to the subjective side, it is possible to attempt through "education" and "propaganda" to affect mass sentiments through influencing various of their manifestations. The phenomena in this field are exceedingly complex and in an elementary stage of analysis. The most important thing to be said is that the chances of successful influence do not depend mainly on the apparent "reasonableness" of what is transmitted but on its relation to the functional equilibrium of the system on which it impinges. This in turn depends on at least three factors: the functional significance of the manifestations it attempts to displace, the potential functions of the new patterns which are put forward, and the appropriateness of the source and manner of influence, that is, the definition of the situation of "being influenced" from the point of view of the recipients.

Again it is important to discriminate sentiments and their manifestations touching remoter objects concerning the society at large, from those touching the immediate interests of its members.

Just as actual situations deviate from institutionally sanctioned definitions of the same situations, so ideological and symbolic patterns associated with the sentiment system do not stand in a simple relation of correspondence with the sentiments manifested. Ideological patterns are inevitably highly selective if not distorted relative to the system of sentiments which support institutions. These and other patterns often involve psychological reactions to strain and thus contain elements of prejection and displacement on "culture heroes" or scapegoats. Finally, symbolism plays a very prominent part in this field.

These considerations, combined with the others already discussed, show that it is not to be expected that the "logical" consequences of ideas will be automatically "acted out." What will happen is rather the resultant of the interaction of verbal patterns with a variety of other elements in the total social system.

The Case of Germany
THE PROBLEM: OBJECTIVES OF A PROGRAM

The members of the Conference agreed that the dominant character structure of modern Germany had been distinguished by a striking dualism between "A: an emotional, idealistic, active, romantic component which may be constructive or destructive and anti-social," and "B: an orderly, hard-working hierarchy preoccupied, methodical, submissive, gregarious, materialistic" component.[5]

In the traditional pre-Nazi German society it is overwhelmingly the B component which has become institutionalized. The A component arises from two principal interdependent sources: certain features of the socialization process in the German family, and the tensions arising from life in that type of institutional order. It is expressed in romantic, unrealistic emotionalism and yearnings. Under other circumstances the dissociation has historically been radical—the romantic yearning has found an outlet in religion, art, music and other-worldly, particularly a-political, forms.

The peculiarity of the Nazi movement is that it has harnessed this romantic dynamism to an aggressive, expansionist, nationalistic political goal—and an internal revolution—and has utilized and subordinated all the motives behind the B component as well. In both cases the synthesis has been dependent at the same time on certain features of the situation and on a meaningful definition of the situation and system of symbols. The first task of a program of institutional change is to disrupt this synthesis and create a situation in which the romantic element will again find an a-political

---

[5] Quoted from Report of the Conference, Appendix 3, p. 10. Compare Erikson, Erik Homburger, "Hitler's Imagery and German Youth," *Psychiatry* (1942) 5:475-493.

form of expression. This will not, however, "cure" the basic difficulty but only its most virulent and, to the United Nations, dangerous manifestation. Its importance, however, should not be underestimated. This may be referred to as a semi-institutionalized feature of the German system.

The second problematical set of features of the German institutional system comprises certain traits associated with the B components of her character structure.[6] Orderliness, industry, and methodicality are not "trouble-making" traits if they are stable. Even, these, however, are skewed by their relation to the dominance-submission element which finds its institutional counterpart in a rigidly hierarchical status system where the superiority-inferiority aspect of roles tends to be emphasized to the exclusion of their positive functional significance, and in a peculiar prominence of relations of authority.

A second conspicuous general trait of German institutions is their "formalism." In part this serves to emphasize status and authority as such. But there is also what to Americans seems a peculiar kind of dissociation between the status system and the "inner" emotional interests and character of persons. This is both a determinant and a consequence of the dualism of German character. Goals *within* the status system fail to satisfy the romantic longings of component A as previously defined. Germans are much more preoccupied with status than Americans, but there has been little romantization of *success* in Germany. Americans are prone to romanticize attainment *within* the institutionalized status system; while Germans have a greater romantic interest in goals *outside* it.

Both these traits permeate the whole role and group structure of German society. But their special incidence varies in the different parts of the social structure. The Prussian state has remained the center of both these patterns. For, long before industrialization, in its civil service it developed a highly formalized hierarchical and authoritarian structure which, with the waning of feudalism, came to hold a position of high prestige in the society. Much the same was true of the other main structure, the military establishment, which shared the same traits but in the officers' corps with even greater emphasis on a prestige status and with this, a highly favorable situation for the dominance of "militaristic" values.

---

[6] For a somewhat fuller analysis of these institutional traits than space allows here, see Parsons, Talcott, "Democracy and Social Structure in Pre-Nazi Germany," *J. Legal and Political Sociol.*, Nov. 1942, reprinted above.

Another important pre-industrial component of the German institutional system was the "conservative" structure of the peasantry
and the older artisan and middle-class groups. Above all, these
lower groups could readily integrate their status in the occupational
system with a patriarchal-authoritarian family structure. For the
most part the significant occupational unit was a family, not an
individual person as such. The father was, as a peasant, for instance,
the actual head of a producing organization in which his familial
and productive roles coincided.

The third fundamental aspect of German society is a structural
tension which in a very broad sense may be described as that between the firmly institutionalized patterns of this older pre-industrial structure and the structure of situations and—in part—sentiments resulting from the impact of modern industrialism and its
principal social accompaniments, notably large-scale urbanization.
It is a case of partial integration and partial conflict. Industrialism
would never have had the spectacular development which, by
contrast with all the Latin countries, it had in Germany unless the
previous institutional structure had been favorable to it. But in
part the result was an industrial system with a different emphasis
from that in the United States. The state has played a much more
prominent role. Within industry itself there has been more emphasis
on hierarchy, authority, formalism, status-consciousness.

But at the same time there has been very serious tension. One
point of tension is between the status system and the patterns of
individual, technical achievement. The enormous German sensitivity to "proletarization" has something to do with the definition of
all but the highest statuses in organization as involving subordination and limitation to a strictly formal definition of role. Another
most important consequence is the change in the kinship situation.
Where the role of father and head of a small economic unit were
combined they reenforced each other. But where a man is an authoritarian father in the family, but a subordinate whose subordination is continually symbolically rubbed in outside, it creates a
serious ambivalence in his own attitudes and in his significance to
his wife and children. The result has been to break down a relatively well integrated patriarchal pattern.

The result of this major internal tension was to arouse intensely
defensive vested-interest behavior on the part of the groups most
closely identified with these conservative patterns and to introduce

a very large element of insecurity into the lives of large numbers who were torn between conflicting patterns. This situation played a large part in the instability of the Weimar régime and accounted for much of the susceptibility of large elements of the population to the appeal of Nazi propaganda.

The problem of control of German institutional structure may be put, therefore, in terms of the following three major objectives:

To eliminate the specific Nazi synthesis of the two major components of German character, or to divert it from its recent distinctive channels of expression if this is possible.

To eliminate, or at least seriously reduce, the structural role of the hierarchical, authoritarian and formalistic elements in the "conservative" German institutional structure—in particular its focus on the army and the military class should be broken.

To displace the conservative pattern and to reduce the tension by systematically fostering those elements of the pattern of modern Germany, especially of industrialism, which are closest to their counterparts in the democratic countries.

REPRESENTATIVE CONTROL OF THE SITUATION

It is clear that the first task, now nearing completion, is to break down the German military effort against the United Nations. Victory for the United Nations can, in combination with other things, have a profound effect on the internal institutional structure of Germany as well as on its immediate power to make war. This is particularly true since the Nazi movement, as an anti-traditional "charismatic" movement, is peculiarly dependent on success to maintain its internal prestige. It is irrevocably committed to success in this war and can scarcely survive a really thorough defeat. Defeat should, if properly managed, not only realistically disrupt the Nazi organization but be the most important factor in permanently eliminating the "Hitler myth" as the primary focus of the romantic elements in German national psychology. For this to happen it is, however, essential that the *moral* prestige of the victorious powers *in Germany* should be maintained. The German propaganda line will surely be that it is an "unfair" victory of material force alone. However stern the victors should be, they should never lose sight of the importance of getting across a sense of the justice of their cause—not of impulsive and arbitrary revenge.

The logical "follow-up" of military victory is to place Germany in a position where it is quite clear that a repetition of her aggression will not be tolerated and cannot be successful. There are many possible ways in which this objective can be achieved. There is no point in trying to decide between them; it is necessary only to indicate that once chosen, they should fulfill three principal conditions:

The control must be effective. To the German type of mentality the idea that objectively it is possible to "get away" with a repetition of aggressive aggrandizement is a direct invitation to attempt it. The security system *must* be strong. This means above all solidarity among those responsible for its enforcement.

It must be such as to maintain the moral position of those who impose it. It is not necessary to be bound by Nazi ideologists' definitions of German rights nor to avoid all just punishment for past derelictions of duty to the community of nations—but the attendant severity must not be such as to be construed, in the long run, as dictated simply by the victors' self-interest or revenge—using main force to hold Germany down. The Germans must be given "a chance" to play a role of honor and dignity in the world.

It must not be such as to interfere with any of the other vital measures to be proposed in following paragraphs. This applies above all to the widely current proposals for de-industrialization of Germany which, while depriving her immediately of the power to make war, would almost certainly confirm the patterns which it is desirable should be changed. Much the same objections apply to most of the proposals for partition of Germany which would be very likely to arouse an irredentist nationalism such as dominated the early nineteenth century there, only more intense.

The effect of these measures should be to eliminate the Nazi synthesis and perhaps accomplish even more. But to accomplish this permanently, it is necessary to think well beyond the problem of German military power as such, toward coping with the psychological repercussions of its collapse. It is here that the combination of effective firmness with a strong *moral* position is so crucial, as is also non-interference with other measures.

The Nazi pattern of aggrandizement is an extreme manifestation of a more general German tendency to be fascinated with power. The flourishing of this tendency is in part dependent on the German nation functioning as a unit of power in a system of competitive politico-military power relationships, where the definition of success consists in achieving a position of ascendancy *over* its competitors. The fundamental remedy for such a situation is to so define the situation that the international order is a *cooperative* order and Germany is not primarily a competitive unit. The moral foundations for such a definition exist but have been overlaid by the competitive power pattern. They must be brought again to the fore.

Successful fulfillment of the conditions just enumerated would force the romantic element into a-political channels, or into internal revolution.[7] By thoroughly discrediting certain crucial elements of the conservative structure—which are already vulnerable because of having "played ball" with the Nazis—it can go farther to facilitate the weakening of this deeper stratum of German institutions. This is particularly true of the military class and tradition.

In the internal structure of Germany the two obvious cases for compulsory suppression are the Nazi party and all its subsidiary organizations and the Junker class. The greater the extent to which both these measures are accomplished by spontaneous internal German movements or agencies, the better, for the principal danger to be avoided is the saddling of the victorious foreigner with responsibility for destroying "legitimate" German institutions. The collapse of the Party should be an almost automatic consequence of thorough military defeat. Allied Military Government will simply have to step into the resulting organizational vacuum.

The case of the Junker class is more difficult because of its deeper-seated status of legitimacy. First, however, it is important that it has been considerably weakened during the events of recent years. The further the Party-Army conflict goes in this direction before final collapse the better. The considerable element which has been closely identified with Nazism should be a victim of the collapse of the Party while another is destroyed in conflict with it.

It may well be that the bulk of what is left will be adequately cared for by Russian occupation of Northeastern Germany. Since the Soviets have not the same tradition of respect for established property rights as Americans, the moral dilemma for them of direct expropriation of Junker estates would not be nearly so serious.

Should this combination of factors prove insufficient, it is probably best to attack the Junkers at their most vulnerable point—their economic basis. Their system of estates has notoriously long rested on an unsound economic basis and could be maintained even in Weimar times only by an elaborate system of agricultural tariffs and

---

[7] This is a case of attitudes toward a "remote" object which, because of their loose connection with the experience of persons, can be relatively easily transferred to another object.

subsidies. These should be swept away and "nature" allowed to take its course.

The main point is to destroy the principal symbolic focus of the historic military tradition in Germany. This is vulnerable because it is out of keeping with "modern" patterns and structures—it can above all be attacked as a case of exclusive *class* privilege. But it is essential to avoid the boomerang effect of the sufferings of the Junkers being defined as the symbol of the "unfair persecution" of Germany.

There are two other structural elements of conservative Germany which raise serious problems because of their previous association with Nazism, and more broadly militarism. These are the traditional higher civil service groups and the big industrialists. In the situation which led to Nazism both tended to behave as typical vested-interest groups and largely threw in their lot with the Nazis although, for most of their members, probably mainly as a choice of what they felt to be the lesser evil.

The two groups are by no means identical in their significance. The higher civil service has had strong pre-industrial traditions which, with its ideal of disinterested service to the state, has made it peculiarly susceptible to an anti-capitalistic ideological appeal—a susceptibility which the Nazis have exploited to the full. But it is overwhelmingly a *conservative* anti-capitalism which can be readily mobilized against all movements of the left. In some respects it is the main citadel of the conservative German patterns which are the source of most trouble, hierarchy, authoritarianism, formalism and status-consciousness. Hence, it is a potentially dangerous focussing point second only to the military.

At the same time, however, it is much more difficult for the Democracies to cope with. The military ideal has little appeal to the Democratic peoples—but an honest, highly trained, technically competent civil service does, largely because Americans are so acutely conscious of their own shortcomings in this respect.[8] Hence, a policy of direct liquidation could scarcely fail to be attended by very formidable guilt feelings. This, and the importance of this group to order and stability in a transitional period in Germany suggests the advisability of an indirect attack. Probably the most important

---

[8] Dr. Margaret Mead points out—in a private communication—that the appeal of a good civil service to Americans and to the British is very different and that, on this point, it may prove difficult to devise a policy satisfactory to both countries.

single defense of the old conservative patterns here is the *class* basis of recruitment of the higher personnel. Nazism itself involved a revolt against the class aspect of the older German society and the general process may be expected to continue after its fall, with a leftward emphasis. The most important policy then is to facilitate *effective,* not merely formal, equality of opportunity in the civil service.[9] It is to be hoped that the stage will have been set for such a development by the disorganization of this class produced during the Nazi régime.

The case of the industrial groups is somewhat different. Part of their orientation has of course, been determined by the internal capital-or management-labor tension—but only part. In Germany industry has developed within a conservative pre-industrial social structure. This has meant that the higher business groups were in a more insecure position than in this country because in a highly status-conscious society the highest prestige statuses were not their own. They have thus tended to become "feudalized" by imitating and attempting to amalgamate with the old upper classes. In the situation which led up to Nazism this tendency was accentuated by the common polarization against the left.

It has also been accentuated by the very prominence of the state in the German economy—for the power of the state has meant in this connection prominence of the role relative to business of the old, conservative, administrative civil service. The same has been true of the close relations of the army to those industries important to war.

Hence, it may be concluded that it is largely by virtue of its close fusion with and dependence on the traditional conservative upper structure of Germany—and more recently with elements of the Nazi party organization—for example, Goering—that German industry has developed institutional tendencies dangerous to the United Nations, and not by virtue of the intrinsic characteristics of indus-trialism. It is above all its integration with a militaristic state and conservative class structure which is the source of this danger.

For other reasons the deindustrialization for Germany seems most

---

[9] A key strategic point here is entrance to the Law faculties of the universities, the most important channel of access to the higher civil service. In the Weimar days there was a striking difference between the Philosophical faculties which leaned on the whole to the left—with students drawn from the middle classes—and the Law faculties which were rightist with students mainly from the Conservative upper groups. The system of student *Verbindungen* played an important part in this situation.

undesirable. But unless the character of the state is greatly changed, socialization would not improve the situation—by giving more power to the conservative bureaucracy it might make it worse. So long as free enterprise is permitted a prominent place in the American and the British economies, an attempt at radical suppression of its German counterpart would arouse a powerful guilt reaction. Hence, it is a reorientation of German business in the direction of a liberal industrialism which seems most desirable.

The cases just discussed have been those of the principal élite groups in pre-Nazi and Nazi Germany. Other groups such as the lower middle class and in certain respects the peasantry have played a very important part in the background of Nazism. But there is little to be said for their compulsory suppression. It is to alterations in the situation and sentiments of their members, and in the remote objects upon which their sentiments become projected, that one must look for any important change in their characters and attitudes.

The case for compulsory suppression in relation to Germany may then be summarized. Both in the case of her power to make war and of the most important élite groups contributing to her aggressive disposition, the United Nations will soon have the physical opportunity to go as far as they deem wise. In using this power two dangers must be avoided. On the one hand certain forms of ruthlessness, while effective, would conflict so radically with democratic values that their repercussions in the society of the victors would be devastating. On the other hand, certain ways of exercising their power would probably arouse a powerful boomerang reaction and thus fail of their purpose. It is not in any simple sense a question of a "hard" or a "soft" peace. It is rather a *technical* question of the measures which will attain the goal on which the members of the Conference were agreed—a reintegration of Germany into the community of Western nations. The technical problem is largely that of protecting security interests but at the same time minimizing the defensive vested-interest reaction to change, the importance of which the whole weight of modern social science emphasizes.

PERMISSIVE CONTROL OF THE SITUATION

As in the case of compulsory suppression, use of control of the situation to open new avenues of action can have consequences at more than one level. It is probably advisable to avoid *all* use of this for the immediate future for the German nation as a whole. But the prospect of future full membership in a cooperative international organization should be offered. The danger is that of making this offer too patronizing. It is essential to safeguard the moral position of those dispensing favors.

With respect to the internal situation in which the various groups of people act, the first problem is that of order and security. The evidence is very strong that the rapid change, the mobility and the complex tensions of an industrial society will in any case produce a high level of psychologically significant insecurity among the masses of the population. The reaction to this state contains an important element of aggression which has in part been displaced upon the foreign enemy. In addition to this, the German people have been subjected to an extraordinary variety of influences making for still greater insecurity. Some of these are consequences of war as such.

But the character of the Nazi régime has a special place in this connection. On the remote level it undoubtedly gave a temporary basis for a greatly enhanced sense of security—although this will be devastatingly shattered by defeat. But on the immediate level in at least two respects, it operated the other way. It subjected millions to an essentially arbitrary hazard to status, property, freedom and life itself which must have stood in terrific contrast to the old orderly German system. Fear and anxiety as to what may come next must play a tremendous role among almost all Germans. In addition to this the Nazis have pursued a systematic policy of breaking up virtually all the independent groupings in the society—from the great Trade Union movement to the family. They have "atomized" the society wherever its older groupings conflicted with the Party, which involved an exceedingly wide area. Since the importance of attachment to such groupings for the security of the individual citizen is known, their disruption must have been attended by an immense heightening of the level of insecurity.[10]

Hence, it can be inferred that the fundamental immediate need of the German people is for order and security—as an essential condition of almost anything else. It seems clear that the immediate agency for providing this will be Allied Military Government, and its role will be crucially important.

There is a most important basis in German tradition for a favorable response to such a change—in the old pattern of meticulous

---

[10] Though emotional enthusiasm for Nazism has compensated for this, to how great an extent no one can say. In any case, this source of security will be gone after the war.

order—of security of property and status, and strictly legal procedure. In this circumstance it is inevitable that important vestiges
of the old conservative pattern should re-emerge, including hierarchy, authoritarianism and formalism. Indeed, the role of the AMG
authorities will itself be defined in terms of these *German* patterns,
more rigidly authoritarian and more formalistic than would be the
case in an Anglo-Saxon country. To be effective in the present sense,
it is essential that AMG should accept this role.

But it is none the less important to avoid two closely interdependent dangers. One is, as the path of least resistance to quick restoration of order, lending too strong a sanction to the older conservative
patterns and the social elements which symbolize them. Above all
it is essential that the occupying authority should not "identify"
with the old, upper classes, but should remain aloof from them.[11]
There is presumably a very tangible limit to the extent to which
such an authority can permit any pattern of order it once allows to
be established to be displaced by violence. But it can do much by
refraining from lending its positive sanction and prestige to an order
and thereby handicapping other groups and patterns. It should
assiduously cultivate as fluid a situation as the basic requirements
of order will permit.

The second danger arises from the fact that in a state of pronounced insecurity spontaneous groupings tend to be largely "defensive" in orientation. There will be a strong tendency to rally
around old traditional patterns. But, in addition, there is ample
evidence that the patterns governing such defensive orientation to
security tend, when seen in relation to the main institutional trends
of modern Western civilization, to be "regressive" in character. In
particular, the elements of universalism in relation to functional
efficiency, and the orientation to functionally specialized roles tend
to disintegrate in favor of particularistic group solidarities. This is
a particularly serious danger for Germany, both because of the high
level of insecurity and because the Nazis have already gone very
far to destroy these patterns in the older German society.

A certain amount of this tendency is a "healthy" reaction in the
circumstances. But it should not be allowed to become too firmly
consolidated. It may be necessary to take positive steps to eliminate
some of its more extreme manifestations. But more important ways

---

[11] It is probable that the extent to which the Allies confirmed the legitimacy
of the position of the conservative elements after the last war was an important
impediment to the strengthening of more liberal forces within Germany.

of mitigating it are to reduce the need for it by improving the level of security, and opening opportunities for alternative patterns of institutionalization.

This type of group formation is a danger for two main reasons. The importance of conservative, militaristic, nationalistic patterns in recent German history is so great that it would be exceedingly difficult to avoid a very close connection and hence a tendency to resurgence. But secondly, if Western civilization is to survive at all, it must be as a relatively mobile, "individualistic," industrial society where such universalistic values as those of science, modern technology, and the rights of the individual citizen play a prominent part. No major unit like Germany in this "Great Society" can be successfully insulated from these patterns. But a great block of the social structure which is institutionalized in a conflicting pattern is a source of serious internal conflict and tension in the society as a whole. It is precisely from such a conflict that, in large measure, the Nazi movement has grown. A policy which would consolidate such tendencies would not conduce to less tension than existed in pre-war European society. It would be laying the foundations of a repetition of the disturbance through which the Western world has lived.

Security, and measures to counteract the above tendencies, important as they are, are probably not enough to start a strong movement of positive institutional change in the right direction. There is, however, a possibility of using control of the situation of action at least to encourage this. In selecting points at which to exert such control three primary considerations are most important: first, accessibility to effective influence; second, strategic significance in the total system of the structure affected; and, third, vulnerability to serious boomerang repercussions which might nullify the desired effect. There are four principal structures which have been widely discussed as possibilities—the family, the educational system, the state itself and economic or, more in sociological terms, occupational situations.

There is little doubt that in terms of strategic significance the family is the most important structure because of its paramount influence on the socialization of the younger generation. It is, however, by far the least accessible to direct influence since it belongs so much to the sphere of private life which is protected from interference. Probably, by far the most important ways of influencing the family are by *indirect* influence. It is to be expected that any substantial change in the occupational structure would profoundly influence the roles of husband and father. Greater security and a removal of the emphasis on hierarchy and relations of authority would greatly reduce the need of a man to "take it out" by being a petty tyrant over his wife and children. This would be a primary objective of the economic policy suggested hereafter.

The second major point touches the position of women. This has been a major source of difficulty in German society because of the deep ambivalence in the child's relation to his mother it has fostered. Any change which can enhance the dignity and position of independent resposibility of women so that they can successfully "stand up" to men, will operate in the right direction. But here also it is probable that occupational changes offer the most important possibilities. The opening of further occupational opportunities for women is only one phase of it. Making domestic service more expensive and servants less submissive would have an important effect in throwing more responsibility on middle-class women. But most important would be a shift in the definition of the masculine occupational role. Germany has been a rather extreme case of status consciousness. This has meant that the position of the married woman has, to a far greater extent than with the democracies, been defined by the status of her husband[12]—and hence her scope for independent development has been very narrowly circumscribed. A change of emphasis in the direction of functional role rather than status would alter this and give a wider scope for feminine independence. The use of this freedom need not take any one direction—it does not do so in the United States. But it would go far to emancipate women from a dependency relationship to particular men.

The case of the educational system is a peculiarly difficult one. To the psychologically minded, it offers a very tempting opening. This is particularly true of the naive "rationalists" who think of the German problem as one of simple indoctrination with the proper attitudes and values. But it is quite positively known, both on the level of psychology and of social structure, that this is not the case. The problem is that of making the desired patterns "stick." The attitudes fostered in democratic schools are not the product of teachers and text books alone—These influences are reinforced by many others, such as those of home, play group and the general social

---

[12] Symbolized by the fact that a married woman takes not only the name, but the *title* of her husband; for example, *Frau Oberst, Frau Professor.*

atmosphere. If all these could be controlled at the same time, the case of the educational system would be difficult. But they almost certainly cannot, as the case of the family shows.

Even if it were possible to mold the school system rather completely to the desired pattern, it is very questionable whether it would be desirable to attempt it, since in the absence of control over the other elements of the situation there would be an especially strong likelihood of a powerful boomerang reaction which would more than nullify the direct effect. The German type of mentality is, with its paranoid characteristics, more than usually likely to resent what it interprets—often irrationally—as gratuitously patronizing "interference." Any United Nations agency or policy which was in the position of "dictating" the education of Germans would be an ideal scapegoat around which to rally all the resentments which will inevitably be produced by the humiliation of defeat. Not only would this produce serious difficulties in the behavior of adults, but it would react so powerfully on the younger generation that it would probably completely destroy the educational program. This is particularly true if it has not proved possible through the family to lay appropriate foundations in character structure for a "democratic" education.

Even more in this field than in many others any fundamental change ought to *appear* to come from spontaneous German sources. And should attempts to alter the institutional balance by other measures succeed, an educational reorientation would automatically follow. But to use imposed educational reform—even with the cooperation of Democratic Germans—as a main direct avenue of change is one of the most dangerous suggestions under discussion.

This does not, of course, by any means preclude a certain amount of negative control of education. But even here the more of it can be a spontaneous result of the revulsion incident to the collapse of the Nazi régime the better.

Somewhat the same considerations apply to proposals for the direct control of government, for this is a critical symbolic focus of the ideological and sentimental structure of a nation. The fate of the Weimar régime in this regard is instructive. It was, in fact, by no means simply imposed by the victorious allies. But the Nazis fully succeeded in getting it defined as such by a large fraction of the German masses—as an "alien" régime which should be replaced by something "truly German." In general it is much better to attempt to control the patterns of government through control of the *situation* in which it has to act. If that is properly handled, the "form" of government can safely be allowed to care for itself. Attempts to influence that directly are in grave danger of boomerang effect.

These two cases suggest two further rather general maxims which should govern United Nations behavior toward Germany. The first is that a quick, easy turning of the German people to patterns and forms closely in accord with democratic values should be regarded with serious suspicion and not too readily and joyfully accepted. This is not so much because it is likely to be "insincere," masking a plot, as because of the ambivalence and instability of the structure of sentiments underlying it. It is likely to represent the dominance of one potentiality of an ambivalent structure. It is after all the major premise of this analysis that basic changes of institutions and character structure are necessary before a stable, permanent reorientation of the German people can take place. It is impossible that such changes should have been completed within a brief period after the war.

Secondly, American functionaries dealing with Germans in any capacity should be on their guard against using those who on a naive level "make a good impression" on them personally. For the probability is that they will be people congenial to American patterns and hence incapable of exercising leadership over those Germans whose attitudes are different and hence most need to be changed. The *first* question to ask about a person, an organization or a group is, what is its position in the *German* social system? Is it in a sufficiently strategic position to exert an important influence in the right direction? Only when this question can be answered in the affirmative does it become even relevant to ask, how can we get along with him or them?

There are two specific directions in which this danger is particularly acute. First, attraction to Germans with good democratic ideas and attitudes is likely. But this very fact may so define their status in their own society as to preclude their effectiveness in doing what is desired. Second, there is an inclination to have a strong predilection for people of the old, established, upper classes—they are "educated," and have good manners, for example. But in a revolutionary situation, identifying with them may directly block the forces which could accomplish the most desirable changes in a larger context.

These considerations suggest one aspect of a policy. It seems unlikely that after the collapse of the Nazi régime there will be anything like a government of Germany. Although a difficult situation in many respects, this will have the great advantage of relieving the occupying forces of the obligation to work with any particular group. In such a situation it would, within the requirements of order, seem highly advisable to allow as much freedom as possible for the spontaneous formation of groups and emergence of leaders. Such a policy could do much to prevent the serious error of premature commitment to people who later prove unable to carry their own followers with them. The basic principle applies all the way from a national government down to the smallest groups.

The fourth major structure to be considered here is the economic-occupational structure. This seems to be much the most promising as a lever of institutional change according to all three of the criteria previously set forth.

First, it is undoubtedly a highly strategic point in the total structure. It is one in which the great bulk of the adult male population, and a considerable fraction of the female, spend nearly half their waking hours. The situation and definition or role in the occupational sphere is of profound, direct significance But through its close structural interdependence with kinship and the class structure an important change there would have major repercussions in these neighboring areas.

The desirable direction of change is in the first place a quantitative spread in the incidence of functionally differentiated roles where functional achievement is the principal emphasis and value. In proportion to this spread, roles in which an established status was the main emphasis, as in large sections of the peasantry, the old *Mittelstand* and the older élite groups, would be correspondingly weakened.

The second aspect of change is one of altered emphasis, away from hierarchy, authority and formalism, in the direction of functional achievement as the dominant value, and status as the reflection of this, not vice versa.

The probable effect on the family has already been indicated—mitigation of the authoritarianism of the husband-father role and opportunity for a more dignified feminine role to develop. On the class structure the principal effect would be to weaken the rigid formalism of the status hierarchy.

Secondly, it is a point of departure which is much less likely than the others to arouse defensive reactions which might be strong enough to defeat its purpose. In the first place, it is, as such, fairly close to ideological neutrality. Most of the required changes, so far as they need advertisement at all, can be justified simply as measures to open opportunities and contribute to the welfare of Germans. Many can be so unobtrusive as to arouse little attention beyond the limited groups most immediately affected. So far as the context is mainly commercial and technical the democratic peoples are used to treating these problems more objectively than others. Above all the status of the German nation need not be dramatically involved.

There is a very solid common basis of shared value here in the admiration for technical and organizational efficiency and achievement. Few Americans will deny the Germans a high rating in these respects and vice versa.

There seems to be one major point at which trouble is likely; namely, German oversensitiveness to alleged American "materialism," and "money-consciousness." For this reason the emphasis should probably be placed on technical—including scientific—development rather than directly on trade and commercial development.

In the field of indirect repercussions there is one major risk, and one factor which might block the process. In the nature of the case the German tendency to military aggression could only be gradually eliminated. It is possible that a policy which increased German industrial power before the deeper structural change had gone far enough would play into the hands of a nationalistically aggressive resurgence. The answer to this objection lies in other features of the control structure. If the latter is strong, no tendency to militarization of the German economy could get well started, however great her industrial potential. Even after Hitler's advent to power, it was the *weakness* of the Allies, who could not bring themselves to intervene before it was too late, not the strength of Germany *before* her rearmament was far advanced, which made it possible for Germany to become a military threat. It is to a better system of international control, not to de-industrialization of Germany, that one must look for a solution of this problem.[13]

---

[13] This paper was written before the public discussion of the so-called "Morgenthau Plan." That discussion has not caused me to alter my fundamental opinion.

The possible block lies in the question of capacity to accept the repercussions of such a policy. The probable consequence is German industrial expansion. In view of Germany's economic position, this would be possible only with considerable expansion of her foreign trade. Protectionism has been a growing tendency all over the world and has not been least prominent in the United States. If the automatic reaction to German trade expansion everywhere were the progressive raising of trade barriers, this would bring the process to a halt or force it into a nationalistic-aggressive pattern.

It has not been possible to consider here the probable repercussions of the opposite policy—the drastic de-industrialization of Germany. Suffice it to say that from the point of view of Western institutional stability they would appear to be even more serious.

But apart from these questions of repercussions, is a control through economic-occupational channels on a scale large enough to be effective, realistically feasible? If it is seriously meant, it should be.

The essential thing is that there should be a policy of fostering a highly productive, full-employment, expanding economy for Germany. The inherent tendencies of the modern industrial economy are such that if this is achieved its influence on institutional change will be automatically in the right direction. Conversely, tendencies to particularism, the breakdown of functional specialization, over-emphasis on group solidarity are overwhelmingly defensive reactions to the insecurity attendant on a contracting field of opportunity. It is not modern industrialism as such, but its pathology and the incompleteness of its development which fosters these phenomena.

Specific means are various. One is relative freedom for trade expansion. Another is fostering fiscal and monetary stability and the measures economists advocate to stimulate high production.

Apart from this type of measures there is another possibility. It has been indicated that the principal area of common value is technical and organizational achievement. It is, therefore, suggested that the first majer steps in the reintegration of Germany into the Western community should be the admission of the professional representatives of these values into the community of their Allied "opposite numbers." This should be true of technologists, trade groups, scientific societies, professional groups, university exchange. The professionally specialized character of their role would do much to reduce their vulnerability to being defined as "traitors selling out" to the enemy, in the German view. At the same time, these groups have a key influence in defining crucially important patterns in democratic society. Genuine integration of the German counterparts would do much to set a right tone for the corresponding development in Germany. It would also help to avoid defining the situation in terms of corrupting German "idealism" with Western commercialism and "materialism," since science, technology and the professions are relatively immune to this charge.

DIRECT CONTROL OF SUBJECTIVE FACTORS

Whatever may be true of the long-run influence of "ideas" in shaping social structures and culture patterns, it is one of the most important results of modern psychological and social science that, except in certain particular areas, ideas and sentiments, both on the individual and the mass levels, are more dependent manifestations of deeper lying structures—character structure and institutional structure, as they have been called here—than independent determinants of behavior. They are, however, *inter*dependent with the other elements of the system and there is always the possibility that in particular instances they may be highly strategic factors. Hence, the problems on this level should be explicitly considered as an integral part of an analysis like the present.

The most obviously important of the mass manifestations in this field is the ideological definition of the situation. The Nazi movement has succeeded in winning acceptance by a large portion of the German people—in varying degrees of intensity and completeness —for a relatively well-integrated complex ideological system. Its principal component elements have been "endemic" in Western society, although part of the combination has been peculiarly German in a pre-Nazi sense. But it is the intensity of affective fixation and the particular combination which are unique.

The most important components, familiar as they are, had best be summarized as follows: first, perhaps, is the conception of the German national community, the *Volksgemeinschaft,* pseudo-biologically defined as a "race," as having a special historic role, a mission to purge the world of the great evils and impurities of the time—of "materialism," "corruption," plutocracy, bolshevism. This purge is to usher in an eschatological millennium, the New Order or *Tausendjaehriges Reich* in which all men will be blissfully happy and noble.

A major aspect of the corrupt world which is to be purged is capitalistic materialism, commercial-mindedness. Over against this is set the "heroic" ideal which serves to rationalize a conspicuous readiness to resort to force in order to execute the providential mission—and thus to idealize "militarism."

The sense of a special mission is also closely associated with the "master race" idea. Since the Germans are the heroic people, it is to be expected that their superiority should be manifested in a position of dominance attained by force and perpetuated that way. All other peoples are thus inferior and to be subordinated—for their own good, of course. The development of democracy, capitalism and bolshevism among the most important of these other peoples demonstrates their decadence and unfitness to perform a role of leadership in the world.

The Jew has of course served as the master symbol of the adversary of the German people and their mission. One of his most important functions is to unify the different evils which beset them in a single tangible symbol—above all to bring capitalism and bolshevism together. The Jew is not only a group enemy but is also a semi-magical source of "infection." So far as the Nazis attack anything, it becomes "Jewish" in sovereign disregard of the alleged biological race doctrine. Thus both American capitalism and Russian communism are essentially Jewish, although J. P. Morgan and Henry Ford, like Lenin and Stalin, would appear to have no Jewish antecedents whatever. Even the British people as a whole have become "white Jews" to certain radical Nazi circles.

The relation of an ideological system to the social system in which it takes root is highly complex, and subject to a great deal of variation in different circumstances. In a well-integrated society the dominant ideology in large measure reflects and interprets a large part of the system of actually institutionalized patterns. But even in the most stable societies the ideological patterns are selective relative to the institutional. Ideological formulation often reflects a need to justify, which may imply a sense of insecurity. Hence, those patterns which are most completely taken for granted are likely to play a small role, if any, in explicit ideology. The system is thus "skewed" in the direction of emphasizing elements which are felt to be "problematical." Consciousness of contrast with other societies is one major factor in this.

Every society has important elements of conflict. Hence, an ideology which has unifying functions will tend to "play down" the elements of internal conflict and thus be "skewed" in another way. In the United States, for example, from the "official" ideology one could get little insight into the actual divergences and conflicts between religious, ethnic and class groups.

Finally, the objects of ideological formulation are mainly in the "remote" category to most persons—or are high-level abstractions with a similar significance. Hence, they are less fully controlled by realistic considerations and constitute particularly favorable opportunities for the operation of such nonrational and irrational mechanisms as projection, displacement, identification. Where there are severe and definitely structured tensions in a society there are almost certain to be ideological patterns which contain conspicuous elements of unrealism, romantic idealization, and distortion.

All these considerations apply in full measure to the various levels of German ideology. The nearest thing to an official ideology of the older Germany was what may be called "Prussian conservatism." This went far toward directly reflecting the institutionalization of the conservative patterns previously discussed. It took relatively little account of the A component of German character. To some extent, however, this was expressed in religious form, and in the valuation of various forms of a-political romanticism—in the arts and philosophy. Germany as a land of poets and idealistic dreamers fits into this situation.

Perhaps the most important aspect of this underlying conservative ideology for the present problem is its bearing on the readiness with which Germans respond to an "anti-capitalistic" appeal. The basic value and prestige symbols of this pattern are *pre*-industrial, centering on class traditions, the enormous dignity of the state, a *noblesse oblige* code of honor, and an ideal of disinterested service and duty. This made it easy to define profit-making business as a form of corruption of these high ideals, and the countries particularly marked by its prominence, like England and the United States, became very vulnerable to the stigma of "materialism"; for example, England as the "nation of shopkeepers" and the United States as ruled by the "Almighty Dollar." The Anglo-Saxon "business ideology" has served to make these countries all the more vulnerable. The German devil could only too easily find scripture to quote.

It may be assumed that the sentiments expressed in this ideological complex are still very powerful in Germany and that their definition of Anglo-Saxon character as materialistic by contrast with their own noble idealism is a very serious impediment to the Allies acquiring a role of moral prestige relative to Germany. It is also one primary foundation of the appeal of the symbol "socialism" there.[14]

This background is important to understanding the role of the ideology of the "left" in Germany also. This took over the patterns of rationalism and the Enlightenment, and of course opposed German conservatism. But *it too* was, although from a very different point of view, anti-capitalistic. It may even be suggested that the latent anticapitalism of the conservative background, plus the prestige of the state, was an important positive factor in the wide appeal of Marxian socialism in Germany—which gave it the largest socialist party in Europe. At any rate, "liberalism" tended to be ground down between these two millstones and was far weaker than elsewhere in the Western world.

From an ideological view Nazism is a kind of synthesis of these two basic currents plus a highly emotionalized nationalistic-political expression of the A component of German character as an eschatological political romanticism. It has presented an extraordinarily wide combination of symbolic appeals calculated to catch virtually every main strain of German sentiment with which it is difficult for Anglo-Saxons to cope.

What are the prospects and possibilities following the collapse of Nazism? First, the immediate collapse is likely to be devastatingly thorough and to give rise to a profound convulsion of sentiment and thought. The Germans are likely to be the most badly disoriented people of modern history for a considerable period. This is, in part, because in accepting emotional adherence to such a drastically romantic doctrine as Nazism, they have gone extraordinarily far to isolate themselves both from the reality and from the moral community of Western civilization. Hence, the awakening from their "hypnotic self-intoxication" will produce a very severe national "hangover." But it is also in part because of a fundamental factor of instability. As a charismatic movement par excellence Nazism has lacked the security given by an established basis of

---

[14] For an expression of this antithesis on a very high level, see Troeltsch, Ernest, *Deutscher Geist und Westeuropa*, Tübingen Mohr, von Hansbaron, 1925 (ix and 268 pp.). A much more vulgar version is that of Sombart, Werner, *Händler und Helden*, Munchen, Duncker and Humblot, 1915 (vii and 145 pp.). Both are *pre*-Nazi.

legitimacy. Lacking this, it has to be legitimized by success and is overwhelmingly dependent on this. Hitler has unequivocally committed the movement to the definition of this war as the ultimate test by ordeal of his mission. Its definitive loss cannot but result in the deflation of the whole Nazi myth and an acute crisis of confidence.[15]

But though the Nazi ideological structure may, except for a group of fanatical die-hards who will go underground, be expected to disintegrate, its components will remain "endemic" in the German situation. What are the prospects of restructuring?

The selectivity of ideologies is such that in the German case it is highly probable that there are more favorable starting points for integration with American—and British—patterns on the institutional level than on the ideological. Institutionally German society has been rather conspicuously unintegrated. A dominant national ideology tends to concentrate on defining the situation for the nation as a unit; it has to unify and therefore play down actual structural elements which do not fit well. Furthermore, orientation to other national units plays a very prominent role with a need to feel a strong contrast and assert a "real" superiority to those which seem to enjoy the dominant external position in the world.

Given the forces underlying the formation of ideology in Germany on the character structure and institutional levels, it seems most unlikely that before these are greatly changed there is any prospect of stimulating the formation and dominance of a national ideology which could be closely integrated with those of the democratic countries and also be made to "stick." A repetition of the 1918–1919 romantic-utopian enthusiasm for Wilsonian democracy seems unlikely. But if it should appear it should be regarded with even more skepticism than the study of this experience would suggest. For a firm basis for it almost certainly could not exist.

It is more likely that a revolutionary situation may develop in Germany which would bring a communist ideology to a commanding position. By interpreting the defeat as a victory for the working classes and the revolution, and thoroughly liquidating the old upper classes, this could do much to eradicate the humiliation of de-

---

[15] These considerations remind one of the importance of insuring that in every *symbolic* as well as realistic respect it is a *definitive* victory of Allied arms. It seems quite possible that a major motive of the tenacity of German resistance at certain conspicuous points—as in Italy and at Brest—is to preserve the myth that a German force is not "really" beaten. It is only eventually "unfairly" overwhelmed by superior force. It has won a moral victory.

feat.[16] But it is scarcely likely that Britain and the United States will wish actively to promote this solution, although they may adapt to it more or less gracefully if it should happen spontaneously or through Russian influence.

These considerations play an important part in determining the emphasis placed in foregoing paragraphs upon approach to the German problem through situational factors. Above all the view so common among Americans that it is "conversion" to democratic values which is the key to bringing Germany "around" is one of the most dangerous misconceptions currently in the air. To attempt to do so by propaganda or other means of indoctrination would almost certainly intensify a tendency to ideological reaction which would give the Germans the unique role they so desperately feel they need and deserve.

The main conclusion from the foregoing analysis is that the ideological problem needs to be handled with especial care, and most important, an attempt to define the situation for the German *nation* as a unit in "democratic" terms is dangerous. But before considering what can be done, it is necessary to discuss one possibility of spontaneous development.

One of the keynotes of German attitude structure for a very long time has been dualism. Although the best-institutionalized, the conservative pattern has never had the sanction of more than *one* side of this duality. This fact has been fundamental to the "formalism" of German institutions. There has been a strong feeling that somehow the fulfillment of institutionalized roles did not provide a field of expression of the "real" inner personality. It was rather a set of duties and obligations laid down by Providence—or "fate"—which merely demonstrated the tragic element in life. In earlier times this "inner" life was predominantly defined in religious terms, with a specific Lutheran slant. More recently it has been in artistic or philosophical terms.

But this romanticism has not remained individualistic. It has in later times gotten linked to a conception of the "real" life, that is mission, of the German people, which was not to remain a prosaically conservative system of order. The ability to mobilize the romantic urge was one of the most important sources of strength of the Nazi movement.

---

[16] This possibility was suggested to me by Dr. Robert Waelder—unpublished correspondence.

This dualism goes to the very roots of the German structure. It will not and cannot be overcome until the long process of fundamental change is nearly complete. Furthermore, the romantic element cannot be permitted political expression in terms of national power. The immediate effect of suppressing this expression will be to bring the conservative component back to a dominant position. But the romantic component will not disappear—it will have to find expression in some other form.

It is of course possible that the link with the mission of the German nation will be broken and a purely individualistic romanticism reappear. But particularly in a world where nationalistic feelings run high everywhere, this seems unlikely. It is more likely that it will take another direction. The element of aggression may well be turned inward upon themselves. The defeat may be interpreted masochistically as just punishment for their own derelictions—surely there must be an enormous reservoir of guilt available for this purpose.[17]

But if this happens it is likely to be associated with a new expression rather than an elimination of the national sense of mission as a specially chosen people. If this can be completely sublimated into a cultural mission perhaps, well and good. But it is more likely to contain an undercurrent of a sense of persecution and an orientation to the day of fulfillment when revenge can be taken.

The analogy to the Jewish people in the time of the Prophets is striking. Acceptance of the same order of deposition from all immediate hopes of worldly glory as a judgment of God would solve the immediate problem of German aggression. But it would not insure against its eventual revival, and it would preserve a basis for it because it would consolidate the separateness of the German people instead of assimilating them into the larger community of Western civilization. It would probably favor alteration of their institutional structure in a direction different from that envisaged here.

Whether or not such a development will take place is probably considerably more dependent on processes on the situational and institutional levels, and thus the direct influence on them of Allied policies, than on those on the ideological level as such. But Allied ideological policy can at least avoid measures which would favor

---

[17] The existence of this reservoir has been questioned by Dr. Margaret Mead. A good deal of evidence, however, seems to indicate its great importance. This is surely one of the most important problems for further research about Germany.

it—or the perpetuation of Nazism—and can exert some pressure toward influencing a balance of forces if it is at all close.

The most fundamental consideration is that of the moral position of the victorious Western powers. This is a field where actions speak louder than words and a propaganda deliberately emphasizing a strong moral case would probably be interpreted as self-righteous cant. But the Western Allies are rather unlikely to indulge in this. A more serious danger is succumbing to a wave of guilt and self-depreciation. This could hardly fail to have a serious effect on Germany since it would confirm their own arrogance. To retain moral self-confidence without "protesting too much" is one of the most important conditions of exerting the right influence.

Western civilization as a whole has been a moral community historically—although never anywhere nearly perfectly integrated. This has been based on the values of Christianity and certain derived or closely related secular values—such as those of science, and free inquiry, the dignity and freedom of the person, even equality of opportunity. Despite differentiated versions, distortions, and contradictory values there, these values are by on means dead in Germany. Their wholesale violation must have produced much guilt-feeling however deeply repressed it may now be.

A cautious propaganda appeal to these sentiments may be considered—by word and deed. In doing so, two especial precautions should be observed. First, the appeal should as far as possible be *dissociated* from anything to do with the status of the German nation as a unit. It should be made to the rights and duties of persons or citizens and groups as such, not as Germans, and to impersonal patterns such as truth or freedom. The obviousness of the inclusion of Germans under the universality of such values should be the main context.

Second, the form in which they are expressed should so far as possible avoid association with or suggestion of those aspects of Western societies which have served as widespread negative symbols in Germany. Thus, expressions of the values of freedom should not emphasize freedom to make profits, or even, in many contexts, of trade. Similarly suggestion of a direct connection of adherence to such values with the British or American position of power in the world should be avoided.

Although major effects cannot be expected from positive propaganda of this sort, it is undoubtedly worth promoting on the principle that "every little bit helps." But in the field of ideology and sentiments the most important conclusions from sociological and psychological analysis are those concerning the dangers to avoid.

One general methodological point may be emphasized in conclusion. A complex social system like the German is composed of many variable elements which are interdependent in complex ways. It is highly unlikely that there is any one sovereign "key" to the practical solution of the German problem. The Germans do not suffer from a unified disease syndrome for which a specific remedy is known. Confronted with this kind of problem the basic orientation of policy is clear. Although some openings for control are far more strategic than others, in general there are two fundamental maxims:

Utilize every opening for control which is practicable and can be shown to influence the system in the right direction, but

Analyze the repercussions of such change throughout the system as carefully as possible.

Where there is reason to believe that these, as will frequently be the case, include processes which tend to neutralize or nullify the change, make sure that one or more of the following conditions is fulfilled: that the counteracting force is of sufficiently small magnitude so that the net gain is substantial; that measures are feasible which can be expected effectively to neutralize it; or, that the proposal for change is abandoned.

XIII

Population and the Social
Structure of Japan

THE STRUCTURE AND trends of population of an area constitute both
an important index to the deeper-lying social structure and situation, and a very important set of conditions which will affect its
future development. The population situation of Japan reflects the
most fundamental fact about Japanese society: that it has been a
society in transition from a "feudal" preindustrial organization—of
a very distinctive type—to a modern urbanized industrial society
closer to the social type of the great industrial countries of the
West than any other Oriental country.

Available evidence indicates that before the Meiji restoration
the population of Japan had long been relatively stable at a level
of approximately thirty millions. As in practically all other preindustrial societies this stable balance was achieved in terms of a
high birth rate balanced by a high mortality rate, with all the familiar concomitants of that situation, such as high infant mortality
and high disease rates in many fields. The most authoritative recent
study states: "The pattern of mortality in Japan . . . was similar to
that of mediaeval Europe, or that of the isolated regions of contemporary China. The ultimate controls to growth were famine and
epidemics. . . . Even abortion and infanticide appear to have been
techniques that flourished after the great calamities—not techniques . . . to forestall the calamities."[1]

With the dramatic change in Japan's situation in the mid-nine-
teenth century, there began a rapid process of industrialization and
urbanization. As in the corresponding phases of the process in the
Western world, it was marked by a rapid increase of population, to
a total of over seventy millions by 1940. Only in the latest recorded

---

[1] Irene B. Taeuber and Edwin G. Beal, "The Dynamics of Population in
Japan," *Demographic Studies of Selected Areas of Rapid Growth* (New York:
Milbank Memorial Fund, 1944), p. 6.

census period—between 1935 and 1940—did the rate of increase begin to slacken.

Certain notable facts stand out in the more detailed picture. Apparent increases in death rates are almost certainly explicable in terms of improved registration of deaths. Hence the increase seems almost wholly due to a progressive lowering of death rates without a compensating reduction of birth rates—again typical of the earlier stages of industrialization in the Western world. A further striking fact is that the rural population, as closely as can be ascertained, had remained almost exactly constant during the period. The whole increase has gone to the cities, and until the most recent period to the largest cities. A very large part of this urban increase, however, came from the surplus of rural births. Finally, the process which has marked all Western industrial countries also has set in unmistakably in Japan—the decline in birth rates in urban communities. By 1940 the total rate of growth was beginning to slacken, but it still was very rapid. On the basis of extrapolation of the curve, a stage comparable to the approaching stabilization, or actual decline, in Western countries would not be reached for a long time.

Thus the process of declining rate of increase has probably been setting in more slowly than in the West. But the above are the fundamentals of it. Nothing could better reflect the basic importance of Japan's emergence from rural isolation to industrialism, nor the fact that the social consequences, at the outreak of the war, were very far from complete.

The population history of the Western world seems to indicate that even a major war does not necessarily change the fundamental course of development of a population. In both Germany and Great Britain the birth and death rates continued to decline after 1918, though the process probably was accelerated by the war. For Japan, however, defeat may mean a profounder population crisis very closely connected with the major problems of her whole society.

The great urban population has not been supported primarily by interchange with the countryside of the home islands; "foreign trade," whether in the free markets of world trade or in a closed imperial system, has played an essential part. The very stability of the rural population seems to indicate great tenacity in a rural standard of living which has risen only gradually during the period of great economic expansion. If Japan is forced back economically upon herself, the rigidity of the whole structure is such that it might force her population balance back into the old pattern of high rural-type birth rates compensated in a correspondingly high death rate—with eventually a new stabilization at a figure probably somewhere between the thirty millions of Tokugawa and the seventy millions of the present. If this happens, however, it will both condition and reflect profound changes in Japanese tendencies of social development—a drastic check to the process of internal change which has dominated the society for the better part of a century.

The recent characteristics of Japanese social structure and its potentialities of adaptation to the consequences of defeat must be understood in terms of the dynamic consequences of this process of industrialization. This process, curiously, has combined features resembling the Western counterpart with striking differences and peculiarities of its own. To understand this in turn it is necessary to sketch briefly the main outline of the older authentically Japanese components and the particular type of Western industrialism which has come into Japan.

The base, and the part which has been changed least fundamentally, is the social structure of the rural villages in which, on the eve of the war, about 70 per cent of the population still lived. In main outline this base has been similar to that of peasant societies in many parts of the world. The basic unit has been the kinship group responsible for the tillage of an agricultural holding. With a good many local variations this still is the common element. The kinship unit is patrilineal, with status inherited by primogeniture, so that the normal household contains three rather than two generations. The eldest son remains in his father's household, brings a wife from outside, and with the retirement or death of the father becomes proprietor and head of the household. Younger sons must find places outside since the holding is passed down intact and undivided. In the last couple of generations much the commonest outlet for younger sons has been migration to the cities, without complete severance of ties with the home village and family. Daughters always go out, either to marry into a similar farm family—perhaps in a neighboring village—or to migrate to the city. Until she is married a daughter is very strictly under the control of her parental family.

The tradition of continuity of family on the ancestral holdings is very strong. If there is no son to inherit, it is common practice to adopt a young man to marry a daughter. In this case the usual pattern is reversed. The new son-in-law takes the name of his wife's family and becomes a member of their household. Holdings are so small that doubtless there have been processes of subdivision in the past. Recently, however, the dominant facts are the tenacity with which they are kept together, and the stability of the village community as a group of family units which have held this status for an indefinite period and intend to maintain it indefinitely in the future.

This fundamental pattern has not depended on the extent of independent proprietorship or tenancy. Though varying in different places, the general situation in that regard has been mixed. A very few farmers have owned enough land to rent some of it to others, and there has been a fairly large class who have owned all that they and their families have cultivated. The largest class includes those who have owned some land but have rented the rest in varying proportions. A substantial minority have been entirely tenants with no land of their own. This situation has been facilitated by the fact that most holdings are split up; a family cultivates a number of different plots scattered through the village lands, not a single consolidated "farm" in the American sense.

In spite of the prevalence of tenancy, modern rural Japan is characterized by relative lack of a prominent rural landowning class in the social structure. At first sight this is surprising in view of her feudal history. The explanation lies largely in the fact that the samurai of the Tokugawa period were not a landed gentry in the European sense, but were attached to the court of the *daimyo* who owned the land and paid them "rice stipends" out of the proceeds. Continuity of status bound to specific holdings of land thus applied to the peasantry and the high feudal nobility, but not to the gentry class.

In modern Japan there are landowners in the villages who are "gentlemen" rather than cultivators. But they are not decisively important to the social structure. Of the rural land owned by non-cultivators, town- or city-dwelling landlords probably hold a larger proportion. A certain prestige seems to attach to landownership as compared to other sources of income, but by no means a decisive one when compared to China or "county" England. On the whole, owners of rural land tend to merge with the larger middle class of people of business and professional status, which, though much smaller and weaker, is very similar to our own in basic social characteristics.

The most distinctive feature of rural Japanese social organization, which it shares with the rest of the society, is the family council. The most important structural implication of this is the solidarity of a considerable number of household units which are related by kinship on both the paternal and maternal sides, though the former tends to predominate. All major decisions—such as the purchase or sale of land, marriage of a child, unusual steps in education, a new business venture—must be referred to the family council. The prestige of seniority or other high status works effectively in attaining unanimity within the family council.

Through the mechanism of the family council, kinsmen whose places of residence have become scattered are kept close together in mutual support. Property is managed in the light of common interest. The most promising youths of the various collateral lines may be picked for united backing in getting higher education or in a business venture. In particular the branches of rural families that have migrated to the cities are kept closely bound to relatives in their native villages. This pattern has certainly done a great deal to preserve the older patterns of life in the urban population and to slow up the process of social change which urbanization inevitably sets in motion. Finally it should be noted that the system of family councils produces an interlocking network of overlapping kinship groups. There is a slightly different council for each household. Members who are central for one will be peripheral for another. This seamless web binds every individual in a very tight system of traditional obligations.

On top of this peasant base in preindustrial Japan was erected a highly stratified class system based on rigid primogeniture and continuity of kinship groups in their hereditary status. The family council system and the sharp subordination of the individual have been at least as marked on this level as on that of the peasantry. The two most important elements of this higher structure were the *daimyo* nobility and the samurai gentry.

The most important features of these older upper classes for the understanding of modern Japan account both for the surprising lack of resistance to "modernization" in the Meiji period, and for certain peculiar features of the society which emerged as a result. The Tokugawa regime was a unique kind of feudal dictatorship. Though built up on a decentralized feudal structure of society, it did not in fact put the *daimyo* class in a very firm position in the total society, largely because the principle of the regime was that of divide and rule. The "inner lords" (*fudai daimyo*) who were directly integrated with the regime were made so heavily dependent on it that their position was inherently weak. At the same time they were set over against the "outer lords" (*tozama*) who were kept impotent by exclusion and isolation from each other. The initiative for the restoration came from the latter; but the situation did not encourage a new equilibrium on a feudal basis. Having upset the delicate balance of the Tokugawa regime itself, they set up a highly centralized structure in which the socially dominant classes and the government were bound up closely with each other.

The samurai class, as noted above, were in a slightly different position, the dominant characteristic of which was their lack of independent roots in the land and the local community, with corresponding direct dependence on the *daimyo* to whom each was bound by ties of personal loyalty. One consequence was sharp differentiation in the power and wealth of different samurai. The most prominent and powerful were those who held positions of trust and influence at the courts of outstanding *daimyo*, especially the outer lords. In the restoration these men were in fact more influential than the *daimyo* themselves, though each acted in his lord's name. Already they constituted a kind of higher civil service group.

With the success of the political overturn it was natural that the nobility—including the *kuge* or court nobility—should be amalgamated with these ambitious and influential samurai to form a new centralized national nobility. Outside their traditional loyalty to their particular *daimyo* the samurai had no vested interest to bind them to their local community. The position of the *daimyo* was weak, so it did not prove very difficult to deprive them of their special feudal status, to buy out their rights, and set up almost overnight one of the most highly centralized political structures of modern times.

One additional important group was involved. In the absence of modern technology, transportation, and communications, there had been little organization of production in Japan beyond the handicraft level. But, as is common in such societies, an upper class with considerable wealth and everything that was to be found in the capital of a centralized regime in Yedo had produced a situation favorable to a considerable growth of mercantile trade and finance. This was further favored by the long period of internal peace of the Tokugawa regime. As a result mercantile houses of very considerable wealth and extensity of interests grew up. Even the *daimyo*, especially the outer lords, engaged in manufacturing and commerce—at first surreptitiously, then openly.

Here was an extreme example of such a new "bourgeois" class having to fit into the interstices of the existing social structure. "Feudal" Japan was dominated by aristocratic classes of the type which idealized the military virtues and a corresponding code of honor and looked with extreme contempt on the merchant and tradesman. Traditionally even the humble peasant ranked higher in the social scale than the merchant. In fact considerable wealth and influence developed, but in a setting which promoted maximum dissatisfaction with the existing regime.

The wealthier merchant classes thus were natural allies of the rebellious elements and played a prominent part in financing and otherwise facilitating the restoration. They were rewarded by admission to the new national aristocracy, with seats in the House of Peers, patents of nobility for many of the most prominent, and a general tendency to intermarry and fuse with the older families. This, however, was very different from the "bourgeois revolutions" which took place in much of Europe. In various respects the older aristocratic groups remained dominant; it was their values and patterns of life which set the principal tone for the new Japan. Important as the mercantile elements were as the direct vehicle of Japan's economic modernization, it was only for brief periods, as in the 1920's, that they acquired anything like the upper hand.

Japan thus made the transition to modernization with minimum immediate disturbance of her preindustrial social structure. The peasant base remained essentially intact. The old upper classes faced greatly altered conditions, but on the whole as a group remained in the top positions of prestige, wealth and power. The military values and code of the samurai had an opportunity for a new field of expression in the form of the armed forces of a modern nation, supported by a nationalistically tinged system of universal education.

With these older patterns and values there also remained intact the Japanese family system with its rigid system of obligations subordinating all individual interests to those of family units. Through long centuries of conditioning by a hierarchical social system, these patterns of subordination of the individual to his larger family, of the young to the old, of women to men, shaded almost imperceptibly into a subordination of people of lower to those of higher status in a highly crystalized class system, and of general predisposition to accept legitimate authority. The imperial institution—master symbol of this highly hierarchized and integrated system—not only remained intact but was also exalted to a new position of prestige which was exploited systematically by the new ruling group.

The dynamic significance of this older component of Japanese social structure is greatly heightened by its exceedingly close integration with the magico-religious tradition of Shinto. It is important to understand the radical difference of this from the Christian tradition in its relation to social obligations. The rather sharp segregation of spiritual from temporal affairs which is characteristic of the Occident is unknown to Japan. From the highest pinnacle of government in the person of the emperor to the humblest household, virtually every status has at the same time a magico-religious and a secular aspect. The obligations of everyday social life are not merely derived ultimately from religious authority, they are immediately and directly ritual obligations. The pressure to conformity which inheres in every well-integrated system of social relationships is greatly heightened by this situation as long as general acceptance of the whole pattern of Shinto remains untouched.

While much of ordinary social obligation in Japan carries a directly sacred character unknown to Occidentals, at the same time it involves an attitude toward these sacred sanctions quite different from our own. The Western emphasis is on the individual's own responsible conscience; social pressures are minimized and submission to them is felt to be unworthy. Our concept of moral heroism idealizes the person who stands up for his convictions *against* others and against tradition. The predominant feeling of the individual who transgresses his obligations is that of guilt—while that of others is one of moral indignation.

In Japan the emphasis is quite different. Obligations are not imposed by a principle in which one "believes" but by specific acts of oneself or others in traditionally defined situations, or by the accepted patterns of one's status. "Responsibility" is the willingness to accept the implications of these obligations and carry them out regardless of personal cost. The individual's own emotional reaction to transgression is shame that the honor due to his status is besmirched, while that of others is that he has disgraced the *group* with which he is identified—the consequences are not personalized in his *own* character. Moral idealism is to take responsibility in the above sense, not to stand out for principles. Moral conflict is a matter of being caught between conflicting obligations, not of conflict between principle and pressure of practical necessity as it is predominantly with Occidentals.

This mode of incidence of sacred sanctions in a "moral" context is an indispensable background for understanding Japanese behavior in the situations presented by the social structure. Though highly formalistic it is a system characterized by a moral rigor in many respects greater than in Western societies.

There is every reason to believe that the rigor is so great that, even apart from the special insecurity introduced by the consequences of Westernization, it does not operate without severe strains on most individuals. Whatever these may be there is no doubt that they are intensified by the juxtaposition with radically different Occidental values.

There is a good deal of evidence that, with all its outward stability, the Tokugawa system had been accumulating tensions over a long period and in fact was far from completely static. However that may have been, the new society was inherently dynamic. It not only grew rapidly in population, in industrial organization and productive facilities, in foreign trade and political prestige—emerging as the only Oriental unit in the system of great powers—but it also underwent a rapid and drastic internal social transformation. Many of the tensions generated by this internal change were certainly expressed in heightened nationalistic feeling and thus formed the popular basis of Japanese expansionism.

The new regime speedily created a highly centralized organization into which all the most influential social elements were drawn. Second only to consolidation of its own power, it was dedicated to a program of swift modernization of the country through adoption of Western patterns of organization and technology, both industrial and military. The combination of centralization and modernization set the fundamental pattern of those aspects of recent Japanese society which most closely resemble the West.

Very early there was established a system of universal education following the Continental European model. Schools on all levels were organs of the state. Teachers of even the village schools were appointed and controlled by the prefectural governments. Fundamental policies were determined by the Ministry of Education in Tokyo, which closely supervised both prefectural agencies and local schools. On the higher levels an important immediate objective was the training of a civil service after the Continental model. The primary entry to that civil service was through attainment of academic distinction in the universities, particularly the Imperial University of Tokyo. Once on the ladder a very strict merit system prevailed. For a considerable period, however, the class balance was not upset very seriously; considerations of status and wealth were so important in controlling access to higher education that in fact sons of the higher groups predominated.

Industrial development, to an extent quite unfamiliar in the Anglo-Saxon world, was conducted in direct collaboration between the business firms and the state, which supervised and subsidized. Conditions generally favored the rise to power of a relatively small number of large firms with widely distributed holdings and interests. The top financial control of these firms remained in the hands of family groups, the famous Zaibatsu, which were organized and governed in traditional Japanese fashion through family councils. New talent indeed was brought into these families from time to time through the adoption of able young men of humble origin—often through marriage to a daughter. But lower down, with steady expansion of the scale of operations, there was increasing need for technical and administrative personnel too numerous to fit into this traditional pattern. Here also the tendency was to organize the firms bureaucratically, to recruit, relatively regardless of origin, from able, well-trained graduates of the institutions of higher education, and to open to talents opportunities for a career that might lead far.

Rapid expansion of industry led to growth of cities even more pronounced in their concentration than in other industrial countries. To these cities flocked the surplus population of the rural areas. There was opportunity for rise in status to a degree unknown to a relatively static, predominantly rural society. Urban conditions and exposure to Western cultural influences undermined in many elements the traditionalism and familistic solidarity of the older rural population, and this even began to have repercussions in the rural areas themselves. Individualism on the Western model seemed to be—and indeed was—making great strides in Japan. To be sure, the country was governed largely by an aristocracy headed by a rather antiquated type of emperor, but this was not so very different from several European countries.

In two respects, however, even on this level there was an important difference from Europe, to say nothing of the United States. In the first place, even in the cities large elements of the population clung tenaciously to the old patterns of organization. Not only small retail shops, but also innumerable manufacturing processes were carried on in households by family units working together much as peasant families work. Such units were bound together by family ties with each other and with peasant units in country villages. Within the limits of the pattern of primogeniture, children remained with the family. Unless numbers were too large, hired help was virtually taken into the household or slept on the work premises. As an observant European writer remarked, the Japanese working class resisted proletarization to an extraordinary degree.[2] It is not inappropriate to refer to very large elements of them as an "urban peasantry." With all this went a tenacious clinging to many old Japanese customs and patterns of life such as type of house, kimono, and the like. Too rapid acquisition of Western habits was undoubtedly checked by the low income levels of the masses—in turn a function of the swift increase of population.

In the second place, the very resistance to the spread of individualistic and directly competitive patterns served to accentuate certain strains in the society which presumably were present already in considerable degree. In its contrast with Western types of individualism, social scientists tend to assume that a strong system of group solidarity—subordination of the individual to the family, for instance—protects and supports the individual in such a way that breakdown of this solidarity intensifies insecurity. There can be no doubt of the strength of Japanese group solidarity, especially in the family, but its relation to the security of the individual seems to be the reverse of that usually assumed. Instead of protecting the indi-

---

[2] Emil Lederer and Emy Lederer-Seidler, *Japan in Transition* (New Haven, 1938).

vidual member and giving him security, the tendency, according to his status, is to push him into relations outside the group where he functions as a representative of the entire group rather than as an individual. He carries responsibility for its good name in the above sense. His success reflects credit on the group and is admired by them; but if he fails he disgraces the whole group and he is blamed and punished by their disapproval or in extreme cases by ostracism.

An inevitable tendency of Westernization in Japan has been to widen progressively the area of competitive relationships. This is just as characteristic of a merit system of promotion within large-scale organizations as it is of the "individualistic" competition of businessmen in the market. Participating in such competition as a representative of his family and other groups, the Japanese experiences heightened insecurity that has been an important factor in the remarkable dynamic energy evidenced in the speedy transformation of his nation. But at the same time all this increases a level of anxiety which already must have been relatively high. The consequences to the individual of failure to succeed are so serious that he *must* not fail; in the extreme case his position becomes completely intolerable.

The growth of nationalistic sentiment in Western countries has been associated with rising levels of insecurity resulting from the breaking up of the old traditional structures and solidarities of pre-industrial society. In Japan the very refusal of these structures to break up has contributed to the increase of insecurity. This certainly has much to do with the susceptibility of many of the urban elements to a nationalistic appeal, since other aspects of the situation were favorable.

In Japan, however, nationalism has assumed a special character through its relation to the religio-magical traditions of State Shinto. These have provided a pattern for a definition of the situation which was ideally suited to symbolize and canalize nationalistic sentiment. The imperial restoration not only symbolized the religio-political unity and solidarity of the nation, but also provided the rationale, in the increasingly prevalent and official interpretation, of giving the Japanese nation as a whole a position of special prominence among other nations. In Western nations—short of the Nazi revolution—violent nationalism was a kind of pseudo-religion in sharp conflict with the universalistic elements of Christianity. In Japan it could fuse with a major indigenous tradition to give a peculiarly powerful sacred sanction to the goal of military aggrandizement.

Nevertheless, to many Western observers the development of Japan seemed to be following broadly the path of "liberal industrialism" which in time might be expected to overcome both mass tendencies toward nationalism and the influence of older patterns inherited from the earlier background in the upper groups. There probably was much wishful thinking in this judgment. But in the absence of another set of factors it might have been much more nearly correct than events proved it to be.

A major aspect of Japanese feudalism, as of its Western counterpart, lay in the position of prestige and privilege occupied by a specifically military class—the samurai. Considering this background, the part played by the feudal classes in the overturn, and the circumstances, it is not surprising that strengthening and modernization of the armed forces was one of the cardinal early policies of the new regime. In implementing this policy, however, there were two particularly significant features of the new Japanese military structure. First the European system of universal military service was adopted. Second, officers were to be selected and promoted by a relatively rigid merit system. In so rigidly aristocratic a society with a military background it is remarkable that a decision, apparently deliberate, was taken that an officer did not need to be a "gentleman" in the sense in which that was true of practically all European armies at the time.

Conscription meant that army service was the most important connection the ordinary village youth had with the big outside world—and the considerable majority of conscripts have remained rural, with many more from small towns. He had this experience under rigidly controlled conditions highly favorable to indoctrination. Moreover, through the veterans' associations the army reached down into the daily life of the village. Along with the schools, this provided a channel of propagandistic influence over the masses of a population already predisposed to accept authority. This influence was exceedingly powerful. Only a government in which army and civil authority saw eye to eye could command this double channel—and that, given the tone of the Japanese armed forces, was apt to mean one in which the military predominated.

In the circumstances, especially with the background of Shinto nationalism, it was almost inevitable that this power over the masses should be used in an anti-Western sense. By their very constitution the armed forces were bound peculiarly to the imperial institution with its embodiment of what was distinctively Japanese in a traditional sense—to say nothing of the pronounced ethnocentrism of the myth of the Sun Goddess. On top of this, however, the predominantly rural composition of the army was bound to put a premium on a type of reaction well known in the Western world: that of simple rural folk against the corruption and wickedness of the cities. The profound tensions which the process of urbanization and industrialization was inevitably creating in Japanese society could very readily become polarized about the rural-urban antithesis—secondarily about the antithesis of a wealthy exploiting class (the predominantly urban Zaibatsu) and the poor and struggling masses. In this situation the army naturally became the champion both of traditional Japanese values and of the people, who after all were mostly peasants, against the moneyed interests and against the corrupting influence of the West.

In this setting considerable tension would certainly have developed anyway. Conceivably an urbane and cosmopolitan aristocracy in full control of the armed forces might have held it in line. This did not happen. The free road to talent in the armed forces opened the opportunity for a new type of element to rise to the top within the army. These no longer were the aristocratic Choshu samurai of earlier days, but men of humble origin, sons of small town businessmen or even peasants. They were proud of their professional records and of the fact that they could rise and compete with their erstwhile betters. At the same time they were caught up in a cause. They were the champions of the little man and of the best religiously sanctioned traditions of old Japan against the destructive influence of the foreigner. They, predominantly, were the "militarists" who upset the more stable equilibrium of Japanese affairs at home and who initiated the career of conquest abroad which was the primary dynamic precipitating factor of Japan's clash with the powers.

The rise of this new group culminated in the early 1930's. It was not surprising that, given the situation, the whole Japanese social structure should swing over into their control and accept the path of conquest on which they were bent. They acted in the name of the emperor; this gave them a formal legitimacy far stronger than in most societies. They appealed to sentiments which went very deep in the masses of the population. Finally the whole structure—government, business, and the dominant social classes—had become very highly centralized. There was such a close integration of interests that, despite severe internal conflicts between different elements, the structure as a whole virtually had to follow the lead of the element which was able to gain the highest political control. The only kind of opposition which could have hoped to be effective would have been so disruptive to the system that it would have dragged down its leaders with the rest. Only when faced with disastrous and imminent defeat in war could the break come.

The Japanese society which was caught up into the war thus was undergoing a highly dynamic process of change and was in a state of unstable equilibrium. The fundamental components of that situation certainly are still present. The question of the future is in large part the question of what are the principal possibilities of re-structuring which the new situation will allow, and what kinds of further dynamic change may be expected under the conditions which probably will exist. Obviously there are so many unknown factors that there can be no question of an attempt at "prediction." The best that can be done is to make a contribution to clarification of the problems which will have to be faced by all who deal with policy toward Japan. This includes the humblest American citizen who by his vote and expressed opinion exercises influence even as an individual.

Clearly there is no formula by which measures taken in the immediate future—short of extermination—could remove, certainly and permanently, the possibility of revival of a Japanese militarism which might become a future threat to American security. There seem to be three major possibilities of the direction Japanese social development might take. All three have the potentiality either of making the Japanese more amenable to adjustment in a peaceful world order, or of their again becoming truculently aggressive and, in the absence of adequate repressive controls, acquiring the means to make themselves unpleasant. In all three cases, the alternative that works out will depend substantially on the international environment of Japan rather than on her internal development alone.

The first of the three major possibilities is reversion to an essentially preindustrial agrarian society in which an overwhelming majority are peasants. In this case the structures with higher integrative functions might vary within a wide range of alternatives. Secondly, it is conceivable that power should be secured by a revolutionary regime of the communist type which, within a relatively short period, would drastically liquidate the older traditional patterns. What might emerge from such a situation in positive terms is exceedingly difficult to foresee. Finally, it is possible that the fundamental trend of development since the Meiji restoration should be continued, but that the nationalistic-militaristic element should be prevented from predominating. Then the general evolution should take the direction of approximation to the Western "democratic" type of society with emphasis on either its individualistic or its socialistic version.

Certain fundamental features of the situation, relevant to selection among these possibilities, can be taken for granted. First is the fact that, whatever the losses resulting from the war and from immediate postwar economic and social chaos, the fundamental factors making for rapid increase in population would still operate. The only immediate alleviations of this tendency to be expected involve the incidence of higher death rates from disease, malnutrition, and the like, and the kind of decline in birth rates associated with chaotic social conditions in which levels of insecurity are exceedingly high. Even if such conditions should lead to an absolute decline the prospect is that with restoration of order and a minimum of security the upward tendency would be resumed immediately—unless held in check by very nearly absolute limitations of resources.

Secondly, there may be a very serious crisis in the economic sphere—not merely a cyclical depression—caused by the interruption of foreign trade and the cutting off of the islands from the foreign raw materials and markets on which the economy has been dependent. The problems of this crisis are beyond the scope of this paper. The present concern is only with its social consequences. It will mean a considerable period of economic contraction, lowering of standards of living, diminishing fields of individual opportunity, and insecurity.

Finally it may be assumed that there will be rather thorough demilitarization. This includes not only removal of armaments and certain potential facilities for their production, but also complete demobilization of the armed forces, prohibition of the renewal of universal military service, and elimination of the privileged constitutional position of the service ministries. The principal specific social mechanisms which in prewar Japan were instrumental in tipping the balance in favor of aggressive militarism will thus be eliminated from the picture—at least for as long as control is effective.

The combination of the first two factors is certain to mean that there is a heightened state of general insecurity and, for a considerable period, a contracting rather than expanding field of opportunity for the majority of individuals. There also will be an initial revulsion from the regime, and to some extent from the values which are associated with the disastrous defeat. Whether this is of long-run significance will depend on the subsequent development of the situation. The case of Germany after the last war should not be forgotten.

If Japan is permitted to stew in her own juice after demilitarization by being virtually cut off from international trade and cultural relations, it will almost certainly serve to consolidate the traditional indigenous patterns more firmly than ever. The urban and industrial sector of the society has provided the main focus of the forces making for their weakening, and this sector would be diminished greatly in relative significance. Millions of urban people would be forced back into the villages and absorbed into the traditional kinship groupings.

Such a situation would produce many explosive tensions, starting with sheer overcrowding of the land. Perhaps the most important, however, would result from the system of inheritance. The powerful tradition of primogeniture would inhibit subdivision of holdings; but at recent rates of population growth—which, as noted, are likely to be resumed—there would be no satisfactory status available in the rural community structure for the surplus—to say nothing of food. The system certainly could give here and there, but it is sufficiently rigid so that one of two major outcomes is probable. On the one hand the lid may be kept on; i.e., discipline might be maintained in terms of the old patterns and the explosive tensions mastered. The result of these pressures then would be to bring population into balance, presumably on a partly preindustrial basis with reduced rate of increase through higher death rates rather than fewer births. Presumably some reduction through postponement of marriage is also possible. On the other hand the lid may blow off and some kind of an internal revolution occur which would break up the traditional peasant system.

Which of these possibilities is actually realized and what the consequences may be will not depend mainly on the social structure of the masses of the population, but on the higher integrative structures. In this respect the situation is such that a stable situation in a sense favorable to the United States is not likely. A foundation for a revival of aggressive tendencies would probably be laid which could be kept in check only by an external system of political order so strong that any challenge to it would be suicidal.

Tensions within the masses will be so powerful that only a relatively strong higher structure will presumably be able to master them. It is of the first importance that the basic traditions of Japanese society are strongly hierarchical and authoritarian. Any appeal to order is certain to include this aspect in a prominent place. In detail it is impossible to predict just what the outcome might be. With the relative disappearance of the armed forces, of the industrial organizations of the Zaibatsu and their like, the highly centralized structure of Japan might give way and local elements rise to considerably greater prominence. Whatever the emphasis as between centralization and decentralization, hierarchy and authority seem certain to be prominent. The dominant groups, whoever they are, will certainly have to depend largely on force for maintenance of their position. This will favor crystallization of a rigidly stratified social system on the pattern of old Japan, with reestablishment of aristocratic groups. It is also very difficult to see how it could avoid reinstating the militaristic values among these dominant tone-setting groups. It should be remembered that the genesis of these values was not primarily in nationalistic ambitions against the outside world, but in the internal situation in Japan, in the interest of advantage over feudal rivals in the chronic civil wars and of maintenance of a position of dominance over a demilitarized and hence politically impotent peasantry. Hence the outcome might well be a Japan impotent to make war in the modern sense—even more so in the coming atomic age. A Japan genuinely peaceful in sentiment, however, cured of the combination of a propensity to resort to force with an oversensitive suspicious attitude toward others, would seem to be very unlikely. It would be a Japan which, given another Meiji restoration to unify and modernize the nation, and a favorable external situation, could be expected almost automatically to embark on another career of conquest. Such a Japan would offer a maximum of resistance to integration with the cosmopolitan community of world society, since maintenance of its precarious internal equilibrium would depend on keeping intact a set of ideological and symbolic patterns continuous with those of old Japan. It would have to insulate itself from the cultural currents of the world.

Particularly in the earlier stages, however, the equilibrium of such a system would be very precarious. Almost certainly the masses would be seething with unrest. The relative weakness of the middle class has been one of the most important facts of modern Japan, relative to other industrial countries. This middle class has been small numerically and lacking in cultural, political, and economic autonomy, and has been very open to influence from above. It has offered, for instance, practically no resistance to being taken along in the militaristic-nationalistic wave of the last generation. If and when the highly centralized structure on which the integration of the nation has depended is weakened sufficiently, the way may well be open for a revolutionary movement.

If internal disorders once get under way—which is quite likely after withdrawal of occupation forces—there will probably be some kind of struggle for power. Thorough demobilization will have operated to cancel the advantage of the groups previously dominant. A small, well-organized group might be able to seize and consolidate power. Under the circumstances it is overwhelmingly probable that such a group would hold communist ideology and would have affiliations with the communists in Soviet Russia and North China.

It should be remembered that the Russian Revolution did not take place in a maturely industrial country. In the first instance, its position was based on the discontent of the peasantry in an overwhelmingly agricultural country. In Japan too there exists much agrarian discontent which will be accentuated enormously by forcing so much of the urban population back onto the land. Moreover, in the nationalistic phase this has already had an anti-capitalistic animus against the Zaibatsu. This agrarian anti-capitalism and anti-urbanism can be exploited without too much difficulty in a radical rather than a conservative direction. Secondly, though the Japanese industrial worker has been far less proletarized than his Western brother and there has been no strong labor movement, there is no reason to believe that the mass of workers and "urban peasantry" would resist such a movement or would not indeed be strongly susceptible to its propaganda. Russia in 1917 had no strong labor movement, whereas in Britain with a powerful and well-established trade unionism there is only a negligible communist movement.

If such a revolutionary movement should gain control in Japan one inevitable consequence would ensue. The basic patterns of authoritarianism would not be eliminated but would be reincarnated in the new system. In Japan a radical dictatorship, as readily as a reactionary one, would find conditions relatively favorable. Most of the basic patterns of Japanese social tradition could be maintained despite radical changes in the system of ideological symbols. Two generations of relative Westernization certainly have gone far to lay the foundations of such a change.

A conservative, traditionalist Japan would tend to isolation from the rest of the world as the only possible way of maintaining its system. A communist Japan, of course, would not do so. It would have natural allies on the continent of Eastern Asia. But in addition its consolidation as a system would be highly dependent on a return to industrialization and urbanization. In the Japanese case this is allied particularly closely with the question of foreign trade. Relations with the Soviet sphere of influence would open up possibilities which do not exist in the older capitalist sphere. It could and probably would offer a prospect of hope to the Japanese masses which the traditionalist possibility could not.

Just as Japan's underlying authoritarianism would not disappear but would reappear in another form in a communist system, so also her tendency to militarism probably would remain. It is of the first importance that modern Japanese militarism has not rested on aristocratic foundations but has developed deep roots in the masses of the people; the army itself is a popular organ of protest against the "interests." Preservation of this tendency is not in the least incompatible with a communist system. If, as seems entirely possible, communism generally tends to an aggressive policy backed by force, a communist Japan would almost certainly play a prominent role.

The third possibility of development is one that would bring Japanese society closer to the model of the Western democratic nations. The foregoing analysis indicates that this, of the three possibilities, is the most difficult to effect and would require the most favorable—which presumably means the most carefully regulated—conditions. This is not only because there are serious factors of instability involved in such a development in any society, but also because of two types of specific features of the Japanese case. First, the immediate practical situation which must be expected is peculiarly unfavorable, and second, from a long-run point of view, the obstacles in the pre-Westernized Japanese society and the part of it which has survived are more formidable.

If the development which came closest to begin the dominant trend in the 1920's is to go forward to a stage of relative stability, it is indispensable that conditions should favor the continual extension of "individualism" in the fundamental sense. This is not incompatible with the British Labour Party's kind of socialism. It means fundamentally a situation where the individual can become emancipated from the pressure of the particularistic group solidarities which have been so prominent in traditional Japanese society. It means that he must learn not only to take responsibility in the sense of preserving his group, but also to be responsible for independence *from* such group pressures, to value achievement as such, not merely as the enhancement of his family's (or nation's) prestige.

The conditions of peasant society of the Japanese type are such that it is impossible for this type of value to become predominant. By far the most favorable conditions are those of the Westernized type of urban society with occupational roles of the type best exemplified in modern industry. Therefore a situation is essential that places large masses of the population in a position where their fundamental interests and security are bound up with further extension of this type of pattern. This condition cannot be given where the general field of opportunity is contracting. Opportunity for reasonable economic expansion along peaceful lines is an essential prerequisite.

A second fundamental prerequisite touches the higher integrative groups. Demilitarization, including elimination of the privileged position of the armed services, goes without saying. Also a definite change in the previous trend of centralization of the top integrative structure is very important. The monopoly position of the Zaibatsu families should be broken up and governmental subsidy to their firms eliminated. In many different fields governmental administration should be decentralized and responsibility at lower levels built up.

It seems highly undesirable, however, to attempt to secure these ends by means that are too abruptly revolutionary. Restoration of relative stability which can enhance security is essential to such a development. Conditions should be organized so as to weaken the older undesirable elements gradually rather than to eliminate them by violent action, since this would arouse a reaction which probably would endanger the whole policy. Above all conditions should aim at building up into a progressively stronger position those persons who have an important stake in a liberal system: professional and technical people, individuals with substantial administrative positions either public or private, small and moderate businessmen, trade union leaders, and the like.

It goes without saying that a major factor in tipping the balance of prewar Japanese development in the wrong direction was the system of repressive controls which inhibited the natural expression of many of the aspects of a movement of "liberalization," especially the control of "dangerous thoughts." Above all there must be regular cultural and intellectual contact with the outside world so that the roles which are favored by the situation can become integrated with ideological and cultural factors.

The above argument is not in any simple sense a defense of the imperial institution, of Shinto, and all the other things which democratic people feel have been objectionable in Japan. It is hoped profoundly that the course of development will be such as progressively to weaken those elements and correspondingly to strengthen those which are more in line with democratic values. But the evidence of the above analysis does point to the conclusion that an attempt at drastic and sudden elimination of these things by action of the victors is not likely to produce the result desired. A democratic society in the best sense cannot be produced by fiat; it has to grow relatively slowly through the influence of favorable conditions. Drastic intervention of the type so often advocated is likely to drive Japanese society into one of the two other alternatives discussed above.

Perhaps the most important condition of a democratic direction of development in Japan is sufficient stability so that the forces which can effect the desired change have opportunity to operate steadily over a long enough period. Continuity with the situation which has brought Japan as far as she went before the war seems essential. There is no fundamental reason why that continuity should involve "selling out" the aims for which Americans fought— if it is combined with steady, responsible pressure to keep Japan on an even keel by preventing a revival of the tendencies that previously interfered with this development. This means, above all, prevention of revival of the militaristic trend with a new position of privilege and prestige for the militaristic element, while keeping open the channels for outside cultural and ideological influence, and finally giving Japan economic opportunities sufficient so that the hope which is essential to embark on new ventures will not be lost.

XIV

Certain Primary Sources and Patterns of Aggression in the Social Structure of the Western World

The Problem of Aggression

THE PROBLEM OF power and its control is not identical with that of aggression.[1] Without any conscious intent on the part of one individual or collectivity to gain at the expense of another, or even any unconscious disposition to do so, there would still be important sources of instability in the relations of individuals and social groups into which the use of power could and would play. There can, however, be little doubt that the widespread incidence of aggressive tendencies is the most important single factor in the dangerously disruptive potentialities of power relationships; and if these could

---

[1] "Aggression" will here be defined as the disposition on the part of an individual or a collectivity to orient its action to goals which include a conscious or unconscious intention illegitimately to injure the interests of other individuals or collectivities in the same system. The term *illegitimately* deliberately implies that the individual or collectivity in question is integrated, however imperfectly, in a moral order which defines reciprocal rights and obligations. The universality of the existence of a moral order in this sense is a cardinal thesis of modern social science. This is not to say that world society constitutes one integrated moral order in this sense; on the contrary, the diversity of such orders is a primary problem of integration, but it is *not* as such the problem of aggression. Thus friction and hostility arising from lack of mutual understanding or mere thoughtlessness or insensitiveness to the position of the other party are not as such acts of aggression, although aggressive dispositions become attracted to these situations as fields of expression perhaps more readily than any others, because they are easier to rationalize.

The use of the term aggression here is thus narrower than in some psychological, particularly psychoanalytic, discussions. In particular "self-assertion" the "drive to mastery"—for example, of a technical skill—without meaningful hostility to others, will not be treated as aggression. It will not be an issue in the present analysis to decide as to whether, on deeper psychological levels, aggression in the sense here meant, and nonaggressive self-assertion, or mastery, are fundamentally different or whether they derive from the same roots. On the level of *social behavior* the difference is fundamental, and that is what matters in the present context.

be notably lessened, the prospects of effective control would be correspondingly enhanced.

Modern sociological and psychological analysis has greatly improved understanding of the factors and situations which produce aggressive dispositions. This understanding in turn carries with it the potentiality of devising and applying measures of deliberate control, although it is naive to suppose that control will follow automatically on knowledge of causes. Indeed the problem of utilizing what knowledge we have for control is so complex that no attempt will be made to deal with it in this brief paper, which will be confined to sketching a few of the diagnostic considerations on which any program of control would have to be based. This is not to depreciate the importance of an action program, but is merely an application of the principle of the division of labor. It is better to do one thing reasonably well than to attempt too many things and do none of them well.

All social behavior, including the "policies" of the most complex collectivities like nation-states, is ultimately the behavior of human beings, understandable in terms of the motivation of individuals, perhaps millions of them, *in the situations* in which they are placed. Therefore the psychological level of understanding of individual motivation is fundamental to even the most complex of mass phenomena. At the same time, however, the complications and modifications introduced by the facts of the organization of individuals in social systems are equally crucial. If it were possible to arrive at a statistically reliable estimate of the average strength of aggressive tendencies in the population of a nation, it would *by itself* be worthless as a basis of predicting the probability of that nation embarking on an aggressive war. The specific goals and objects to which these aggressive dispositions are attached, the ways in which they are depressed, deflected, projected, or can be directly expressed according to the forces which channel or oppose them, and the structure of situations into which they come—all these are equally important with any aggressive potential in general in determining concrete behavioral outcomes. Indeed they may be far more important to understand, since many of these factors in aggressive behavior may be far more accessible to control than are the ultimate reservoirs of aggressive motivation themselves. The present analysis therefore will be largely concerned with the social structuring of aggression in Western society, rather taking for granted that there is an adequate reservoir to motivate the familiar types of aggressive behavior.

A few elementary facts about the psychology of aggression need, however, to be stated since they will underlie the analysis on the social level. There does not seem to be any very clear understanding of how far or in what sense aggressive dispositions in the sense here meant are inherited. It is, however, highly probable that there are very wide variations in hereditary constitution in this as in other respects and that the variations within any one ethnic population are far more significant than those between "races" or national groups. But whether on the individual or the group level, it is at least very doubtful how far anything like a human "beast of prey" by heredity exists. Ideas to that effect almost certainly contain far more projection and fantasy than solid empirical observation and analysis. Indeed there is much to be said for the hypothesis that aggression grows more out of weakness and handicap than out of biological strength.

Far more definite and clear is the relation between aggression on the one hand and insecurity and anxiety on the other. Whatever the hereditary potential, and whatever it may mean, there is an immense accumulation of evidence that in childhood aggressive patterns develop when security in some form, mostly in human relationships, is threatened, and when realistic fears shade over into anxiety of the neurotic type. This is a very complex field and only a few points can be brought out here.

Insecurity, as the term is used in psychology, certainly has a number of dimensions. One of the most important generalizations concerns the extent to which the specific patterning of reactions to insecurity is a function of the human relationships in which the child is placed rather than of its physical safety and welfare alone. One of the major human dimensions is unquestionably that of love or affection, which in most social systems centers on the relationship of mother and child. The absolute level of maternal affection is undoubtedly of fundamental significance, but equally so is its consistency. The withdrawal of love to which the child has become accustomed, or ambivalence, however deeply repressed, may have devastating effects. Similarly, relative distribution of affection between siblings is important. Frustration through withdrawal, if not absolute low-level or absence, undoubtedly is normally reacted to with aggression. A common example is provided by the fantasies of children that they will die or commit suicide so the parents will be sorry for their maltreatment.

Another major dimension of security touches expectations of achievement and of conformity with behavioral standards. Here two contexts seem to be particularly important as sources of anxiety and aggression. The first is the sense of inadequacy, of being expected to do things which one is unable to achieve, and thus incurring punishment or the loss of rewards. The second is the sense of unfairness, of being unjustly punished or denied deserved rewards. In both cases the comparative context is fundamentally important. Inadequacy is highlighted by the superior achievements of others with whom one feels himself to be in competition, and unfairness almost always involves specific examples of what is felt to be unjust favoritism toward others. Again in both cases the consistency of the standards which are held up to the child and of adults in applying them is crucial. In this general context the sense of inadequacy or injustice may generate aggressive impulses, on the one hand toward those who are held to have imposed such unfair standards or applied them unfairly, and on the other hand toward more successful rivals or beneficiaries of unfair favoritism.

Two further facts about these structured patterns of aggression in childhood are particularly important. First, they are rooted in normal reactions to strain and frustration in human relations at the stages of development when the individual is particularly vulnerable, since he has not, as some psychologists say, yet attained a strong ego-development. But unless they are corrected by an adequate strengthening of security, these reactions readily embark on a cumulative vicious circle of "neurotic" fixation. The child who has reacted with anxiety and aggression to inadequate or ambivalent maternal love builds up defenses against re-exposure to such frustrating situations and becomes incapable of responding to genuine love. The child who has felt inadequate in the face of expectations beyond his capacity to fulfill becomes neurotically resistant to stimuli toward even the achievements he is capable of and aggressive toward all attempts to make him conform. Unless re-equilibration takes place in time, these defensive patterns persist and form rigid barriers to integration in a normal system of human relationships. The result is that the individual tends either to react aggressively, without being able to control himself, in situations which do not call for it at all, or to overreact far more violently than the situation calls for.

The second important fact is a result of the conflict of the aggressive impulses, thus generated and fixated, with the moral norms current in the family and society and the sentiments integrated with them. In childhood the persons in relation to whom such affects are developed are primarily the members of the child's own immediate family. But solidarity with them and affection toward them is a primary ethical imperative in the society. Indeed it is more than an ethical imperative, since these attitudes become "introjected" as part of the fundamental attitude system of the child himself. The hostile impulses therefore conflict both with his own standards and sentiments and with the realistic situation, and cannot be overtly expressed, except under strong emotional compulsion, or even tolerated as conscious thoughts. They tend therefore, to be dissociated from the positive, socially approved attitude system and "repressed." This repressed attitude system, however, persists and seeks indirect expression, especially in symbolic form. This may be purely in fantasy, but there is one particularly important phenomenon for the present context, namely displacement on a "scapegoat." If the father or mother or sibling cannot be overtly hated, a symbolically appropriate object outside the circle of persons who must be loved is chosen and gratification of the impulse indirectly secured. Precisely because his aggressive impulses are repressed, the person is unaware of the fact of displacement and by rationalization is convinced that this is a reasonable reaction to what the scapegoat has done or is likely to do if given a chance. There can be no doubt but what an enormously important component of group hostility has this psychological origin and character.

The Kinship System

"Western society" is a very complex entity with many different variations on national, regional, cultural, class, and other bases. There are, nevertheless, a small number of structurally distinctive features of it which, though unevenly distributed in different parts, are of such strategic significance for the whole that they can be singled out as presenting in the most accentuated form the problems which are crucial to the whole. These are, above all, those features associated with the development of the modern type of urban and industrial society, which is far more highly developed in the modern Western world than anywhere else or at any other period.[2]

In attempting to analyze the genesis and channeling of aggression in modern Western society, four aspects or structural-functional contexts appear to stand out as of paramount importance, and will be discussed in order. They are: First, the kinship system in its context in the larger society, since this is the environment in which the principal patterns in the individual personality become crystallized. Second, the occupational system, since this is the arena of the most important competitive process in which the individual must achieve his status. Third, the fundamental process of dynamic change by which traditional values and sentiments are exposed to a far more drastic and continuing disintegrating influence than in most societies. And fourth, the set of institutional structures through which aggression becomes organized in relation to a small number of structurally significant tensions, rather than diffused and dissipated in an indefinite variety of different channels without threatening the stability of the social system as a whole.[3]

The dominant feature of the kinship system of modern Western urban and industrial society is the relatively isolated conjugal family which is primarily dependent for its status and income on the occupational status of one member, the husband and father. This role, however, is segregated from the family structure itself, unlike the role of the peasant father. Work is normally done in separate premises, other members of the family do not cooperate in the work process and, above all, status is based on individual qualities and achievements which specifically cannot be shared by other members of the family unit.

It follows that sons on maturity must be emancipated from their families of orientation and "make their own way in the world" rather than fitting into a going concern organized around kinship. Determination of occupational status by family connections threat-

---

[2] Modern Japan and the Early Roman Empire are the two cases outside this sphere which have gone farthest in approaching the modern Western situation.

[3] The study which comes closest to the present attempt in approach and analytical method is Clyde Kluckhohn's *Navaho Witchcraft*, Papers of the Peabody Museum of American Archaeology and Ethnology, Harvard University, (1944) 22: no. 2, (see also the author's review, *Amer. J. Sociology* [1946] 51:566-569). Naturally because of the vast extent of Western society, the facts must be determined on a basis of broad general impressions rather than on specific field observation. This does not, however, invalidate the comparability of the two analyses. There is a very important sense in which nationalism in the Western world is the functional equivalent of Navaho witchcraft.

ens the universalistic standards so important to the system as a whole. Daughters become overwhelmingly dependent on their marriage to the right individual man—not kinship group—for their status and security. In practice their parents cannot greatly help them—marriage becomes primarily a matter of individual responsibility and choice.

This kinship system in its larger setting involves a variety of influences on the child which favor high levels of insecurity structured in relatively definite and uniform ways and correspondingly a good deal of aggression. In the first place, the affective orientations of the child are concentrated on a very small number of persons, particularly since the family size is likely to be small. Of adult objects, particularly in the early years, the mother overwhelmingly predominates, because the care of household and children traditionally falls to her, and because the father is normally away from the household, at work most of the child's waking hours. This creates a very high degree of sensitivity to the emotional attitudes of the mother and of vulnerability to anything disturbing about them. To reinforce this, most associations outside the immediate family in the neighborhood play group and school are those in which the child cannot take security of love and status for granted but is placed in competition with others either directly or for adult approval by the teacher and parents. The fact that his mother loves him does not solve his problems; he must stand on his own feet. Furthermore doing well in such situations is highly valued in the society, and this attitude is apt to be shared by the mother, so that her own love and approval tend to become contingent on the child's objective performance rather than unconditional as it is in many societies.[4] This love is therefore more acutely needed than in most societies and more precarious. The situation is favorable to a high level of anxiety and hence of aggression. But because of the very acuteness of the need for affection and approval, direct expression of aggression is more than normally dangerous and hence likely to be repressed.

On top of this situation come factors which are differential between the sexes and not only intensify insecurity but have much to do with the direction aggressive tendencies take. Our kinship situation, it has been noted, throws children of both sexes overwhelm-

---

[4] See Mead, Margaret, *And Keep Your Powder Dry*, N. Y., William Morrow, 1942, for a discussion of the pattern of "conditional love" and its consequences.

ingly upon the mother as *the* emotionally significant adult. In such a situation "identification" in the sense that the adult becomes a "role model" is the normal result. For a girl this is normal an natural not only because she belongs to the same sex as the mother, but because the functions of housewife and mother are immediately before her eyes and are tangible and relatively easily understood by a child. Almost as soon as she is physically able, the girl begins a direct apprenticeship in the adult feminine role. It is very notable that girls' play consists in cooking, sewing, playing with dolls, and so on, activities which are a direct mimicry of their mothers'. But the boy does not have his father immediately available; in addition —especially in the middle classes, but increasingly perhaps in the lower—the things the father does are intangible and difficult for a child to understand, such as working in an office, or even running a complicated machine tool.

Thus the girl has a more favorable opportunity for emotional maturing through positive identification with an adult model, a fact which seems to have much to do with the well-known earlier maturity of girls. The boy on the other hand has a tendency to form a direct feminine identification, since his mother is the model most readily available and significant to him. But he is not destined to become an adult woman. Moreover he soon discovers that in certain vital respects women are considered inferior to men, that it would hence be shameful for him to grow up to be like a woman. Hence when boys emerge into what Freudians call the "latency period," their behavior tends to be marked by a kind of "compulsive masculinity." They refuse to have anything to do with girls. "Sissy" becomes the worst of all insults. They get interested in athletics and physical prowess, in the things in which men have the most primitive and obvious advantage over women. Furthermore they become allergic to all expression of tender emotion; they must be "tough." This universal pattern bears all the earmarks of a "reaction formation." It is so conspicuous, not because it is simply "masculine nature" but because it is a defense against a feminine identification. The commonness with which "mother fixation" is involved in all types of neurotic and psychotic disorders of Western men strongly confirms this. It may be inferred also that the ambivalence involved is an important source of anxiety—lest one not be able to prove his masculinity—and that aggression toward women who "after all are to blame," is an essential concomitant.

One particular aspect of this situation is worthy of special attention. In addition to the mother's being the object of love and identification, she is to the young boy the principal agent of socially significant discipline.[5] Not only does she administer the disciplines which make him a tolerable citizen of the family group, but she stimulates him to give a good account of himself outside the home and makes known her disappointment and disapproval if he fails to measure up to her expectations. She, above all, focuses in herself the symbols of what is "good" behavior, of conformity with the expectations of the respectable adult world. When he revolts against identification with his mother in the name of masculinity, it is not surprising that a boy unconsciously identifies "goodness" with femininity and that being a "bad boy" becomes a positive goal. It seems that the association of goodness with femininity, and therewith much of our Western ambivalence toward ethical values, has its roots in this situation. At any rate there is a strong tendency for boyish behavior to run in anti-social if not directly destructive directions, in striking contrast to that of pre-adolescent girls.

As would be expected if such a pattern is deep-seated and has continued for several generations, it becomes imbedded in the psychology of adults as well as children. The mother therefore secretly —usually unconsciously—admires such behavior and, particularly when it is combined with winning qualities in other respects, rewards it with her love—so the "bad" boy is enabled to have the best of both worlds. She may quite frequently treat such a "bad" son as her favorite as compared with a "sissy" brother who conforms with all her overt expectations much better.

It should be particularly noted that this is not the functionally dominant pattern of the adult masculine role. It combines an emphasis on physical prowess with a kind of irresponsibility. But the adult man predominantly gains his place by using his mind rather than his brawn and by accepting responsibility, not by repudiating it. There must therefore, in a large majority of boys, be a further transition as they grow to maturity; they must come to value other lines of achievement and accept responsibilities. It is to be presumed that this transition in turn is not accomplished without further repressions. At least this "bad boy" pattern did permit a direct outlet of aggression in physical terms, though to be sure this could not be

---

[5] In this she is followed by a teacher who in the United States is almost always a woman until quite a late stage in the process of schooling.

directed against mothers. But the discipline of most adult masculine roles sharply limits that, although a sublimated form in competitive activities is still possible. It is however probable that this is one important source of a reservoir of latent aggression susceptible of mobilization in group antagonisms, and particularly war, because it legitimatizes physical aggression as such.

With girls the situation is different, but not intrinsically or necessarily more favorable. In childhood a girl has the opportunity to mature primarily through identification with the mother and hence introjection of the mother role pattern. But girls later face a situation of realistic insecurity which profoundly disturbs the continuity of transition to adulthood in this role. In many societies marriages are arranged by the older generation who are primarily concerned with providing good mothers for their grandchildren, and the qualities of this pattern are then a positive asset. But increasingly in Western society a girl must seek her fundamental adult security—which, inherently in the structure of the situation, depends overwhelmingly on her relation to the one particular man she marries—by direct appeal to the personal sentiments of men—and she must do so in competition with the other girls of her age group. Compared with the masculine problems of becoming established in a satisfactory occupational career line, it is a more severe type of competitive insecurity, because so much depends on the one step which is almost irrevocable and the average age of marriage is such that the occupational prospects of a suitor are necessarily still indefinite. In addition to this, she must compete for the personal favor of a young man who, in the nature of the influences to which he has been exposed, tends to be deeply ambivalent about the primary role his future wife is going to play, hence severely handicapped in making rational decisions on such matters.[6]

The undoubted predominant tendency in this situation is for the plane of competition in the process of selection of marriage part-

---

[6] An additional feature of this ambivalence not touched above concerns attitudes toward sex. The fact of the incest taboo plus the intensity of emotional concentration on the mother makes for strong inhibitions against sexual attachments, since the sexual relation to the mother becomes the ideal of love. The revolt against this attachment in the "bad boy" pattern thus very readily draws the attitude toward sex into the polarity, and sexual interests become "bad" but attractive. Indeed frequently the hedonic aspect of sex becomes tinged with aggression; sexuality is, so to speak, a means of taking revenge on women for their maltreatment of boys as children. It is notable that the sentimentally idealized stereotype of the "good" woman is strikingly asexual. It may be presumed that this stereotype is largely the product of masculine fantasies.

ners to be deflected markedly from attraction to "good wives and mothers" (and husbands and fathers) toward an accent on "romantic love," certain rather immature types of sexuality, and "glamor"—the exploitation of certain specifically feminine assets of attraction.

Psychologically speaking, this situation implies two very fundamental sources of frustration for the growing girl. The first is the discovery of what is, in the relevant sense, "masculine superiority," the fact that her own security like that of other women is dependent on the favor—even "whim"—of a man, that she must compete for masculine favor and cannot stand on her own feet. This is a shock because in her early experience her mother was the center of the world and by identifying with her she expected to be in a similar position. Secondly, it turns out that the qualities and ideals which were the focus of her childhood identification and personality development are not the primary asset in solving her fundamental problem, are even to a degree a positive handicap. The severity and relative abruptness of this transition cannot but, in a large proportion of cases, be a source of much insecurity, hence the source of a high level of anxiety and of aggressive impulses. The primary source of this aggression is the sense of having been deceived, of being allowed to believe that a certain path was the way to security and success only to find that it does not seem to count. The aggression, it may be presumed, is directed both against men and against women: the latter because they are the primary "deceivers," they are not what they seem to be; the former because it is they who seem to have forced upon women this intolerable fate of having to be two or more incompatible things. This undoubtedly underlies the widespread ambivalence among women toward the role of motherhood, which is a primary factor in the declining birth rate, as well as toward sexual relations and the role of being a woman in any other fundamental respect.[7]

The upshot of the above analysis is in the first place that the typical Western individual—apart from any special constitutional

---

[7] In this and other previous discussions, emphasis has been deliberately placed on the negative aspect of the situation, the strains and their disruptive consequences. This is because present interest is in sources of aggression. The positive side is not evaluated; hence the reader should exercise great care not to take this discussion as a general appraisal of the emotional qualities of the Western kinship system. Furthermore it should go without saying that these patterns have a very unequal incidence in the population, ranging from virtual negligibility to pathological intensity.

predispositions—has been through an experience, in the process of growing to adulthood, which involved emotional strains of such severity as to produce an adult personality with a large reservoir of aggressive disposition. Secondly, the bulk of aggression generated from this source must in the nature of the case remain repressed. In spite of the disquieting amount of actual disruption of family solidarity, and quarreling and bickering even where families are not broken up, the social norms enjoining mutual affection among family members, especially respectful affection toward parents and love between spouses, are very powerful. Where such a large reservoir of repressed aggression exists but cannot be directly expressed, it tends to become "free-floating" and to be susceptible of mobilization against various kinds of scapegoats outside the immediate situation of its genesis.

In addition to establishing the basis for the existence of a large reservoir of repressed aggression, the above analysis tells us something of the directions which its indirect expression may be likely to take and the "themes" of grievance which are most likely to arouse aggressive reactions. In the first place, Western society is one in which most positions of large-scale responsibility are held by men. In this connection the cult of "compulsive masculinity" cannot but be of significance. Western men are peculiarly susceptible to the appeal of an adolescent type of assertively masculine behavior and attitude which may take various forms. They have in common a tendency to revolt against the routine aspects of the primarily institutionalized masculine role of sober responsibility, meticulous respect for the rights of others, and tender affection toward women. Assertion through physical prowess, with an endemic tendency toward violence and hence the military ideal, is inherent in the complex and the most dangerous potentiality.

It is, however, not only masculine psychology which is important in this respect. Through at least two channels the psychology of women may reinforce this tendency. First, there is undoubtedly widespread if repressed resentment on the part of women over being forced to accept their sex role and its contradictory components. This is expressed in an undercurrent of aggression toward the men with whom they are associated, which, given the latter's hypersensitiveness toward women's attitudes toward them, can be expected to accentuate the pattern of compulsive masculinity.

But this feminine resentment against men is only one side of an ambivalent structure of attitudes. The situation by virtue of which women have to accept an inferior position in crucial respects leads to an idealization of precisely the extreme type of aggressive masculinity. It is quite clear that Western men are peculiarly dependent emotionally on women and therefore feminine admiration of them will powerfully stimulate any pattern of behavior which can evoke it.[8]

The childhood situation of the Western world also provides the prototypes of what appear to be the two primarily significant themes or contexts of meaning in which it is easiest to evoke an aggressive reaction, since these are the contexts in which the people of the Western world have been oversensitized by the traumatic experiences of their childhood.

The first of these is the question of "adequacy," of living up to an acceptable standard of achievement or behavior. There is a tendency to be hypersensitive to any suggestion of inferiority or incapacity to achieve goals which have once been set. This in turn is manifested in two ways of primary significance for present purposes. On the one hand the peoples of Western society are highly susceptible to wishful and distorted beliefs in their own superiority to others, as individuals or in terms of any collectivity with which they are identified, since this belief, and its recognition by others, tends to allay anxiety about their own adequacy. On the other hand, since such a belief in superiority has compulsive characteristics, those who have to deal with such people find it "hard to take," even when the former have a highly realistic attitude. But it also stimulates a vicious circle of resentment on the part of those who, sharing the same hypersensitivity, are treated as inferior. It is, in other words, inordinately easy for either individual or group relationships in the Western world to become defined as relations of superiority and inferiority and to evoke aggressive responses, if the assumption of superiority is, even justly, questioned, or if, again even justly, there is any imputation of inferiority.

The second major context of meanings is that of loyalty, honesty, integrity, justice of dealing. Both in competition with others and in relation to expectations which he has been allowed to build up, the Western child has usually had the traumatic experience of disillusionment, of being "let down." The boy has not been allowed

---

[8] The indications are that this feminine admiration, not to say adulation, of the "heroic" "He-man" pattern played a major role in the spread of the Nazi movement in Germany.

to emulate the ideal of his mother; when he has been "good," he has been punished rather than rewarded for it, and his "bad" brother has been preferred. The girl has found out both that her mother as a woman is an inferior being and that to be a "good woman," that is a mother, does not pay. These experiences are the prototype of a certain hypersensitivity to the question of whether others can be trusted either as individuals or collectivities. In sex relations there is a tendency to be compulsively preoccupied with the fidelity of the partner. In general there is an overreadiness to believe that the other fellow will attempt to deceive or injure one. Naturally, since this hypersensitivity is associated with repressed aggression, it is very easy for the aggressive impulse to be projected on the other party to the relation, producing the "paranoid" pattern of over-readiness to impute hostile intentions where they do not exist, or to exaggerate them grossly where they do. In its extreme form the rest of the world is apt to be seen as mainly preoccupied with plotting to destroy one or one's group. The Western tendency is to be "thin-skinned," unable to "take it," when frustrations must be faced and to place the blame on others when most of it belongs at home.

The Occupational System

The other most fundamental institutional structure of modern Western society, the occupational system, can for present purposes be dealt with much more briefly—especially since a good deal has been anticipated in dealing with kinship, the two being so closely interdependent. Its most essential feature is the primacy of functional achievement. This implies the selection of people on the basis of their capacities to perform the task, of innate ability and training, not of birth or any other antecedent element of status. It further implies the segregation of the technical role from other aspects of the incumbent's life, most of which are in the nature of the case governed by other types of standards. This takes the form in the type case of physical segregation and of segregation of personnel and activity, so that it involves a distinct system of relationships. Finally, it implies a peculiar type of discipline in that any type of personal feeling which might come in conflict with these relationships is subordinated to the requirements of the technical task, which are often highly exacting and often narrowly specialized.

There is an inherently competitive dimension of the occupational system. Even when competitive victory is not as such a major direct goal, but rather is subordinated to functional achievement as such, a selective process, which among other things governs access to opportunity for all the higher achievements, is inherent in the system. A man has to "win" the competition for selection, often repeatedly, in order to have an opportunity to prove his capacity for the higher achievements. The inevitable result of the competitive and selective processes is the distribution of the personnel of the system in a relatively elaborate hierarchy of prestige which is symbolized and expressed in manifold ways.

It is furthermore relevant that in the aggregate, particular roles, and still more organizations, undertake functions which are altogether unknown in simpler societies. Men are more frequently subjected to the discipline and strains of more exacting skills. But even more important are two other consequences. One is the involvement of people in systems of social relationship of very great complexity which, because of their newness and rapidly changing character, cannot be adequately governed by established and traditionalized norms. The other is the fact that explicit responsibility, in that great consequences hinge on the decisions and competence of individuals, is a far greater factor than in simpler societies. In view of what we know of the deep-seated tendencies to dependency and the psychological difficulties involved in assuming responsibility, this is a fact of prime importance.

When these features of the occupational system are brought into relation to the personality structure discussed above, two classes of conclusions touching the problem of aggression appear to follow. The first set concerns the relation to the general levels of aggression in the society, the second the channeling of what exists into different actual and potential types and directions of expression.

Though it is difficult to arrive at more than a very rough judgment, it seems clear that the balance is rather heavily on the side of increasing rather than reducing the levels of insecurity and hence of anxiety and aggression—the foundations of which are laid in the process of socialization in the family. It is true that the wide field for competitive activity provides some outlets which are constructive for sublimating aggression by harnessing it to the motivation of constructive achievement, and at the same time "winning." But the other side of the medal is the condemnation of probably a considerably larger number to being "losers"—since success in such a system is to a considerable degree inherently relative—and thereby feeding any tendency to feel unduly inadequate or unjustly treated. At the same time, participation in the occupational system means subjection to a severe discipline. It means continual control of emotions so that repression and dissociation are favored rather than counteracted.[9] Perhaps most important of all, however, the competitive process is governed by a rather strict code which is very often in conflict with immediate impulses. In particular it is essential to be a "good loser" and take one's misfortunes and disappointments with outward equanimity. This reinforces the need to repress feelings of resentment against unfair treatment, whether the feelings are realistically justified or not, and hence their availability for mobilization in indirect channels of expression.

The above considerations apply primarily to men since they are the primary carriers of the occupational system. Conversely, however, by the segregation of occupational from familial roles, most women are denied a sense of participation with *their men* in a common enterprise. Moreover, it is in the occupational sphere that the "big things" are done, and this drastic exclusion must serve to increase the inferiority feelings of women and hence their resentment at their condemnation by the accident of sex to an inferior role.

In respect to the channeling of aggression as distinguished from its absolute level, two things are of primary importance. First, if there are no reasons to suppose that, on the average, absolute levels are lowered, at the same time few direct outlets are provided for most types of aggressive impulse. Hence the general need for indirect channels of expression, particularly by displacement on scapegoats, is reinforced by experience in this sphere of life.

Secondly, it is above all in the occupational sphere that the primary institutionalization of the basic themes of the above discussion takes place—childhood is an apprenticeship for the final test which

---

[9] This discipline includes adherence to sharply objective standards in the face of the strains growing out of the emotional complexity of the system of social relationships of the work situation, and the additional strains imposed by high levels of responsibility for those who have to assume it. In addition, the mobility which is inherent in such a system has two further significant consequences. Status is inherently insecure, in that it cannot be guaranteed independently of performance—to say nothing of the results of economic fluctuations in causing unemployment and the like. Then technological and organizational change, as well as promotion and job change of the individual, are also inherent and make it difficult to "settle down" to a complete emotional adjustment to any one stable situation; it is necessary to make continual new adjustments with all the attendant emotional difficulty.

the adult world imposes on man. Ability to perform well and hold one's own or excel in competition is the primary realistic test of adult adequacy, but many, probably the considerable majority, are condemned to what, especially if they are oversensitive, they must feel to be an unsatisfactory experience. Many also will inevitably feel they have been unjustly treated, because there is in fact much injustice, much of which is very deeply rooted in the nature of the society, and because many are disposed to be paranoid and see more injustice than actually exists. To feel unjustly treated is moreover not only a balm to one's sense of resentment, it is an alibi for failure, since how could one succeed if he is not given a chance?

Thus the kinship and the occupational systems constitute from the present point of view a mutually reinforcing system of forces acting on the individual to generate large quantities of aggressive impulse, to repress the greater part of it, and to channel it in the direction of finding agencies which can be symbolically held responsible for failure and for deception and injustice to the individual and to those with whom he is identified.[10] Perhaps the most important mitigation of the general situation which the working of the occupational system brings about is that occupational success may do much to reduce the pressure toward compulsive masculinity. But the difficulty here is that sufficient success to have this effect is attainable only to a minority of the masculine population. Lack of it would seem to have the opposite effect, and this is just as much a consequence of the system as the other.

The Structure of Group Hostility

The occupational system of the Western world is probably the most important institutional "precipitate" of a fundamental dynamic process which Max Weber has called the "process of rationalization." Through it, as well as other channels, this process has had a fundamental part in structuring attitudes in the Western world which is relevant to the problem of aggression and hence calls for a brief discussion.

---

[10] If anything, probably the kinship system has to absorb more strains originating in the occupational system than vice versa. In any case the effect of these strains is to accentuate the sources of aggression inherent in the kinship system rather than to mitigate them. This would appear to operate above all through the influence on children of parents who themselves are showing the effects of tension. In so far as a man "takes out" the frustrations of his occupational situation on his wife she may in turn "take it out" on the children.

The progress of science and related elements of rational thought is the core and fundamental prototype of the process. Science is an inherently dynamic thing. Unless prevented by influences extraneous to it, it will continually evolve. Moreover, unless science is hermetically insulated from the rest of social life, which is manifestly impossible, this dynamic process of change will be extended into neighboring realms of thought, for example, philosophical and religious thought, and in the direction of practical application wherever rational norms play a significant role in the determination of action. Hence through this dynamic factor, a continuing process of change is introduced, both into the primary symbolic systems which help to integrate the life of a society, and into the structure of the situations in which a large part of the population must carry on their activities.

The significance of this arises in the first place from the fact that there is much evidence that security in the sense relevant to this analysis is to a high degree a function of the stability of certain elements of the socio-cultural situation. This is true especially because certain aspects of the situations people face are involved in the actual and, as they feel it, prospective fulfillment of their "legitimate expectations." These expectations are, even apart from any neurotic distortions, apt to be highly concrete so that any change, even if it is not intrinsically unfavorable, is apt to be disturbing and arouse a reaction of anxiety. It should above all be noted that technological change inevitably disrupts the informal human relationships of the members of working groups—relationships which have been shown to be highly important to the stability and working efficiency of the participants.[11] On the other hand, the corresponding process of change on the level of ideas and symbols tends to disrupt established symbolic systems which are exceedingly important to the security and stability of the orientation of people.

The weight of evidence seems to be that the amount of such change to which even the best-integrated personalities can adapt without the possibility of upsetting the smooth functioning of personality is rather limited; but in proportion as there is a neurotic type of insecurity, there tends to be a compulsive need for stability in these respects. The capacity to adapt to both types of change is a function of "emotional maturity," and the above analysis has

[11]Cf. Roethlisberger, F. J., and Dickson, William J., *Management and the Worker;* Cambridge, Harvard University Press, 1941.

shown that there must be serious limitations on the levels of emotional maturity which most members of Western society can have attained. There seems, therefore, to be no doubt that the continuing incidence of dynamic change through the process of rationalization is one major source of the generalized insecurity which characterizes our society. As such it should also be a major factor in maintaining the reservoir of aggressive impulses at a high level. It is a factor so deep-seated in our society that it must be expected to continue to operate on a major scale for the foreseeable future; only profound changes in the whole social situation which would invalidate the greater part of this analysis would produce a situation where this would not be true.

It is not, however, the significance of the process of rationalization, as a source of quantitative addition to the reservoir of aggression, which is most important, but rather the way it operates to structure the direction of its actual and potential expression. It is a major factor in the polarization of attitudes in the society, especially as they are distributed between different groups in the population in such a way as to focus anxiety and aggression on a single structured line of tension.

It must be remembered that the incidence of the process of rationalization is highly uneven in the social structure. With respect to any given level of traditionalized values, symbols, and structuring of situations, there are always relatively "emancipated" and relatively traditional groups and sectors of the society. Certain of the emancipated groups, like the best of the professions for instance, become relatively well institutionalized so that the dynamic process of which they are agents is not so disturbing to them. They always, however, contain at least a fringe, if not more, where insecurity is expressed in compulsively distorted patterns of extreme emancipation which are highly provocative to the more traditionalized elements, which lead into a vicious circle in proportion as elements of both groups are compulsively motivated.

The process is, however, always tending to spread into the relatively traditionalized areas of the society and thereby tending to threaten the security of the population elements most dependent on traditionalized patterns. Partly these elements already have serious insecurities and are compulsively dependent on traditionalism; partly change introduces new insecurities. In either case, the result is to stimulate what has elsewhere been called a "fundamentalist reaction," a compulsively distorted exaggeration of traditional values and other related patterns.[12] This above all attaches to those elements of culture and society which are not so readily and in the same sense susceptible of rationalization as are the areas of science, technology, and administrative organization—namely, religion, family, class attitudes, the informal traditions of ethnic culture, and the like, where non-logical symbolic systems are heavily involved.

The reverse side of the exaggerated assertion of these traditional patterns is the aggressive attack on the symbols which appear to threaten them, science as such, atheism and other antireligious aspects of liberal rationalism, the relaxation of traditional sex morality —especially in the larger urban communities and in "bohemian" circles—political and economic radicalism, and the like. The compulsive adherents of emancipated values on the other hand tend to brand all traditional values as "stupid," reactionary, unenlightened, and thus a vicious circle of mounting antagonism readily gets started. This polarization in fact corresponds roughly to structured differentiations of the society, with latent or more or less actual conflicts of interest as between rural and urban elements, capital and labor, upper and lower class groups, and the like, which feed fuel to the flames.

It is above all important that the values about which the fundamentalist pattern of reaction tends to cluster are those particularly important in the constitution and symbolization of informal group solidarities—those of families, social class, socio-religious groups, ethnic groups, and nations. Many of these solidarities are seriously in conflict with the explicit values of the Western world which largely stem from the rationalistic traditions of the Enlightenment.[13] They are hence particularly difficult to defend against rationalistic attack. Since, however, they are of fundamental emotional importance, the consequence more frequently than not is their "defensive" assertion rather than their abandonment. This very difficulty of rational defense when rational values are in fact accepted, favors this context as a field for the mobilization of repressed aggression, since it is in a state of bafflement that people are most likely to react with "unreasonable" aggression.

These circumstances seem to go far toward explaining the strik-

---

[12] Cf. Parsons, Talcott, "Some Sociological Aspects of the Fascist Movements," *Social Forces,* Nov. 1942, reprinted as Chapter VII above. Also: "The Sociology of Modern Anti-Semitism" in *Jews in a Gentile World,* Graeber & Britt [eds.]; N. Y.; Macmillan, 1942.

[13] Cf. Gunnar Myrdal's discussion of "The American Creed" in *An American Dilemma;* N. Y., Harpers, 1944 (2 vols.).

ing fact that aggression in the Western world tends to focus so much on antagonisms between solidary groups. Some of these groups are, to be sure, those growing out of the formal and utilitarian structure of modern society, like the conflict of business and the labor unions. Probably more important, however, are the lines of conflict which cut across these groups, particularly those between religious and ethnic groups within nations and, above all, the conflict of nationalisms. Group conflict seems to be particularly significant because on the one hand solidarity with an informal group, the appeal of which is to "infrarational" sentiments, is a peculiarly potent measure for allaying the neurotic types of anxiety which are so common; on the other hand an antagonistic group is a peculiarly appropriate symbolic object on which to displace the emotional reactions which cannot be openly expressed within one's own group lest they threaten its solidarity. In this whole context, it is peculiarly appropriate that groups be available in regard to which the ambivalent structure of emotions in relation to the two dominant themes discussed above can be expressed. The "out-group" should, that is, be a group in relation to which one's own group can feel a comfortably self-righteous sense of superiority and at the same time a group which can be plausibly accused of arrogating to itself an illegitimate superiority of its own. Correspondingly it should be a group with strong claims to a position of high ethical standing of its own which, however, can plausibly be made out to be essentially specious and to conceal a subtle deception. The Jews have in both these connections furnished almost the ideal scapegoat throughout the Western world.

Latent aggression has thus been channeled into internal group conflicts of various sorts throughout the Western world: anti-semitism and anti-laborism, and anti-negro, anti-Catholic, and anti-foreigner feeling are found in this country. There are, however, potent reasons why nationalism should be the most important and serious focus of these tendencies. The first is the realistic basis of it. The organization of our civilization into nation-states which are the dominant power units has been a crucial realistic fact of the situation. Above all, in the chronic tendency to resort to war in crisis situations the loyalty to one's government has been to be in one sense the ultimate residual loyalty, the one which could claim any sacrifice no matter how great if need be.

At the same time it is highly significant that as between the fundamentalist and the emancipated poles of modern attitude structure, nationalistic loyalty as such is largely neutral. It is, however, a particularly suitable focus for fundamentalist sentiments in accusing their opponents of a specious sincerity since it does tend to be an ultimate test of altruism and sincerity. The "foreigner" is, moreover, outside the principal immediate system of law and order; hence aggression toward him does not carry the same opprobrium or immediate danger of reprisal that it does toward one's "fellow-citizen." Hostility to the foreigner has thus furnished a means of transcending the principal, immediately threatening group conflicts, of achieving "unity"—but at the expense of a less immediate but in fact more dangerous threat to security, since national states now command such destructive weapons that war between them is approaching suicidal significance.

Thus the immense reservoir of aggression in Western society is sharply inhibited from direct expression within the smaller groups in which it is primarily generated. The structure of the society in which it is produced contains a strong predisposition for it to be channeled into group antagonisms. The significance of the nation-state is, however, such that there is a strong pressure to internal unity within each such unit and therefore a tendency to focus aggression on the potential conflicts between nation-state units. In addition to the existence of a plurality of such units, each a potential target of the focused aggression from all the others, the situation is particularly unstable because of the endemic tendency to define their relations in the manner least calculated to build an effectively solidary international order. Each state is, namely, highly ambivalent about the superiority-inferiority question. Each tends to have a deep-seated presumption of its own superiority and a corresponding resentment against any other's corresponding presumption. Each at the same time tends to feel that it has been unfairly treated in the past and is ready on the slightest provocation to assume that the others are ready to plot new outrages in the immediate future. Each tends to be easily convinced of the righteousness of its own policy while at the same time it is overready to suspect the motives of all others. In short, the "jungle philosophy" —which corresponds to a larger element in the real sentiments of all of us than can readily be admitted, even to ourselves—tends to be projected onto the relations of nation-states at precisely the point where, under the technological and organizational situation of the modern world, it can do the most harm.

Conclusion

In conclusion, to forestall misunderstanding, it is well to call explicit attention to some of the limitations of the analysis just developed. That it is specifically limited to analyzing sources of aggression and their channeling has already been stated. It needs, however, to be repeated that the more positive sides are deliberately omitted. It is thus not in any sense a complete or balanced picture of the dynamic psychological balance of Western society, even so far as such a picture could be drawn in the light of present knowledge and on a comparable level of generality and abstraction. Above all, it should not by itself be taken as an adequate basis for any suggestions of remedial action. By omitting consideration of the positive aspects, it has precisely neglected the principal assets on which any such program would have to rely. It is confined to a specifically limited diagnostic function. Its results must be combined with those of other studies before they have any practical value beyond this.

This analysis has been couched in terms of a very high level of "ideal-typical" abstraction. It has presumed to deal with the social structure and psychological dynamics of the Western world as a whole, in full consciousness of the fact that there are and have been innumerable ranges of variation within this enormously complicated sociocultural system, many of which are of prime significance to any practical purpose.

In the first place, within any one national society this analysis applies unequally to different elements of its population. In fact it applies most completely and directly to the urban, middle-class elements, those which have been most heavily involved in the consequences of the industrial revolution. Substantial modifications need to be made in dealing with rural populations. The same is true of the highest elite groups, particularly those whose position was firmly institutionalized before the major social changes of the industrial era took place. This is especially true of the older European hereditary aristocracies. It is even necessary to make substantial modifications for the case of social groups which have so low a status that their being in the major competition for places on the general scale of prestige cannot be realistically supposed, thus for large parts, at least, of the "proletarian" elements. These are only among the most conspicuous of the qualifications, each of which would have important consequences for the psychological reaction patterns of the relevant groups.

Similarly, most of the "secondary" complications of the system of dynamic relationships under consideration have perforce been neglected. It is a fact of the first importance that, for instance, in American adult culture there is a fundamentally important institutionalization of "adolescent" values which is in continual competition with the main system.

Finally, it is quite clear that there are extremely important national variations in the relevant patterns. To a considerable degree the analysis has been focused on American conditions. Their greater familiarity favors this. But it is not necessarily a source of serious bias, since in certain respects the United States represents a closer approach to the "ideal type" of structure which is of prime strategic significance for the whole Western world—significant because the fundamental patterns of industrial society have been less modified by powerful institutional complexes which were present in the pre-existing society.

France, for instance, has developed less far along these lines than most Western countries, and has integrated more of the older society with the new tendencies. There seems, for instance, to have been far less isolation of the immediate conjugal family there than in this country.

Certain of the consequences most important to the practical situation have appeared most highly developed in Germany and greatly accentuated under the Nazi regime.[14] The peculiarly virulent nationalistic aggressiveness of Nazi Germany certainly cannot be adequately explained in terms of the factors analyzed in the present paper. It depended on other elements which were either peculiar to Germany, or relatively far more important there than for instance in this country. This is true of the strongly authoritarian character of the father-son relationship, and of the much more sharply subordinated position of women in Germany. There was also a much

---

[14] Cf. Parsons, T., "Democracy and Social Structure in Pre-Nazi Germany," *J. Legal and Political Sociology*, Nov. 1942, and "The Problem of Controlled Institutional Change," *Psychiatry* (1945) 8:79-101, both reprinted here. See also Ericson, Eric Homburger, "Hitler's Imagery and the Dream of German Youth," *Psychiatry* (1942) 5:475-493.

more rigidly formalistic and hierarchical occupational system there, and conditions were much more favorable to the development of a strongly militaristic variety of nationalism.

Nevertheless, differences of this sort do not invalidate the analysis presented here. They are, however extremely deviant, variations on the same fundamental themes. Much of the general foundation of the situation has been in fact common to all the major nations of the Western world where the process of industrialization and rationalization has taken strong hold. It is a question, not of a right and a wrong analysis, but of the appropriate adaptation of one which is in the nature of the case general and abstract, to the concretely variable circumstances of different particular situations. This adaptation is achieved, not by substituting a new "correct" for an incorrect explanation, but by introducing an analysis of the effect of specific modifications of the generalized structure presented here, and by taking account of additional factors which the generality of this analysis has not permitted to be treated.

XV

Social Classes and Class Conflict in the Light of Recent Sociological Theory

I. *The Marxian View as a Point of Departure*

NINETEEN HUNDRED AND FORTY-EIGHT is the centenary of the Communist Manifesto—the first major theoretical statement of Marxism—and some stocktaking of where Marx and Engels stood in an important line of the development of social science rather than only as the ideological founders of "scientific socialism" is in order.

The president of the American Economic Association, Professor Schumpeter,[1] has particularly clearly distinguished these two aspects of Marx's work. He has also within the scientific component distinguished Marx, the economic theorist, from Marx, the sociologist. In both respects I should like to follow Professor Schumpeter.

From my point of view, looking toward the development of modern sociological theory, Marx represented a first major step beyond the point at which the Utilitarian theorists, who set the frame of reference within which the classical economics developed, stood. Marx introduced no fundamental modification of the general theory of human social behavior in the terms which this school of thought represented. He did, however, unlike the Utilitarians, see and emphasize the massive fact of the structuring of interests rather than treating them as distributed at random. The structure of the productive forces which Marx outlined for capitalist society is real and of fundamental importance. Naturally, many refinements in the presentation of the structural facts and their historical development have been introduced since Marx's day, but the fundamental fact is certainly correct. The theory of class conflict is an integral part of this. It is of great interest to sociology.

---

[1] J. A. Schumpeter, *Capitalism, Socialism and Democracy.*

Marx, however, tended to treat the socioeconomic structure of capitalist enterprise as a single indivisible entity rather than breaking it down analytically into a set of the distinct variables involved in it. It is this analytical breakdown which is for present purposes the most distinctive feature of modern sociological analysis, and which must be done to take advantage of advances that have taken place. It results both in a modification of the Marxian view of the system itself and enables the establishment of relations to other aspects of the total social system, aspects of which Marx was unaware. This change results in an important modification of Marx's empirical perspective in relation to the class problem as in other contexts. The primary structural emphasis no longer falls on the orientation of capitalistic enterprise to profit and the theory of exploitation but rather on the structure of occupational roles within the system of industrial society.

Thus class conflict and its structural bases are seen in a somewhat different perspective. Conflict does not have the same order of inevitability, but is led back to the interrelations of a series of more particular factors, the combinations of which may vary. Exactly how serious the element of conflict is becomes a matter of empirical investigation. Similarly, the Marxian utopianism about the classlessness of communist society is brought into serious question. There is a sense in which the Marxian view of the inevitability of class conflict is the obverse of the utopian factor in Marxian thought.

It should, however, be clearly noted how important Marx was in the development of modern sociological thought. All three of the writers who may be regarded as its most important theoretical founders—Vilfredo Pareto, Emile Durkheim and Max Weber—were profoundly concerned with the problems raised by Marx. Each of them took the Marxian view with great seriousness as compared with its Utilitarian background, but none of them ended up as a Marxian. Each pushed on to a further development in a distinctive direction which in spite of the diversity of their backgrounds contains a striking common element.[2]

II. *The Approach to the Analysis of Social Stratification in Terms of Modern Sociological Theory*

On the basis of modern sociological approach, it may perhaps be said that Marx looked at the structure of capitalistic enterprise and

---

[2] Talcott Parsons, *The Structure of Social Action.*

generalized a social system from it, including the class structure and, to him the inevitable conflicts involved in it. Conversely, the concept of the generalized social system is the basis of modern sociological thinking. Analyzed in this framework, both capitalistic enterprise and social stratification are seen in the context of their role in such a social system. The organization of production and social stratification are, of course, both variable in these terms, though also functionally related to each other. For the functional basis of the phenomena of stratification, it is necessary to analyze the problem of integrating and ordering social relationships within a social system. Some set of norms governing relations of superiority and inferiority is an inherent need of every stable social system. There will be immense variation, but this is a constant point of reference. Such a patterning or ordering is the stratification system of the society.

As with all other major structural elements of the social system, the norms governing its stratification tend to become institutionalized; that is, moral sentiments crystallize about them and the whole system of motivational elements (including both disinterested and self-interested components) tends to be structured in support of conformity to them. There is a system of sanctions, both formal and informal, in support; so that deviant tendencies are met with varying degrees and kinds of disapproval, withdrawal of co-operation, and positive infliction of punishment. Conversely, there are rewards for conformity and institutionalized achievements.[3]

It follows that in relation to the problem of social class as in other fields, the general problem of economic motivation must be viewed in an institutional context. Even the system of profit seeking of modern capitalism is, there is abundant evidence, an institutionalized system. To be sure, it grew up as a result of emancipation from previous institutional controls in a pre-capitalistic order, but it could not have become established and stabilized to the extent that actually happened had it not had a positive system of moral sentiments underlying it and had it not acquired an institutional status of its own. The Marxian interpretation of this problem tends to see the structuring and control of self-interest only in terms of the realistic situation in which people are placed. Modern socio-

---

[3] See Talcott Parsons, *Essays in Sociological Theory*, for a variety of different discussions of the problem of institutionalization and its relation to motivation on the psychological level.

logical theory accedes fully to the importance of this aspect, but insists that it must be seen in combination with a structure of institutionalized moral sentiments as well, so that conformity is determined by a system of mutually reinforcing situational pressures and subjective motivational elements, which in one sense are obverse aspects of the same process.

III. *The Fundamentals of Stratification in a Modern Industrialized Social System*

The distinctive feature of this structure called "social stratification" is that it ranks individuals in the general social hierarchy in generalized terms, not in any one specific context. For the sake of simplicity, we may first speak specifically of the importance of two such contexts in a modern industrial society and then of the articulations between them.

Looked at in the large, by far the most prominent structure of modern Western society is that organized around the "work" people do, whether this work is in the field of economic enterprise, of governmental function, or of various other types of private nonprofit activity, such as that of our own academic profession. The extremely elaborate division of labor, which permits a tremendous specialization of functions of this sort, of course necessitates an equally elaborate system of exchange, where the products of the work of specialized groups (whether they be material or immaterial) are made available to those who can utilize them, and vice versa, the specialist is enabled to live without performing innumerable functions for himself, because he has access to the results of the work of innumerable others. Similarly, there must be a property system which regulates claims to transferable entities, material or immaterial, and thereby secures rights in means of life and in the facilities which are necessary for the performance of function. This whole complex of structural elements in our society may be called "the instrumental complex." Its three fundamental elements—occupation, exchange, and property—are all inextricably interdependent.

On a high level of the structural differentiation of a social system, the occupational system seems to be the least variable of the three and thus in a certain sense structurally the most fundamental. Elaboration of the system of exchange and its segregation from functionally irrelevant contexts are certainly essential. But there may be great variation in the extent to which the units in the exchange process enjoy autonomy in their decisions and are thus free to be oriented to their own "profit" or act merely as agents of a more comprehensive organization. Similarly, though presumably something like the Roman-modern institution of ownership is called for, the organization units in which such rights inhere may also vary, and with them the line between property and contractual rights.

Within such ranges of variation, a highly developed system of occupational roles, with functional considerations dominating them, will tend to have certain relatively constant features. Perhaps the most important of these features, seen in comparative perspective, is its inherently "individualistic" character. That is, the status of the individual must be determined on grounds essentially peculiar to himself, notably his own personal qualities, technical competence, and his own decisions about his occupational career and with respect to which he is not identified with any solidary group.

This is, of course, not in the least to suggest that he has complete freedom; he is subject to all manner of pressures, many of which are from various points of view "irrational." It is nevertheless fundamental that status and role allocation and the processes of mobility from status to status are in terms of the individual as a unit and not of solidary groups, like kinship groups, castes, village communities, etc.

There is, furthermore, an inherent hierarchical aspect to such a system. There are two fundamental functional bases of the hierarchical aspect. One is the differentiation of levels of skill and competence involved in the many different functional roles. The requirement of rare abilities on the one hand and of competence which can only be acquired by prolonged and difficult training on the other make such differentiation inherent. Secondly, organization on an ever increasing scale is a fundamental feature of such a system. Such organization naturally involves centralization and differentiation of leadership and authority; so that those who take responsibility for co-ordinating the actions of many others must have a different status in important respects from those who are essentially in the role of carrying out specifications laid down by others. From a sociological point of view, one of the fundamental problems in such a system is the way in which these basic underlying differentiations get structured into institutionalized status differentiations.

The second major context of an industrialized social system which is relevant to its stratification is that of kinship. The fundamental principle of kinship relationships is that of the solidarity of the members of the kinship unit which precludes individualistic differentiation of fortune and status in the sense in which this is fundamental to the occupational system In other societies, extended kinship units are very prominent indeed. In our society, the size of the unit has been reduced to a relative minimum—the conjugal family of parents and immature children. Only on this basis is it compatible with our occupational system at all. Nevertheless, this minimum is fundamental to our social system and differentiations of status, except those involved in age and sex roles, cannot be tolerated within it. The same individual who has a role in the occupational system is also a member of the family unit. In the latter context, his status must be shared within broad limits by the others, irrespective of their personal competence, qualities, and deserts. The articulation of the two is possible only by virtue of the fact that in the type case only one member of a family unit, the husband or father, is in the fullest sense normally a functioning member of the occupational system. Important though this degree of segregation of the two is, for it to be complete would be functionally impossible.

Wives, by virtue of at least different qualities and achievements than those of their husbands, must in the relevant contexts share their status. This means that criteria and symbols of status relevant to the family must be extended to realms outside the sphere of the same order of functionally utilitarian considerations on which a woman's husband's status in his occupation is based. The style of life of a family and its implication in the realm of feminine activities, however dependent it may be on a husband's income, precludes that total status should be a simple function of the "shop" concerns of a man's occupational world. Equally important, children must share the status of their parents if there is to be a family system at all. If the status of the parents is hierarchically differentiated, there will inevitably be an element of differential access to opportunity.

It is only in terms of the articulation of these two fundamentals, the instrumental complex and kinship, that I should speak of social class in a sociological sense. A class may then be defined as a plurality of kinship units which, in those respects where status in a hierarchical context is shared by their members, have approximately equal status. The class status of an individual, therefore, is that which he shares with the other members in an effective kinship unit. We have a class system, therefore, only insofar as the differentiations inherent in our occupational structure, with its differential relations to the exchange system and to property, remuneration, etc., has become ramified out into a system of strata, which involve differentiations of family living based partly on income, standard of life and style of life, and, of course, differential access for the younger generation to opportunity as well as differential pressures to which they are subject. There is no doubt that everywhere that modern industrial society has existed there has been a class system in this sense. There are, however, considerable variations from one society to another, particularly between the European versions of industrial capitalism and the American.

In certain respects, the above considerations might be regarded as obvious. It has been necessary to enter into them, however, because of their bearing on the perspective in which the modern class system is seen. "Liberal" economic thought has for understandable reasons paid primary attention to the market system and therefore views the economy as a system of market-oriented units rather than concerning itself with occupational structure, most of which is internal to such units. Marxian thought shares this emphasis with the addition of the capitalist-labor division in its bearing on the market process. Neither has had much concern for the family. The importance of the difference of perspective will become evident in the analysis of class conflict which follows.

IV. *The Analysis of Class Conflict in Sociological Terms*

The above sociological analysis of social stratification is based heavily on the general view that stratification is to an important degree an integrating structure in the social system. The ordering of relationships in this context is necessary to stability. This is necessary precisely because of the importance of potential though often latent conflicts. Therefore, the problem of class conflict may be approached in terms of an analysis of these latent conflicts and of the ways in which the institutional integration of the system does and does not succeed in developing adequate control mechanisms. The following principal aspects of the tendency to develop class conflict in our type of social system may be mentioned.

1. There is an inherently competitive aspect of our individualistic occupational system. Because it is differentiated on a prestige scale and because there is individual choice of occupation and a measure of equality of opportunity, there will inevitably be some differentia-

tion into winners and losers. Certain psychological consequences of such situations are known. There will be certain tendencies to arrogance on the part of some winners and to resentment and to a "sour grapes" attitude on the part of some losers. The extent to which the system is institutionalized in terms of genuine standards of fair competition is the critical problem.

2. The role of organization means that there must be an important part played by discipline and authority. Discipline and authority do not exist on a grand scale without generating some resistance. Some form, therefore, of structuring in terms of an opposition of sentiments and interests between those in authority and those subject to it is endemic in such a system. The whole problem of the institutionalization of authority so as to insure its adequate acceptance where necessary and protect against its abuse is difficult—doubly so in such a complex system.

3. There does seem to be a general tendency for the strategically placed, the powerful, to exploit the weaker or less favorably placed. The ways in which such a tendency works out and in which it is controlled and counteracted are almost infinitely various in different societies and social situations. Among the many possibilities, Marxian theory of capitalistic exploitation selects what it claims to be an integrated combination of reinforcing factors, the principal components of which are the use of positions of authority within organizations (the capitalistic "boss"); the exploitation of bargaining advantage in market relations (e.g., the labor market); and the use of the power of the state to the differential advantage of certain private interests ("executive committee of the *bourgeoisie*"). In my opinion, the Marxian view of this factor needs to be broken down into such components which are certainly independently variable and related to a variety of other factors which Marx did not consider. In the face of ideology and counterideology, this is particularly difficult but it is essential if one is to reach a basis for a scientific judgment of the Marxian doctrine of the dynamics of capitalism.

4. There seem to be inherent tendencies for those who are structurally placed at notably different points in a differentiated social structure to develop different "cultures." There will tend to be a differentiation of attitude systems, of ideologies, and of definitions of the situation to a greater or less degree around the structure of the occupational system and of the other components of the instru-

mental complex, such as the relation to markets and profits. The development of these differentiated cultures may readily impede communication across the lines of these groups. Under certain circumstances, this tendency to develop a hiatus may become cumulative unless counteracted by effective integrative mechanisms. A leading modern example is the opposing ideologies of business and labor groups in modern industrial society. Marx provided a beginning of analysis in this direction—but it did not go far enough.

5. It is precisely in the area of such a subculture, which is integrated with a structural status, that the problem of articulation with kinship becomes most important. The differences in the situation of people placed at different points in the occupational system and of the consequences for family income and living conditions seem to lead to a notable differentiation of family type. In American urban society, a relatively clear differentiation of this kind has been shown to exist between "middle-class" and "lower-class" groups as they are generally called in the sociological literature. These differences are apparently such as to penetrate into the deepest psychological layers of attitude determination. There are indications from our society that the family structure of the lower groups is such as to favor attitudes which positively handicap their members in competition for status in the occupational system. The role of the integration between occupation and kinship, therefore, under certain circumstances can become an important factor in pushing toward cumulative separation of classes and potential conflict between them.

6. Absolute equality of opportunity in the occupational system, which is, in a sense, the ideal type norm for such a system, is in practice impossible. There seem to be two main types of limitation.

a) Certain of these are, as noted above, inherent in the functional requirements of family solidarity. Children must share the status of their parents, and insofar as this is differentiated, the more favored groups will have differential access to opportunity. This seems to be counteracted by certain compensating mechanisms, such as leading some of the children of the upper groups into paths which positively handicap them in occupational competition (e.g., the playboy pattern). It may also be pointed out that a differential birth rate has a functional significance in leaving relatively more room at the top for the children of the lower groups.

b) There are important reasons to believe that the complete

institutionalization of the universalistic and functionally specific standards so prominent in our occupational world is not possible in a large scale social system. Such problems as the difficulty in establishing comparability of different lines of achievement, the lack of complete adequacy of objective standards of judgment of them, and similar things necessitate mechanisms which avoid too direct a comparison and which favor a very rough, broad scale rather than one of elaborately precise comparison. To take just one example in the academic profession, there is a wide variation of degrees of distinction between the senior members of any large university faculty. The tendency, however, is to play down these variations in favor of a broad similarity of status; for instance, as full professor, to conceal differentiations of salary within this group from public view, and to concentrate the most highly competitive elements at certain very narrowly specified points, such as the appointment to permanent rank. Considerations such as these lead to the view that there will be elements in an occupational system which run counter to the main structural type but which have the function of cushioning the impact of the latter on certain "human factors" and thus protect the stability of the system.

The fundamental problem then is how far factors such as these operate to produce deep-seated and chronic conflict between classes and how far they are counteracted by other factors in the social system such as the last mentioned. It should first, of course, be pointed out that these are not the only directions in which a structuring tending to conflict takes place. There is considerable evidence that in the modern Western World, national solidarity tends generally to take precedence over class solidarity and that, even more generally, the solidarity of ethnic groupings is of particularly crucial significance. One cannot help having the impression that in these matters Marx chose one among the possibilities rather than proving that there could be only one of crucial significance.

Furthermore, in Europe the precapitalistic residues of the old class structure in the ways in which they got tied in with the consequences of the developing industrial society have a great deal to do with the acuteness of class conflict. A good example of this is Germany with the continuing powerful position during the imperial and even the Weimar periods of the nobility and the old civil service and professional groups which were certainly not the product of the capitalistic process alone. The problem of the "threat of communism" in Germany just before Hitler was certainly colored by their role. Class conflict certainly exists in the United States, but it is different from the German case and much less influenced than the latter by precapitalistic structures. Marxian theory inhibited the recognition of differences such as this—all class conflicts in a society in any sense capitalistic had to be reduced to a single pattern. Another most important set of conclusions from this type of analysis is that there must be certain elements of fundamental identity of the functional problems of social stratification and class in capitalist and socialist societies, if we have given two really fundamental elements: the large-scale organization and occupational role differentiation of industrial society and a family system. The history of Soviet Russia would seem to confirm this view. The role of the managerial and intelligentsia class, which has been progressively strengthened since the revolution, does not have a place in the Marxist utopia. In certain major respects, the role of managers and technical personnel closely resembles American society. I, for one, do not believe that there is a sharp and fundamental sociological distinction between capitalist society and all noncapitalist industrial societies. I believe that class conflict is endemic in our modern industrial type of society. I do not, however, believe that the case has been made for believing that it is the dominant feature of every such society and of its dynamic development. Its relation to other elements of tension, conflict, and dynamic change is a complex matter, about which we cannot attempt the Marxian order of generalization with certainty until our science is much further developed than it is today.

It is relevant to this set of problems that since Marx wrote, our knowledge of comparative social structures has immensely broadened and deepened. Seen in the perspective of such knowledge, the sociological emphases on the interpretation of modern Western society have shifted notably. Capitalist and socialist industrialisms tend to be seen as variants of a single fundamental type, not as drastically distinct stages in a single process of dialectic evolution. Indeed, to the modern sociologist the rigid evolutionary schema of Marxian thought appears as a strait jacket rather than a genuine source of illumination of the immensely variant facts of institutional life.

V. *Conclusion*

The Marxian theory of class conflict seen as a step in the development of social science rather than as a clarion call to revolution thus represents a distinct step in advance of the ultilitarian background of the predominant economic thought of a century ago. Though couched in terms of a neo-Hegelian evolutionary theory of history, it was, seen in terms of subsequent developments of social science, an advance more on the level of empirical insight and generalization from it than of the analytical treatment of dynamic factors in social process. The endless exegetical discussions of the "relations" or "conditions" of production and of what was meant or implied in them is an indication of this.

As a point of focus for the subsequent development of modern sociological theory, however, the Marxian ideas have had an important place, forming a point of departure for the formulation of many of the fundamentals of the theory of social institutions. The Marxian view of the importance of class structure has in a broad way been vindicated.

When the problem of the genesis and importance of social classes and their conflicts is approached in these modern sociological terms, however, considerable modifications of the Marxian position are necessitated. Systems of stratification in certain respects are seen to have positive functions in the stabilization of social systems. The institutionalization of motivation operates within the system of capitalistic profit making. The Marxian ideal of a classless society is in all probability utopian—above all so long as a family system is maintained but also for other reasons. The differences between capitalist and socialist societies, particularly with respect to stratification, are not as great as Marx and Engels thought.

In both types there is a variety of potential sources of class conflict centering about the structure of the productive process. Those lying within the Marxian purview are not so monolithically integrated in the process of capitalist exploitation as Marx thought, but are seen to be much more specific and in certain degrees independently variable. Some of them, like the relation to family solidarity, lay outside the Marxian focus of emphasis on the relations of production.

Insofar as Marx and Engels were true social scientists, as indeed in one principal aspect of their role they were, we justly celebrate their centennial in a scientific meeting. They promulgated ideas which were a notable advance on the general state of knowledge in the field at the time. They provided a major stimulus and definition of problems for further notable advances. They formed an indispensable link in the chain of development of social science. The fact that social science in this aspect of their field has evolved beyond the level to which they brought it is a tribute to their achievement.

XVI

Psychoanalysis and the Social Structure

The Basic Common Frame of Reference

BOTH PSYCHOANALYTIC THEORY and the type of sociological theory which is in process of developing a new type of analysis of social structure and its dynamics go back to the same basic conceptual scheme or frame of reference which it is convenient to call the theory of action. This theory conceives the behaving individual or actor as operating in a situation which is given independently of his goals and wishes, but, within the limits of that situation and using those potentialities which are subject to his control, actively oriented to the attainment of a system of goals and wishes. Studying the processes of action, the scheme takes the point of view of the meaning of the various elements of the system to the actor. Meaning may be of several different types, of which, perhaps, the most important are the cognitive and the affective or emotional. Finally, the mutual orientation of human beings to each other, both as objects of meaning and as means to each other's goals, is a fundamental aspect of the scheme. Though it is logically possible to treat a single individual in isolation from others, there is every reason to believe that this case is not of important empirical significance. All concrete action is in this sense social, including psychopathological behavior.

There are two main foci of theoretical organization of systems within the broad framework of this conceptual scheme. One is the individual personality as a system, and the other is the social system. The first is, according to this point of view, the primary focus of the subject matter of the science of psychology; the second that of social science in the specific sense. The same fundamental conceptual components are involved in the treatment of both, and on a broader level whatever theories exist in both are part of the same fundamental theoretical system. Nevertheless, it is extremely important to differentiate the various levels and ways in which these conceptual components are involved or combined. It is dangerous to shift from the one level to the other without taking adequate account of the systematic differences that are involved.

The Social System
as a Structural-Functional System of Action

It is essential from the point of view of social science to treat the social system as a distinct and independent entity which must be studied and analyzed on its own level, not as a composite resultant of the actions of the component individuals alone. There is no reason to attribute any fundamental logical or ontological priority to either the social system or the personality. In treating the social system as a system, structural categories have proved to be essential in the same sense as in the biological sciences, and presumably also in psychology.[1] In the present state of knowledge of social systems, it is not possible to treat a total social system directly as a dynamic equilibrium of motivational forces. It is necessary to treat motivational problems in the context of their relation to structure, and to raise dynamic problems in terms of the balance of forces operating to maintain or alter a given structure. At this point, however, psychological categories in social science play a fundamental role which is in some respects analogous to biochemistry in biological science. In this context what is meant by social structure is a system of patterned expectations of the behavior of individuals who occupy particular statuses in the social system. Such a system of patterned legitimate expectations is called by sociologists a system of roles. In so far as a cluster of such roles is of strategic significance to the social system, the complex of patterns which define expected behavior in them may be referred to as an institution. For example, in so far as the behavior of spouses in their mutual relationships is governed by socially sanctioned legitimate expectations in such a sense that departure from these patterns will call forth reactions of moral disapproval or overt sanctions, we speak of the institution of marriage. Institutional structures in this sense are the fundamental element of the structure of the social system. They constitute relatively stable crystallizations of behavioral forces in

[1] *Cf.* Cannon, Walter B. and Higginson, George: *The Wisdom of the Body.* Second Edition. New York: W. W. Norton & Co., 1939; Freud: *The Ego and the Id.* London: Hogarth Press, 1927; Parsons, Talcott: The other essays in the present volume.

such a way that action can be sufficiently regularized so as to be compatible with the functional requirements of a society.

From the psychological point of view, institutionalized roles seem to have two primary functions. The first is the structuring of the reality situation for the action of the individual. They define the expectations of behavior which are generalized in the attitude patterns of other individuals with whom he may come in contact. They tell him what the probable consequences of various alternative forms of action are likely to be. Second, they structure the 'superego content' for the individual. It is fundamentally the patterns institutionalized in role structure which constitute the moral standards which are introjected in the process of socialization and become an important part of the personality structure of the individual himself, whether he conforms to them or not. It may be stated as a fundamental theorem of social science that one measure of the integration of a social system is the coincidence of the patterns which are introjected in the average superego of those occupying the relevant social statuses with the functional needs of the social system which has that particular structure.

The Discrepancy Between Personality Structure and Institutional Motivation

One of the most important reasons why it is dangerous to infer too directly from the psychological to the social structure level and vice versa is the extremely important fact that there is not a simple correspondence between personality structure and institutional structure. On the level of clinical diagnosis, the persons occupying the same well-defined status in the social system will be found to cover a wide range of personality types. It is true that seen in sufficiently broad perspective there will be modal types which differ from one society to another, but this is a statistical correspondence and not one of the social pattern to the personality pattern of each individual. This means that there must be mechanisms by which the behavior of individuals is motivated to conform with institutional expectations, even though personality structure as such does not give an adequately effective background for it.

It is convenient to refer to the fundamental mechanism involved here as the 'structural generalization of goals'; thus there is a level of the structuring of motivational forces which is essentially a function of the institutional situations in which people are put, rather than of their particular personality structures. It may be said to operate within the range of flexibility which personality structures permit, and, of course, to involve a greater or less amount of strain to carry out that conformity. This, however, is one area of the analysis of motivation where the relation of psychology to social structure is particularly important. To cite just one example, most attempts at a direct psychological attack on the problem of so-called economic motivation, or the profit motive, have proved to be singularly unfruitful. The essential reason for this is that the uniformities of social behavior do not directly correspond to uniformities on the psychological level independent of the institutional context. Anything like the profit motive of modern Western society is not a psychological universal, and the corresponding behavior would not be found in many, for instance, nonliterate and other societies.[2]

The Problem of the Use of Motivational Categories in Dynamic Explanations on the Sociological Level

The most notable direct contributions of psychoanalytic theory to the empirical understanding of behavior would seem to fall in the dynamic theory of motivation of the individual in the context of the structure of personality. The most important problem of the relation of psychoanalysis to social structure from the point of view of the sociologist is how these categories can be used for explanatory purposes on the level of the analysis of social structure and its changes as such. This is a field in which it is particularly dangerous to attempt too direct an explanation. The lack of correspondence between personality structure and social structure should make this clear.

The sociologist is, in the first instance, concerned with behavior and attitudes which are of strategic significance to the social system. In the terms stated, this means tendencies which either support the structure of an existing social system or tend to alter it in specific ways.[3] The judgments of significance on which the statements of sociological problems of motivation are based must there-

---

[2] Cf. Parsons, Talcott: The Motivation of Economic Activities, Chap. III above.

[3] This excludes behavior which varies at random, relative to structural patterns, from being treated as sociologically significant.

fore be couched in terms of the frame of reference of the social system, not of personality, though of course they must be compatible with established knowledge of personality.

Such problems must in turn be approached in terms of constructs of typical motivation, typical of the persons occupying given statuses in the social structure. The most obvious of the ingredients of such constructs will of course be derived from the situation in which a given incumbent of such a status is placed—a situation principally compounded of the behavior and attitudes of others. But psychoanalytic theory shows that these alone are not sufficient; certain typical elements of structure of the particular personality, such as superego content and ways in which the instinctual components are organized, are also involved. It is furthermore often necessary to link these elements in a developmental sequence so that the motivational structures resulting from an earlier situation in the life cycle become elements in shaping the situations of a later stage.

There is involved throughout this procedure a peculiar process of abstraction from the frame of reference of personality as a functioning system. Psychologists and psychoanalysts tend to take this frame of reference for granted and thus find it difficult to accept the sociologist's mode of abstraction. They feel it is psychologically inadequate, as indeed it is. But adequacy is not an absolute; it is relative to the problems which facts and conceptual schemes can help to solve. The typical problems of the psychologist and the sociologist are different and therefore they need to use the same concepts at different levels of abstraction and in different combinations.

In general it may be said that psychological analysis is oriented to the explanation of the concrete acts, attitudes, or ideas of individuals. Both motivational elements and the social structure come into this, the latter as describing the situation in which the individual must act or to which he has been exposed. Adequacy is judged in terms of the completeness of accounting for one given act, attitude, or idea as compared to another. The frame of reference is, as has been said, the personality of the relevant individual treated as a system.

The sociologist's problems are different. They concern the balance of motivational forces involved in the maintenance of, and alteration in, the structure of a social system. This balance is a peculiar sort of resultant of very complex interaction processes. It can only be successfully analyzed by abstracting from the idiosyncratic variability of individual behaviors and motivations in terms of strategic relevance to the social system. Conversely the psychologist abstracts from what are to him the equally idiosyncratic variations of social situations in reaching psychological generalizations about such matters as the relations of love and security.

If we had a completely adequate dynamic theory of human motivation it is probable that this difference of levels of abstraction would disappear. Then the use of structural categories, on the levels of either personality or the social system, would be unnecessary, for such categories are only empirical generalizations introduced to fill the gaps left by the inadequacy of our dynamic knowledge. In the meantime, however, we must put up with the complications involved in the diversity of levels.

It follows from these considerations, if they are accepted, that the motivational constructs needed for the solution of any sociological problem will generally turn out to be inadequate to explain the action of any particular individual involved in the very concrete events being studied. They will be concerned with certain elements in this motivation, but the combinations of these elements with others, and hence what will be the order of their strategic significance to the psychological problem, cannot be inferred from the sociological analysis.

Conversely, psychologists, whether they are aware of it or not, categorize the social structure. But by the same token, the conceptualizations they find adequate for their purposes will generally turn out to be inadequate to the explanation of a single process of change in a social structure in which the same concrete persons and action-sequences were involved.

It is, in my opinion, neglect of the indispensability of distinguishing these levels of abstraction which, more than errors or differences of opinion about facts, has accounted for the difficulties. These difficulties, from the sociologist's point of view, have been prominent in much of what may be called psychologically (psychoanalytically) oriented sociology which attempts to generalize about societies from *Totem and Taboo* to Geoffrey Gorer's *American People*. In the absence of very careful discrimination of these levels it was almost inevitable that the analyst would 'extrapolate' directly from what he found in the personalities he had studied in the clinical situation. He would then necessarily categorize social structures *ad hoc* in the light of these references without systematic reference to the social system as a conceptual scheme and the criteria of relevance inherent in such a reference.[4] Certain sociologists likewise indulge in *ad hoc* psychological constructions without reference to technical psychological considerations.[5]

An Example of the Use of Motivational Categories for Sociological Purposes: American Youth

To give concrete content to the abstract analysis presented above, a brief account of one example of what may be considered the most fruitful level of use of psychoanalytic categories in sociological interpretation is given. The essential facts are matters of common observation.

Starting at about high school age young Americans, especially in the urban middle classes, embark on patterns of behavior and attitudes which do not constitute a stage in a continuous transition from childhood to adulthood but deviate from such a line of continuity. Instead of gradually assuming increasing responsibilities there is a tendency to such irresponsible acts as reckless driving. A major aspect of increasing maturity would seem to be progressively greater freedom from needs to conform with rigidly detailed patterns of the group. On the contrary, there is in youth a rather extreme pressure to conformity in details of dress and behavior. Finally, maturity seems to involve increasing capacity for realistic orientation to emotionally significant objects, but in youth there is a resurgence of romanticism—a resurgence of unrealistic idealization not only in relation to age-peers of the opposite sex, but also in the form of hero worship; moreover, such figures as athletic stars whose functions are of quite secondary importance in the adult world tend to be idealized far more than eminent statesmen, executives or scientists.

This pattern of attitudes and behavior is sufficiently general and pronounced to be singled out as a distinctively structured complex conveniently called the youth culture. Its principal characteristics may be summarized.

1. Compulsive independence of and antagonism to adult expecta-

---

[4] In extreme instances, the history of social change has tended to be interpreted as the simple consequence of the collective 'acting out' of the emotional tensions observed in personalities.

[5] In essence this is what Max Weber did on a high level in his construction of ideal types of motivation. *Cf.* Parsons, Talcott: Introduction to: *The Theory of Social and Economic Organization* (Sec. 2) by Max Weber. New York: Oxford University Press, 1947.

tions and authority. This involves recalcitrance to adult standards of responsibility and, in extreme instances, treating the conformist —who, for instance, takes school work seriously—as a 'sissy' who should be excluded from peer-group participation.

2. Compulsive conformity within the peer group of age mates. It is intolerable to be 'different'; not, for example, to use lipstick as soon as the other girls do. Related to this is an intense fear of being excluded, a corresponding competitiveness for acceptance by the 'right' groups, and a ruthless rejection of those who 'don't make the grade'.

3. Romanticism: an unrealistic idealization of emotionally significant objects. There is a general tendency to see the world in sharply black and white terms; identifications with one's gang, or team, or school tend to be very intense and involve highly immature disparagements of other groups.

There is thus a well-defined sociological problem. In the socialization of the younger generation in the American social system, there is a specifically structured deviation (a mass phenomenon) from the path of asymptotic approach to 'maturity'. What is this all about? Comparative evidence adequately disposes of the popular view that it is a consequence of physiological maturation because there is no reason to believe that Samoans or Chinese 'adolesce' differently from Americans in a physiological sense.[6] It is therefore plausible to suggest that the American social structure through its impact on the human material may provide a field of interpretation.

The essential structural facts are very simple but must be considered at two age levels. American middle class children, unlike many others, are reared in small conjugal families normally separated in place of residence and other respects from other close kin. There is a very small circle of emotionally significant persons on whom the child's object cathexes must be focused: father, mother, and one, two or three siblings. Of these the mother occupies a particularly central place for both sexes because no other women have a remotely similar role, and because the father works away from home and is thus absent a great deal of the time; moreover, there is a very sharp distinction between relations inside the home and those outside. In the neighborhood play group and later in school,

---

[6] *Cf.* Mead, Margaret: *Coming of Age in Samoa.* New York: William Morrow & Co., 1928, and Levy, M. J., Jr.: *The Family Revolution in Modern China.* Cambridge: Harvard University Press, 1949.

the child must 'find its own level' in competition with others with whose parents his parents have no clearly ordered status relationship, who are just neighbors.

Approaching adulthood the American youth faces a situation very different from the youth of many other societies. Both sexes look forward to the 'independence' of leaving the parental home and setting up a home of their own. The choice of a partner in marriage is their personal responsibility, without major parental participation in the decision. Boys must make their own way, achieving status and income in a competitive occupational system. Most girls can look forward to support by a husband, but they must choose the husband on their own responsibility, and their own status and welfare and that of their children depends most crucially on the wisdom of the choice.

What is the impact of these two successive situations on the human material exposed to them, taking due account of differentiation according to sex? Insights into motivation which stem from psychoanalysis more than any other source provide the principal clues.

In the first place, the sharp limitation of the circle of objects of cathexis tends to intensify emotional involvements. This is particularly true of the common significance of the relation to the mother since she is unique and the father tends to be remote. This intensity is reinforced by early exposure to a competitive process outside the family in which it seems reasonable to assume that the insecurity generated tends to be compensated by greater dependence on familial cathexes. Thus more than other family systems the American makes the child highly dependent emotionally on its parents, particularly the mother.

The child is then placed in a situation, as it approaches adulthood, where it must, if it is to live adequately up to expectations, break away from these ties far more drastically than is necessary in most societies. If a male, he must choose his own occupation and make his own way in it. He must make the complicated emotional adjustment to a sexual partner and spouse on his own initiative and responsibility. A girl must 'catch' an acceptable man by exercise of her own feminine attraction in sharp competition with other girls and without adult support.

For boys the situation is greatly complicated by the tendency to feminine identification inherent in the especially intense relation to the mother and the remoteness of the father. This seems to account for a reaction-formation of 'compulsive masculinity' which appears in the latency period and is carried, in a socially structured way, over into adolescence and beyond. With it goes a deep ambivalence toward moral values (since these tend to be felt as feminine) and toward the acceptability of sexuality. For girls there seems to be greater stability in childhood through identification with the mother which probably accounts for much of their precocity. When, however, they face the 'mancatching' situation, to be too much of a motherly figure is, in the face of masculine ambivalence, by no means an unambiguous asset. The conflict between 'glamor' and the domestic pattern seems to have its roots in this situation.

Thus the compulsive independence of the youth culture may, according to well-established psychological principles, be interpreted as involving a reaction-formation against dependency needs, which is for understandable reasons particularly prominent among boys. The compulsive conformity, in turn, would seem to serve as an outlet for these dependency needs, but displaced from parental figures onto the peer group so that it does not interfere with the independence. The element of romanticism finally seems to express the ambivalence and insecurity which are inherent in the emotional patterning of both sexes when faced with highly crucial decisions. It is a tonic stimulus to confidence and action in the face of potentially paralyzing conflicts.

The above is a highly schematic and simplified interpretation of the psychological dynamics of American youth culture. Any experienced analyst can add many more nuances of motivation, as a sociologist would on the details of the social structure. The analysis is carried only far enough to illustrate concretely an application of psychoanalytic concepts to sociological usage. This is not 'psychoanalytic sociology' in the sense of generalizing from clinical insights in terms of their 'implications' for society. It involves the use of technical sociological theory in the statement of problems and the analysis of social structure; nevertheless, the contributions of psychoanalysis are crucial. Without them a far cruder level of dynamic interpretation would have to be accepted. By further refinement of both components of the scheme, far more refined and subtle interpretations are likely to be attainable.

Conclusion

Psychoanalytic theory can make a crucially important contribution to the problems of the sociologist, though not, of course, to the exclusion of other traditions of psychological theory. This contribution is, however, likely to be much more fruitful if it is made in the form of the adaptation of psychoanalytic concepts and analyses of motivation to the technical needs of sociological theory in terms of problems stated in sociological terms.

This way of using psychoanalytic theory, it has been pointed out, involves putting it into a frame of reference, the social system, which is not usually familiar to the clinical analyst and which is not reducible to terms of his own clinical experience and standards of expectation, couched as these are, implicitly or explicitly, in terms of the frame of reference of personality. To make the transition requires such a shift in perspective and problems that it must be held that the analyst, no matter how well trained, is not per se competent to apply psychoanalytic theory to sociological problems. To do this he must be a trained sociologist, he must learn to think in terms of social systems, and he does not automatically learn this from clinical experience as an analyst but only from studying sociology as such.

But if the sociologist is to utilize the potential contributions of psychoanalysis to his problems, he can only do so competently by going to the authentic sources, by learning psychoanalysis himself, as far as possible by the regular training procedures. To some important degree the same people must have real competence in both fields. Only from such a solid base is the diffusion of psychoanalytic knowledge into such a neighboring field possible without distortion.

If the general position here taken is sound, there is a further implication which may be briefly noted in conclusion. If psychoanalytic theory is as important to sociology as it certainly seems to be, the converse relationship should also be important. This is indeed strongly indicated by the fact that analytic theory has laid so much emphasis on the psychological importance of social relationships—of the child to parents, of the adult to love objects, etc.

Concretely, these relationships are aspects of social systems; the family, for example, is a small-scale social system. The sociological aspects of the family as a social system have, understandably, not been explicitly considered by psychoanalysts because they have concentrated on the particular relations of each patient to each of the members of his family in turn. There has been little occasion to consider the total family as a social system, though this might well yield insights not derivable from the 'atomistic' treatment of each relationship in turn.

Unfortunately the sociologists as yet have not provided as much help as they might. The science is in general very immature (but then, psychoanalysis is not yet very old) and the principal preoccupation of sociologists has so far been with 'macroscopic' social systems. But the evidence is strong that the same fundamental conceptual scheme, the social system, is applicable all the way from the largest-scale societies (like the United States) to groups of such small size as the family.[7] But the sociological study of small groups is in its barest beginnings and, paradoxically, only suggestions of the technical analysis of the family as a social system exist.

But in relation to the family the problem for the psychoanalyst is the obverse of that outlined above for the sociologist. Supposing that in the near future we attain something which could respectably be called a sociology of the family; this would no more as such solve the analyst's problems about family structure than a psychoanalytic theory of personality solves the sociologist's problems of motivation. But such a theory would contain the essential conceptual bases on which the analyst could construct a theory of family structure adapted to his needs.

The sociologist must face the problems of human motivation whether he wants to or not. If he does not acquire a genuinely competent theory, he will implicitly adopt a series of *ad hoc* ideas which are no less crucial because they are exempted from critical analysis. Turning to psychoanalysis with the proper adaptations can provide him with a way out of the dilemma. Perhaps the situation is not altogether incomparable in reverse. The analyst is in fact dealing with social systems. His ideas about them have tended to be *ad hoc* and common sense. Such ideas may be adequate for many empirical purposes but tend to break down as subtler levels of generalization are attempted. There is the possibility that this gap can be filled by the products of genuinely technical analysis. Originating as they do in another frame of reference, to be useful to the analyst these would have to be adapted to his problems and needs. But can he in the long run do without them any more than the sociologist can do without the insights of psychoanalysis?

---

[7] This is also true of the classical mechanics, e.g., celestial mechanics, terrestrial mechanics, and the kinetic theory of gases.

XVII

The Prospects of
Sociological Theory

TWO YEARS AGO at the annual meeting of this Society it was my
privilege to act as chairman of the section on theory and thus to be
responsible for a statement of its contemporary position, as part of
the general stock-taking of the state of our discipline which was the
keynote of that meeting. As that meeting was primarily concerned
with taking stock of where we stood, the present one, with the
keynote of frontiers of research, is primarily concerned with looking
toward the future. It therefore seems appropriate to take advantage
of the present occasion to speak of the future prospects of that
aspect of sociological science on which more than any other I feel
qualified to speak.

The history of science testifies eloquently to the fundamental importance of the state of its theory to any scientific field. Theory is
only one of several ingredients which must go into the total brew,
but for progress beyond certain levels it is an indispensable one.
Social scientists are plagued by the problems of objectivity in the
face of tendencies to value-bias to a much higher degree than is
true of natural scientists. In addition, we have the problem of selection among an enormous number of possible variables. For both
these reasons, it may be argued that perhaps theory is even more
important in our field than in the natural sciences. At any rate, I
may presume to suggest that my own election to its presidency by
the membership of this society may be interpreted as an act of recognition of this importance of theory, and a vote of confidence in
its future development.

Though my primary concern this evening is with the future, perhaps just a word on where we stand at present is in order. Some
fifteen years ago two young Americans, who, since they were my
own children, I knew quite intimately, and who were aged approximately five and three respectively at the time, developed a little

game of yelling at the top of their voices: "The sociology is about to begin, said the man with the loud speaker." However right they may have been about their father's professional achievements up to that time, as delivering a judgment of the state of the field as a whole I think they were a bit on the conservative side. It had already begun, but especially in the theoretical phase that beginning did not lie very far back. The historians of our discipline will have to settle such questions at a future time, but I for one would not hesitate to label *all* the theoretical endeavors before the generation of Durkheim and Max Weber as proto-sociology. With these figures as the outstanding ones, but with several others including a number of Americans like Sumner, Park, Cooley, and Thomas, in a somewhat less prominent role, I feel that the real job of founding was done in the generation from about 1890 to 1920. We belong to the second generation, which already has foundations on which to build. But as for the building itself, a post here and there, and a few courses of bricks at the corners, are all that is yet visible above the ground. After all, two or, more correctly, one and a half generations, in the perspective of the development of a science, is a very short time.

When, roughly a quarter of a century ago, I attained some degree of the knowledge of good and evil in a professional sense, this founding phase was over. The speculative systems were still taken seriously. But the work of such writers as Sumner, Thomas, Simmel, Cooley, Park, and Mead, was beginning to enter into thinking in a much more particularized sense. In fact, a research tradition was already building up, in which a good deal of solid theory was embodied— as in Sumner's basic idea of the relativity of the mores, Thomas' four wishes, and many of Park's insights, as into the nature of competitive processes. This relatively particularized, attention focusing, problem selecting, use of theory in research, so different from the purely illustrative relation between theory and empirical fact in the Spencerian type of system, has continued to develop in the interim. Such fields as that of Industrial Sociology, starting from the Mayo-Roethlisberger work, and carried further at Chicago and Cornell, the study of Ethnic Relations and that of Social Stratification will serve to illustrate. At the same time controversies about total schools, which in my youth centered especially about Behaviorism, have greatly subsided.

Our own generation has seen at least the beginnings of a process of more general pulling together. Even when a good deal of theory was actually being used in research much of the *teaching* of theory was still in terms of the "systems" of the past, and was organized about names rather than working conceptual schemes. Graduate students frantically memorized the contents of Bogardus or Lichtenberger with little or no effect on their future research operations, and little guidance as to how it might be used. But this has gradually been changing. Theory has at least begun no longer to mean mainly a knowledge of "doctrines," but what matters far more, a set of patterns for habitual thinking. This change has, in my opinion, been considerably promoted by increased interest in more general theory, especially coming from study of the works of Weber and Durkheim and, though not so immediately sociological, of Freud. There has thus been the beginning at least, and to me a very encouraging beginning, of a process of coalescence of these types of more or less explicit theory which were really integrated importantly with research, into a more general theoretical tradition of some sophistication, really *the* tradition of a working professional group.

Compared to the natural sciences the amount of genuine empirical research done in our field is very modest indeed. Even so, it has been fairly substantial. But the most disappointing single thing about it has been the degree to which the results of this work have failed to be cumulative. The limitations of empirical research methods, limitations which are being overcome at a goodly rate, are in part responsible for this fact. But *probably the most crucial factor* has been precisely this lack of an adequate *working* theoretical tradition which is bred into the "bones" of empirical researchers themselves, so that "instinctively" the problems they work on, the hypotheses they frame and test, are such that the results, positive or negative, will have *significance* for a sufficiently generalized and integrated body of knowledge so that the mutual implications of many empirical studies will *play directly into each other*. There are, as I have noted, hopeful signs which point in this direction, but the responsibility on theory to promote this process is heavy indeed. So important is this point that I should like to have the view of the future role of theory in sociology, which I shall discuss in the remainder of this address, understood very largely in relation to it.

When, then, I turn to the discussion of the prospects of theory in our field I can hardly fail to express my own hope as well as a diagnosis. I hope to combine in my suggestions both a sense of the strategic significance of certain types of development, and a realistic sense of feasibility, if sufficient work by able people is done. I shall also be talking of the relatively near future, since the shape of our science two centuries hence, for instance, cannot, I fear, be realistically foreseen.

Here I should like to discuss five principal types or fields of theoretical development, which are by no means independent of one another; they actually overlap considerably as well as interact. They are:

1) General theory, which I interpret primarily as the theory of the social system in its sociologically relevant aspects.

2) The theory of motivation of social behavior and its bearing on the dynamic problems of social systems, its bearing both on the conditions of stability of social systems and the factors in their structural change. This of course involves the relations to the psychological level of analysis of personality and motivation.

3) The theoretical bases of systematic comparative analysis of social structures on the various levels. This particularly involves the articulation with the anthropological analysis of culture.

4) Special theories around particular empirical problem areas, the specific growing points of the field in empirical research. This involves their relations to general theory, and the bases of hypothesis construction in research.

5) Last, but in no sense least, the "fitting" of theory to operational procedures of research and, vice versa, the adaption of the latter to theoretical needs.

The field of general theory presents peculiar difficulties of assessment in sociology. The era of what I have above called "proto-sociology" was, as I have noted, conspicuous for the prominence of speculative systems, of which that of Spencer is an adequate example. The strong and largely justified reaction against such systems combined with a general climate of opinion favorable to pragmatic empiricism, served to create in many quarters a very general scepticism of theory, particularly anything that called itself general or systematic theory, to say nothing of a *system* of theory. This wave of anti-theoretical empiricism has, I think fortunately, greatly subsided, but there is still marked reluctance to recognize the importance of high levels of generality. The most important recent expression of this latter sentiment, which in no sense should be confused with general opposition to theory, is that of my highly esteemed friend and former student, Robert Merton, first in his discussion paper directed to my own paper on the *Position of Sociological Theory*, two years ago, then repeated and amplified in the Introduction to his recent volume of essays.

The very first point must be the emphatic statement that what I mean by the place of general theory in the prospects of sociology is *not* the revival of speculative systems of the Spencerian type, and I feel that Merton's fears that this will be the result of the emphasis I have in mind are groundless. We have, I think, now progressed to a level of methodological sophistication adequate to protect ourselves against this pitfall.

The basic reason why general theory is so important is that the cumulative development of knowledge in a scientific field is a function of the degree of *generality of implications* by which it is possible to relate findings, interpretations, and hypotheses on different levels and in different specific empirical fields to each other. If there is to be a high degree of such generality there *must* on some level be a common conceptual scheme which makes the work of different investigators in a specific sub-field and those in different sub-fields commensurable.

The essential difficulty with the speculative systems has been their *premature closure* without the requisite theoretical clarification and integration, operational techniques or empirical evidence. This forced them to use empirical materials in a purely illustrative way without systematic verification of *general* propositions or the possibility of empirical evidence leading to modification of the theory. Put a little differently, they presumed to set up a theoretical system instead of a systematic conceptual scheme.

It seems quite clear, that in the sense of mechanics a *theoretical system* is *not* now or foreseeably possible in the sociological field. The difficulties Pareto's attempt encountered indicate that. But a *conceptual scheme* in a partially articulated form exists now and is for practical purposes in common use; its further refinement and development is imperative for the welfare of our field, and is entirely feasible.

In order to make clear what I mean, I would first like to note that there is a variety of ways in which what I am calling general theory can fruitfully influence research in the direction of making its results more cumulative. The first is what may be called a set of general categories of orientation to observation and problem choice in the field which defines its major problem areas and the directions in which to look for concealed factors and variables in explanation. Thus modern anthropology, by the "cultural point of view," heavily documented with comparative material, has clearly demonstrated the limits of purely biological explanations of human behavior and taught us to look to the processes by which culturally patterned modes are learned, transmitted and created. Similarly in our own field the reorientation particularly associated with the names of Durkheim and Weber showed the inadequacy of the "utilitarian" framework for the understanding of many social phenomena and made us look to "institutional" levels—a reorientation which is indeed the birthright of sociology. Finally, in the field of motivation, the influence of Freud's perspective has been immense.

Starting from such very broad orientation perspectives there are varying possible degrees of further specification. At any rate in a field like ours it seems impossible to stop there. The very basis on which the utilitarian framework was seen to be *theoretically* as well as empirically inadequate, required a clarification of the structure of systems of social action which went considerably farther than just indicating a new direction of interest or significance. It spelled out certain inherent relationships of the components of such systems which among many other things demonstrated the *need* for a theory of motivation on the psychological level of the general character of what Freud has provided.

This kind of structural "spelling out" narrows the range of theoretical arbitrariness. There are firmly specific points in the system of implications against which empirical results can be measured and evaluated. That is where a well-structured empirical problem is formulated. If the facts then, when properly stated and validated, turn out to be contrary to the theoretical expectation, something must be modified in the theory.

In the early stages these "islands" of theoretical implication may be scattered far apart on the sea of fact and so vaguely and generally seen that only relatively broad empirical statements are directly relevant to them. This is true of the interpretation of economic motivation which I will cite presently. But with refinement of general theoretical analysis, and the accumulation of empirical evidence directly relevant to it, the islands get closer and closer together, and their topography becomes more sharply defined. It becomes more and more difficult and unnecessary to navigate in the uncharted waters of unanalyzed fact without bumping into or at least orienting to several of them.

The development of general theory in this sense is a matter of degree. But in *proportion* as it develops, the generality of implication increases and the "degree of empiricism," to quote a phrase of President Conant's, is reduced. It is precisely the existence of such a general theoretical framework, the more so the further it has developed, which makes the kind of work at the middle theory level which Merton advocates maximally fruitful. For it is by virtue of their connections with these "islands" of general theoretical knowledge once demonstrated that their overlaps and their mutual implications for each other lead to their incorporation into a more general and consistent body of knowledge.

At the *end* of this road of increasing frequency and specificity of the islands of theoretical knowledge lies the ideal state, scientifically speaking, where *most* actual operational hypotheses of empirical research are directly derived from a general system of theory. On any broad front, to my knowledge, only in physics has this state been attained in *any* science. We cannot expect to be anywhere nearly in sight of it. But it does not follow that, distant as we are from that goal, steps in that *direction* are futile. Quite the contrary, *any* real step in that direction is an advance. Only at this *end* point do the islands merge into a continental land mass.

At the very least, then, general theory can provide a broadly orienting framework. It can also help to provide a common language to facilitate communication between workers in different branches of the field. It can serve to codify, interrelate and make available a vast amount of existing empirical knowledge. It also serves to call attention to gaps in our knowledge, and to provide canons for the criticism of theories and empirical generalizations. Finally, even if they cannot be systematically derived, it is indispensable to the the systematic clarification of problems and the fruitful formation of hypotheses. It is this organizing power of generalized theory even on its present levels which has made it possible for even a student like myself, who has done only a little actual empirical research, to illuminate a good many empirical problems and formulate suggestive hypotheses in several fields.

Though it is not possible to take time to discuss them adequately for those not already familiar with the fields, I should like to cite two examples from my own experience. The first is the reorientation of thinking about the field of the motivation of economic activity. The heritage of the classical economics and the utilitarian frame of reference, integrated with the central ideology of our society, had put the problem of the "incentives" involved in the "profit system" in a very particular way which had become the object of much controversy. Application of the emerging general theory of the institutionalization of motivation, specifically pointed up by the analysis of the contrast between the orientation of the professional groups and that of the business world, made it possible to work out a very fruitful reorientation to this range of problems. This new view eliminates the alleged absoluteness of the orientation to "self-interest" held to be inherent in "human nature." It emphasizes the crucial role of institutional definitions of the situation and the ways in which they channel many different components of a total motivation system into the path of conformity with institutionalized expectations. Without the general theoretical reorientation stemming mainly from Durkheim and Weber, this restructuring of the problem of economic motivation would not have been possible.

The second example illustrates the procedure by which it has become possible to make use of psychological knowledge in analyzing social phenomena without resort to certain kinds of "psychological interpretations" of the type which most sociologists have quite correctly repudiated. Such a phenomenon is the American "youth culture" with its rebellion against adult standards and control, its compulsive conformity within the peer group, its romanticism and its irresponsibility. Structural analysis of the American family system as the primary field of socialization of the child provides the primary setting. This in turn must be seen both in the perspective of the comparative variability of kinship structures and of the articulation of the family with other elements of our own social structure, notably the occupational role of the father. Only when this structural setting has been carefully analyzed in sociological terms does it become safe to bring in analysis of the operation of psychological mechanisms in terms derived particularly from psychoanalytic theory, and to make such statements as that the "revolt of youth" contains typically an element of reaction-formation against dependency needs with certain types of consequences.

Again this type of analysis would not have been possible without the general reorientation of thinking about the relations between social structure and the psychological aspects of behavior which has resulted from the developments in general theory in the last generation or more; including explicit use of the contributions of Freud.

Perhaps I may pause in midpassage to apologize for inflicting on you on such an occasion, when your well-filled stomachs predispose you to relaxation rather than close attention, such an abstruse theoretical discourse. I feel the apology is necessary since what I am about to inflict on you is even more abstruse than what has gone before. Since I am emphasizing the integration of theory with empirical research, I might suggest that someone among you might want to undertake a little research project to determine the impact on a well-fed group of sociologists of such a discourse. I might suggest the following four categories for his classification.

1) Those who have understood what I have said, whether they approve of it or not.

2) Those who *think* they have understood it.

3) Those who do not think they have but *wish* they had, and

4) Those who didn't understand, know it and are glad of it.

I can only hope that the overwhelming majority will not be found to fall in the fourth category.

With relatively little alteration, everything I have said up to this point had been written, and has deliberately been left standing, when I underwent an important personal experience which produced what I hope will prove to be a significant theoretical advance precisely in the field of general theory. With the very able collaboration of several of my own Harvard colleagues and of Professors Tolman of California and Shils of Chicago, the present semester has been devoted to attempting to practice what I have preached, namely to press forward with systematic work in the field of general theory. Partly because of the intrinsic importance of the fields, partly because of its urgency in a department committed to the synthesis of sociology with parts of psychology and anthropology, we have been devoting our principal energies to the *inter*relations and common ground of the three branches of the larger field of social relations.

This new development, which is still too new for anything like adequate assessment, seems to consist essentially in a method of considerably increasing the number of theoretically known islands in the sea of social phenomena and thereby narrowing the stretches of uncharted water between them. The essential new insight, which unfortunately is not easy to state, concerns the most general aspects of the conception of the components of systems of social action and their relations to each other.

It seems to have been the previous assumption, largely implicit, for instance, in the thinking of Weber, of W. I. Thomas, and in my own, that there was, as it were, *one* "action-equation." The actor was placed on one side—"oriented to" a situation or a world of objects which constituted the other side. The difficulty concerned the status of "values" in action, not as the motivational *act* of "evaluation" of an object, but as the *standard* by which it was evaluated —in short, the concept "value-attitudes" which some of you will remember from my *Structure of Social Action*. I, following Weber, had tended to put value-standards or modes of value-orientation into the actor. Thomas and Znaniecki in their basic distinction between attitudes and values had put them into the object-system.

We have all long been aware that there were three main problem foci in the most general theory of human behavior which we may most generally call those of personality, of culture, and of social structure. But in spite of this awareness, I think we have tended to follow the biological model of thought—an organism and its environment, an actor and his situations. We have not *really* treated culture as independent, or if that has been done, as by some anthropologists, the tendency has been for them in turn to absorb either personality or social structure *into* culture, especially the latter, to the great discomfort of many sociologists. What we have done, which I wish to report is, I think, to take an important step toward drawing out for *working* theory the implications of the fundamental fact that *man is a culture-bearing animal*.

Our conclusion then is that value-standards or modes of value-orientation should be treated as a *distinct* range of components of action. In the older view the basic components could be set forth in a single "table" by classifying the modes of action or motivational orientation which we have found it convenient to distinguish as cognitive mapping (in Tolman's sense), cathectic (in the psychoanalytic sense) and evaluative, against a classification of the significant aspects or modalities of objects. These latter we have classified as quality complexes or attributes of persons and collectivities, action or performance complexes, and non-human environmental factors. By adding values as a fourth column to this classification, this had seemed to yield an adequate paradigm for the structural components of action-systems.

But something about this paradigm did not quite "click." It almost suddenly occurred to us to "pull" the value-element out and put it into a separate range, with a classification of its own into three modes of value-orientation: cognitive (in the *standard*, not content, sense), appreciative and moral. This gave us a paradigm of *three* "dimensions" in which *each* of the three ranges or sets of modes is classified against *each* of the other two.

This transformation opened up new possibilities of logical development and elaboration which are much too complex and technical to enter into here. Indeed the implications are as yet only very incompletely worked out or critically evaluated and it will be many months before they are in shape for publication. But certain of them are sufficiently clear to give *me* at any rate the conviction that they are of considerable importance, and taken together, will constitute a substantial further step in the direction of unifying our theoretical knowledge and broadening the range of generality of implication, with the probable consequence of contributing substantially to the cumulativeness of our empirical research.

Certain of these implications, which in broad outline already seem clear, touch two of the subjects on which I intended to speak anyway and can, I think, now speak much better. The first of these is the very fundamental one of the connection of the theories of motivation and personality structure on the psychological level with the sociological analysis of social structure. The vital importance of this connection is evident to all of us, and many sociologists have been working away at the field for a long time. Seen in the perspective of the years, I think great progress has been made. The kind of impasse where "psychology is psychology" and "sociology is sociology" and "never the twain shall meet," which was a far from uncommon feeling in the early stages of my career, has almost evaporated. There is a rapidly increasing and broadening area of mutual supplementation.

What has happened in our group opens up, I think, a way to eliminating the sources of some of the remaining theoretical difficulties in this field, and still more important, building the foundations for establishing more direct and specific connections than we have hitherto been able to attain. I should like to indicate some of these in two fields.

The first is the less radical. We have long suspected, indeed on some level, known, that the basic structure of the human personality was intimately involved with the social structure as well as vice versa. Indeed some have gone so far as to consider personality to be a direct "microcosm" of the society. Now, however, we have begun to achieve a considerable clarification of the bases on which this intimacy of involvement rests, and to bring personality, conceptually as well as genetically, into relation with social structure. It goes back essentially to the insight that the major axis around which the expectation-system of any personality becomes organized in the process of socialization is its *interlocking* with the expectation-systems of others, so that the mutuality of socially structured relationship patterns can no longer be thought of as a *resultant* of the motivation-systems of a plurality of actors, but becomes directly and fundamentally *constitutive* of those motivation systems. It has seemed to us possible in terms of this reoriented conception to bring large parts both of Tolman's type of behavior theory and the psychoanalytic type of theory of personality, including such related versions as that of Murray, together in a close relation to sociological theory. Perhaps the farthest we had dared to go before was to say something like that we considered social structure and personality were very closely related and intimately *interacting* systems of human action. Now I think it will probably prove safe to say that they are in a theoretical sense different phases or aspects of the *same* fundamental action-system. This does not in the least mean, I hasten to add, that personality is in danger of being "absorbed" into the social system, as one version of Durkheim's theory seemed to indicate. The distinction between the personality "level" of the organization of action and the social system level remains as vital as it ever was. But the *theoretical* continuity, and hence the possibility of using psychological theory in the motivation field for sociological explanation, have been greatly enhanced.

The second point I had in mind is essentially an extension of this one or an application of it. As those of you familiar with some of my own writing since the *Structure of Social Action* know, for some years I have been "playing" with a scheme of what I have found it convenient to call "pattern variables" in the field of social structure, which were originally derived by an analytical breakdown of Toennies' *Gemeinschaft-Gesellschaft* pair into what seemed to be more elementary components. This yielded such distinctions as that between universalism, as illustrated in technical competence or the "rule of law," and particularism as given in kinship or friendship relations, or to take another case, between the "functional specificity" of an economic exchange relationship and the "functional diffuseness" of marriage. Thus to take an illustration from my own work, the judgment of his technical competence on which the choice of a physician is supposed to rest is a universalistic criterion. Deviantly from the ideal pattern, however, some people choose a physician because he is Mary Smith's brother-in-law. This would be a particularistic criterion. Similarly the basis on which a physician may validate his claim to confidential information about his patient's private life is that it is necessary if he is to perform the specific function of caring for the patient's health. But the basis of a wife's claim to a truthful answer to the question "what were you doing last night that kept you out till three in the morning?" is the generally diffuse obligation of loyalty in the marriage relationship.

Again I cannot take time to go into the technicalities. But the theoretical development of which I have spoken has already indicated two significant results. First it has brought a scheme of five such pattern variables—the four I had been using, with the addition of the distinction of ascription and achievement which Linton first introduced into our conceptual armory—into a direct and fundamental relation to the structure of action systems themselves. These concepts can now be systematically derived from the basic frame of reference of action theory, which was not previously possible.

Secondly, however, it appears that the same basic distinctions, which were all worked out for the analysis of *social* structure, can, when rephrased in accord with psychological perspective, be identified as fundamental points of reference for the structuring of personality also. Thus what sociologically is called universalism in a social role definition can be psychologically interpreted as the impact of the mechanism of generalization in object-orientation and object choice. Correspondingly, what on the sociological level has been called the institutionalization of "affective neutrality" turns out to be essentially the same as the imposition of renunciation of immediate gratification in the interests of the disciplined organization and longer-run goals of the personality.

If this correspondence holds up, and I feel confident that it will, its implications for social science may be far reaching. For what these variables do on the personality level is to serve as foci for the structuring of the system of predispositions or needs. But it is precisely this aspect of psychological theory which is of most importance for the sociologist since it yields the *differentiations* of motivational orientation which are crucial to the understanding of socially structured behavior. *Empirically* we have known a good deal about these differentiations, but *theoretically* we have not been able to connect them up in a systematically generalized way. It looks as though an important step in this direction had now become possible. With regard to its potential importance, I may only mention the extent to which studies of the distribution of attitudes have come to occupy a central place in the empirical work both of sociologists and of social psychologists. The connection of these distribution data with the social structure on the one hand and the structure of motivational predispositions on the other has had to a high degree to be treated in empirically *ad hoc* terms. Any step in the direction of "reducing the degree of empiricism" in such an area will constitute a substantial scientific advance. I think it is probable that such an advance is in sight, which, if validated, will have developed from work in *general* theory.

Let us now turn to the other major theoretical field, the systematization of the bases for *comparative* analysis of social structures. First I should like to call attention to the acute embarrassment we have had to suffer in this field. On the level of what I have made bold to call "proto-sociology" it was thought that this problem was solved by the implications of the evolutionary formulae which arranged all possible structural types in a neat evolutionary series which *ipso facto* established both their comparability and their dynamic relationships. Unfortunately, from one point of view, this synthesis turned out to be premature; but from another this was fortunate, for in one sense the realization of this fact was the starting point of the transition from proto-sociology to real sociology. At any rate, in spite of the magnificence of Max Weber's attempt, the basic classificatory problem, the solution of which must underlie the achievement of high theoretical generality in much of our field, has remained basically unsolved.

As so often happens there has been a good deal of underground ferment going on in such a field before the results have begun to become widely visible. There are, I think, signs of important progress. One of these is the great step toward the systematization of the variability of kinship structure which our anthropological colleague, Professor Murdock, has reported in his recent book. For one critically important structural field we can now say that many of the basic problems have been solved. But this still leaves much to be worked out, particularly in the fields of more complex institutional variability in the literate societies, in such areas as occupation, religion, formal organization, social stratification and government.

Just as in the problem of the motivation of socially structured behavior our relations to psychology become peculiarly crucial and intimate, so in that of systematizing the structural variability of social systems, our relations to anthropology are correspondingly crucial. This, of course, is because of the ways in which the basic cultural orientations underlie and interpenetrate the structuring of social systems on the action level. Anything, therefore, which can help to clarify the most fundamental problems of the ways in which values and other cultural orientation elements are involved in action systems should sooner or later contribute to this sociological problem.

In general, anthropological theory in the culture field has in this respect been disappointing, not that it has not provided many empirical insights, which it certainly has, but precisely in terms of the present interest in systematization. I am happy to report that my colleague, Dr. Florence Kluckhohn has, in yet unpublished work, made some promising suggestions the implications of which will, I think, turn out to be of great importance. In what follows I wish gratefully to acknowledge my debt to her work.

In this connection it is important that the central new theoretical insight to which I have referred above came precisely in this field, in a new view of the way values are related to action. The essence of this is the *analytical* independence of value-orientation relative to the psychological aspects of motivation. It introduces an element of "play" into what had previously been a much more rigid relation, this rigidity having much to do with the unfortunate clash of sociological and anthropological "imperialisms."

The independence of value-orientation encourages the search for elements of structural focus in that area. The "problem areas" of value-choice seem to provide one set of such foci, that is, the evaluation of man's relation to the natural environment, to his biological nature and the like. But along with these there are foci differentiating the alternatives of the basic "directionality" of value-orientation itself. In this connection, it has become possible to see that a fundamental congruence exists between at least one part in the set of "pattern variables" mentioned above, that of universalism and particularism, and Max Weber's distinction, which runs throughout his sociology of religion, between transcendent and imminent orientations, the Western, especially Calvinistic orientation, illustrating the former, the Chinese the latter.

Bringing such a differentiation in relation to basic orientation-foci together with the problem foci seems to provide at least an initial and tentative basis for working out a systematic classification of some major possibilities of cultural orientation in their relevance to differentiations of social structure. Then through the congruence of these with the possible combinations of the values of pattern variables in the structuring of social roles themselves, it seems possible further to clarify some of the modes of articulation of the variability of cultural orientations with that of the structure of the social systems which are their bearers and, in the processes of culture change, their creators.

In this field even more than that of the relation between social structure and motivation, what I am in a position to give you now is not a report of theoretical work accomplished, but a vision of what *can* be accomplished if the requisite hard and competent work is done. This vision is not, however, I think, mere wishful thinking. I think we have gone far enough so that we can see real possibilities. We are in a position to organize a directed and concerted effort with definite goals, not merely to grope about in the hope that something will come out of it.

It seems to me that the importance of progress in this field of structural analysis which attempts to establish the bases of comparability of social structures can scarcely be exaggerated. I have indeed felt for some time that the fact that we had not been able to go farther in this direction was a more serious barrier to the all-important generality and cumulativeness of our knowledge than was the difficulty of adequately linking the analysis of social structure to psychological levels of the understanding of motivation.

The problem of the importance of structural variability and its analysis is most obvious when we are dealing with the broad structural contrasts between widely differing societies. It is, however, a serious error to suppose that its importance is confined to this level. Every society, seen close to, is to an important degree a *microcosm* of the various possibilities of the structuring of human relationships all over the world and throughout history. The variability *within* the same society, though subtler and less easy to analyze, is none the less authentic.

Of course in any one society *some* possibilities of structural variability are excluded altogether, or can appear only as radically deviant phenomena. But it must not be assumed that in spite of its conformity to a broad general type, the American middleclass family for instance is, *precisely in terms of social structure,* a uniform cut-and-dried thing. It is a complex of many importantly variant sub-types. For some sociological problems it may be precisely the structural differentiations between and distribution of these sub-types which constitute the most important data. To say merely that these are middle-class families will not solve such problems. But it is not necessary for the sociologist to stop there and resort to "purely psychological" considerations. He can and should push his distinctive type of structural analysis on down to these levels of "minor" variability.

In the present state of knowledge, or that of the foreseeable future, we are bound to a "structural-functional" level of theory. There will continue to be long stretches of open water between our islands of validated theory. In this situation we cannot achieve a high level of dynamic generalization for processes and interdependences even *within* the same society, unless our ranges of structural variability are really systematized so that when we get a shift from one to another we know *what* has changed, *to what* and *in what degree.* This order of systematization can, like all theoretical work, be verified only by empirical research. But experience shows that it cannot be worked out by sheer *ad hoc* empirical induction, letting the facts reveal their own pattern. It must be worked out by rigorous theoretical analysis, continually stimulating and being checked by empirical research. In sum I think this is one of the very few most vital areas for the development of sociological theory, and here as in the other I think the prospects are good.

The above two broad areas of prospective theoretical advance are so close to the most general of general theory that they would scarcely qualify as falling within the area of "special theories," which was the fourth area about which I wanted to talk. I have precisely taken so much time to discuss these because of their importance for more special theories. I am very far indeed from wishing to disparage the importance of this more special and in one sense more modest type of theoretical work; quite the contrary. It is here that the growing points of theory in their direct working interaction with empirical research are to be found. If the state of affairs at that level cannot be healthy we should indeed despair of our science.

I will go farther. It seems to me precisely that the fact that real working theory at the research levels did not exist and was not developed in connection with them was perhaps the most telling symptom that the "speculative systems" of which I have spoken were only pseudo-scientific, not genuinely so. Most emphatically I wish to say that the general theory on which I have placed such emphasis can *only* be justified in so far as it "spells out" on the research level, providing the more generalized conceptual basis for the frames of reference, problem statements and hypotheses, and many of the operating concepts of research. In these terms it underlines the problem-setting of research, it provides criteria of more generalized significance of the problem and its empirical solution, it provides the basis on which the results of one empirical study become fruitful, not merely in the particular empirical field itself, but beyond it for other fields; that is for what above I have called its *generality of implication*. In my opinion it is precisely because of its orientation to a sound tradition of general theory, however incomplete and faulty, that the particular theories which are developing so rapidly in many branches of the field are so highly important and promising for the future. Let us, by all means, work most intensively on the middle theory level. That way lies real maturity as a science, and the ultimate test of whether the general theory is any good. And of course many of the most important contributions to general theory will come from this source.

This brings me finally to the fifth point on my agenda, the fitting in of theory with the operational procedures of research. Thus far I have been talking to you about theory, but I was careful to note at the outset that however important an ingredient of the scientific brew theory may be, it is only one of the ingredients. If it is to be *scientific* theory it must be tied in, in the closest possible manner, with the techniques of empirical research by which alone we can come to know whether our theoretical ideas are "really so" or just speculations of peculiar if not disordered minds.

Anyone who has observed the social science scene in this country over the past quarter century cannot fail to be impressed by the very great development of research technique in our field, in very many of its branches. Sampling has come in to make it possible for the social scientist to manufacture his own statistical data, instead of having to work only with the by-products of other interests. Techniques of statistical analysis themselves have undergone an immense amount of refinement, for example, in the development of scaling procedures. An altogether new level has already been attained in the collection and processing of raw data, as through questionnaire and interview, and the development of coding skills and the like. I used to think that the construction of a questionnaire was something any old dub could dream up if he only knew what information he wanted. I have learned better. The whole immense development of interviewing techniques with its range from psychoanalysis to Gallup and Roper lies almost within the time period we are talking about. The possibilities of the use of projective techniques in *sociological* research are definitely exciting. The Cross-Cultural Survey (now rechristened) and Mr. Watson of I.B.M. vie with each other to create more elaborate gadgets for the social scientist to play with. We have even, as in the communications and the small groups fields, begun to get somewhere with relatively rigorous experimental methods in sociology, no longer only in psychology among the sciences of human behavior.

This whole development is, in my opinion, in the larger picture *at least* as important as that of theory. It is, furthermore, exceedingly impressive, not merely for its accomplishments to date, important as these are, but *still more* for its promise for the future. There is a veritable ferment of invention going on in this area which is in the very best American tradition.

If I correctly assess the recipe for a really good brew of social science it is *absolutely imperative* that these two basic ingredients should get together and blend with each other. I do not think it fair to say that we are still in the stage of proto-science. But we are unquestionably in that of a distinctly *immature* science. If it is really to grow up and not regress into either of the two futilities of empiricist sterility or empirically irrelevant speculation, the synthesis must take place. In this as in other respects the beginning certainly has already been made but we must be quite clear that it is *only* a beginning.

This is a point where a division of labor is very much in order. It surely is not reasonable to suppose that all sociologists should become fully qualified specialists in theory and the most highly skilled research technicians at the same time. Some will, indeed must, have high orders of competence on both sides, but this will not be true of all. But the essential is that there should be a *genuine* division of labor. That means that all parties should directly contribute to the effectiveness of the whole. For the theoretical side this imposes an obligation to get together with the best research people and make every effort to make their theory researchable in the highest sense. For the research technician it implies the obligation to fit his operational procedures to the needs of theory as closely as he can.

It has been in the nature of the circumstances and processes of the historical development of theory that much of its empirical relevance has heretofore been made clear and explicit only on the level of "broad" observations of fact which were not checked and elaborated by really technical procedures. The value of this, as for instance it has appeared in the comparative institutional field, should not be minimized. But clearly this order of empirical validation is *only* a beginning. For opening the doors to much greater progress it is necessary to be able to put the relevant content of theory in terms which the empirical research operator can directly build into his technical operations. This is a major reason why the middle theories are so important, because it is on that level that theory will get *directly* into research techniques and vice versa. Again in this field the beginnings I happen to know about are sufficiently promising so that I think we can say that the prospects are good.

Theory has its justification *only* as part of the larger total of sociological science as a whole. Perhaps in closing I may be permitted a few general remarks about the prospects of sociology as a science. I have great confidence that they are good, a solider and stronger confidence than at any time in my own professional lifetime, provided of course that the social setting for its development remains reasonably stable and favorable.

These prospects are, however, bound up with the fulfillment of certain internal as well as external conditions. One of the most important of these on which I would like to say a word, is a proper balance between fundamental research, including its theoretical aspect, and applied or "engineering" work. This problem is of course of particular interest to our friends in the Conference on Family Welfare. Both the urgencies of the times and the nature of our American ethos make it unthinkable that social scientists as a professional group should shirk their social responsibilities. They, like the medical profession, must do what they can where they are needed. Indeed it is only on this assumption that they will do so that not only the very considerable financial investment of society in their work, but the interferences in other people's affairs which are inevitably bound up with our research, can be justified.

It is not a question of *whether* we try to live up to our social responsibilities, but of *how*. If we should put the overwhelming bulk of our resources, especially of trained talent, into immediately practical problems it would do some good, but I have no doubt that it would have to be at the expense of our greater usefulness to society in the future. For it is only by systematic work on problems where the probable *scientific* significance has priority over any immediate possibility of application that the greatest and most rapid scientific advance can be made. And it is in proportion as sociology attains stature as a science, with a highly generalized and integrated body of fundamental knowledge, that practical usefulness far beyond the present levels will become possible. This conclusion follows most directly from the role of theory, as I have tried to outline it above. If the prospects of sociological theory are good, so are, I am convinced, those of sociology as a science, but *only* if the scientifically fundamental work is done. Let us, by all means, not be stingy with the few golden eggs we now have. But let us also breed a flock of geese of the sort that we can hope will lay many more than we have yet dreamed of.

One final word. Like all branches of American culture, the roots of sociology as a science are deep in Europe. Yet I like to think of sociology as in some sense peculiarly an American discipline, or at least an American opportunity. There is no doubt that we have the leadership now. Our very lack of traditionalism perhaps makes it in some ways easier for us than for some others to delve deeply into the mysteries of how human action in society ticks. We certainly have all the makings for developing the technical know-how of research. We are good at organization which is coming to play an increasingly indispensable part in research.

It is my judgment that a great opportunity exists. Things have gone far enough so that it seems likely that sociology, in the closest connection with its sister-sciences of psychology and anthropology, stands near the beginning of one of those important configurations of culture growth which Professor Kroeber has so illuminatingly analyzed. Can American sociology seize this opportunity? One of our greatest national resources is the capacity to rise to a great challenge once it is put before us.

We can do it if we can put together the right *combination* of ingredients of the brew. Americans as scientists generally have been exceptionally strong on experimental work and empirical research. I have no doubt whatever of the capacity of American sociologists in this respect. But as *theorists* Americans have, relative to Europeans, not been so strong—hence the *special* challenge of the theoretical development of our field which justifies the theme of this address. If we American sociologists can rise to this part of the challenge the job will really get done. We are not in the habit of listening too carefully to the timid souls who say, why try, it can't be done. I think we have already taken up the challenge all along the line. "The sociology," as my children called it, is not *about* to begin. It has been gathering force for a generation and is now really under way.

XVIII

A Sociologist Looks at the
Legal Profession *

AS A SOCIOLOGIST I am in no sense an expert in the law or the affairs of the legal profession. Worse than that, even from my own professional vantage point I have never made any special study of the law or of lawyers. My only claim to be able to say anything of interest to a group of lawyers on this occasion is that I have been concerned in a broad way with the structure and functioning of modern societies, particularly that of the United States and, in that connection have had a special interest in the place of the professions in such societies. What I can provide, therefore, is only the kind of perspective an outsider is capable of, not the intimate knowledge that a direct student or participant would have.

I should like to begin with two very general observations, one about our society in general, the other about the historic place of the legal profession in it. The great ideological conflict of our time throughout the whole western world, has been between the proponents of the merits of "capitalism" or "free enterprise" as a "system" and "socialism" as a system, whether or not in its communist variety. The proponents of the former have freely included the "profit motive" among the central features and, from their point of view virtues, of the free enterprise system, while the proponents of socialism have looked askance on the entrusting of any serious social responsibilities to agencies other than those of public authority.

It is curious that in this conflict the ideologists of both camps have, as interpreters of the contemporary scene, almost completely overlooked the presence and strategic significance in our society of a set of occupational groups which are not either in their own opinion or by and large in the public estimation, devoted mainly

---

*The substance of this paper was presented at the first symposium on the occasion of the fiftieth anniversary celebration of the University of Chicago Law School, Chicago, Ill., Dec. 4, 1952.

to the goal of their own profit, but rather in some sense to "service," but which equally are not composed primarily of civil servants, though a considerable proportion of them are in government employ, namely the professions. But the comparative historical evidence about societies shows very clearly that the status of the professions in our society is unique in history. Famous as the Roman lawyers were, the development of law as a profession is certainly far greater today, and the doctor, the engineer, the university professor, and a variety of others were only in their barest beginnings at that time compared with their present status. It is a curious paradox that this key group, who are the primary spearheads of the development of science and its practical applications, of the education of our people and the trustees of its legal traditions, should not find an important place in *either* of the great competing ideological systems of the time. A proper appraisal of their significance seems to me an important part of an adequate orientation of our people to their world.

The second observation concerns a very broad fact about the history of the legal profession. As it emerged into some prominence in the late Middle Ages, particularly with the revival of Roman Law in the Italian Universities, though closely connected with the development of the modern secular state, it is probably correct to say that from the beginning the lawyers maintained a certain independence of political authority as such. The lawyer, though in many respects dependent on princes, was to some extent always an independent expert whose doctrines with respect to the law were by no means simply a special mode of expression of the power interests of his political superiors. This is a fact which is characteristic of the professions generally and has been so of the law from the beginning of its modern history.

In the following brief discussion, a certain kind of abstraction will necessarily be observed. Some in particular, including some lawyers, will feel when I am through that too "rosy" a picture of the legal profession has been painted. This is almost inevitable when the aim is to bring to attention certain aspects of what sociologists call the "latent functions" of a set of social institutions. This analysis will be devoted mainly to this task and should therefore *not* be considered a *general* appraisal of the value of the legal profession. A few indications will be given of points at which deviant tendencies take hold, as in overcompliance with the pressures of client interest, sentimentality and formalism. But assessment of just how far these, and possible other types of deviance go, is a complex question which should not be prejudged. There is almost certainly some truth in the old adage "where there is smoke there must be fire." But at the same time there is ample sociological evidence of ideological distortion in the other direction. There are many reasons why the legal profession is a convenient scapegoat for a variety of groups in society. Any competent analysis and appraisal of these less rosy aspects of the place of the profession in our society would require analysis and extensive research. A proper appreciation of the positive side of the case is an essential condition of evaluation of the other side of the coin.

I would now like to review a few considerations about the modern American legal profession in the context of the general place of the professions in our society. In sociological terminology, a profession is a cluster of "occupational" roles, that is roles in which the incumbents perform certain functions valued in the society in general, and by these activities, typically "earn a living" at a "full-time job." Among occupational role-types, the professional is distinguished largely by the independent trusteeship exercised by the incumbents of a class of such roles of an important part of the major cultural tradition of the society. This means that its typical member is trained in that tradition, usually by a formally organized educational process, so that only those with the proper training are considered qualified to practice the profession. Furthermore only members of the profession are treated as qualified to interpret the tradition authoritatively and, if it admits of this, to develop and improve it. Finally, though there usually is considerable division of labor within such a group, a substantial proportion of the members of the profession will be concerned largely with the "practical application" of the tradition to a variety of situations where it can be useful to others than the members of the profession itself. The professional man is thus a "technical expert" of some order by virtue of his mastery of the tradition and the skills of its use.

In view of the central importance of expertness is relation to the mastery of a cultural tradition as a criterion of a professional role, a few words need to be said about what, from a sociologist's point of view, are the most important features of the Law as a cultural tradition and its place in the society. Law, of course, consists in a body of norms or rules governing human conduct in social situations, that is involving the relations of men to other men. Following Dean Pound I may distinguish law from other bodies of such rules, such as those governing the affairs of "private" organizations, as such rules as have come to be considered to be of sufficient public concern as to be formally sanctioned by "politically organized society." It is first essential to keep in mind that there is no clear and inherent line between what is and is not the concern of politically organized society and thus of the law as such. It is a rather indefinite line and with legislation and court decision, even with administrative ruling, a continually shifting line. That the "formal" law in this sense merges into what sociologists call "informal social control" is a fact of the first importance.

To use a classification entirely familiar to lawyers it may be said that legal rules fall into four categories. They may be said to include first prohibitions, second explicit permissions, that is sanctioning of acts about the legitimacy of which doubt might be raised (this is an important aspect of what are called "rights") and prescriptions, that is injunctions that under defined conditions certain positive performances (obligations) must be undertaken. Back of these more specific "doctrines" of law of course lie certain "standards" of applicability such as "due process of law," "due care" or "knowledge of the difference of right from wrong." The fourth class of rules are the procedural which state not substantively what men are expected to do or not to do, but what in relation to legal agencies is the proper procedure for determining or enforcing their rights, or, vice versa, for agencies of the law in determining and enforcing obligations. The central importance of the procedural component of our own legal tradition is of course evident.

This legal tradition of ours exists in an extremely complex and dynamically changing society. It rests on certain authoritative written sources of which the federal and state constitutions are of course the focus, and certain formally legitimized processes of change, of which ordinary legislation and the processes of constitutional amendment are the obvious ones. But the very existence of the legal profession as an entity in the society is a result of the fact that the maintenance of such a tradition in terms of its own integration and continuity, and its application in relation to our multifarious system of social interests would not be possible without some powerful intermediate mechanism operating between the political organs which carry ultimate legal authority, the constitutional documents and the formal acts of legislatures, and the actual implementation of legal control of going social processes.

The legal profession is not the only mechanism which operates in this context. The various other channels through which both legislation and the executive action of government are influenced are also involved.[1] The legal profession is, however, one of the most important of these, in a broad perspective, probably *the* most important.

As such the profession has certain exceedingly important sociological characteristics. First it is in a curiously ambiguous position of dependence and independence with reference to the state. The laws for which it is responsible are official enactments of the state. Part of its structure, the courts, the departments of justice, the attorneys general et cetera, are directly organs of the political authority. The member of the bar is formally an "officer of the court," and for example, disbarment is an act of the political authority.

At the same time, and at least equally important, the profession is independent of political authority. Even judges, though public officials, are treated as in a special class with special immunities. The ordinary member of the bar is not paid by public authority but by his clients. The bar associations are most definitely not organs of the state, but private associations of their members. Finally, and by no means least, the law schools, with their critically important functions in the training of lawyers, are equally definitely not organs of the state, but integral parts of the universities. Thus, as I have said, the profession is, subject to certain checks on the part both of the state and of the non-legal elements of the control of universities, to say nothing of the influence of clients, given an *independent* position. That, however, this is regarded as a position of "trusteeship" is above all evident in the classification of the law as a profession and not as a "business." The relation of attorney and client is a relation of "trust" not of competition for profit; the client's fee is for "service," not simply the best "bargain" he can get in a competitive market; his communications to his attorney are pro-

---

[1] For example "lobbying" is a favorite scapegoat of much public discussion, and there are undoubtedly many abuses in this field. But if legislators attempted to act only in terms of their independent "convictions" without continual communication with their constituents as to what was needed and what would be workable, it is likely that very serious trouble would result. What is needed is not to prevent people outside legislatures from having any influence on legislation but to insure that the channels of influence are "representative," that competition between different "interests" is "fair" and hence that influence is not "undue.")

tected by law as confidential and cannot be revealed in the attorney's or any other interest.[2]

The position of the legal profession in the social structure is thus an "interstitial" one, and this is one of the most important facts about it. It is, in the first place, not only "oriented to" but to an important degree "integrated with" the structure of political authority. But secondly, it is organized around partly independent trusteeship of the legal tradition, with respect to which it has independent, formally and informally recognized monopolistic prerogative; thus in general only properly trained and validated lawyers are elected or appointed to judicial office. Finally, third, the profession has most of its dealings with private persons, individual and corporate, and is very closely involved with their affairs and interests, so much so that the charge of being merely a "tool" of these interests is not uncommon. I shall discuss each of these facets" of the interstitial position of the profession in turn, and then comment on some of the sociological implications of the situation.

It seems best to start with problems of the relation to the cultural tradition of the law. First it may be noted that apart from the difficulties of enforcement of legal rules, for which of course the legal profession as such is not primarily responsible, there is a critically important problem of "interpretation" in at least a double sense. The first of these concerns primarily the relation to the client and will be commented upon further below. It is the "application" to the specific practical situations faced by clients. Here the problem of the client is by no means simply his motivation to conform with or evade the law, but to *know* what his rights and obligations are. And, the very fact that so often he must come to a lawyer with his questions indicates that, in spite of the lawyer's superior knowledge, even for him this interpretation presents what are very often far from easy questions. Even in so far as the final resolution rests either with legislatures or with judges, the importance of the work of members of the legal profession in formulating the questions and marshalling the evidence on which final decisions are made should not be underestimated.

The second is the set of questions involved in the internal consistency and hence stability, in the sense which includes *orderly* change, of the legal tradition itself. The severity and difficulty of

---

[2] In sociological terms the role of lawyer is defined, along with that of other professional roles, as "collectivity-oriented" not, like that of the business man, as "self-oriented." Cf. Parsons, *The Social System*, Chap. II for definition of these terms.

the problems of conflicts between mutually contradictory statutes is well known to lawyers. Anglo-American law of course relies heavily on the processes of judicial decision and through these the accumulation of precedents. But the problem of maintaining the internal consistency of the precedent system even to a tolerable degree is a very formidable one. Furthermore there must be orientation to the authority of the basic constitutional documents, which naturally means continual reinterpretation of them, and to the positive acts of legislation which are continually being produced.

The problems faced by our legal profession in this respect may be compared with two other types of situations. One is the analogy to the professions concerned with the application of scientific knowledge, such as engineering and medicine. In these cases it is a sociologically central fact that the available knowledge is far from adequate to cover the practical needs. Nevertheless established scientific knowledge does constitute a highly stable point of reference. Hence the "authority" of the relevant professional groups for interpretations can always be referred to such established knowledge. This is, moreover, a basis of reference which is steadily growing in stability. The other type of case is very different, namely that in which there is a fountain-head of authority beyond which there is no appeal. The Roman Catholic Church is perhaps the most conspicuous large-scale example, though the Soviet Communist Party is in certain respects similar. The essential point is that the "correct doctrine" is assumed not to be dependent on any human will, but to be infallibly specific and definite, with a clearly authorized human agency for its implementation.

As compared with both of these our secular law is considerably looser in its points of reference. The Constitution is considerably less clear-cut than the authoritative canons of the church and even the Supreme Court is less "canonical" than is the papacy. The legal profession then has to maintain difficult balances in a tradition which is in itself exceedingly complex, which is applied to very complex and changing conditions, subject to severe pressures from interest groups, authoritatively based only on very general and partly ambiguous documents, and subject to change within considerable limits by the more or less arbitrary and unpredictable "will of the people."

We know from analysis of a great many such situations that responsibility for such functions under conditions where no clearly "right" answers can be attained within considerable limits, is a source of strain. We also know that in relation to such strains tendencies to various types of "deviant" behavior are likely to develop. One of these is probably yielding to expediency, above all through financial temptations and pressures from clients. Ideological trends in our society are such that there is almost certainly serious exaggeration in the views of many circles about lawyers on this point, but that the tendency to abdicate responsibilities in the service of financial "self-interest" or merely "peace" in the face of severe pressure, is there, can scarcely be doubted.

A second type of deviance consists in exaggerated legal "formalism" the tendency to insist on what is conceived to be the "letter" of the law without due regard to a "reasonable" balance of considerations. Legal "technicalities" may of course be, and often are, invoked as tactical weapons in various types of procedures, a point which will be discussed briefly below, but apart from their instrumental use, undoubtedly there is a tendency is many legal quarters to exaggerate the importance of being formally "correct" down to the last detail. In psychological terms, the legal profession probably has at least its share, if not more of "compulsive personalities" as compared with other occupations. The essential present point is that this tendency in the profession is not simply a result of certain types of people "happening" to be lawyers, but grows out of the situation in which lawyers as a group are placed.

The third type of deviant tendency prominent in the law may be said to be the "sentimental" exaggeration of the substantive claims of clients or other "interests" represented by the lawyer. Thus corporation lawyers may often become more lyrical about the rights of "property" than the main tradition of the law warrants, or labor lawyers about "human rights" and the like. Or, to take another example, the lawyer who identifies with an injured client to the extent of fighting very hard to get for him what, on cooler consideration look like highly excessive damages, is guilty of "sentimentality" in this sense.[3]

---

[3] In more technically sociological terms, I may point out that this classification of typical deviances of lawyers corresponds closely to a more general classification. Yielding to "expediency" seems to be the most relevant version of the "alienative" tendency in this case. ("Active alienation" the "rebellious" attitude toward law, is hardly compatible with the professional role itself, though it operates in particular contexts.) "Formalism" may in a broad way be identified with "passive compulsive conformity" while "sentimentality" seems to fit the category of "active compulsive conformity." For the general classification see Parsons, *The Social System*, Chap. VII.

Problems of the relation of the profession to the state need relatively little comment, since several points have been noted above. But first I may note again that some lawyers are public officials and some public offices are reserved exclusively for lawyers, notably the judiciary. Furthermore every lawyer, by virtue of his admission to the bar becomes in a limited and qualified sense a public official, as an "officer of the court." The profession is thus an entity which as it were penetrates the boundary between public and private capacities and responsibilities. Its members act in both capacities and the profession has major anchorages in both.

This position, though of course it impinges differently on different sectors of the profession, subjects the profession in its independent aspect, to a whole series of strains in its relations to political authority. In the first place, as noted, the private attorney in advising clients and the judge in deciding cases are both placed in a difficult if not sometimes impossible position in saying what in fact the law is. Partly this is the problem of interpretation of vague or ambiguous phraseology in the authoritative documents. Partly it is a matter of the fact that legislatures sometimes flatly contradict themselves so that either there must be legislative correction, which is so cumbersome a process as to be impossible within any reasonable length of time or some kind of "extralegal" compromise. Finally, there may be questions of sheer impracticality. The law taken literally sometimes requires the citizen to do what is either impossible for him, or if possible, only with what in terms of public sentiment is undue hardship.

What is true in relation to legislation, is, with differences, also true with reference to the executive organs of government. These are charged with the responsibility of implementing the decisions of legislatures. But they are faced with the same difficulties of interpretation as are the courts and lawyers. They have corporate interests which predispose them to one rather than another interpretation. This may lead to a clash of interests with private persons in the public (individual or corporate) or as between different organs of government.

Just as from a certain point of view the law-making process itself is a mechanism for settling conflicts in the society and establishing rules, so then the legal profession is a kind of "secondary" line of defense against the disruptive consequences of conflict. It acts as a buffer between the legislature, the executive organ and the general public, helping to iron out inconsistencies and unrealism in the law, to protect against special interests of the executive branch of government, or particular units of it and the like. In performing this mediating function the most important point to note is the independent responsible position of the profession. It is not exclusively an organ either of the state or of the private interests of private clients. This independent position rests on the institutionalization of its own tradition, on the balance of interests, and on integration with other structures of the society which are relatively independent, notably the universities through the Law Schools.

Finally a few things may be said about the relation of the legal profession to the public, i.e. to "private" clients. One of the most important facts to emphasize is the enormous range of things done by lawyers for clients. This appears both in the range of different kinds of specialties within the profession, from Judges, to tax specialists, patent lawyers, admiralty lawyers, and many others. It also appears in the many different things done by particular lawyers, and particularly the fact that technical mastery of the law is involved in only some of them and in many situations is not the most important element. A few of these points may be commented upon briefly.

The first set of considerations derives from the fact that a private attorney's job is to advise his client in relation to a *concrete* situation. In this connection his understanding of the situations clients of the type he deals with get into is just as important as is his knowledge of the law. Furthermore, his function is not confined to understanding these situations and the relation of the law to them, but in various ways involves actively taking a hand in them. Here above all what may be called "knowhow" about the relevant situations, such as how to go about defining a problem or what the chances of reaching a settlement are become most important. Finally lawyers of course are called upon to carry out a great deal of negotiation on behalf of their clients, sometimes with the attorneys representing the other side, sometimes directly with private persons. Knowledge of the law is, in such situations, often an essential tool of successful negotiation, but by itself it does not suffice to give the skill in handling other people which makes the good negotiator. These considerations are obviously related to the very large amount of settlement of actual or potential conflict carried out by lawyers without the direct involvement of public authority at all. This ranges all the way from forestalling a conflict of interest by giving advice as to how to deal with a situation in advance, or possible actively taking part in handling it, through "settlements out of court" without ever reaching a court, to cases brought before a court but settled without trial.[4]

The second major context I wish to discuss briefly concerns the fact that the lawyer represents his client in situations which very frequently involve direct conflict of interest with an opponent of the client, a situation most highly dramatized of course when the case is tried in court. Here the mediating role of the profession is clearly evident in the fact that the attorneys for the two sides do not have the same personal involvement in the case that their principals do and can often negotiate with each other without being swayed by their emotions to the same degree. At least they are "brother" lawyers bound by the solidarity of their profession, and not infrequently they know each other well, have no personal antagonism, and are accustomed to working together.

In the same connection the procedural aspect of the law and the lawyer's mastery of it, show their importance. For adherence to procedure narrows and defines the issues, and makes the parties and public opinion more ready to accept a settlement when it is arrived at. Procedure, however, has another importance in mitigating the strain on the lawyer. The fact that the case can be tried by a standard procedure, relieves him of some pressure of commitment to the case of his client. He can feel that, if he "does his best" then having assured the client's case a fair trial, he is relieved of responsibility for an unfavorable verdict if it comes. He may even take a case with considerable reservations about its soundness, counting on procedurable fairness to protect the interests of the opponent. The very fact that the lawyer is given a position of independent, though partly informal and unofficial responsibility, both for the interests of his client and for those of "the law" means that there must be mechanisms which mitigate the pressure to which he is subject in this position. The procedural emphasis of our legal system seems to fit in this context.

Mention should also be made here of another aspect of the lawyer's independent responsibility, namely the protection of the con-

---

[4] In this connection Judge Barnes' statement (in the paper following this one) was interesting that in his long experience on the bench about six cases brought to the court were settled without trial for every one actually brought to trial.

fidential nature of his relation to his client. He is, in a certain sense, in a position to protect his client against himself, in that if the latter says intemperate or unwise things in conference with his attorney he can be assured they will go no farther. But similarly the attorney himself is protected in that he is enabled to participate in private affairs without himself becoming too deeply involved, either in judgment of the legality of the client's position, or in responsibilities to his client going too far beyond their professional relationship.

The above discussion has cited facts which are familiar to every lawyer and are in no sense new to him. I have done so, however, in order to establish that the legal profession has a place in our social structure, and performs functions on its behalf, of which probably the average lawyer himself is only partly aware. He does his job, on the bench, on behalf of his client etc. according to his lights and with justification feels that this job is also important to the society. The essential point to be made in conclusion is to show in certain ways how it is that by and large, with due allowance for the incompetence and chicanery found to some extent in every large group, these functions are useful to society.

With the appropriate qualifications for specific features of its role and situation, the legal profession shares certain fundamental characteristics with the other professions. Its members are trained in and integrated with, a distinctive part of our cultural tradition, having a fiduciary responsibility for its maintenance, development and implementation. They are expected to provide a "service" to the public within limits without regard to immediate self-interest. The lawyer has a position of independent responsibility so that he is neither a servant only of the client though he represents his interest, nor of *any* other group, in the lawyer's case, of public authority.

Above all the member of a profession stands *between* two major aspects of our social structure; in the case of the law between public authority and its norms, and the private individual or group whose conduct or intentions may or may not be in accord with the law. In the case of the physician it is between the world of sickness and of health; he himself is defined as not sick, but he participates more intimately with the sick than any other well person. In the case of the teacher it is between the world of childhood, or, on advanced levels, of relative "untrainedness" and the full status of being trained.

The professions in this sense may, sociologically, be regarded as what we call "mechanisms of social control." They either, like the teaching profession, help to "socialize" the young, to bring them into accord with the expectations of full membership in the society, or they bring them *back* into accord when they have deviated, like the medical profession.[5] The legal profession may be presumed to do this but also two other things, first to forestall deviance by advising the client in ways which will keep him better in line, and also "cooling him off" in many cases and, second, if it comes to a serious case, implementing the procedure by which a socially sanctioned decision about the status of the client is arrived at, in the dramatic cases of the criminal law, the determination of whether he is innocent or guilty of a crime.

Except for the formal determination of innocence or guilt which has certain special features, analysis has shown that effective performance of these functions depends on whether the role in which they are performed meets certain broad sociological conditions. These have been worked out most clearly in connection with the psychotherapeutic functions of the medical profession. It can however, be shown that they are of considerably more general significance, applying to "socialization" both in family and in school, to some aspects of religious ritual, and to various other situations. In conclusion I may briefly outline these conditions and indicate how they apply to the legal case.[6]

In the first place, in situations of strain, there seems to be required scope for a certain permissiveness for expression of attitudes and sentiments which, in ordinary circumstances, would not be acceptable. If this permissiveness is to operate effectively it must be associated with relief from anxiety. In order to be capable, psychologically, of "getting things off his chest" a person must be assured that, within certain limits, otherwise ordinary or possible sanctions will not operate. In general this implies a protected situation. The confidential character of the lawyer's relation to his client provides just such a situation. The client can talk freely, to an understanding and knowledgable ear, without fear of immediate repercussions. What is relayed beyond this confidential relationship is selected through the screen of the lawyer's judgment.

[5] Illness, in this context can be defined as a form of deviant behavior. Cf. Parsons, *The Social System*. Chap. X.

[6] A more extensive discussion of these conditions will be found in Parsons, *The Social System*, Chaps. VII and X.

To some extent the same kind of thing occurs in other phases of the legal process, notably the hearing by judges of some evidence in chambers. It could be a feature of the process of trial itself, and under the most favorable circumstances probably is. This tendency is, however, counteracted by the publicity of trials, which has developed rather special features in this country on account of certain of the characteristics of our press.

In the case of the law, the situations of strain with which it deals focus to a large extent on conflicts. One of the very important aspects of legal procedure is to provide mechanisms for "cooling off" of the passions aroused in such situations. Undoubtedly the private attorney does a great deal of this. Like the physician, he helps his client to "face reality," to confine his claims to what he has a real chance of making "stand up" in court or in direct negotiation, and to realize and emotionally to accept the fact that the other fellow may have a case too. The element of delay in bringing things to a head may, though doubtless often carried too far because of crowding of court calendars and the like, have a similar function. The important thing here is that a person under strain should have some opportunity for "tension release" which is treated as institutionally legitimate.

Secondly, it is a feature of the types of situation I am thinking of, that there is some assurance of "support" or "acceptance" within broader limits than would otherwise be the case. The physician in one sense tends to be particularly "tolerant" of human beings; he does not judge them morally, but tries to "help" them as best he can. Certain features of legal practice also seem to fit into this pattern. Though there are expectations that the attorney will not consciously attempt to "get off" a person he knows to be guilty of a crime, there is on the other hand the presumption that the client is entitled to a "fair trial" not only in the formal sense, but a hearing from his attorney, and any help within the bounds of reason and professional ethics. The lawyer is not easily shocked in the way the general public may be; he is familiar with the complexities of human living and ready to "give a break" to the person who has become involved in a difficult situation. Perhaps the presumption of innocence, not only as a canon of formal trial procedure, but as a deepseated trend of the ethos of the profession, is the primary focus of this feature of the institution of the law. It is strikingly symbolized by the fact that, like the medical profession, payment for the services of lawyers is not on an ordinary "commercial" basis, but on a "sliding scale" with a presumption that the lawyer will be willing to help his client relatively independently of whether it is financially worth his while.

But while the lawyer tends to be both permissive and supportive in his relations with his clients, there is another side to the picture. He is after all schooled in the great tradition of the law. As a member of a great profession he accepts responsibility for its integrity, and his whole position in society focuses that responsibility upon him. His function in relation to clients is by no means only to "give them what they want" but often to resist their pressures and get them to realize some of the hard facts of their situations, not only with reference to what they can, even with clever legal help, expect to "get away with" but with reference to what the law will permit them to do. In this sense then, the lawyer stands as a kind of buffer between the illegitimate desires of his clients and the social interest. Here he "represents" the law rather than the client. His tendency under certain circumstances to give way to the pressures of client interest is one way in which, as noted above, he can be "deviant." But in this connection he can retreat into the formalism of the law as a way of resisting these pressures. From the present point of view the significant point is that *both* these two functions are combined in a particular way in the same agency.

What I have referred to above as permissiveness and support are relatively "unconditional" in that the lawyer will not betray his client's confidence, or refuse to give him the presumption of innocence while he is hearing his story. But there is another class of his services which are to be treated as conditional, namely the specific positive services he is willing to provide, especially those performed in public where the lawyer's own reputation may be involved. The negative aspect of this has just been discussed, the things which the lawyer will refuse to do for his client, but there is also a positive aspect. His legal competence, his knowledge of situations and of people, his skill in negotiation, etc., are at the service of his client but, even after he has taken on the case, not wholly on the client's terms, but to an important degree on his own terms. From a sociological point of view, that is to say, he is "manipulating rewards" in such a way as to have an important effect in influencing the behavior of the client. This influence operates, not only through what the client "gets" in the sense of achieving his original goals for which he consulted a lawyer, but through the impact on the client of the *attitude* of the lawyer, his expressed or implied approval of this as so legitimate that a lawyer is willing to help him get it, whereas other elements of the client's goals are disapproved and help in getting them is refused.

The upshot of these commonplace considerations is that the sociologist must regard the activities of the legal profession as one of the very important mechanisms by which a relative balance of stability is maintained in a dynamic and rather precariously balanced society. The most significant thing is that a pattern of analysis, worked out in an entirely different context, the psychotherapeutic aspect of the role of the physician, turns out to be applicable in this field as well. This is something of which I myself was not aware until I attempted to put together some thoughts about the legal profession for this occasion.

XIX

A Revised Analytical Approach
to the Theory of
Social Stratification*

IT HAS COME to be rather widely recognized in the sociological field that social stratification is a generalized aspect of the structure of all social systems, and that the system of stratification is intimately linked to the level and type of integration of the system as a system.

The major point of reference both for the judgment of the generality of the importance of stratification, and for its analysis as a phenomenon, is to be found in the nature of the frame of reference in terms of which we analyze social action. We conceive action to be oriented to the attainment of goals, and hence to involve selective processes relative to goals. Seen in their relations to goals, then, all the components of systems of action and of the situations in which action takes place, are subject to the process of evaluation, as desirable or undesirable, as useful or useless, as gratifying or noxious. Evaluation in turn has, when it operates in the setting of *social* systems of

---

*This paper was written especially for *Class, Status and Power: A Reader in Social Stratification*, Bendix & Lipset, Eds. It may be regarded as a revision of the author's earlier paper, "An Analytical Approach to the Theory of Social Stratification," first published in the *American Journal of Sociology*, May 1940, and reprinted in the *Essays*, both the first edition (Chapter VII) and the present one (Chapter IV). The Editors of the stratification volume originally proposed reprinting of this older paper in it. However, so much work had intervened in the meantime, both in the field of general theory and more specifically on social stratification, that it seemed much better to attempt a new statement of a general approach to the field. The more recent phases of the work in general theory on which the present paper relies most heavily will be found discussed in three publications in which the author has had a major part: Parsons and Shils, Editors, *Toward a General Theory of Action* (Harvard University Press, 1951); Parsons, *The Social System* (Free Press, 1951); and Parsons, Bales, and Shils, *Working Papers in the Theory of Action* (Free Press, 1953). In addition Bales' *Interaction Process Analysis* (Addison-Wesley Press, 1950) has played a very important part in the background.

On the empirical side the author has, over a considerable period, been engaged in a study of social mobility among high school boys in collaboration with Samuel A. Stouffer, Florence Kluckhohn, and a research staff. Though results of this study are not yet ready for publication, the work on it has exaction, two fundamental implications. First the units of systems, whether they be elementary unit acts or roles, collectivities, or personalities, must in the nature of the case be subject to evaluation. To say that all acts were valued equally, that it did not "matter" what a person did or how he did it, would simply be to say that the category of evaluation was irrelevant to the analysis of action. But given the process of evaluation, the probability is that it will serve to differentiate entities in a rank order of some kind. Exactly equal evaluation of two or more entities may of course occur, but it is a special case of evaluative judgment, not a demonstration of its irrelevance. Just how great the differentiations may be, how permanent or generalized they are, and by what criteria they are made is of course the focus of a whole series of analytical and empirical problems, but *that they should be* imputed to actors in a system is inherent in the frame of reference we employ for the analysis of social interaction.[1]

erted a major influence on my theoretical thinking about the general field. In addition, in collaboration with Dr. Bales and two assistants, an attempt is being made to link together the study of stratification in the large-scale society and in small groups, using in a broad way the conceptual scheme outlined in this paper. Both projects have been carried out under the auspices of the Harvard Laboratory of Social Relations. Besides the general funds of the Laboratory, the study of mobility has received financial support in the first instance from the Russell Sage Foundation, but also from the Rockefeller Foundation and the Harvard Graduate School of Education. I would like herewith to express gratitude to all these agencies for their assistance.

The paper is, therefore, by no means a product of individual work, but is essentially collaborative in nature. In the work in general theory I am particularly indebted to my collaborators, Shils and Bales, and to the co-authors of *Toward a General Theory of Action.* With reference to the field of stratification there is a special debt to Samuel Stouffer and Florence Kluckhohn, and to staff members who have worked intimately with me on relevant aspects of the two empirical projects, especially most recently Frank E. Jones, Bengt G. Rundblad, and Joseph Berger. I am, however, solely responsible for the specific formulations which are here set forth. I am greatly indebted to Professor Stouffer, Dr. Bales, and Messrs. Jones, Rundblad and Berger for criticism of the first draft of this paper.

[1] It should be clear that this process of differentiation, with respect to ranking as in other respects, is a process *internal* to the social system. In its development extra-system phenomena, such as sex, age, individual differences serve as points of reference. These may determine what concrete units will occupy what place and in part sometimes affect the range of differentiation, but they never determine the basic pattern itself which derives from the exigencies of process in the system as such.

Furthermore, differentiation and integration are, in social as in biological systems, correlative phenomena. The differentiation of units in a system *from* each other in rank as in other respects, involves ipso facto the integration of the components of the units. In the stratification aspect this means that by the same process by which collectivities are differentially ranked the *members* of any one come to be treated as equals—thus the equality of members of a family unit is a corollary of the differentiation in class status of the family from other families.

The second implication is the well-known one that it is a condition of the stability of social systems that there should be an integration of the value-standards of the component units to constitute a "common value-system." Again the content of such a common value system and the degree and modes of its integration with the actual action of the units in a social system vary empirically. But the existence of such a pattern system as a point of reference for the analysis of social phenomena is a central assumption which follows directly from the frame of reference of actions as applied to the analysis of social systems.

Stratification *in its valuational aspect* then is the ranking of units in a social system in accordance with the standards of the common value system. This ranking may be equal but obviously from a logical point of view this is a limiting case, and there are good reasons to believe that from an empirical point of view it should also be so regarded, the more so the larger and more complex the system. The valuational aspect must be analytically distinguished from the others entering into the total "power" system of a society.

In the above statement care has been taken to use the very general term "unit" as the "that which" to which ranking evaluation is applied. One of the most important ranges of problems in the field of stratification is the discrimination of the different kinds of units to which the categories of stratification can be applied, and the order of relations of these different kinds of units to each other.

It will simplify our analysis if in a strict sense we focus attention on social systems, and hence confine the technical discussion of the bases of social stratification to the ranking of the units of a *given* system of specific reference in terms of scope and time-span. We may then maintain that for a given social system, in the theoretical sense, there can be only one kind of unit, which is the "membership" role, or status-role complex. The "actor" of whom this is a role may, however, be either an individual human being or a collectivity, and it is particularly important to keep in mind that these two cross-cut each other, a collectivity by definition is composed of a plurality of roles pertaining to actors each of whom has roles in several different collectivities. Strictly speaking we will not refer to a personality as having a place in a scale or system of social stratification, because even in the case of the total society an individual's membership does not exhaust his personality as a system.

This focus on the specific social system is, we believe, exceedingly important. But the familiar sociological fact that a given actor has a plurality of roles, calls our attention to the fact that the particular system which is isolated for analysis never stands alone but is always articulated with a plurality of other systems, specifically though not exclusively, the systems in which the same actors have other roles, such for example as kinship units and occupational organizations in our society. We have found by experience that a great many of the problems of empirical sociological analysis can most effectively be handled by treating more than one system at a time. We shall have occasion below to consider a number of problems in these terms, but in the meantime it is most important to define our terms and the basic relationships with which we are concerned in terms of a single system of reference, and then to introduce the further complications involved in the articulations of more than one system with each other.

Specific judgments of evaluation are not applied to the system unit as such—except in a limiting case—but to particular properties of that unit—always by comparison with others in the system. These properties may be classificatory, in the sense of characterizing the unit independently of its relations to other objects in a system as in the case of sex, age or specific abilities, or they may be relational, characterizing the way in which it is related to other entities as in the case of membership in a kinship unit.[2]

Looked at on another basis the properties to which a judgment may be applied may be classified as qualities, performances (including their reward significance as sanctions) and possessions.[3]

Qualities are those properties of a unit which can be evaluated independently of any change in its relations to objects in its situation, but may be ascribed to the unit as such. Thus when we say a man "has an I.Q. of 120" we describe a quality usually called "intelligence." When, however, we say, "he gave the right answer to the question" we describe a performance, which is thus a process of change in his relation to a situational object, the questioner, which

---

[2] This distinction will be recognized as an application of the pattern variable, universalism-particularism.

[3] More accurately qualities and performances are attributable to the system unit as such, whereas possessions are situational objects in some sense independent of such a unit. Qualities (including performance-capacities) may be modified by learning processes, but they are not transferable. Possession, however, is a relation to an object which can be transferred from one actor to another. Qualities (or performances) may be instrumentally or expressive-symbolically significant. This distinction is parallel to that between facilities and rewards, as categories of the meaning of possessions.

can be ascribed to his "agency." Qualities may be interpreted, of
course, in whole or in part, as consequences of previous processes of
performance, on the part of the system-unit in question and/or of
others in the system, and performances are never understandable
without reference to an ascriptive or quality point of reference
which describes "that which" is the starting point of the performance and that which brings it about. Thus to give the right answer
the man had to be "intelligent." Or to say a man is now a member
of the American Sociological Society is to describe a quality, but he
got there by a variety of performances including (if an "active"
member) getting a Ph.D., applying for membership and paying
his dues. Hereditary status is the limiting case where only qualities
and no prior performances are the requisites, the "ascriptive base,"
of a social status.[4]

Possessions are situational objects which are intrinsically transferable and to which an actor (individual or collective) in a social
system has a specific relationship of "control" such that he has in
the institutionalized case rights to their use, control or disposal differentiated from those held by other units in the system. In the
nature of the case possessions are valued objects, valued directly by
their possessor and either actually or potentially by others in the
system. Possession is thus a category not of the "intrinsic" nature of
the object, but of its *relation* to a unit in a system as distinguished
from its relation to other units in the same system. Possessions in
turn may be of two primary orders of significance in social systems,
either of which may have primacy. On the one hand they may be
"facilities," i.e. means-objects relative to instrumental goal-attainment processes, on the other hand "rewards," i.e. objects which
either are objects of direct gratification or are symbolically associated with such objects.[5]

It is quite clear that the concrete hierarchical "position" of a
system-unit in a social system cannot be only a function of its place
in the scale of valuation relative to an integrated common value-
system, because no social system is ever perfectly integrated in this
sense. It is convenient to conceptualize this element of discrepancy

---

[4] The reader who is interested in more technical developments of the theory
of action, may think of qualities in this sense as describing a given location of
a system unit in action-space, whereas performances describe a change of
location from one point to another. Cf. Parsons, Bales and Shils, *Working
Papers*, Chaps. 3 & 5.

[5] Cf. Parsons, *The Social System*, Chaps. III and IV for an extensive discussion of these categories.

between the normatively defined "ideal" ranking order and the actual state of affairs, in terms of the relation between ranking in value terms and "power." Power we may define as the realistic capacity of a system-unit to actualize its "interests" (attain goals, prevent undesired interference, command respect, control possessions, etc.) within the context of system-interaction and in this sense to exert influence on processes in the system.[6]

Power in this sense we may conceive to be the resultant of three sets of factors which are cognate with the above aspects of institutionalized ranking but are treated differently in order to permit the analysis of discrepancies between institutionalized standards and the empirical state of affairs. The first of these is the valuation of the unit in the system according to value standards, whether completely common throughout the system or not, and including both the quantitative and the qualitative aspects of judgment in relation to the standards. The second is the degree to which and the manner in which actors in the system permit deviance from these standards in performance. The most obvious way in which this factor can be seen to operate is the permission of other actors to allow any one (ego) to do things which are more or less out of line with the common value standards. The third set of factors is the control of possessions, which is a source of differential advantage in bringing about a desired result (including preventing one not desired). The assumption is that these three sets of factors are interdependent and hence that "position" with respect to any one of them will be correlated with position with respect to each of the others, but they will also be to some degree independent.

From this point of view one type of measure of the integration of a social system (that in terms of pattern consistency) should be the degree to which ranking in terms of paramount common value standards does in fact correlate with all three of the above sets of factors. Any such correlation would, however, be a complex resultant of a variety of considerations. Thus there is no reason to believe that all of the units in the system conform or are expected to conform equally with the common value-standards. If ego—the unit of reference—conforms relatively more fully than the others this may

---

[6] It will be noted that this definition confines the relevant "interests" to those *within* the system of reference. The use of one system-membership to promote interest in influencing events in another system in which the same concrete entity, e.g. personality, is involved, presents further complications, which need to be handled independently and not in this elementary set of definitions.

diminish ego's power relative to that of the others because he is less willing to exploit opportunities forbidden by the norms. On the other hand his own deviance, if it happens to mesh with that of others, may increase his power, because he is allowed to "get away with it." The effect of deviance on power naturally depends on just what the nature of the deviance in question on both sides is. Similarly, access to possessions is always to some degree a function of factors which are "adventitious" from the point of view of the value-standards of the system; these discrepancies may or may not be corrected by the equilibrating mechanisms of the system.[7]

The problems of the place of power in social systems shade directly over into those of authority. Both root in the most elementary fundamentals of social interaction on the one hand, its normative control on the other. Interaction, as we will discuss further below, is a continual interplay of what we call "performance" and "sanctions." What people do has an influence on the state of the system as a system, and on each other as members; the latter is the sanction aspect. In so far as influence on the action of others in the system becomes an institutionalized expectation of a role, we have the roots of authority. Authority, finally, is full blown when this institutionalized expectation comes to include the legitimation of "coercive" sanctions, that is the right to impose consequences deprivational to alter in case he fails to act as ego has an institutionalized right to expect he will, and of course to use the "threat" of such consequences to motivate alter to "conform."

Authority in this sense is an aspect of power in a system of social interaction; it is institutionalized power over others. In the nature of the case it must be evaluated, and therefore like other evaluated aspects, be stratified. In the strictest sense we probably ought to say that every member of a social system has some authority, at the very least he would be felt to be justified in passively resisting "unreasonable" demands upon him by others, in effect saying nega-

---

[7] It will be remembered that in the earlier paper, of which the present one is considered to be a revision, six criteria of differential evaluation were distinguished, namely, membership in a kinship unit, personal qualities, achievements, possessions, authority and power. Three of these, membership, authority and qualities have now all been consolidated under the one general category of qualities, but this is defined more broadly than before to include any qualities of a unit of a social system, not only "personal" qualities. It was not seen at that time that what we here call "relational" qualities, e.g. memberships, could be treated as qualities of the unit. Furthermore authority, as will be discussed below, is a quality of the "status" of a unit. Finally, power is redefined as a resultant rather than as a residual factor.

tively "if you do this, I won't—" do something expected. This is certainly a coercive sanction. In common usage however we tend to restrict the term authority to the higher ranges of the stratification of institutionalized power; thus we speak of parental authority over children but seldom of children's authority over their parents.

It should also be noted that authority, as legitimizing the use of power involving coercive sanctions, is not an isolated phenomenon. It is part of a much larger family of mechanisms of social control each of which may involve an element of authority, but also other elements as well. Thus patterns of religious ritual, of therapy, and of facilitation of ecological adjustment through intervention in the distribution of possessions or communication may serve this type of function. We will comment briefly on some of these problems below.

Empirically the imperfections of integration of social systems formulated by the two non-valuational components of the power of a unit may be extremely important. However, the point of view from which we approach the analysis of stratification prescribes that analysis should focus on the common value-pattern aspect. Only through this can we gain stable points of reference for a technical theoretical analysis of the empirical influence of the other components of the system-process. This is essentially because on general theoretical grounds we can state that the "focus" of the *structure* of a system of action lies in the common value-pattern aspect of its culture.

We have throughout treated the stratification of a social system as an aspect of its fundamental structure. It may be regarded as one of the most important conclusions of sociological theory that the distinction between the normative and the factual aspects of a social system must be regarded as relative. The basic categories in terms of which we describe a system as a structure, i.e. as a set of objects seen from the point of view of an observer, are *the same* as those in terms of which we describe the norms which regulate behavior or performance. This does not *in any way* imply that deviance from normative expectations is not to be treated as important, but concerns only the nature of the categories in terms of which social phenomena are to be described and analyzed.

Every unit in a system of action, e.g. the actor in a social role, is treated both as an object having ascertainable qualities, and as an entity performing the functions of a role. In the quality aspect we may, so far as his position in the system is concerned, speak of an actor's *status;* in the performance aspect we may speak of his *role* in the narrower technical sense. The value-standards of the common value system then will on the one hand categorize the units of the system as objects in status terms, and the units will be stratified in this respect so far as application of these status categories leads to differences of evaluation according to the common standards. At the same time, for objects having the qualities in question there will also be expected performances. These in turn will be evaluated in terms of norms, and the actual performances will be differentially evaluated.

The distinction of performance and quality is, it is important to recognize, relative. Every performance implies what may be called an ascriptive or a "quality-base," a description of "that which" acts. The evaluation of performances is always relative to that base; we never literally mean that a performance is to be judged with no reference to *who* is responsible for it. Thus we say "pretty good, considering he is only twelve years old" or "Somebody with all his experience ought to have done better." Naturally we very often think or speak eliptically, and just say "well done" or the reverse; but the quality-base may always be regarded as implicit if it is not explicit.

At the same time performances have consequences. If these concern only the situation of action, they may be ignored, not from the point of view of evaluation of the performance, but in the quality context. If, however, these consequences involve change in the properties of the actor (through learning), then we may speak of a change in his own quality-patterns. A child, as actor in a social system, does not remain unchanged, but his qualities develop as a function of the socialization process itself.

On the basis of recent theoretical work it seems possible to treat the standards on the basis of which both object-qualities and performances are evaluated as reducible to four fundamental types which correspond to what we believe to be the four dimensions of action systems.[8] Any concrete system, including a single role-status unit considered as a sub-system, will be subjected to all four types of standard, but they will stand in different orders of precedence in

---

[8] For the theoretical basis of these statements and the derivation of the four standard types see the *Working Papers,* op. cit. See especially Chapter V, Figure 2, p. 179 and Sec. V of that chapter.

different kinds of systems. We will first take up the four types of standard in their relation to the normative control of performances, and then speak of their application to the evaluation of status-qualities.

The first type of standard we wish to consider, in relation to the evaluation of objects and performances, involves in its cognitive aspect, what we call universalism. In relation to performance its dominance defines what we call "technical" norms which maximize universalistic values in the adaptation of action to the intrinsic properties of the situational object-system in the service of a specific goal. This is what in common sense terms we ordinarily mean by "efficiency." The only reference is to the effectiveness with which objects in the situation are utilized (including adaptation to its uncontrollable features) in the interest of attainment of the goal. There is no consideration of the justification or usefulness of this particular goal-state itself nor of the consequences of the performances taken for other units in the system, i.e. in an integrative context, nor of change in qualities of the system. Cognitive knowledge of the situation is at a premium in defining a technical norm, but a certain level of effort or commitment to the goal is presumed as well.

The second basic type of standard is that having to do with the definition of goals of an action process themselves, what in pattern-variable terms we have called performance or achievement. As a system-norm, it will either specify the system-goal or goals to which the unit is expected to contribute, (this we may call the prescriptive case) or it will define the limits of permissible "private" goals of the unit (the permissive case). As such, an achievement norm does not define the instrumental or technical means-acts which are expected but only the goal itself, and of course it is not concerned with other kinds of consequences either relative to system-integration or to changes in the qualities of the system or its units.

The third type of standard *does* concern integration and may be called the system-integrative. It defines expectations with respect to a unit's contribution to the maintenance of solidarity with other units in the system. The focus is on the quality of attitude, on positive action expected to be taken in the interest of inter-unit solidarity. The standards are particularistic, not universalistic, in that it is the status of both units in their relation of common membership in the same system which constitutes the basis of the expectations of showing solidarity. It focuses on the integrative or particularistic dimension.

Finally, the fourth type of standard concerns the maintenance and/or regulation of changes in the ascriptive-qualitative "base" from which other performances take their departure. There are two primary types of expressive action concerned. The first comprises those which are expressive of, or implement the value-patterns ascribed to the unit in its status in the system independent of specific adaptive problems, specific goals or the inter-unit integration of the system in the particularistic solidarity sense. The second type is that oriented to bringing about changes in the qualities of the unit itself through learning processes. In system terms, that is, socialization is governed by qualitative-ascriptive norms.

From the dynamic or performance point of view social interaction is a continual back-and-forth alternation between performances and "sanctions." Sanctions may be thought of as actions which express attitudes toward the action or performance of others through reward and punishment. The distinction, it should be made clear, is an analytical one. Every (concrete) act has potential consequences for the maintenance or change of system state, and is in some degree oriented to these consequences—this is the aspect we have just been discussing under the heading of performances. At the same time every act is in some degree a reaction to the acts of others, and involves at least an implicit evaluation of the acts of other actors in the system. It thereby exerts an influence on their subsequent actions; this is the sanction aspect.

For every type of norm for evaluating performance there is a norm which defines the corresponding "appropriate" type of sanction. The formulae for the performance norms look from the dimension of primary focus "forward" to the next stage of the action process, i.e. a technical norm is defined in relation to the specific goal. The sanction norm on the other hand looks "backward" to the phase from which the process is emerging and thus "rewards"—in the positive case—successful transition to a new phase. Thus in the first type of sanction, which corresponds to technical norms, we may speak of "approval" as referring both to universalistic standards, and to the quality base from which the performance takes its departure; the attitude of "neutrality" protects this quality base and universalistic orientation from being "diverted" into premature enjoyment of the goal in question or of other available goal-states.[9]

The sanction norms corresponding to the four performance norms outlined above are, in the same order, first "approval" which is characterized by attitudes of "specificity," i.e. relativity to the specific goal to which the action-process in question is committed, and "neutrality" which is relativized to the initial quality-base and inhibits consummatory gratification or diversion prior to attainment of the goal-state. The second is "response" characterized by attitudes of specificity and affectivity which is appropriate to the consummatory goal-state itself, and directly rewards the actor with access to goal-objects. It should therefore be conditional on the attainment of an approval goal. The third, appropriate to the system-integrative performance norm is "acceptance" in the form of reciprocation of the showing of solidarity and characterized by attitudes of affectivity and diffuseness and the fourth, finally, we have called "esteem," the evaluation of the unit as a unit in terms of the whole complex of its qualities, i.e. its total status in the system and characterized by attitudes of diffuseness and neutrality.

The standards governing the evaluation of the qualities of system units as objects are exactly the same as those governing performances. In this context, corresponding to technical norms we would speak of standards evaluating the adaptive or technical performance-capacities or "competence" of the actor as object, corresponding to the goal-defining norm simply of his goal-orientations, corresponding to the system-integrative, to his quality of system-loyalty, and finally corresponding to the qualitative-ascriptive standard, we would speak of his residual-qualities. What binds the performance norms and the quality-standards together is simply the fact that we think of both as defining the stable state of system-process. When the system and its units are looked at "statically," i.e. as objects in abstraction from the processes going on within the system, then these norms define the qualities of the object and the sub-objects or "parts" of which it is composed.

In the light of these considerations the formal composition of the stratification of a social system may be summed up as follows. The categories in terms of which social objects (actors) and systems of

[9] The relations between performance-norms and sanction-norms will be found discussed in *Working Papers*, Chap. V, Sec. IV. Cf. especially Figure 5, p. 203.

them in roles are analyzed, are categories which in one aspect are value-standards. Value-standards, then are classified in terms of the same dimensions or variables which differentiate units in the social system in a structural sense *and* which define the types of sanctioned performance of those units and hence the appropriate sanctions relative to those performances. The evaluation of qualities and performances has inherently a hierarchical aspect because according to any value-standard some will rank higher than others. The next crucial problem we have to face, then, is that of how the different standards are *organized* relative to each other in a given social system; how, that is to say, they constitute a *system* of standards.

From this point of view any given social system will have a "paramount" value pattern which, in ideal type terms, we may classify as belonging to one of the four major types we have outlined. Thus the paramount values may emphasize efficiency of technical achievement as such without primary reference to the specification of goals; they may emphasize a paramount system-goal as the focus of valuation, they may emphasize the integration of the system, the relations of solidarity of the units with each other, or finally, they may emphasize the implementation and preservation of ascribed system-qualities.[10] This is an ideal type classification and hence it can be taken as a point of departure in order to deal with mixed types. However, the problem we are now dealing with is quite sufficiently complex without just now complicating it further by taking these explicitly into account.

Given the paramount value system, there will be a specification of the primary aspects of the system as a total object in relation to each of the four types of standard. As such the system will have ascriptive base-qualities, it will exist in a situation with concrete specification of the adaptive problem and hence norms for dealing wth them—or level of competence to do so; there will be a definition

---

[10] It is fully realized that this classification of types of basic value-patterns is highly" formal" and thus by no means concretely adequate for empirical purposes. It must be filled in by the concrete content of the cultural categories under consideration, which are given in the concrete belief systems and the concrete system of expressive symbolism. The reason why this classification is crucial for our present purposes and why its formality is not a handicap but a great advantage, is that it expresses the fundamental categories of the structure of the social system. If stratification is to be treated as a generalized aspect of social structure it must be analyzed in terms which are general to all instances and sub-classes of the type of system we are considering. In terms of the logical structure of our conceptual scheme, what we are dealing with here is analogous to the "primary qualities" of Locke's picture of the physical world, whereas, specific cultural content is analogous to "secondary" qualities.

of paramount system-goals and limits of commitment to them; there will be definitions of the appropriate modes and levels of solidarity of the units with each other.

After specifying these aspects of the system, which means "spelling out" the paramount value system in each of the primary functional contexts of system process, we can then approach the problem of analyzing the structural differentiation of roles in the system. It should be remembered that we are dealing with this on a purely descriptive structural level. We are aware that the number of units belonging to a system, for example, is itself a function of system-process over time, and from a dynamic point of view should not be assumed as given, but for present purposes we will ignore this.

The first level of structural analysis is, we may say, the distinction of "primary" sub-systems, i.e. those which may be interpreted to constitute direct differentiations of the major system itself. There will, then, be one of these primary subsystems which is the one given most stress by the common value system, the one in which the paramount values are most directly embodied. Since we interpret the American value system to be very closely described in terms of the universalism-achievement (or performance) pattern, we may say the strategic subsystem is the "occupational" i.e. the subsystem organized about the adaptive problems of the total system. There should then be a sub-system oriented to system-goal attainment, one to system-integration and one to expression and maintenance (including socialization) of the institutionalized ascriptive-qualitative pattern-complex, i.e. a subsystem with primarily "cultural" functions.

At this point, however, two very important sets of analytical, to say nothing of empirical, difficulties, arise. The first concerns the fact that concrete structures do not follow the lines of differentiation of system-function exactly. The functional or dimensional classification is a frame of reference in terms of which this differentiation may be analyzed, but because of the empirical interrelations between the units, the segregation of their properties from each other does not neatly follow the lines of such a classification. The situation is closely analogous to that in the biological sciences. Without the categories of metabolism, respiration, locomotion, coordination and the like, it would be impossible to analyze the structure and functioning of complex organisms, but speaking of any one concrete organ-system as serving only one organic function is seldom legitimate. Exactly what the "blurrings" of the analytical lines we have drawn will be in any concrete case will vary with the type both of value system and of level of its differentiation as a social system. Rather than attempting to get into these problems here, it will be better to touch them briefly in relation to concrete illustration of this analysis.

The second set of difficulties concerns the complexities of system-subsystem relationships in a full scale social system. At one extreme we have the type of differentiation found in small groups which Bales has so ably analyzed.[11] In a five-member group for example the possibilities of such differentiation are very strictly limited, but even here the question must be raised of whether each member's role should be treated by itself, or whether it is not better to think of sub-collectivities as already present. It would be appropriate, for example, to speak of these as "coalitions" or "cliques." Similar considerations are important in the analysis of family units as systems.

At the other extreme we have the problem of treating such a complex entity as American Society. For purposes of empirical analysis the problems seem to center on the relations between three principal different levels of unit. The one we speak of most commonly is the role of the individual actor, not in his total societal membership but in specific interaction subsystems such as his conjugal family or the particular occupational organization, etc. The second is that of the interactive system of which such a role is itself a unit, e.g. his conjugal family, or the particular occupational organization in which he works. The third level then concerns subsystems of the society which are aggregates of such units grouped in relation to common paramount function, such as the occupational function type or the governmental function and the like. Again, it seems best merely to call attention at this point to this immensely difficult field, and to reserve any further treatment of it for the illustrative analysis of the American stratification system.

Let us return to the problem of the relationships of different types of evaluative standards to each other. It was stated above that the type of paramount value-system will establish the primacy of the norm-type which directly "embodies" these values, in our American case, universalistic-performance values. "Commitment" of the system to such a set of values we may interpret to mean a tendency to maximize their implementation in action and thus in concrete

---

[11]Cf. *International Process Analysis* and *Working Papers*, op. cit. Ch. IV.

system-structure. This tendency is, however, subject to certain exigencies, those of adaptation to the conditions of the extra-system situation—which of course includes other *social* systems—the integrative exigencies involved in the maintenance of solidary relations in a system consisting of the kind and number of units in question and those concerned with maintenance of the institutionalization of these patterns and management of the attendant motivational tensions. Thus we would class "size" of the society as defined by its population as constituting an integrative exigency, as would its composition for example in terms of the ethnic origins of the population.

Whatever the type of value system, it is this which defines the primary ascriptive-qualitative base in terms of which the other aspects of its structure must be analyzed. Thus the general dimensional scheme we have outlined must be applied on *two* different levels, first to define the type of system with which we are dealing in terms of its type of paramount value-system, and second, to analyze the internal differentiation of the system using this paramount value-pattern type as the ascriptive base from which to carry out the analysis.

Then we must ask what are the implications of the value system for the definition of goals. First this must be asked on the level of a goal or goals for the system as such, and then for the units on whatever level is being considered. Implications for unit goals in turn may be either prescriptive—both relatively continuous as with reference to a governmental unit or a university, and in special circumstances, as in relation to a national emergency—or permissive. Furthermore, it must be noted that it is fundamental to the nature of differentiation of a system, that the goals of units should also be differentiated. Differentiated unit-goals then must be defined either as "contributions" to system function, or permissively as falling within limits allowed.

Clearly, what differentiated unit goals will be prescribed or permitted will be a function, in turn, of the three sets of exigencies we have noted in their relation to the paramount value-system. Even in very simple systems there is reason to believe that some differentiation on the axis of the distinction between adaptive and integrative functions will take place, i.e. of units whose paramount function and therefore sub-system goals are more adaptive than anything else, and of units whose paramount functions are more integrative than anything else. Both these may however be combined in subtle ways with system-goal-oriented and pattern-maintenance or ascriptive functions and hence subsystem goals.

In general we may say that the criteria of relative priority of these functions and hence sub-system goals will be defined in terms of the *consequences* of performance, in the expected way, of the system-functions or the maintenance of the system and its institution-alized value-patterns; it will, that is to say, be a matter of the *strategic* significance of the unit-functions in the system process. It is evident that this significance will vary as a function both of the type of value system and its cultural content and of the concrete adaptive, integrative and regulatory exigencies to which it is subject. We cannot therefore lay down any general priority scales independent of these factors. In general, however, we can say that the function most directly institutionalizing the paramount value will have first place; the problems for analysis concern the ranking of the other principal functions. In other words what we have developed here is not an empirical generalization about rank-ordering, but only a set of categories in terms of which the empirical problem may be approached.

There remain two further general analytical problems before we can attempt to illustrate through the analysis of certain aspects of the American stratification system. The first of these is that of the way in which the analysis of the place of possessions is to be fitted into the scheme outlined above. The second is the problem of the modes and degrees of integration of the different criteria of differential ranking to form a single "general prestige continuum."

The key to the analysis of possessions lies in the distinction between facilities and reward objects. Facilities are to be categorized according to performance-norms, rewards according to sanction norms. It should, of course, be kept in mind, as noted above, that a concrete object may be—indeed in principle always is—both a facility and a reward, but one or the other aspect of its significance may be of primary importance in a given context. Facilities and rewards are, strictly speaking, categories of the *meaning* or significance of objects, they are not *classes* of concrete objects.

In the facility or performance aspect the basic classification of types of possession is that relative to the system-functions in relation to which they serve as facilities, i.e. relative to the role of the possessing unit, and its various sub-differentiations. Thus for the unit all facilities have instrumental functions, but for the system the functions of the facilities will be relative to those of the unit in the system. A blast furnace has instrumental functions for a steel-manufacturing concern, but pews and priestly robes have instrumental functions as facilities for a church. This duality of reference must always be kept in mind in judging the categorization of an object of possession. Of course the same distinction may be repeated if the unit itself is treated as a system. Then there will be facilities for its adaptive functions, for its goal-consummation phase, or its own integrative functions and for its pattern-maintenance and tension-release function.

The allocation of roles and that of facilities in a system must, as a condition of integration of the system, have some kind of ordered correspondence. This is to say that this is a condition of the stable state of the system, that is of conformity with or integration in terms of, its value system. The basic principle of optimum allocation would seem to be "the facilities to those who need them most to promote whatever goals or values are relevant to the system as defined in its specific culture." The standard of effectiveness of course is contribution to system-function. It therefore includes both a component of "technical" efficiency and one of commitment to an institutionalized role, with its various functions in the system. The relevant questions therefore are first to what end are the facilities used and second, how effectively are they used? The first question includes adherence to "regulative" rules which protect the interests of other system-units and functions. The most important general inference from these considerations seems to be that in so far as a social system is stratified on the basis of the differential strategic contributions of its units to system-function, there will tend to be a corresponding differentiation in the facilities allocated to those units. This becomes particularly important in the situations where there are mechanisms of generalization of the control of facilities, of which money is an outstanding example. Then we would say that the rank order of control of facilities should tend to correspond to the rank order of the evaluation of unit-function in the system; any lack of such correspondence may be regarded as a disturbing factor in the situation. Furthermore this broad generalization should with better knowledge, be subject to progressively more minute specification.

The case of rewards is very closely parallel. However a certain setting of the more concrete problems needs to be kept in mind. There is a partial lack of symmetry in the two categories of possession because of the fact that adaptive functions require control of objects which are inherently independent of the interaction process itself, whereas it seems to be one of the crucial features of human action systems that this is not so much the case with the functions of rewards. What we mean to say is that the most basic rewards are the *attitudes* of actors and therefore that possession of reward-objects which are not themselves social objects, is primarily significant through the fact that this possession can be treated as the symbolic manifestation of the attitudes of one or more actors. This can be brought out most clearly in the case of social interaction, but even in empirical independence of this, it can be said that a person's valuation of self-acquired reward-objects is a function of *his* attitude toward the object in essentially the same sense; its possession symbolizes his "success" in achieving a valued goal in the same way as if it had been "given" to him by another.

Rewards then are to be classified in terms of their appropriateness as sanctions to the corresponding categories of performances. A duality of system-reference is as essential in this field as in that of the analysis of facilities. The overall, superordinate classification of types of reward must be made from the point of view of system-function. Then we would speak of approval and its symbols in relation to adaptive performances, of response and its symbols with reference to system-goal attainment, acceptance with reference to system-integration, etc. But the unit is itself a subsystem and the same logical pattern of differentiation applies to it in turn but with different specific content. Then for a unit with primarily adaptive functions, approval and its symbols are rewards for technical operations effectively performed, but not for "success" in goal-attainment. The right to the "proceeds" as available for "consumption" is essential in the latter context and this is to be classified as a response-reward. Acceptance in turn implies recognition of "contribution" to the system, which goes beyond either of the above types of reward for unit-success alone.

There is an essentially parallel relation between the integration of possession of reward-objects and the rank-ordering of units by direct evaluation as prevails in relation to facilities. The principle here is the very simple one of reward in proportion to "desert," interpreted in the broad sense which includes rewarding of desirable qualities as well as of performances; it is not to be interpreted in terms of our value system alone. Generally speaking, then, we may say that it is a condition of the stable state of a system that the reward system should tend to follow the same rank order as the direct evaluation of units in terms of their qualities and performances.[12]

Before leaving the subject of possessions a word should be said about symbolism in relation to stratification, though it is too big a subject to do more than mention here. We have said above that possession is a category of the *meaning* of objects (also the distinction of their facility and reward aspects) not of their "intrinsic" properties. This is essentially to say that the situational object is always treated symbolically. Thus instrumental utility of facilities is a category of meaning of objects, and must be analyzed in the same basic terms of symbolic process as other types of meaning are.

Without attempting to carry the analysis farther we may distinguish here roughly cognitive-instrumental meanings of objects of possession and expressive-integrative meanings. It is the latter broad category which presents most of the analytical problems. A fundamental part is played in stratification systems by the expressive "style of life" symbolism which is integrated with the various status-categories, and this is one of the most important fields of the function of possessions. It is implicit in the whole theory of action that objects of consummatory gratification shade into symbols of status. Thus obviously hunger-gratification is essential to maintain life, and food-objects must have the necessary minimum nutritional properties. But in *what* human beings eat, and how and under what circumstances they eat it—as distinguished from *the fact that* they eat—an enormous part is played by the—often unconscious—symbolic significance of the choice. Thus to have steak for dinner is on one level an assertion that "I can afford something especially

---

[12]It should be clear that we are here speaking directly only of *objects* of possession, whether significant as facilities or as rewards. Objects of possession separable from the possessor shade, however, in their analytical significance, into qualities and performances of the actor. Thus membership in a collectivity may from one point of view be treated as a possession which can be acquired by active effort, or used as a facility in attaining a goal. It may also be regarded as a quality of the actor. These two points of view must be distinguished as involving different system-references, in some and different stages of the process through time. Thus membership in a collectivity cannot be used as a facility for attaining goals ascribed by the membership-status itself; it can however be used as a facility toward goals in other systems. Similarly the same actor may be rewarded by membership in a collectivity which he has been striving to attain, and this membership may be treated as one of his qualities. These considerations are of course of great significance in the analysis of social mobility, and will be touched upon below in that connection.

good," or of the special occasion which it is meant to symbolize. Essentially then we may say that expressively symbolic objects of possession form a continuum with status-qualities themselves, a kind of "extension" of the status-qualities of the possessor, and a reinforcer of their evaluation, positive or negative. They can thus, among other things, serve as an instrument of power.

Our final broad analytical problem is that of the value-integration of a social system in its bearing on the problem of stratification. We have classified the standards of evaluation in terms of functions of the social system. Since any going system must meet all of the fundamental functional prerequisites there must be positive evaluation of conformity with each of the four types of norm somewhere. This is true in a functionally integrated (as distinguished from pattern-integrated) system. This is to say that there may be romantic" or "utopian" values which make it a positive virtue to act in violation of necessary conditions of system-function. In full self-consciousness this of course would be rare; there is generally a veil of rationalization drawn over such situations.

Then, as we have said, the broad rank-order of procedence will be, below the paramount value-pattern, the order of relative strategic importance of the exigencies relating to the other three major functional problem-contexts of the system. Thus in our system the primary value-focus is universalism-achievement. It may be suggested that the second order precedence goes to the cultural-latent area (universalism-quality) in the maintenance of the strategic cultural patterns on the one hand (e.g. science, education) and the regulation of personal motivation in relation to the basic value-system (family, health, etc.) Probably the system-integrative comes next, and except for situations of national emergency, system-goal attainment last; this last is primarily what we mean by our "individualism." Or, to take a contrasting case, in a society where a transcendental religious orientation occupies the paramount position, the first order priority of values will rest in the ascriptive-qualitative norms. Then according to whether it is an actively "proselyting" religion or a more static-traditionalistic type, the next order would tend to be the system-goal attainment or the system-integrative type, with, presumably the adaptive in the last place. In the case of Calvinism, however, system-goal came second (the "kingdom of God on Earth") and because of the nature of this goal, the

remaking of secular society in the image of God, adaptive considerations apparently outranked the system-integrative.

This broad rank-ordering of value-standard types, however, still
leaves two vital problems unsolved. The first of these concerns
what may be called the "spread" of the evaluative system, i.e. the
relative independence of different sub-system hierarchies, while the
second concerns the patterning of the "interlarding" of high rank
on one scale with lower rank on another; thus in our system how
would a rather high-ranking politician rank compared with a middle ranking business executive?

Systems of stratification undoubtedly differ greatly with respect
to the first problem, that of the relative importance of a tightly integrated "general prestige continuum." Thus in the European
Middle Ages there seems to have been great importance attached
to maintaining the unequivocal superiority of the nobility-gentry
over any "bourgeois" classes, and of these in turn over any peasantry. In our system on the other hand it is much less easy to say
that there is any specific elite group which ranks unequivocally at
the top—is it the business elite, or the "best families," or the top
professionals, or the top ranges in government? The most significant thing to be said in answer to the question apparently is that
there are no unequivocal standards by which one or the other could
be given first place, as there were in the Middle Ages, and still more
in the case of Brahman supremacy in India.

Broadly it may be said that the amount of "looseness" or spread
is a function of the relative ascendancy of universalistic-performance values, of the paramountcy of adaptive functions from the
system point of view. A departure from this pattern in the direction
of any of the other three seems to increase pressure toward tighten-
ing up the scale. If it is the system-goal direction then the standard
of contribution to the goal becomes paramount; a hierarchy of
which the instrumental organization is the prototype gains dominance. The Soviet system, dominated by the goal of Communism, is
close to this type. If it is the "cultural" ascriptive-qualitative focus
then the tendency is to measure all groups in terms of this quality-
standard, i.e. to integrate the system in terms of a diffuse hierarchy
of general esteem. Pre-Nazi Germany was not very far from this
type. Finally, if it is a system-integrative emphasis, the tendency is
to assign each unit a stably accepted place in the system, so that

potentialities of disturbance of the system-equilibrium will be minimized. The "traditionalism" of the classical Chinese system fits into this type.[13]

These considerations lead over into two problem areas which need to be briefly dealt with, namely those of ascription and of authority. We have tried to make clear throughout that every system-unit must have an ascriptive quality-base from which its performances are to be evaluated. Certain of these qualities, however, may be the consequences of past performances, such as achieved collectivity membership. Others on the other hand are beyond control in various respects and hence the only problem is how they are to be evaluated, not whether or not they are to be acquired or renounced. The type cases at the latter extreme of course are the biological characteristics of individuals such as age, sex, and biological relatedness through descent. The hereditary principle is the extreme of using such an unalterable ascriptive point of reference as a basis for status-allocation in a social system. In general, I think it may be said that the adaptive and system-goal emphasis will lay least stress on ascription in this sense, while the system-integrative will lay most stress on it. The case of quality-emphasis will vary, depending on the specific content of the valued qualities. Since a very important class of such cases are those institutionalizing a transcendental religious value system, there seems to be a strong likelihood that this will also favor ascriptive bases; the extreme case is India, but our own Middle Ages went quite far in that direction.

There are important relations of interdependence between these radically ascriptive foci and other more contingent bases of ascription. An excellent example is territorial location. Since all action involves human organisms one potentially relevant basis for analyzing an action is always *where* the actor is located at the time, including of course, changes in his location in the course of an action. One prominent case is that of location of residence and its connection with the family as a solidary unit; in all known kinship systems the two aspects are inherently interdependent, since the basic func-

---

[13]This problem of looseness is being considered at present *only* with reference to the total stratification "profile" and thus involving the mode and degree of integration of ranking according to all four types of standard. On a more microscopic level a further problem of the mode of differentiation with respect to any one type of standard arises. We cannot take space to go into this problem here.

tions of the family imply sharing of residence in most cases. Another example is the relation between territorial location and political jurisdiction; political units are always organized relative to territorial areas of jurisdiction. To be sure an individual may change his residence or other location of activity under certain conditions from one political jurisdiction to another; but the consequences of such change and the constraints on it may be so formidable that it is for many purposes almost as inescapable as one's sex or parentage.

The case of authority is quite different. Authority is one particularly important type of superiority, that which involves the legitimized right (and/or obligation) to control the actions of others in a social relationship system. It thus belongs, as we noted above, among the mechanisms of social control. The factor of legitimation means that authority is always an aspect of a status in a collectivity; in so far as this is not the case but there is only realistic ability to control others, we speak of power.

The primary point is that authority *over* someone must mean in *some* sense and in some respect *superiority to* him. It is a status-quality involved in hierarchical evaluations. The legitimation of the authority is ipso facto that of the superiority. But the nature and bases of this superiority may of course vary widely. If it is specific rather than diffuse it need not imply any *generalized* superiority and may be compatible with the reverse; thus a traffic policeman has authority to stop the car of a prominent citizen who in general prestige terms is greatly his superior.

As Weber made clear, types of authority are to be classified in terms of the bases of their legitimation, i.e. in terms of the value-patterns which define the particular mode of superiority which the authority involves. This may of course be relative to any one of the functions of a system-process.

There are two kinds of inferences which may be drawn from this set of references. First, authority will tend to be relatively more prominent as a function of the priority of either goal-attainment or system-integrative values. In the one case the focus of the need for authority is the need to coordinate the contributions of the various units of the system to the goal. Authority will tend to be a function of the urgency of "getting things done." The system-integrative case presumably gives a somewhat lesser emphasis on authority for getting things done; it is based mainly on the negative need to *prevent* units from disturbing the integration of the system, the

need to keep them "in line." The first is more "prescriptive" authority, the second more "regulative." The primacy of adaptive functions tends to transfer the problem of authority to the next level
down. The unit is evaluated in terms of its achievement, but
authority may be exceedingly important as one of the conditions of
bringing about this achievement. Thus in our society the authority
of the business executive is not a direct but a "derived" authority,
it is legitimized in terms of its contribution to the efficiency of the
firm. If ascriptive-qualitative values have primacy, the situation
will tend to resemble that in the system-integrative case, but with
perhaps a somewhat greater emphasis on authority. It would seem
safe to infer that the adaptive emphasis would lead to the least
emphasis on authority unless it were a case of ascriptive values with
a strictly anti-authoritarian cast.

Secondly, the problem of authority is very much involved in the
complexities of system-sub-system relationships. It has been emphasized that authority is an aspect of a status in a collectivity. The
position of authority, therefore, is very much a function not only of
the unit's status in the specific collectivity, but of the position of
this collectivity in any larger system of which it is a part. The question of competing loyalties involved in the different collectivity
memberships of the same persons necessarily limit authority in any
one.

This leads us over to the problem mentioned above, that of the
"inter-larding" of the hierarchical scales set forth in terms of each
of the major types of value-standard. In a complex system, there
must be mechanisms which establish levels of relative equivalence,
as well as mechanisms which insulate against too rigid and specific
comparisons of status. Part of this function is carried out by what
may be called direct evaluation of qualities and performances. Thus
there is no doubt that any occupational role which can be adequately filled by almost any normal adult will not be considered
the equal of one which is both highly valued and requires qualifications which only a few can fulfill, whatever the combination of
training and native ability which may be involved. But there are
serious limitations on the adequacy of the mechanisms of direct
evaluation. One is the level of competence necessary for an adequate judgment, and hence the problem of how the judgment of
the competent few is to be brought to bear, and to become generalized through the system. A second problem concerns the in-

herent element of indeterminacy of many of the standards of relative evaluation even within a class of cases, while a third concerns the comparability of different *kinds* of qualities and performances, even if the standards are relatively clear and definite with reference to each kind.

This gap tends to be filled, in part, by the processes of "ecological" distribution of possessions and of evaluative judgments, both as facilities and as reward-objects, but particularly the latter, and in part through the allocation of attitudinal rewards. In our type of society these mechanisms function through two main types of channels, the monetary market system and the fluid public communication system. In the first context it is above all financial resources as *generalized* access to possessions which come to be distributed; in the latter context, in the evaluative aspect, it is especially "reputation" which is allocated. In both cases we may speak of an ideal type of "free" competitive market process as a kind of base line. But equally in both cases, this fails to operate fully automatically even under what are empirically the best conditions. Hence various kinds of modifying "intervention" tend to take place which "even" the balances. Thus government or private philanthropy channels funds into uses to which, under competitive conditions they would not be put, such as health care or higher education, thereby increasing both the facilities and the rewards available to those working in those fields and the beneficiaries of their work. Similarly a person prominent in a field goes out of the way to praise the work of a younger less known person. By enhancing his reputation he also shifts the balance of facilities and rewards in the latter's favor. Essentially what seems to be going on is a kind of continual series of comparative judgments which say in effect, class A of roles is receiving too little, class B too much, and then a shift from B to A takes place.

It is obvious that it is particularly in processes such as these that the relation between the three components of power which we discussed above comes to be particularly crucial in the integrative functions of a system of stratification. It is essentially a question of the effectiveness of operation of the mechanisms of social control. Control of possessions is inevitably correlated with high status, hence there is a source of power independent of the direct evaluative legitimation of the status. Similarly potential deviance on either ego's or alter's part may enhance these possibilities of power.

The function of the mechanisms of social control is to keep the *independent* i.e. the illegitimate, use of this power at a minimum.[14]

It may prove helpful to the reader in following the rather involved theoretical analysis of this paper if he is given a schematic outline of the principal conceptual elements used and some of their most important relations.

The most important point of reference is the accompanying figure (Fig. 2, Chap. V, p. 182 of *Working Papers*). This is necessarily a highly schematic and hence in certain respects arbitrary representation, but it does show certain fundamental components and relations.

The four dimensions of our action space or directions of process are represented at the four corners of the figure—the adaptive (A), the goal-attainment or gratification (G), the integrative (I), and the latent-expressive (L). The *order* of the four is not arbitrary but is fundamental, e.g. that G is between A and I.

The four types of standards defining object-qualities and performance and sanction norms are described by the combinations of pattern variables clustering at each of the corners of the figures. These are respectively:

    A. Qualities of "technical competence"
        Performance norms: "technical efficiency"
          (Pattern variables: universalism-performance)
        Sanction norms: "approval-disapproval"
          (Pattern variables: specificity-neutrality)

    G. Qualities of a) "system-goal-commitment" or
              b) "legitimation of unit-goal-commitment"
        Performance Norms: a) system or "relational" responsi-
                    bility
                   b) regulative "rules of the game"
          (Pattern-variables: performance-particularism)
        Sanction norms: conditional response-reward
          (Pattern-variables: affectivity-specificity)

---

[14]The ecological allocation of possessions and of communication may, as mechanisms of social systems, be treated as analogous to the "internal environment" of which physiologists have made so much. The stability of expectations with respect to the kind of evaluative judgments to be expected from qualities and performances, and with respect to their relation to control of facilities and reward-objects, is a condition of the integration of the system as a system. Thus there is functional significance in the constancy of this internal environment of the social system, an environment which is non-situational for the system as a whole, but situational, for the action of the units taken as subsystems. We shall attempt to analyze this somewhat further in connection with our own system of stratification presently.

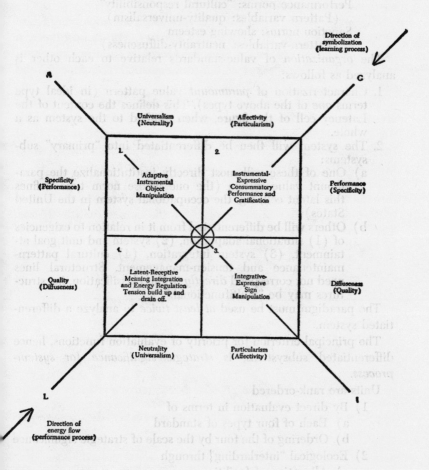

Figure 2

Phases in the Relationship of a System to its Situation

Direction of
symbolization
(learning process)

A

C

Universalism
(Neutrality)

Affectivity
(Particularism)

1.

2.

Specificity
(Performance)

Adaptive
Instrumental
Object
Manipulation

Instrumental-
Expressive
Consummatory
Performance and
Gratification

Performance
(Specificity)

3.

Quality
(Diffuseness)

Latent-Receptive
Meaning Integration
and Energy Regulation
Tension build up and
drain off

Integrative-
Expressive
Sign
Manipulation

Diffuseness
(Quality)

4.

Neutrality
(Universalism)

Particularism
(Affectivity)

L

I

Direction of
energy flow
(performance process)

KEY

A—Adaptive Phase

G—Goal Gratification Phase

3. I—Integrative Phase

4. L—Latent Pattern Maintenance Phase

I. Qualities of "loyalty"
  Performance norms: showing solidarity
    (Pattern variables: particularism-quality)
  Sanction norms: diffuse acceptance
    (Pattern variables: diffuseness-affectivity)
L. Qualities of "cultural value-commitment"
  Performance norms: "cultural responsibility"
    (Pattern variables: quality-universalism)
  Sanction norms: showing esteem
    (Pattern-variables: neutrality-diffuseness)

The *organization* of value-standards relative to each other is analyzed as follows:

1. Characterization of *paramount* value pattern (in ideal type terms *one* of the above types). This defines the content of the Latency cell of the figure, when applied to the system as a whole.
2. The system will then be differentiated into "primary" sub-systems:
   a) One of these will most directly institutionalize the paramount value system (the one whose norm type defines this latent cell, e.g. the occupational system in the United States)
   b) Others will be differentiated from it in relation to exigencies of (1) situational adaptation, (2) system and unit goal attainment, (3) system integration, (4) cultural pattern-maintenance and tension-management. Structural lines need not correspond *directly* to this classification, i.e. structures may be "multifunctional."

The paradigm must be used *at least twice* to analyze a differentiated system.

The principal criterion for priority of evaluation functions, hence differentiated subsystems, is *strategic significance for system-process.*

Units are rank-ordered
  1) By direct evaluation in terms of
     a) Each of four types of standard
     b) Ordering of the four by the scale of strategic significance
  2) Ecological "interlarding" through
     a) Allocation of facilities
     b) Allocation of reward-objects and reputation

To analyze the concrete system we should distinguish
  1) A hierarchy of evaluative ranking which is a function of
     a) A "general prestige continuum"—more or less "tight or loose."

    b) Four major sub-hierarchies of direct evaluation in rough interlarded rank-order.
2) A hierarchy of power as a function of
    a) The above direct evaluations
    b) Conformity-deviance balances
    c) Allocation of possessions

We may now attempt to illustrate the abstract conceptual scheme just outlined by a brief sketch of certain highlights of the American system of social stratification, and the problems of analyzing the processes of mobility within it. On particular points contrasts with other systems will be discussed, but there will be no attempt to present a systematic comparative analysis.

As has been several times noted, we treat American society as having a value-system very close to the universalistic-achievement or performance ideal type. This gives first place to unit qualities and performances which have adaptive functions for the system. Furthermore, and very important, the lack of stress on a specific system-goal means that the valuation of adaptive functions is not relativized to such a specific goal, but goals are mainly permissively defined. In general then we may speak of contribution to the *production of valued facilities and reward-objects* for unit-goals, whatever, within the permissible limits, these may be, as the *primary* basis of positive evaluation of unit qualities and performances.

This puts the primary emphasis on productive activity in the economy, and also it is the source of what in a certain sense is an "individualistic" slant in the value system. This latter must, however, be very carefully interpreted. It definitely does not mean that only achievements of individuals in which they have not cooperated with others are valued or even that these are given priority. The achievements of collectivities such as business firms loom very large indeed. The major point is rather what may be called a "pluralism of goals" so that there is no overriding system-goal to which all activity in the system must be conceived to be oriented.

We might put it a little differently by saying that the primary system goal is the maximization of the production of valued possessions and cultural accomplishments which can facilitate the attainment of legitimate unit goals—whether the units be individual persons or various types of collectivities. This orientation places a particularly strong emphasis on the generalization of control of possessions through the money and market mechanisms, and on the generalization of evaluative communication through the allocation of direct attitudinal rewards, i.e. through "reputation." The first-order presumption is that the money value of a "product," i.e. as an exchangeable possession, is a measure of its value relative to others in the total productive process and similarly that money remuneration can serve as a workable index of the "reputation" of a unit in the system, individual or collective. This is of course only a first order orienting point of reference, and certain of its inadequacies will have to be taken up below.

If this general orientation is correctly designated as the central one, then the most directly valued achievement is what may be called in a special American sense a "practical" one, one which visibly eventuates in "production" in this sense. Next in order of evaluation then would seem to be the functions which are most important in insuring the conditions on which effective productive activities in this sense are dependent. In terms of our functional paradigm these involve as we have noted above, three main types or directions. The one next in order to the adaptive is probably the ascriptive-qualitative in a special content sense, then the integrative aspect and finally the system-goal. We may take up each of these in turn.

The significance of values in the ascriptive-qualitative sphere is perhaps best brought out in terms of its relation to the universalistic component of the basic value-orientation type. There seems to be two main contexts of its application. One of these concerns the standards by which productive activities themselves are to be judged, and of course is generalized to cover other functions so far as such standards can be implemented in such a field. The place of science in our cultural system is the most important single example of this generalization. It is true that there is a sense in which its valuation is derivative rather than primary; the order runs from technology to science rather than vice versa. But once technology has attained a certain level of development the connection between it and science becomes exceedingly close. The most important single manifestation of this in the role structure of our present society is the place of the professions which require scientific training, notably of course engineering and medicine. The universities as the primary location of "pure" scientific investigation are also the places for training of professional personnel who then practice throughout the occupational system. Very broadly, then, contribution to the maintenance and development of a cultural tradition which can feed into the productive processes is one of the main classes of functions fitting into the ascriptive-qualitative value category. These functions rank high, but one may suspect it would take a real shift of the major value system to displace the "applied" functions from their position of priority.

The second context of application of universalism concerns the allocation of performance-capacities and opportunities for productive achievement. The focus of it is the universalistic definition of "equality of opportunity" as applied both to individuals and to collectivities. The differences of hereditary capacity must of course be accepted as "facts of nature." But within this framework there is a strong predilection to universalize opportunity. This seems to be the primary source of our high valuation of health and of education. Without good health and without as much training as a person has capacity to utilize, he cannot realize his potentialities for productive achievement. It is notable that these are two fields where there is the strongest consensus that "competitive" forces should not be permitted to operate unmodified, especially that access to health and to education should not be a simple function of ability to pay for them.

Two other particularly important fields of activity also fit into this context. One is the whole field of the regulation of the subtler balances of personality, both in respect to socialization and to maintaining emotional balance. This is above all the field in which our modern type of family, as distinguished from other kinship systems, has come to be specialized; hence perhaps it is not too far fetched to suggest that this is a main focus of evaluation of the feminine role. Formally professionalized handling of similar problems is, it may be noted, assimilated to the same basic context, and treated for the adult mainly as a problem of health through psychiatry, for the child as formal education. The other field concerns the regulation of the ecological processes of the distribution of possessions and of communication, especially reputation. It is here for example that a large part at least of the functions of the legal profession should be placed,[15] but also certain of the regulatory

---

[15]Cf. Chapter XVIII above.

functions of government, and of course, of informal "public opinion."

Integration of the system as a whole may be regarded as next in order in the scale of function-priorities. Generally speaking we expect this to work out to a large extent through spontaneous consensus and through a process of relatively free adjustment of interest groups to each other, through legislative negotiation, lobbying, etc. In general of course this set of functions merges over into the regulative aspects of the ascriptive-qualitative functions; the basic standard is that of "fair" opportunity for all legitimate interests. The doctrine of the separation of powers institutionalizes both our suspicion of commitment to overly specific national system-goals and of overly definite measures of system-integration. With changing conditions it would also seem that certain of the most severe strains in the functioning of the system were likely to appear at these points.

Finally, we have noted that functions of promoting system-goals directly are low in the priority scale because of the lack of a specific positive system-goal. Hence the positive position of government is relatively weak, and also dependent on its articulation with other functions. This also has to do with the wide variation between our attitudes toward government in ordinary circumstances, and in emergency conditions, where the goal of protecting the system from disruption from without becomes urgent. It would seem that the present position of high responsibility of the United States in the world would imply the necessity for a shift in the direction of a higher valuation of governmental function in this aspect; and, given our background this involves difficult processes of adjustment. The shading off of the ascriptive-qualitative into the system-goals aspects should be kept clearly in mind. Thus a primary occasion for relatively recent expansion in the functions of government was severe economic depression, which may be regarded as an emergency situation from the ascriptive-qualitative point of view, whereas the other most important occasion has been the problem of national defense and other closely related aspects of our position of international responsibility, i.e. an adaptive and system-goal problem.

It should be kept clearly in mind that the same order of problems of valuation-priority appear again when we shift from consideration of the overall system as a whole to that of specific subsystems. But the incidence of these judgments must be changed as a function of the place of the subsystem, especially if it is a collectivity, in the structure of the superordinate system. The paradigm must, that is, be applied at least twice in order to place a specific role of an individual in any kind of hierarchical order.

Thus the focus of the executive role as we ordinarily understand it, is on responsibility for system goal-attainment, i.e. of the organization in which the executive is placed. Because this is a highly strategic role for maximizing the contributions of the organization, while we do not necessarily give top priority to responsibility for overall societal goal-attainment, except in emergency, we do give high status to the executive role in productive organizations, other things equal probably higher than to that of technical roles. Furthermore, while in the general value system instrumental functions tend to be ranked higher than expressive, from the point of view of functioning of the unit in the system in relation to the "internal environment" of the superordinate system, capacity to influence the action of others through expressive communication may be a highly strategic factor. Therefore the good negotiator, or the good "salesman" may have a highly strategic position because of the importance of his functions for the unit, even though *its* function in the larger system is of a totally different order. Because of this discrepancy in the two orders relative to the two levels of system reference, however, we might expect a good deal of ambivalence in the evaluation of such capacities and their resultant performances. In the extreme case the fact that they are practiced in the requisite occupational groups may be treated as almost sub-rosa. Thus the symbolic focus of competence in the legal profession centers on knowledge of the law. But the actual functions of practicing lawyers often involve a very large component of capacity to negotiate and persuade which is only loosely connected with intellectual mastery of the law.

We may now turn to a different order of analysis, looking at certain key features of our actual social structure in their bearing on the problems of stratification. Very roughly, and for our specific purposes, we may think of a society as composed of three major types of collectivities. First the "specific function" collectivity or organization of which the business firm, the school, the hospital may be treated as prototypes. Here, except for the recipients of service or the consumers of products, roles are organized in the occupational form, the collectivity is composed of executives, technicians,

workers, teachers, physicians, nurses, etc. The second type, of
which political units and churches are prototypes, are diffuse-function "associations" which represent their constituencies but which
in proportion to their size and extensiveness of interests also tend
to become organized in occupational-type roles for the more responsible and specialized functions, but with many limitations on
how far this mode of organization, i.e. their "bureaucratization"
can be carried. (There are of course innumerable specific-function
associations like labor unions, professional associations, trade associations, etc., but these will be neglected here.) Finally, there are
what may be called the "diffuse solidarities" in which individuals
are embedded, of which local community, kinship and ethnic group
are the most important for our purposes.

The relations of these three types of collectivities to each other
are critically important to the system of stratification because the
normal individual is a member of at least two of them, and if he is
an adult male almost necessarily of a third, i.e. in the occupational
system. He may within limits, of course, be a member of more than
one such collectivity in a type which poses further problems of relationship and integration.

We have seen above that the field of most direct institutionalization of our paramount value system is that of occupational roles.
It is true that some of what are defined as occupational roles are
not primarily in the adaptive subsystem, but in the cultural ascriptive-qualitative subsystem as in the case of the scientist, the teacher
or the minister of religion, or in the system-goal-integrative systems
as in the case of officials of government. However, even though the
collectivities in these different subsystems may have different characters related to their differences of function, they have what in the
narrower sense are occupational subsystems within which the roles
are of the same fundamental type as those in the primarily adaptive
subsystem. Furthermore of course a significant, though decreasing
class of occupational roles, like the completely independent "private
practitioner" of a profession, or completely independent craftsman,
are not imbedded in the context of organization at all. There is one
further type of role of which that of farmer is the type case where
the otherwise normal segregation between kinship unit and productive function does not obtain; similar situations exist for small
stores and in some other fields.

Nevertheless the massive fact is that the normal adult male is the incumbent of a "full-time" occupational role and that in the increasingly typical case this is part of an organization and is rather strictly segregated in physical premises, property control and "management" from his kinship unit. Furthermore the great majority of the unmarried female population have such roles, beyond the educational ages, and an increasing proportion of the married women. Broadly we may say that in the occupational system thus defined status is a function of the individual's productive "contribution" to the functions of the organizations concerned, hence of his performance capacities and his achievements on behalf of the organization.

We have said that this is "broadly" true. Of course there are innumerable ways in which it fails to work out, for the kinds of reasons mentioned above such as difficulty of implementing standards of judgment, indefiniteness of such standards, and difficulty of comparison between qualitatively different performances and qualities. Differences of power as a result of command of possessions, of blocks in communication and the like can serve to protect and increase such discrepancies. These factors are of the greatest importance for detailed empirical analysis, but are secondary from the point of view of the broad characterization of our stratification system.

The same individuals who are the incumbents of occupational roles are of course members of kinship units. The most important thing about the American kinship system from the present point of view is how far the process of "isolation" of the conjugal family has gone. In the first place this means of course that the standard or "expected" unit is the "family" household consisting of the married couple and their still dependent children. Though other relatives do often live in the household it can pretty definitely be said that this is structurally anomalous, particularly under urban middle class conditions. Furthermore there is a very close approach to symmetry in the relations between this family and the families of orientation of the spouses, though one may perhaps speak of a slight "matrilineal" trend through a tendency to special solidarity of mother and married daughter. Beyond this the conjugal family has, as is well recognized, been very largely stripped of functions in the larger society other than those in the ascriptive-qualitative sphere, above all those in "production" which otherwise are so fundamental to our type of society. This means essentially that its primary function significance is as a maintainer of certain "style patterns" of life which are integral to the general cultural tradition, as a regulator of the personality equilibria of its members, and as a socializer of children into this cultural tradition.

This "whittling down" of the American kinship unit as compared with those in other societies, both with regard to membership and to function, is obviously intimately connected with the functional requirements of our type of occupational system. But there is a limit beyond which this process cannot go if the remaining functions are to be effectively performed. There seems to be little doubt first that these functions are vital to the society and second that there is, in a broad sense, no alternative way of taking care of them in sight.

The family is essentially a unit of diffuse solidarity. Its members must, therefore, to a fundamental degree share a common status in the larger system; which means that they must, in spite of their differentiation by sex and age, be evaluated in certain respects as equals. The family as a unit has a certain order of "reputation" in the community. Its members share a common household and therefore the evaluation of this in terms of location, character, furnishings, etc., in the system of prestige symbolism. They have a common style of life. If the position of the parents in the community is relatively high, its advantages must to some extent be shared by the children, whether they "deserve" it or not; similarly of course the sharing of the disadvantages of low parental status. From these considerations it follows that the preservation of a functioning family system even of our type is incompatible with complete "equality of opportunity." It is a basic limitation on the full implementation of our paramount value system, which is attributable to its conflict with the functional exigencies of personality and cultural stabilization and socialization.

Another aspect of the consequences of our family system concerns its impact on sex role differentiation. Even though its typical membership is so small, a conjugal family is an internally differentiated system. The adaptive exigencies of its maintenance as a system in our society focus above all on the reputation and income to be earned through the husband-father's occupational role. This is strategically so fundamental that by virtue of it alone he must be accorded the "instrumental leadership" role. But we know that groups of such size strongly tend to develop a differentiation between instrumental and expressive leadership. At the same time the exigencies of the socialization process demand a certain type of relation to children which it is exceedingly difficult for the father to combine with his occupational responsibilities. Hence the mother role in specific personal relation to the child, and the "expressive leadership" role in the family, combined with primary *internal* instrumental responsibilities in the family (as "homemaker") tend to form the center of gravity of the feminine role.

Inherent in this situation is a whole set of forces making for relative segregation of the sex roles, and in general to "shunt" the feminine role out of primary status in the occupational system or competition for occupational success or status. Probably the main positive functional basis of this is the crucial functional significance to the society of the mother role *within* the context of the family. From this follows the importance of equality of status of husband and wife, but occupational competition tends to disperse in status rather than to equalize. Broadly married women in our society are not in direct competition for occupational status and its primary reward symbols with men of their own class. On the other hand it may also be said that the segregation of sex roles serves to keep men integrated in the family so that the extremely important socialization functions of the father role are preserved. Obviously the whole situation, however, produces another fundamental limitation on full "equality of opportunity," in that women, regardless of their performance capacities, tend to be relegated to a narrower range of functions than men, and excluded, at least relatively, from some of the highest prestige statuses.[16]

A striking manifestation of this segregation of the sex roles is to be found in the style-symbolism of dress and personal appearance generally. Masculine dress in our society is virtually a uniform, except for certain types of sports clothes. Feminine dress on the other hand emphasizes considerable elaboration and individuality of taste, supplemented by relatively elaborate embellishment of the hair, the face, etc., which is strongly taboo for men. That this order of differentiation is not to be regarded as "human nature" may be brought out by two contrasting examples. Anyone familiar

---

[16]The relevant aspects of the American kinship system and its relation to occupation and stratification are more fully discussed in Chapters V, IX and XIV above. See also on the whole American system, Robin M. Williams, Jr., *American Society,* especially Chap. 5.

with conservative farm communities knows that there tends there to be a much closer parallelism between the clothes of the two sexes, work clothes for every day, and "Sunday best" with about the same order of relative elaborateness for both sexes. At the other extreme we may mention the aristocratic society of the European eighteenth century where masculine dress approached feminine in its elaborateness and scope for taste. Powdered wigs, lace ruffles and cuffs, varicolored coats and waistcoats, satin breeches and silver buckles were not deemed in the least "effeminate" for a gentleman whereas they would be unthinkable for a man in our society.

Very broadly, again, the main lines of our system of stratification seem to be understandable as a resultant of the tendencies of institutionalization on the one hand of the occupational system—including of course roles in the ascriptive-qualitative and governmental systems—and on the other hand of the kinship system. Local community might be an independent basis and to some extent is with respect to rural-urban and regional differentiations. But compared with other societies the notable thing about our patterns of residence is their high mobility, so that above all community of residence tends to be a function of occupational role rather than vice versa. Similarly within a community neighborhood of residence tends, within the limits of access to occupational premises, to be a function of income and family taste rather than an independent determinant.

Ethnic belongingness is another possible basis in diffuse solidarity for differentiation of status. It is probably, along with certain aspects of religion, the most important basis which is independent of occupation and kinship in the narrower senses, except perhaps for the rural-urban and the regional aspects of community. The case of the negro, even in the North, is the most conspicuous one. But in spite of the dispersion of the members of given ethnic groups through the different levels of the main class structure, ethnicity to some degree tends to preserve relatively independent "pyramids" in the more general system. Its importance would, in the normal course of development of our type of society, be expected to decrease. How far this is actually happening is exceedingly difficult to judge. On the one hand our system is, as noted, the kind which allows a much greater degree of looseness than most others, and this permits the preservation of ethnic distinctiveness. These tendencies are reinforced by ethnic traditionalism as a defense against insecurity. On the other hand there are very powerful forces of acculturation at work which tend to break down distinctive ethnic traditions. Broadly we may regard the ethnic factor as a secondary basis of modification of the stratification pattern but as by no means unimportant.

The ethnic problem seems to modify the system of stratification through two principal types of process. In the first place the value-system of an ethnic group may vary from that paramount in the dominant society. Then within certain limits of tolerance it may tend to form a variant subsociety within the larger society, more closely approximating implementation of its own values. In these respects the actions of an ethnic group should be interpreted in terms of its own distinctive culture, including its own internal stratification and the ways in which it can, according to its values, appropriately articulate with the main class system.[17]

The second mode of modification derives from the fact that the ethnic group, with regard both to its value-patterns and to many other aspects of its status in the larger society, constitutes an entity somewhat apart, to which non-members react in patterned ways which in turn help to determine the reactions of the members of the group. Discrimination, as in the non-acceptance of ethnic members in certain statuses for which they are otherwise qualified, is a type example. A reaction to discrimination is not understandable *only* in terms of the value-patterns of the ethnic group, but the source and character of the discrimination must also be taken into account.

In general it should be said that until fairly recently perhaps the major modifying influence of ethnic groups in American society has been in the lower reaches of the stratification scale. With upward mobility on a large scale, however, this has come to be modified and the place of Jews or of Catholic Irish in the upper middle classes, for instance, present problem areas of considerable empirical importance.

Of the two major types of what above were called diffuse-function associations, the political may be treated as a relatively minor factor except for the groups actively participating in political func-

---

[17]The case of the Negro in American society would be that where an independent ethnic culture was of minimal importance; those of Italians or East European Jews would be cases where this culture was of considerable significance.

tion. The high level of horizontal mobility means that membership in the local political unit is of secondary significance and easily changed. Similarly party affiliation is for most of the "public" loose and easily changed except at the numerically small extremes involved in political activism of the protofascist or communist variety. The question of where those actively engaged in political careers belong presents another order of problem. Perhaps the most important point to note is that in sharp contrast to many societies, a "political elite" or "ruling class" does not have a paramount position in American society, but at best those most successful in making a political career are only *among* the elite elements, not the distinctively paramount one. Moreover, there is little continuity from generation to generation in this type of affiliation.

The case of religious organization and affiliation is different and is of great sociological interest. The main structure is, we may say, that of Protestant denominational pluralism with a great deal of congregational autonomy of the local units, even in the Episcopal and Methodist churches. This has tended to work out, in close correlation with residential neighborhoods, in terms of an assimilation of religious affiliation in a broad and rather loose way with social stratification. Thus the main membership of certain churches is drawn from the upper class groups, and there is from here down a rough gradation of denominations corresponding to the class structure. If differentiation of parishes within the same denominations is taken into account the relationship is even closer. The main exception to the pattern is the Roman Catholic Church with its close relationship to the ethnic origins of its constituents. Again by contrast with other societies it is notable that a clergy does not occupy any very distinctive position in the class structure. Though in many respects a very special kind of occupational role, with the exception of the celibate Catholic clergy, it tends to be assimilated to the general occupational role system. The status of a clergyman is roughly a function of the prestige of his parishoners.

If we treat "politics" as at least partially an occupational role, (as indeed civil service and careers in the armed services certainly can be) then we need broadly abstract only from the ethnic problem, from the type of local community, and from the special position of the Catholic Church, to justify the broad generalization that our system of stratification revolves mainly about the integration between kinship and the occupational system. Obviously the most important direct links between the two concern the fact that what from the point of view of family status is the primary occupational role, that of husband-father, is occupied by the same person who is "instrumental leader" of the family, and that his occupational earnings constitute the main—though decreasingly often perhaps the only—source of family income, i.e. of facilities and symbolically significant reward-objects.

Hence there *has to be* a broad correlation between direct evaluation of occupational roles, income derived from those roles, and status of the families of the incumbents as collectivities in the scale of stratification. It is essentially this broad correlation to which we would like to apply the term "class-status," so far as it describes American conditions. Somewhat more broadly we may repeat the definition of class status given in the earlier paper[18] as that component of status shared by the members of the most effective kinship unit. In this respect the distinctive features of the American system are the constitution of the typical kinship unit, the isolated conjugal family, and the fact that one of its members occupies a status-determining occupational role. In classical China, for example, the distinction between peasantry and gentry families—which as kinship units were also differently constituted—rested on a quite different basis; essentially whether or not they owned sufficient land to make the "scholarly" pattern of life possible, without the family members themselves engaging in manual labor.

As thus defined, class status is, it should be clear, not a rigid entity, but a fairly loosely correlated complex. Family status relative to specific occupation and to income may be enhanced (or depressed) by canons of taste in the fields of expressive symbolism, by connections with other families of certain orders of prestige, through kinship or for example through memberships in voluntary associations or purely informal mutual entertainment relations. It may also be enhanced or depressed through choice of residential location, through prestige of educational institutions which members have attended or children are currently attending, and through various other channels. To a considerable degree it is arbitrary where the "constitutive" elements of class status are held to end, and their "symbolic" penumbra to begin. All that is here contended is that the family-occupation-income complex is by and large the core of the wider complex. We have deliberately abstracted from

---
[18]Chapter IV above.

ethnic status which might be brought in. In a sense it is taken account of by way of the family. Perhaps the best single case for another element would be education. The most important reason for not including it in the core, but placing it on the "periphery" here is that in *our* society the primary meaning of education seems to be that it serves as a path to future occupational (and partly marital) status. This differentiates American society from that of most European countries where the "quality" status of the educated man as compared with "what he does" is relatively much more important. This is, however, a difference of degree; thus attendance at an "ivy league" college does indeed stamp a man to some extent independently of his future occupational status.

However this question may be treated, it is of the greatest importance that it is only in the broadest sense that this class complex can in American society be made to yield a single unequivocal scale of classes. Some such broad classification as "upper"—carefully defined—"middle" and "lower" makes sense. Furthermore it is often useful to sub-divide these for specific purposes—as is done at a number of points in this paper. But care should be taken not to imply that the finer differentiations are even nearly uniform "across the board" or that the lines between adjacent classes are very clear-cut.

The main bases for such caution are three. First, as we have seen, from the point of view of direct evaluation of occupational roles themselves there has to be a complex process of "interlarding" of the different qualitative role types, not only in terms of *one* application of our qualitative classification, but of *at least two.* Thus high business executives, people highly placed in government, and people highly placed in the ascriptive-qualitative functions such as scientists, writers, etc., are extremely difficult to rank relative to each other in any unequivocal way. Certain "situses" as Hatt[19] calls them, are easier to arrange in a relatively clear-cut rank order—broadly within the same qualitative types. Secondly, the relation between occupational and family status is relatively loose. It is true that there is a *tendency* through the consolidation of advantage, for the families of the successful to consolidate their position and perpetuate it as hereditary "upper class," but this has not been notably effective on a nationwide basis. It is most conspicuous in

---

[19]Hatt, Paul K., "Occupation and Social Stratification," *American Journal of Sociology*, 55, May 1950.

smaller communities, not least because the occupationally more ambitious tend to be drained off from these communities. Even here there seems to be considerable change over time. In general any expressive-symbolic scale of ranking of family—such as the Chapin living room scale—will correlate, but only loosely, with one of occupational status of father, the more narrow the range relative to the total scale, the more loosely.

The third reason for looseness is the relative independence relative to the other components, of the factors involved in the processes of allocation of possessions. Inherited wealth plays some part, but compared to other systems a relatively minor one. (Its place in the upper reaches of the system, including what is ordinarily called the upper middle class is, however, undoubtedly worthy of more careful study than it has yet received). Earnings of members of the family other than the husband-father are also by no means negligible, but probably by far the most important factor is that of difference in the mechanisms through which income is allocated to occupational remuneration in different fields. Three main types of such mechanisms may be distinguished. The first is the "classical" distribution by free competition, whereby income of the individual is a direct function of his own "entrepreneurial" activity, through selling services or products on a free market. Formally this should include the independent craftsman, professional, etc., as well as the proprietor of a business in the usual sense. This has led to the greatest inequality, and is of course the source of the fortunes which are so much less prominent now than in our past. The second is payment by the firm on the basis of its earning in a competitive—though not necessarily unregulated—market, e.g. salaries, wages, bonuses, commissions, etc., (dividends on securities belong in another category). The third is the class of occupations which have to be "subsidized" in the sense that funds have to be "raised" through some mechanisms other than those of the free market, e.g. through taxation or philanthropic contribution.[20] Government employees and those of "non-profit" organizations like hospitals, universities, etc., are the most important cases. The most important broad generalization seems to be that the first two mechanisms lead to a considerably wider range of differentiation, and thus a considerably higher "top" than does the third. It is very

---

[20]The "sliding scale" which is a prominent feature of the market for professional services, is intermediate between these.

much an open question how far these discrepancies of occupational income and hence of course of family standard of living correspond to clear-cut differentiations of direct evaluation of function.[21] It is easy to cite cases where discrepancy is clear—as for instance that between the salary of a high Federal Judge and what the incumbent could usually earn in the private practice of law.

The point of this relative "looseness" need not be labored. But these kinds of discrepancies necessitate mechanisms of adjustment so that they do not disturb the integration of the social system too greatly. Two sets of such mechanisms may be briefly mentioned. One, which is very conspicuous by comparison with European societies, especially a generation or more ago, is the relatively wide range of facilities open to the "public" without specific status-implications; thus travel facilities, hotels, restaurants, etc. Such small things as the fact that "almost everybody" smokes standard brands of cigarettes of about the same price, and even that many very high status people drive Fords and Chevrolets, (and some not-so-high drive Cadillacs) are undoubtedly significant. Related to this broad "band" of objects with relatively little "invidious" significance, is the degree of insulation which exists between these different groups so that they do not come into much direct contact in spheres where the comparison would lead to acute strain. Thus the families of civil servants, officers, professors whose incomes are lower than those of comparable occupational statuses in business, have little to do with the families of the latter, so that strain is minimized. There are of course standards below which serious strain would be felt—a very important field is the education of children. But the existence of these mechanisms is a very important fact in a society where "keeping up with the Joneses" figures so prominently in the folklore. It illustrates the importance of assaying particular facts in the context of the social system as a whole, not one isolated context.

In brief, particularly as seen in comparative perspective, one of the most notable features of the American system of stratification is its relative looseness, the absence of a clear-cut hierarchy of pres-

---

[21]The evidence of the North-Hatt study which places scientists and certain professional groups *above* even rather high business personnel would indicate that money income did not reflect relative evaluation *across* these types very accurately. Cf. North, Cecil C., and Hatt, Paul K., "Jobs and Occupations; A Popular Evaluation," *Opinion News*, Sept. 1, 1947, pp. 3-13; reprinted in *Sociological Analysis*, Logan Wilson and William L. Kolb, eds., New York: Harcourt, Brace & Co., 1949, pp. 464-473.

tige except in a very broad sense, the absence of an unequivocal top elite or ruling class; the fluidity of the shadings as well as mobility between groups and, in spite of the prestige-implications of the generalized goal of success, the relative tolerance for many different paths to success. It is by no means a "classless society," but among class societies, it is a distinctive type.

Another notable fact, the broader significance of which will have to be assessed in the light of the very long run trends of the development of the society, is the amount of "compression" of the scale, so far as the income aspect is concerned, which has occurred in about the last generation. This has come from pressures on both "ends." On the one hand, related of course very largely to the development of the labor movement, with very considerable political support, but also involving the slowing up of immigration, there has been a very great rise in the relative incomes of most of the lower groups, though it has been uneven, and the "White collar" groups have not risen comparably. On the other hand high progressive taxation, both of incomes and of estates, and changes in the structure of the economy, have "lopped off" the previous top stratum, where the symbols of conspicuous consumption were, in an earlier generation most lavishly displayed. A notable symbol of this is the recent fate of the Long Island estate of the J. P. Morgan family, which had to be sold at auction in default of payment of taxes. One wonders what Veblen would say were he writing today instead of at the height of the "gilded age."

We may sum up the main pattern from top to bottom very broadly as follows: the "top" is a broad and diffuse one with several loosely integrated components. Undoubtedly its main focus is now on occupational status and occupational earnings. Seen in historical as well as comparative perspective this is a notable fact, for the entrepreneurial fortunes of the period of economic development of the 19th century, especially after the Civil War, notably failed to produce a set of ruling families on a national scale who as family entities on a Japanese or even a French pattern have tended to keep control of the basic corporate entities in the economy. Members of these families have retained elite position but broadly through their own occupational or occupation-like achievements rather than on a purely ascriptive basis of family membership. This is true in spite of the fact that mechanisms of safe investment have made it possible to keep inheritances intact more effectively (not of course allowing for voluntary dissipation through distribution to heirs and through philanthropic gifts and bequests) than in most other societies. The basic phenomenon seems to have been the shift in *control* of enterprise from the property interests of founding families to managerial and technical personnel who as such have not had a comparable vested interest in ownership. This critical fact underlies the interpretation that what we may call the "family elite" elements of the class structure (the Warnerian "upper-uppers") hold a *secondary* rather than a primary position in the overall stratification system. On the whole their position is far stronger locally than nationally, and on the whole in smaller than in larger communities—least so in metropolitan centers—and in economically less rather than more progressive communities. The burden of proof certainly rests upon him who would allege that we were well on the way to the development of a hereditary top class in the precapitalistic European sense. The development of our taxation system in the last generation would clearly not be understandable on the hypothesis of the increasing predominance of such a group.

Only in a rather loose and insecure way can one speak of the business managerial elite as the unequivocal top class in an occupational sense. There is strong competition from the professional elite groups, greatly reinforced by the increasing importance of scientifically based technology, both in industry and in the military field. Some groups of professionals are of course very close to business, notably lawyers and engineers, but they shade off into other groups, notable in the universities. With the kinds of qualifications already suggested we may speak of a rather open shifting elite.

The next point to note is that there is no clear break between elite groups in this sense and a broad band of what is usually called the "upper middle class," of business and professional people and, increasingly with the expansion of the functions of government, of civil servants and professional military officers.

The lack of distinctness of this line, and the next one down, is strongly accentuated by another circumstance. This is an implication of the independence of the conjugal family which in turn means that young married couples who are destined by ability or even birth for elite status often start off their married lives with a standard of living which might well be characterized as "lower middle class." The fact that on the whole we have so much less presumption than in European tradition that a son will follow in his father's footsteps, in status if not exact occupation, and that he will only marry when he can support his wife in "the style to which she has been accustomed," means that the lines are much more blurred by the circumstances of stages of career than is the case in other types of stratification system.

Probably the best single index of the line between "upper middle" class and the rest of the middle class is the *expectation* that children will have a college education, as a matter that is of status-right not of the exceptional ability of the individual. This also is blurred above all by the wide qualitative and other variation of institutions of higher education, but it seems to be a fairly clear-cut line.[22] It is important to be clear about the meaning of this expectation. It is, primarily, that the son of such a family will thereby be able to qualify for an acceptably high-level occupational role rather than that he should become a sufficiently educated man to have the manners and humanistic interests appropriate to the cultural status of the family.

Traditionally the line between "middle" and "lower" class status in the Western world has of course been drawn in terms of the distinction between "white collar" and "labor" occupations. Development in this country has gone far to blur the distinctness of this line. A major contribution to this blurring has been the high income of the elite labor groups, largely though not wholly enforced by strong union pressure, so that there is a very considerable overlap in income. But along with that has gone the assimilation of styles of life so that it is difficult to draw clear differentiations. A most important point, documented by Centers[23] is that expectation of advancement in status for children runs throughout these groups. We have relatively little of the traditional "laboring class" of the European background.

Another major aspect of this problem is the failure (contrary to Marxian predictions) for the industrial labor force to grow in proportion to the growth in productivity of the economy, and the corresponding relative increase in numbers in white-collar and "serv-

[22]As shown in the study of mobility referred to above, this expectation operates relatively clearly in the top two of six occupational status-groups we have distinguished.

[23]Centers, Richard, *The Psychology of Social Classes,* Princeton: Princeton University Press, 1949, p. 147 and 216.

ice" occupations, many of which have many of the characteristics of semi-independent small business, as in the case of the gas-station proprietor.

In any case the changing structure of the lower reaches of the occupational system is of the greatest importance for the future. The occupations consisting of almost sheer drudgery—"pick and shovel work"—have of course been enormously diminished. Now automatic machinery is eliminating whole ranges of the so-called "semi-skilled" occupations. It looks very much as though the traditional "bottom" of the occupational pyramid was in course of almost disappearing. If anything this will tend to make our class structure even more predominantly "middle-class" than it already is.

In the lower reaches of the structure there are tendencies to deviation from this "middle class" pattern which are in some respects complementary to the tendencies near the top to form family as distinguished from occupational elites. Essentially we might say this consists in a shift from predominance of the "success" goal to that of the "security" goal. More concretely it is a loss of interest in achievement, whether for its own sake and for opportunity to do more important things, or for advancement of family status through more income and enhanced reputation. Occupational role then becomes not the main "field" for achievement, but a means for securing the necessities of a tolerable standard of living, a necessary evil. The basic focus of interest is diverted from the occupational field into the family, avocations, friendship relations and the like. Undoubtedly this type of shift, found to some extent at all class levels, increases toward the bottom of the scale in what some have called the "common man" class.[24] It is probably most marked in what Warner and his associates call the "lower-lower" group The exact extent and distribution of these tendencies are uncertain, but again perhaps the most important point to be made, one of which we have direct evidence,—is the lack of definiteness of the line. Evidence from the study of mobility shows clearly that we find considerable "ambition" at all class levels; there is no sharp break.

A word also needs to be said about the place of the farm population in the system of stratification. The first and notable fact is the enormous decrease in the relative proportion of farmers among the gainfully employed; it is now down to not much more than 15% —the contrast with most other societies is striking. Secondly it is

[24]The term is used by Warner, but also by Dr. Joseph A. Kahl in unpublished material.

important that there is a very wide range in size of farm, income, etc., so really we can say that farmers go all the way from equivalents of "upper middle" (excluding "gentleman farmers" to whom it is not really an occupational commitment) to the bottom of the scale in the proverbial poverty-stricken share-croppers of certain areas. Finally it may be suggested that the mechanization of agriculture is contributing to assimilation of farming to the "small business" category of occupations, indeed in a good many cases not very small. Furthermore the phenomena of "rurbinization" have tended to assimilate the style of life of the farming groups greatly to that of the urban population.

The kinds of considerations discussed in the last few pages suggest that while in American politics the great "interest groups" are above all business, labor and agriculture, they are not as blocks nearly as tightly integrated as much ideological stereotyping suggests; each contains a great range of types and status-levels (especially if we include labor-leaders, who often have business-level incomes). These groups are not as loose coalitions as the Democratic and Republican parties, but are very far from being groups whose members have interests which are identical on almost all issues. Above all they interlard in the system of stratification with each other and with other groups; they do not constitute clear cut "strata" in the literal sense, one above another.

Finally, this sketch would not be complete without a brief discussion of the problem of mobility within our stratification system. Though the interest of sociologists in this problem has tended to be focussed on so-called "vertical" mobility, perhaps the first important thing to emphasize is the great importance of "horizontal" mobility. Of this in turn two interrelated types are both crucial, namely residential mobility and shift from one occupational status to another, whether within the same occupational type but from one organization to another, or between occupational types. The volume of residential mobility is very great indeed, and this is a most important condition of vertical mobility, since it makes it possible to escape "tight" situations and try again where opportunity seems more promising. The study of small, economically stagnant communities without systematic accounting for what has happened to persons moving out of the community, has contributed to the impression given by the Warner-group studies of the low level of vertical mobility in the society.

Another extremely important fact about the American occupational system is the large amount of "lateral" movement within the occupational system. For example in Continental Europe, below the highest political levels, it has been much less common than here for people to move in and out of government service; there civil service has had to be a life career. Similarly we "hire away" from other organizations in the same or closely related fields a great deal. There is of course even less continuity of specific occupational status from generation to generation, even on similar levels, and much less than there has been in Europe. Both these types of horizontal mobility have been most important in making it possible to "make end runs" on an upward course rather than having to "break through the line" in the same situation in which one is placed by origin or at a given career stage.

Though it is perhaps less commonly said now than a few years ago, there have recently been a good many flat statements to the effect that opportunities for upward mobility have been drastically declining in American society in the last generation or so. These statements should be regarded with great scepticism. There are to be sure two factors in our past which are not likely to be repeated. The settlement of a continent opens up opportunities for status, particularly in new local communities, which cannot be repeated in a fully settled country. Secondly, the opportunity for whole strata of recent immigrants, coming in at the bottom of the scale, to rise in status relative to their initial status in this country, naturally will not be repeated unless immigration is resumed on a grand scale, which seems unlikely. On the other side of course is the enormous increase in productivity of the American economy which is the big positive opportunity-producing factor. These factors are difficult to balance against each other. The general question is very open and the evidence fragmentary.

Undoubtedly there has been a shift by which mobility through the education-system has been greatly increasing in importance. The "self-made man" is less likely than before to have only a grade-school education, and less likely to have established his own organization rather than to have risen through existing organizations. Evidence from the Boston metropolitan area, and taking going to college as a prognosis of probable "high" status in the future, shows that both relative to occupational status of father and education of both parents there is considerable mobility.[25] If this is true of the

---

[25]The study of mobility in collaboration with S. A. Stouffer and Florence Kluckhohn referred to in Note, p. 386 above.

Boston area, which is perhaps economically one of the more "stagnant" of the larger metropolitan areas of the country, the presumption is that it is more rather than less true of metropolitan America as a whole, though smaller towns are another matter.

On the question of how far sheer economic problems, the access to facilities, play a part in the aspect of mobility we have studied, the evidence is less definite, but an impression is fairly clear. This is that, in a metropolitan area where it is possible to attend college and live at home, the economic difficulties of going to college are not the principal barriers even for those from relatively low income families. Exactly how important this factor is we do not know—it is presumably much more so in communities which do not have a local college—but we feel that the available evidence suggests that it is less important than is generally supposed. If this is correct, then an unexpectedly heavy emphasis falls on the factor of *motivation* to mobility, on the part both of a boy himself, and of his parents on his behalf, as distinguished from objective opportunity for mobility. This is a conclusion which runs contrary to much "liberal" opinion, but is at least well enough validated by evidence to warrant further sociological investigation.[26]

This raises certain problems about the type of sociological analysis which is needed in order to understand the processes of mobility under such conditions. Essentially we may say that, within this framework, the focus is on the determinants of the "free choice" of the individual. Therefore his motivation to "get ahead" and the qualitative direction in which he wishes to do so, must be treated as qualities of his personality, rather than placing the problem primarily in the understanding of the exigencies of the situation in which he must act.

If the problem focuses on qualities of the personality, then the question is, how do these qualities develop? One factor of course is constitutionally given ability, but this is outside the range of the sociologist's competence to analyze. Within the range of variation left open by constitutional abilities, however, qualities are acquired through the processes of socialization. These processes, we feel, operate first in the family as a sub-system of the society, then secondarily in the school and peer group. Essentially, then, we must be concerned with those features of families as social systems, the roles

---

[26]There is, of course, no reason why this lack of motivation to mobility may not be a function of continuing low family status and hence opportunity over generations.

played by the parents and siblings and their impact on the personality of the child, which are significant for socialization in general and in particular for determining the difference between "ambitious" and "unambitious" boys and within the ambitious category, different qualitative types of ambition. (Similarly of course for schools and peer groups.)

From the point of view of American society as a social system this problem leads us into the areas of "microscopic" variability of the social structure, since we have good evidence that the differences in which we are interested are only partly a function of the broad differences of class status of families. But in no way does this circumstance make it any less a sociological problem area than if we were attempting to explain only the broadest differences between mobility (or its lack) in the American system of stratification and in the caste system of India.

In no sense is the above sketch a technically "operational" study of the American system of social stratification. In the context of the present paper its purpose is mainly illustrative; it is meant to give the reader some sense of the empirical relevance of the abstract analytical categories which were developed in the first part of the paper. Essentially its purpose will have been served if it helps to do three things: first to give concrete empirical content to most of the theoretical categories dealt with, second to show that by approaching even so complex and baffling an empirical area as the analysis of the stratification of a very complex society in terms of an articulated conceptual scheme, a firm "base of operations" for such analysis can be gained and, third, to show that by use of such a scheme specific insights about the dynamics of the system may be gained which would either not be possible at all, or would be far more vacillating and uncertain if the same empirical problems were approached in a more ad hoc or common-sense way.

One final note may be sounded about the paper as a whole. It is common by implication, if not quite explicitly, to suggest that it is possible and fruitful to develop "theories" of certain types of social phenomena which are essentially independent of each other and of general sociological theory; thus we might speak of a "theory of juvenile delinquency," a "theory of the family," or a "theory of political behavior" and of course a "theory of social stratification." That any one of these constitutes a legitimate field of specialization is beyond doubt. But unless the theoretical approach taken in this paper is grossly mistaken, the theory of stratification is not an independent body of concepts and generalizations which are only loosely connected with other parts of general sociological theory; it *is* general sociological theory pulled together with reference to a certain fundamental aspect of social systems. Such merits as the present analysis may possess are therefore overwhelmingly the product of advances in general theory which have made it possible to state and treat the problems of stratification in such a way as to bring to bear the major tools of general analysis upon them. It is above all the fact that we have much better general theory than a generation ago which makes a better understanding of stratification on a theoretical level possible, though of course in turn study of the problems of stratification has made a major contribution to the development of general theory.

Bibliography of Talcott Parsons

1928

"Capitalism" in Recent German Literature: Sombart and Weber.
J. Political Economy 36:641-661.

1929

"Capitalism" in Recent German Literature: Sombart and Weber.
J. Political Economy 37:31-51.

1930

Translation of Weber, Max, *The Protestant Ethic and the Spirit
of Capitalism;* London and New York, Allen and Unwin, and
Scribners; xi+292pp.

1931

Wants and Activities in Marshall.
Quarterly J. Economics 46:101-140

1932

Economics and Sociology: Marshall in Relation to the Thought
of His Time. *Quarterly J. Economics* 46:316-347.

1933

Malthus
Encyclopedia of the Social Sciences 10:68-69.
Pareto
Encyclopedia of the Social Sciences 11:576-578.

1934

Some Reflections on "The Nature and Significance of Economics."
Quarterly J. Economics 48:511-545.
Society
Encyclopedia of the Social Sciences 14:225-231.
Sociological Elements in Economic Thought. I.
Quarterly J. Economics 49:414-453.

1935

Sociological Elements in Economic Thought. II.
Quarterly J. Economic 49:645-667.
The Place of Ultimate Values in Sociological Theory.
Internat. J. Ethics 45:282-316.
H. M. Robertson on Max Weber and His School.
J. Political Economy 43:688-696.

1936
Pareto's Central Analytical Scheme.
  J. Social Philos. 1:244-262.
On Certain Sociological Elements in Professor Taussig's Thought.
  Viner, Jacob [ed.], *Explorations in Economics: Notes and
  Essays contributed in honor of F. M. Taussig;* New York,
  McGraw-Hill, 1936 (xii + 539 pp.)—pp. 359-379.

1937
The Structure of Social Action
  New York, McGraw-Hill; xii + 817 pp.
Education and the Professions
  Internat. J. Ethics 47:365-369.

1938
The Role of Theory in Social Research.
  Amer. Sociological Rev. 3:13-20. (An address delivered before
  the Annual Institute of the Society for Social Research, at the
  University of Chicago, summer 1937.)
The Role of Ideas in Social Action.
  Amer. Sociological Rev. 3:652-664. (Written for a meeting on
  the problem of ideologies at the American Sociological So-
  ciety's annual meeting, Atlantic City, N. J., December 1937.)

1939
The Professions and Social Structure.
  Social Forces 17:457-467. (Written to be read at the annual
  meeting of the American Sociological Society in Detroit, De-
  cember, 1938.)
Comte.
  J. Unified Sci. 9:77-83.

1940
An Analytical Approach to the Theory of Social Stratification.
  Amer. J. Sociology 45:841-862.
Motivation of Economic Activities.
  Canad. J. Economics and Political Sci. 6:187-203. (Originally
  given as a public lecture at the University of Toronto and
  also published in *Essays in Sociology* [ed.] by C. W. M. Hart.)

1942
Max Weber and the Contemporary Political Crisis.
  Rev. Politics 4:61-76, 155-172.
The Sociology of Modern Anti-Semitism.
  Graeber, J., and Britt, Steuart Henderson [eds.], *Jews in a
  Gentile World:* New York, Macmillan, 1942 (x + 436 pp.)—
  pp. 101-122.

Age and Sex in the Social Structure of the United States.
> Amer. Sociological Rev. 7:604-616. (Read at the annual meeting of the American Sociological Society in New York, December, 1941.)
Propaganda and Social Control.
> Psychiatry 5:551-572.
Democracy and the Social Structure in Pre-Nazi Germany.
> J. Legal and Political Sociology 1:96-114.
Some Sociological Aspects of the Fascist Movements.
> Social Forces 21:138-147. (Written as the presidential address to the Eastern Sociological Society at its 1942 meeting.)

1943

The Kinship System of the Contemporary United States.
> Amer. Anthropologist 45:22-38.

1944

The Theoretical Development of the Sociology of Religion.
> J. of the Hist. of Ideas 5:176-190. (Originally written to be read at the Conference on Methods in Science and Philosophy in New York, November, 1942.)

1945

The Present Position and Prospects of Systematic Theory.
> Gurvitch, Georges, and Moore, Wilbert E. [eds.], Twentieth Century Sociology, A Symposium; New York, Philosophical Library, 1945.
The Problem of Controlled Institutional Change: An Essay on Applied Social Science.
> Psychiatry 8:79-101. (Prepared as an appendix to the report of the Conference on Germany after the War.)
Racial and Religious Differences as Factors in Group Tensions.
> Finkelstein, Louis, etc. [eds.], Unity and Difference in the Modern World, A Symposium; New York, The Conference on Science, Philosophy and Religion in Their Relation to the Democratic Way of Life, Inc., 1945.

1946

The Science Legislation and the Role of the Social Sciences.
> Amer. Sociological Rev. 11:653-666.
Population and Social Structure.
> Haring, Douglas G. [eds.], Japan's Prospect; Cambridge, Harvard University Press, 1946 (xiv + 474 pp.)—pp. 87-114. (This book was published by the staff of the Harvard School for Overseas Administration.)

1947

Certain Primary Sources and Patterns of Aggression in the Social Structure of the Western World.

> *Psychiatry* 10:167-181. (Prepared for the Conference on Science, Philosophy and Religion at its September 1946 meeting in Chicago, Ill., and also published in the volume issued by the Conference.)

Some Aspects of the Relations Between Social Science and Ethics.

> *Social Science* 22:213-217. (Read at the Annual Convention of the American Association for the Advancement of Science in Boston, December, 1946.)

Science Legislation and the Social Sciences.

> *Political Science Quarterly,* Vol. LXII, No. 2, June 1947.
> *Bulletin of Atomic Scientists,* January, 1947.

Max Weber: The Theory of Social and Economic Organization.

> Parsons, Talcott, editor, and translator with Henderson, A. M.; Oxford University Press, 1947.

1948

Sociology, 1941-46. (coauthor: Bernard Barber)

> *Amer. J. Sociology* 53:245-257.

The Position of Sociological Theory.

> *Amer. Sociological Rev.* 13:156-171. (Paper read before the annual meeting of the American Sociological Society, New York City, December, 1947.)

1949

Essays in Sociological Theory Pure and Applied.

> Glencoe, Ill., The Free Press, 1949; xiii + 366 pp.

The Rise and Decline of Economic Man.

> *J. General Education* 4:47-53.

Social Classes and Class Conflict in the Light of Recent Sociological Theory.

> *Amer. Economic Rev.* 39:16-26. (Read at meeting of the American Economic Association in December, 1948.)

1950

The Prospects of Sociological Theory.

> *Amer. Sociological Rev.* 15:3-16. (Presidential address read before the meeting of the American Sociological Society in New York City, December, 1949).

Psychoanalysis and the Social Structure.

> *The Psychoanalytic Quarterly* 19:371-384. (The substance of this paper was presented at the meeting of the American Psychoanalytic Association, Washington, D. C., May, 1948.)

The Social Environment of the Educational Process.
> *Centennial;* Washington, D. C.: American Association for the
> Advancement of Science; pp. 36-40. (Read at the A.A.A.S.
> Centennial Celebration, September, 1948.)

1951

The Social System.
> Glencoe, Ill., The Free Press, 1951; xii + 575 pp.

Toward a General Theory of Action
> Editor and contributor with Shils, Edward A.; Cambridge,
> Harvard University Press, 1951; viii + 506 pp.

Graduate Training in Social Relations at Harvard.
> *J. General Education* 5:149-157.

Illness and the Role of the Physician: A Sociological Perspective.
> *Amer. J. Orthopsychiatry* 21:452-460. (Presented at the 1951
> annual meeting of the American Orthopsychiatric Association
> in Detroit.)

1952

The Superego and the Theory of Social Systems.
> *Psychiatry* 15:15-25. (The substance of this paper was read
> at the meeting of the Psychoanalytic Section of the American
> Psychiatric Association, May, 1951, in Cincinnati.)

Religious Perspectives in College Teaching: Sociology and Social
Psychology.
> Fairchild, Hoxie N., [ed.], *Religious Perspectives in College
> Teaching;* New York, The Ronald Press Company, 1952 (vii +
> 460)—pp. 286-337.

A Sociologist Looks at the Legal Profession.
> (This paper was presented at the Conference on the Profes-
> sion of Law and Legal Education on the occasion of the
> Fiftieth Anniversary Celebration of the University of Chicago
> Law School on December 4, 1952, and published in the pro-
> ceedings of that occasion.)

The Father Symbol: An Appraisal in the Light of Psychoanalytic
and Sociological Theory.
> (The substance of this paper was read at the meeting of the
> American Psychological Association in September, 1952, at
> Washington, D. C. It will be published in the Thirteenth
> Symposium, 1952, of the Conference on Science, Philosophy
> and Religion.)

1953

Working Papers in the Theory of Action.
   (In collaboration with Robert F. Bales and Edward A. Shils)
   Glencoe, Illinois, The Free Press, 1953; 269 pp.

Psychoanalysis and Social Science with Special Reference to the
   Oedipus Problem.
   Twenty Years of Psychoanalysis (Franz Alexander and Helen
   Ross, editors); New York: W. W. Norton & Co., Inc.; 1953.
   (Read at the Twentieth Anniversary Celebration of the Insti-
   tute for Psychoanalysis, Chicago, in October 1952.)

A Revised Analytical Approach to the Theory of Social Stratifica-
   tion. Bendix, Reinhold, and Lipset, Seymour M. [eds.], *Class
   Status and Power*: A Reader in Social Stratification, Glencoe,
   Illinois, The Free Press.

Illness, Therapy and the Modern Urban American Family.
   (Coauthor with Renée Fox) *J. of Social Issues* 8:31-44.

Psychology and Sociology.
   Gillin, John P. [ed.], *Toward a Science of Social Man;* New
   York, Macmillan Company (in press), Chapter IV.

Family, Socialization, and Interaction Process.
   (Coauthor with Bales, Robert F.; Zelditch, Morris; Olds,
   James; and Slater, Philip) Glencoe, Illinois, The Free Press
   (in press).

Some Comments on the State of the General Theory of Action.
   American Sociological Review 18:618-631.

Index

Acceptance, 397, 404, 413, 414
Achievement (see also Performance)
   and status, 44-5, 60, 65-6, 72-88,
      92, 96, 99, 191-2, 295, 301,
      306, 310-11, 389-90, 343-94 ff,
      408-9
   definition of, 75
Acquisitiveness, 35-6, 43, 66-7
Action
   economic, 23-4, 29-31, 50-68, 221-2
   rational, 22-3, 31, 33n, 37, 45, 152,
      199, 201, 222, 243
   theory of, the, 13-4, 19, 27, 29-32,
      52, 70, 71, 72, 199-200, 208-9,
      225-6, 228-9, 336-347, 357-60,
      386-387 ff.
Action space, dimensions of, 395-6,
   412-15
Actor, the, 21-2, 29-30, 56-7, 72-3,
   149-50, 228-30, 241-2, 336
   (see also Action, theory of, Indi-
      vidual, Personality, Motivation)
Adaptive phase, 395, 397-415
   in U. S. stratification, 415-16, 420
Administration (see Bureaucracy)
Affectivity-Neutrality
   and stratification, 397, 412-14
Aggression, 63n, 67, 137-8, 272, 290,
   292, 294, 314
   definition of, 298n
   free floating, 117, 126
   in Western World, 298-322
Alienation, 377n
Altruism, 35-6, 42, 45, 48, 54
Ambivalence, 345
Analysis (see also Theory)
   functional, 152n, 186, 195, 322,
      325
Anomie, 119, 125-31, 136-9
   definition of, 125
Anthropology, 52, 172, 198, 219, 227
   and sociology, 177, 351, 353, 356-7,
      362, 369

Anxiety, 117, 126, 150, 171, 300-1,
   304, 308, 310, 312, 315, 318, 382
Approval, 397, 404, 412, 413
ARENSBERG, C., 184n
Aristocracy, 62, 80, 81-2, 85, 100, 185
   German, 106-8
   Japanese, 279-80, 285, 287, 288,
      294
Ascription, 408-9. (see also Qualities)
Ascriptive-Qualitative sphere (see also
   Latent Pattern-Maintenance)
   in U.S. stratification, 416-18, 420,
      422
Associations, 420, 425 ff.
Attitudes
   emotional, 45, 59, 70, 72, 93, 117-
      123, 143-4, 149, 157, 161, 164-8,
      174, 241, 244-6, 247, 250, 253n,
      271, 301-2, 304, 306, 308-10,
      317-19, 330, 338, 339, 340, 361,
      382
   moral, 60-1, 206, 384
   structuring of, 131
Authoritarianism, 106, 109, 292, 294
Authority, 37, 90, 109, 128, 167, 195,
   206, 232, 249-52, 327, 330, 343,
   376
   charismatic, 251
   defined, 76, 392-3
   differentiation of, 40, 55
   legal, 373
   legitimate, 56, 171
   moral, 37, 206
   political, 105, 374-5, 379, 381
   professional, 38, 155-7, 160
   and status, 76, 78, 81, 83-4, 139
   and stratification, 409-12
   traditional, 133
   unjust, 133

BALES, R. F., 9, 386n, 390n, 400
BARNES, J. P., 380n
BATESON, G., 119n

BEAL, E. G., 275n
Behavior (see also Action, Motivation)
51, 99, 193-4, 233, 244-5, 309-11, 336-47
economic, 53, 61
Japanese, 283
neurotic, 67, 150-1, 153, 157, 194, 301, 305, 315
social, 144-5, 148, 221, 234, 240, 242, 298
Behaviorism, 349
BENDIX, R., 11, 386n
BENNION, L. L., 26n
BERGER, J., 387n
Biology (see Physiology)
Birth, 74, 76, 77, 78, 81-2, 89, 181, 191
Birth-rate, 275-6, 290, 291, 308, 331
BOGARDUS, E. S., 350
Bohemianism, 136
Brahmanism, 62
BRITT, S. H., 317n
Bureaucracy, 39-40, 42, 47-8, 65, 85, 161, 170
German, 104-123, 254-6, 317
Japanese, 280, 284, 295

Calvinism, 121n, 207, 363, 406
CANNON, W. B., 218n, 337n
Capitalism (see also Society, Modern Western, and Economy)
27ff., 64, 67, 83, 116, 132-4, 135, 137, 140, 207, 323, 325, 329, 330, 332, 334, 370
in Germany, 105, 119, 250-1, 266-7
symbol of, 133-4
Caste, 78, 81
Categories (see Theory)
Catholics, (see also Church, Roman Catholic), 425, 426-7
CENTERS, R., 433
Change, 146, 303, 315-16
cultural, 128-44, 148
economic 82, 333
institutional, 47-8, 140, 232, 238-74
legal, 370-85
social, in Germany, 117-23
social, in Japan, 275-97
Chapin living-room scale, 429
Character (see Personality, Motivation, Psychology)
150, 173-4, 233-5

German, 104-23, 238-74
Japanese, 275-97
Childhood (see also Socialization), 57, 74, 79, 87, 89-90
China, 16, 17, 27 ff, 208, 293, 343, 363, 408, 427
Christian Science, 146n, 154, 163
Christianity (see also Religion)
and Capitalism, 207-8
and science, 131
values of, 166-7, 273, 286
Church
Lutheran, 109, 121n
Protestant, 121, 166-8, 426
Roman Catholic, 110, 166-8, 376, 426-7
Universalist, 46
Clan, 183
Class (see also Stratification), 78-81, 91, 94, 317, 323-34
defined, 77, 328, 427
in Germany, 104-8, 110-14
in Japan, 275-97
lower, 185, 331
middle, 90, 94n, 95, 136, 186, 193, 278, 293, 320, 331, 342-3
upper (see also Aristocracy), 185, 279
in United States, 427-38
Clergy, 140, 166-8, 426
Collectivity (see also Group, Society, Institution, Social System), 310
types of, 419-20
Common value system (see also Values), 388, 390, 393-4
Communism (see also Marx, Socialism), 116, 125, 134, 289, 291, 293-4, 323-4, 333, 370, 376, 407
Community, 86-8, 91, 97, 103, 166, 187, 191, 192, 194
Competence (see also Functional Specificity, Universalism)
technical, 38, 40, 42, 155, 174, 191
Competition, 63, 64n, 80, 85, 92, 94, 96, 101, 132, 191, 192, 221, 285-6, 301, 303-4, 307-8, 311-13, 329-32, 344
Complexes (see also Motivation, Psychology),
institutional, 191, 326
instrumental, 330-1
COMTE, A., 104
CONANT, J. B., 354